KEVIN ZRALY

WINDOWS ON THE WORLD
COMPLETE WINE COURSE

•REVISED & UPDATED EDITION•

STERLING EPICURE
New York

I am indebted to the grape growers, winemakers, and wine friends throughout the world who contributed their expertise and enthusiasm to this project. The signatures on the endpapers come from some of the people whose help has proved invaluable to me.

STERLING EPICURE
New York

An Imprint of Sterling Publishing Co., Inc.
1166 Avenue of the Americas
New York, NY 10036

ISBN 978-1-4549-2106-6

Distributed in Canada by Sterling Publishing Co., Inc.
c/o Canadian Manda Group, 664 Annette Street
Toronto, Ontario, M6S 2C8, Canada
Distributed in the United Kingdom by GMC Distribution Services
Castle Place, 166 High Street, Lewes, East Sussex, BN7 1XU, United Kingdom
Distributed in Australia by NewSouth Books
45 Beach Street, Coogee, NSW 2034, Australia

For information about custom editions, special sales, and premium and corporate purchases, please contact Sterling Special Sales at 800-805-5489 or specialsales@sterlingpublishing.com.

Manufactured in Canada

4 6 8 10 9 7 5

sterlingpublishing.com

Interior design by Ashley Prine

DEDICATION

This book is called *Windows on the World Complete Wine Course* for a reason. Windows on the World was the restaurant atop One World Trade Center in New York City. I worked there from the day it opened in 1976 and for the next 25 years—until September 11, 2001. I continue to title my books, as well as my wine course, with the name of the restaurant to continue the legacy.

I dedicate this edition to all those who worked at Windows on the World, celebrated their birthdays, anniversaries, or bar mitzvahs there, dined there, or just had a glass of wine at the bar.

The Windows on the World Wine School has continued uninterrupted for forty years. Through the first World Trade Center terrorist bombing in 1993 and even after its destruction in 2001, I continued the school at the Marriott Marquis Hotel in Times Square. (Today it takes place at the J. W. Marriott Essex House on Central Park South.) This year, in fall 2016, the Windows on the World Wine School will end its forty-year run. I am pleased to say that I have never missed a class or stopped teaching one because of terrorism.

I also dedicate this edition to the 20,000+ students who have taken the class and learned to enjoy the taste of a great glass of wine!

⚜ CONTENTS ⚜

FOR MORE INFORMATION, INCLUDING LINKS TO VIDEOS,
PRONUNCIATIONS, AND AN ONLINE STORE, VISIT KEVINZRALY.COM.

INTRODUCTION

AS I CELEBRATE my fortieth year of teaching the Windows on the World Wine School, I want to look back in time to describe my wine journey and why I wrote this book. I can say honestly that, after forty-five years of studying wine, I am still having fun on this amazing adventure.

At age twenty-five, I accepted the position of cellar master at Windows on the World, the restaurant opening at the top of One World Trade Center. I had the responsibility of selecting, ordering, and selling all the restaurant's wine. There I was, a kid in a candy store with carte blanche and only one mandate: create the biggest and best wine list New York had ever seen. So I did. Within five years of opening, Windows on the World became the number-one dollar-volume restaurant with more wine sold than any other restaurant in the world.

Wine had been my passion since my college days, when, at age nineteen, I got a job as a waiter to earn some beer money. As fate had it, the restaurant received a four-star rating from *New York Times* restaurant critic Craig Claiborne, and the owner asked me to take over bartending duties. (Luckily, at the time the legal drinking age in New York was eighteen.) I began studying beer, distilled spirits, and wine, learning whatever I could as fast as I could. Then I tasted my first glass of great wine, and that was it. From that moment, wine became my passion, and I quickly switched from Budweiser to Burgundy!

Studying wine isn't merely learning about a beverage but also understanding the history, language, culture, and traditions of the people and countries where each wine is made. Wine is a complicated subject, one that reinvents itself every year with a new vintage. That wines constantly change makes for fascinating, lifelong study.

Over the next five years, I read as many wine books as I could find, attended wine tastings, and traveled to wineries in New York, California, and Europe. I taught my first class when I was twenty and, later, a two-credit wine course while I was still a college student.

All this helped when I interviewed for the job at Windows on the World. In fall 1976, the Windows on the World Wine School began. I had to decide which textbook to use. Unfortunately, most wine books available at the time were encyclopedic and too advanced for my students. So I started with my own handouts for each class. I also had a friend record a year of the wine school. After each class, she gave me a transcript of what I taught, including the students' questions. Those handouts and the transcripts eventually became the basis for this book, which I have been using in the Wine School since the book was first published in 1985. That it has sold over three million copies since then is overwhelming!

In college, one of my favorite authors was George Orwell. In the essay "Rules of Communication," he writes: "Use simple language, simple expressions, and simple style." William Strunk Jr. and E. B. White continue that thought in *The Elements of Style*: "A sentence should contain no unnecessary words, a paragraph no unnecessary sentences." As Shakespeare masterfully said, "Brevity is the soul of wit." In updating this book, I followed that advice, and it continues to work well for my students and readers. The format has stayed very much the same for more than thirty years. To emphasize specific points and supplement the information in the text, I added sidebars. I love statistics, so I have included facts and figures as well as anecdotes, personal commentary, and quotes in the margins to reinforce the ideas in the main text. All these tools keep learning about wine easy and fun.

Faced with the opportunity to revise, my approach over the years has been to add only up-to-date, useful information. Less is more.

In researching "The Greater World of Wine" chapter this past year, I tasted thousands of wines. Some were good, some not so good, and others outstanding, especially in the $20–$30 range. By constantly tasting wine, I learn new things every day. The journey continues.

THE STORY OF WINDOWS ON THE WORLD

WINDOWS ON THE World opened its elevator doors for the first time on April 12, 1976, as a private luncheon club. The press had been writing about its opening for months, speculating whether the whole project—both the restaurant and the World Trade Center complex itself—could succeed. Never before had anyone attempted a project this large. It was designed not only to be the tallest building in the world, but it was going to be one of the largest urban centers ever built, feeding more than 50,000 office workers and more than 150,000 commuters who would pass through the complex on their way to and from work every day.

All eyes fixed on Joe Baum, the man in charge of food services for the World Trade Center complex and mastermind behind the Windows on the World restaurant. Everyone wanted to see and feel and touch what Joe Baum had been working on for the previous six years. After all, Joe had created some of New York's most successful landmark restaurants, including The Four Seasons, La Fonda del Sol, and The Forum of the Twelve Caesars.

Baum's family owned a resort in New York's Saratoga Springs, so Joe grew up in the hospitality world. Shortly after graduating from the Cornell University School of Hotel Administration, he took a job with a major restaurant operator, Restaurant Associates (R.A.). While working at R.A., he developed a reputation: He became known in the industry as a maverick, genius, and pitbull—usually called all these names at the same time. His innovative approach often landed him in trouble, and in the late '60s, Joe left R.A. to form his own consulting company. In 1970, he signed a contract with the Port Authority of New York and New Jersey to design and manage all the restaurant and food-service areas of the World Trade Center.

Joe and his associates conceived and organized twenty-two restaurants located throughout the complex. They planned restaurants with names like Eat & Drink, The Big Kitchen, and The Market Bar and Dining Room and included everything from Coffee Express, where commuters could grab a cup of coffee and a bagel while in transit, to Windows on the World. With almost 200,000 people working or passing through every day, the WTC was a city unto itself.

"To me, Windows on the World will always be about Joe Baum, who knew the significance of establishing an urban oasis atop the tallest towers in New York City. With its exciting architecture and its culinary and wine programs easily accessible to everyone, Windows satisfied the many appetites of body and soul."

—TONY ZAZULA, owner,
Commerce Restaurant, New York City

An early menu from Windows on the World.

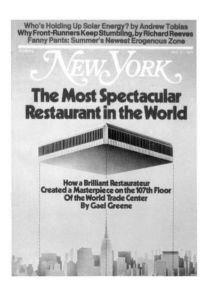

Joe had grandiose ideas for the restaurant on top of the World Trade Center—ideas that would cost a lot of money. In the early '70s, New York City was in the midst of a severe fiscal crisis. Many New Yorkers opposed the building of the World Trade Center in the first palce, and building anything extravagant meant facing intense scrutiny.

With the backing of the Port Authority, more than $17 million were spent developing Windows on the World. The main focus was the 107th floor of One World Trade Center, divided into five parts: The Restaurant (seating nearly 300 guests); The City Lights Bar; Hors d'Oeuvrerie, which served everything except the main course; The Cellar in the Sky, a glass-enclosed working wine cellar that seated just thirty-six guests and served a seven-course, five-wine, one-seating dinner; and six private banquet rooms capable of seating more than 300 people. Altogether, Windows on the World spanned one acre, 107 stories up in the sky.

Joe Baum was a master contractor. He hired the best culinary talent available. He asked food author James Beard and chef Jacques Pépin to help develop the menus, Warren Platner to design the restaurant, and Milton Glaser to design the graphics—all the best in the business.

Joe asked me to handle the wine for Windows on the World and hired me as the cellar master. Friends warned me against leaving my job as a wine salesman to work at Windows, giving me three reasons not to take the job:

1. In 1976, no one went downtown after 6 PM.
2. Rooftop restaurants weren't considered quality operations.
3. Joe Baum had a reputation for being difficult.

On all three counts, it just wasn't so. I knew it was going to be a great restaurant and job when I asked Joe about creating the wine list. He said: "It's very simple. I want you to create the biggest and the best wine list that New York has ever seen, and don't worry about how much it costs!" There I was, a twenty-five-year-old kid in a candy store—only it sold wine!

In May 1976, the cover of *New York* magazine read: "The Most Spectacular Restaurant in the World—How a Brilliant Restaurateur Created a Masterpiece on the 107th Floor of the World Trade Center." Some of the superlatives from that article by the illustrious Gael Greene included: "a miracle," "a masterpiece," "a dream," and "almost unreal." It went on, "Windows on the World is a triumph!" "No other sky-high restaurant quite prepares you for the astonishment of the horizon . . . like a luxury liner sailing through the blue skies," "Everything to hate and fear is invisible."

Teaching the Wine School in the early 1980s.

This was the best article ever written about Windows on the World, and it appeared *before* the public opening! We thought it couldn't get any better, but we were wrong. The best was yet to come.

The World Trade Center and Windows on the World became symbols of the financial turnaround of New York City, and their completion played a key role in the revitalization of Lower Manhattan. The year that Windows on the World opened, 1976, was also the bicentennial of America. From the 107th floor, imagine an unobstructed view of the spectacularly refurbished Statue of Liberty and the entire New York Harbor with its flotilla of tall ships. What a sight! Seeing the bicentennial fireworks from Windows became the hottest ticket in the world.

On that memorable July Fourth evening, I went alone to the top of One World Trade Center (the broadcast antennae and barriers not yet erected) and watched all the fireworks displays within a sixty-mile radius. I remember thinking that life didn't get much better than this. I was serving wine to kings, queens, presidents, sports heroes, and movie stars. During the next five years, I met every celebrity I had ever heard of or read about.

Windows on the World was an instant success and booked up months in advance. What made it so great? Was it the sixty-second elevator ride? The menu concept? The youthful, energetic staff? The extensive and outrageously low-priced wine list? The most spectacular view in the world?

For me, it was all of the above.

A Windows on the World business card with Milton Glaser's memorable design.

"On July 4, 1976, Windows on the World was filled with celebrities for the bicentennial fireworks display. I was given the very pleasant task of escorting Princess Grace of Monaco. As we watched the extravaganza over the Statue of Liberty, Princess Grace held my hand very tightly because the fireworks made her somewhat nervous. I asked if the moment reminded her of To Catch a Thief *and her very famous, very passionate scene with Cary Grant, set to the backdrop of fireworks. She was astounded I knew the film and the scene. So I told her that if she wanted to watch the film again, she could that night, because it was being shown at 11:30, on Channel Two."*

—MELVIN FREEMAN, page, Windows on the World, 1976–1993 and 1996–2001

"Even more than high school and college, my "education" at Windows on the World University has stood me well in tackling the challenges of the world at large."

—MICHAEL SKURNIK, assistant cellar master, Windows on the World, 1977–1978; now president, Michael Skurnik Wines Ltd

An early brochure from the Windows on the World Wine School.

The first five years of Windows on the World were nonstop. Always full for lunch and dinner, it was the restaurant destination of choice for everyone in the world. Combined with all the other World Trade Center restaurants, it proved so successful in the first five years (generating close to $50 million in revenues in 1980 alone) that a ballroom on the 106th floor joined the ranks in 1981. The demand for such a large space was overwhelming; prior to construction, very little banquet space was available to the public in downtown Manhattan. Again, the World Trade Center complex was playing a vital role in both the community and the economic redevelopment of Lower Manhattan.

In 1985, my book, *Windows on the World Complete Wine Course*, made its debut, putting the Wine School in print for the first time.

The first terrorist attack on the World Trade Center took place on February 26, 1993, at 12:18 pm. Six people were killed, including one of our employees who worked in the receiving department in the basement. Andrea Robinson, cellar master at the time, escorted all our patrons down 107 flights of stairs to safety.

Windows on the World shut down after the bombing, leaving over four hundred food-service people without jobs. Within six months I was the last on the payroll, and the restaurant lay dormant from February 26, 1993, until June 1996. I was one of the few people allowed to enter after the 1993 bombing. It was a very lonely time.

The Port Authority knew that the restaurant was going to be closed but wanted to continue the Wine School. It had operated continuously since the restaurant opened in 1976. The school started with a small group of ten lunch-club members in 1976. Members invited their friends, who then invited *their* friends. Soon the friends of club members outnumbered the club members. Still, the class list kept growing. In 1980, we opened

In the Cellar in the Sky.

the school to the public. Since then, more than 20,000 students have attended classes.

Although the restaurant was closed from 1993 until 1996, I continued teaching the classes in three different locations in the World Trade Center complex. I'm proud that the school remained open during those difficult years; it kept the memory of the restaurant alive and became a symbol to everyone that it would return.

"Windows was silent when I ran the wine school, but I relished its solitude. I roamed its floors, inspected its rooms, absorbed all that was left frozen in time. Like Jack Nicholson in The Shining, *I could sense the energy it embodied, feel its buzz, envision its diners, find myself immersed in the dream. But unlike Jack's, my visions embodied warmth and peace. The space lived and breathed even when empty and will continue to do so in our hearts."*

—REBECCA CHAPPA,
Wine School coordinator, 1994–1995;
owner, Wine by the Class
and Tannin Management

In late 1993, the Port Authority began looking for a new operator. Again, requests for proposals went out, and this time more than thirty restaurant operators expressed interest in taking over Windows on the World. A review committee examined each proposal and made recommendations. They narrowed it down to three entries: Alan Stillman, owner of Smith & Wollensky, The Post House, The Manhattan Ocean Club, Park Avenue Café, and Cité; Warner LeRoy of Tavern on the Green, Maxwell's Plum, and later The Russian Tea Room; and Joe Baum, original creator of Windows on the World, then operating The Rainbow Room.

The Port Authority awarded the contract to Joe Baum, and the renaissance of Windows on the World began. Both Andrea Robinson and I were brought back: she to develop the wine list and beverage program, and I to continue the Wine School. In all, the staff totaled more than 400 employees and represented more than 25 nationalities.

The names of many of the old spaces changed as part of the renovation: The old City Lights Bar and the Hors d'Oeuvrerie became The Greatest Bar on Earth. The Cellar in the Sky took up a new location overlooking the Statue of Liberty. The banquet rooms were enlarged.

The reopening of Windows on the World in June 1996, twenty years almost to the month after its first opening, happened because of Joe Baum's usual kinetic energy, joie de vivre, and theatrical hoopla. The celebrities came back, the paparazzi gathered in full force, the view was better than ever, and the wines had aged gracefully over the previous three years. It almost felt like 1976 all over again.

Within a year of reopening, it was decided to make Windows on the World the ultimate American-style food and wine experience. The most important change was hiring Michael Lomonaco, former executive chef of The '21' Club, to oversee all culinary operations as the Windows chef. He was the first American-born chef to run the kitchen.

Under Lomonaco's leadership, Windows on the World received two stars from the *The New York Times*, three stars from *Crains*, a 22 in *Zagat*, and ranked in the top listing in *Wine Spectator* for overall dining. Over the next three years, Windows on the World remained a premier destination for corporate meetings, weddings, anniversaries, birthdays, and bar mitzvahs. We were hosting parties of 10 to 1,200 people.

The Greatest Bar on Earth took on a life all its own. Under its old guise, The Bar closed at 10 PM. The new bar began attracting a younger, more vibrant international crowd that danced 'til the wee hours to the city's

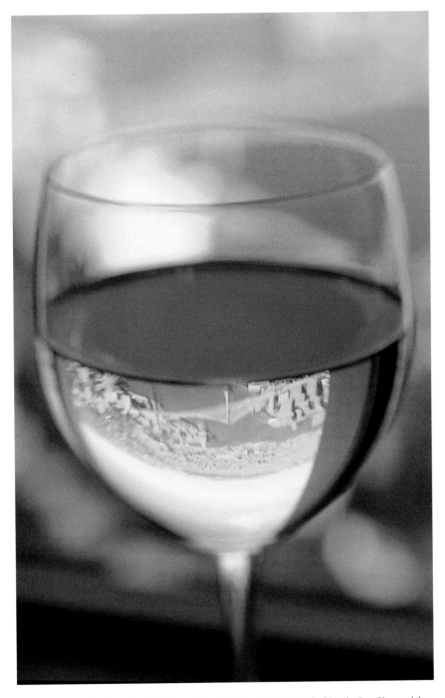

This picture was taken from the 107th floor of One World Trade Center overlooking the East River and the Brooklyn Bridge.

"What I remember most about Windows on the World is the employee cafeteria. It was in that room that friends congregated to eat, talk, and enjoy the view of the three bridges below us. It was here where laughter and happiness prevailed. Windows was my family in New York, my world that I loved so dearly."
—INEZ HOLDERNESs, beverage manager, Windows on the World, 1999–2001; owner, On the Square Restaurant & Wine Store, Tarboro, North Carolina

"Most people saw only the crowds of people and felt the energy of a busy restaurant complex when they came to Windows. We were lucky enough to experience the peace and beauty that surrounded us every day, long after the crowds had gone home. My favorite times occurred long after service was over, when I could turn off all the lights in the dining room and sit with a glass of wine to enjoy the beauty of the city stretched out before me."
—MELISSA TRUMBULL, restaurant manager, Windows on the World, 1997–2001; director, Ian Schrager's Royalton Restaurant

"Windows on the World reopening in 1996 was the launchpad for my career in wine. Working with Kevin and overseeing the award-winning wine list he created have given me tasteful (pun intended) memories to last a lifetime . . . 1989 Coche-Dury Corton Charlemagne, 1989 Comte de Vogue Musigny Blanc and 1975 Joseph Phelps 'Eisele Vineyard' Cabernet Sauvignon to name but a few!"
—Ralph Hersom, cellar master, Windows on the World, 1996-1997; category manager of wine / beer / spirits, Hannaford Supermarkets

Michael Lomonaco.

hottest bands and DJs. The Greatest Bar on Earth became a downtown late-night destination. Windows had learned to change with the times.

The Cellar in the Sky had been an integral part of the old Windows on the World, but by 1996 restaurants around the country were also doing food and wine pairings. It was time to replace The Cellar with something new: a restaurant called Wild Blue. At Wild Blue—a restaurant within a restaurant—Michael and his chefs showcased their culinary skills. Wild Blue received four stars from *Crains*, a 25 in *Zagat*, a spot in the top-ten list of New York restaurants in *Wine Spectator*, and a rating as one of New York's best by *Esquire*.

Windows was the best it could be on September 10, 2001. It was producing more than $37 million in revenues and was the number-one dollar volume restaurant in the country. Of that $37 million, $5 million came from the sale of wines from among our 1,400 different selections. We were enthusiastic about our future and were preparing excitedly for our 25th anniversary celebration the following month, with the opening of the new wine cellar.

But on Tuesday, September 11, 2001, the world changed. What began as a beautiful, pristine September morning ended in a dark nightmare of death and destruction. Seventy-two co-workers, one security officer, and seven construction workers who were building the new wine cellar at Windows on the World died in the worst terrorist attack in American history.

For me, the loss remains incomprehensible. The World Trade Center complex was my New York City. It was a neighborhood. I shopped there. I stayed at the Marriott with my family. My dentist and my bank were there. I lost my home and community of twenty-five years, a community I helped build and watched grow.

Windows on the World no longer exists, but the reflections of those windows will remain with me forever.

After September 11, 2001, I took every memento I had of the restaurant and shared all of it with the New York Public Library as part of a tribute they were holding to the greatest restaurants of the world. Now that the World Trade Center Memorial has opened, it seems only appropriate to share photos, menus, and memories of this very special restaurant once again. It's my way of honoring the legacy and keeping alive the memory of Windows on the World.

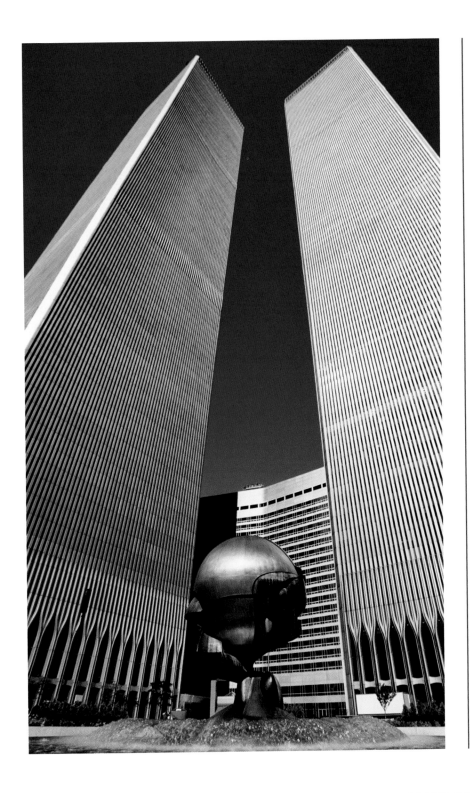

"I was in the 'Skybox' room overlooking The Greatest Bar on Earth Monday night September 10th. I was hosting my class called 'Spirits in the Skybox,' a name that has haunting implications. When we finished, my co-host and head bartender, George Delgado, and I invited a few friends and some members of the press to join us for a quick drink in the bar. I usually have cocktails, but this time we ordered Champagne. There was no particular celebration; the group just seemed to click, so we had several more bottles of Champagne and food. A DJ named Jennifer began spinning records. Someone in our group knew her, so we stayed and ended the evening dancing. I awoke Tuesday morning to the horror of the terrorist attack that finished off that medium-sized city called the World Trade Center. I will cherish the gift I was given of that last spontaneous celebration in the late Joe Baum's majestic Windows on the World. We were unknowingly lifting our Champagne glasses that night in farewell to all those friends and colleagues we would lose the following day."

—DALE DEGROFF,
master mixologist, Windows on the World,
1996–2001; author, kingcocktail.com

The World Trade Center Plaza in the 1980s. Minoru Yamasaki was the designer and lead architect of the World Trade Center. Fritz Koenig's bronze sculpture "The Sphere" stood in the plaza between the World Trade Center towers. It was not destroyed and is on display in Battery Park.

THE WINE REVOLUTION

"May you live in interesting times."

In 1970, when I began my journey in wine, I studied French wines and a little German wine. Those were the only quality wines being made. Then it started to happen: California began to produce outstanding wines, especially Cabernet Sauvignon from the Napa Valley. Next, not in any specific order, Shiraz from Australia, Pinot Noir from Oregon, Sauvignon Blanc from New Zealand, Malbec from Argentina, Cabernet Sauvignon from Chile, Merlot from Washington, Riesling from New York, and more came into the quality category. The resurgence of great wines from Italy and Spain also added to the wine revolution. Wine has become a global community, and today is the golden age for wine in the world.

Here are the changes since 1970 that have altered the course of winemaking and viticulture significantly. Wherever possible throughout the book, I have included sidebars comparing wine statistics from 1970 to 2016.

WINEMAKING AND VITICULTURE

Wine quality has improved enormously over the last four decades, more than at any other time in the history of winemaking. Vast strides have taken place in the science and technology, growers have readapted back-to-the-earth farming techniques, and there has been widespread planting of international grapes, all of which have led to wine's rise in popularity throughout the world.

Here are some of the specific changes in high-quality winemaking and viticulture that I have witnessed.

- More attention paid to individual vineyards, clonal selection, and trellis systems

- More care taken to match grape varieties with specific sites

- Far less filtering of wine, leading to a more complex and natural taste

- Oak used far more judiciously

- Even though wine alcohol levels have reached historic highs, most quality winemakers have adjusted their winemaking techniques to keep all components of a wine in balance.

- Sustainability has become king: Grape growers are using fewer herbicides and pesticides, and many are going organic. There are more than 500 producers of biodynamic wines, including elite wineries such as Araujo, Benziger, Castello dei Rampolla, Chapoutier, Château Pontet-Canet, Domaine Leflaive, Domaine Leroy, Grgich Hills, J. Phelps, Quintessa, and Zind Humbrecht.

- Vine density (number of vines planted per acre) has increased dramatically, which has allowed viticulturists to produce better grapes.

- Screw caps gradually are replacing corks on more than just inexpensive wines: Screw caps seal 75 percent of Australian and 93 percent of New Zealand wines.

- Climate change: Between 1960 and 1969, grape harvesting in Burgundy, France, on average began September 27. From 2000 to 2016, grape harvesting began closer to the first week of September. To help offset the effects of a shorter growing season, some viticulturists plant grapes vertically rather than horizontally to avoid excess sun.

THE WINE REGIONS OF THE WORLD

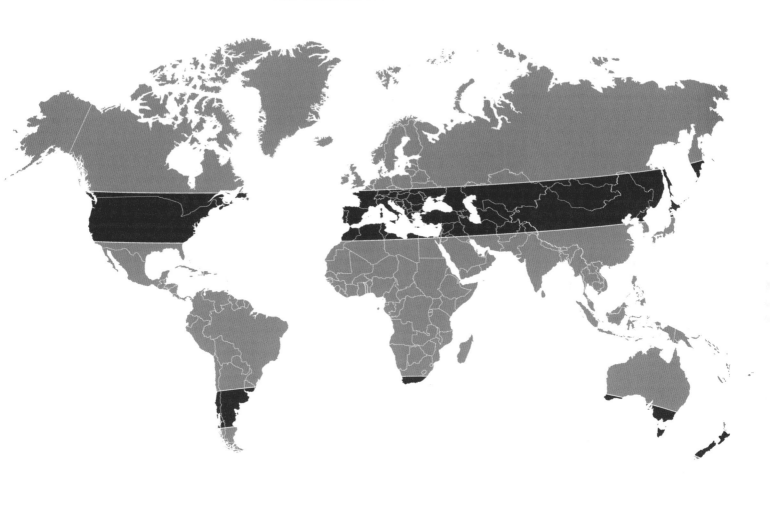

- Chaptalization (adding sugar) now rarely used
- Winemakers increasingly using natural rather than laboratory yeasts
- The European Union has standardized basic wine labeling rules for member nations, and countries exporting to the EU (and worldwide) are following their regulations. For example, one law states that if a grape is on the label, the wine must contain a minimum of 85 percent of that grape.
- Wine consumption in America has increased 70 percent over the last 20 years.

THE BUSINESS OF WINE

Besides the tremendous elevation in wine quality, the wine business has benefited greatly from the global planting of *Vitis vinifera* grapes. Cabernet Sauvignon, Merlot, Pinot Noir, Chardonnay, Riesling, Sauvignon Blanc, and other familiar grapes now grow throughout the world, making it easier for you to buy unfamiliar wines with the expectation that you will be getting a wine familiar in style and of a fairly consistent quality.

Here are a few of the most significant advances in the business of wine:

• About 70 percent of wines sold in the United States retail for $7 or less.

• 2013 was the eightieth anniversary of the repeal of Prohibition. (See page 90.)

• China has become the fifth biggest wine consumer in the world, and the fifth largest producer. Imports have doubled over the last few years, and China is now the number-one importer of Bordeaux. The Chinese are drinking primarily red (their lucky color) wine, and they are the largest consumer of red wine in the world. Consumption has increased more than 150 percent from 2007 to 2016.

• When I began my study of wine in 1970, Europe was by far the number-one producer of wine in the world, with 78 percent of the total. In 2016, Europe dropped to two-thirds and the United States increased to nearly 20 percent of worldwide wine production.

• Wine has enjoyed the largest growth rate of all alcoholic beverages since 2001.

• American wine names are becoming more creative, for example: Gnarly Head, Killer Juice, Mad Housewife, Marilyn Merlot, Kick Ass Red, Ménage à Trois, Pinot Evil, and Red Truck.

• In 2005, the Supreme Court approved the interstate shipping of wine directly to consumers, causing most states to rewrite their wine laws. FedEx and UPS are delivering wine directly to consumers, which is now legal in many states.

• According to the Silicon Valley Bank, fine wine sales—priced at $20 and above—are expected to grow between 14 and 18 percent in 2016.

• The quality of American wine lists has never been better. Although some restaurants have created "monster" lists for promotional purposes, others list only the best wines in each category. You can find wine lists in diners all across America now! Shake Shack has an extraordinary wine list.

• Costco sells more than $1.4 billion in wine annually, making it the largest retailer of wine in the United States. In 2010, Costco spent more than $22 million to help change Washington State's laws from state control to privitization of wine sales.

• Celebrity branding is big, from football players (Drew Bledsoe, Mike Ditka, John Elway, John Madden, Joe Montana, Charles Woodson—your move, Peyton Manning!), baseball stars (Tom Seaver), and race-car drivers (Jeff Gordon, Mario Andretti) to politicians (Nancy Pelosi), actors (Drew Barrymore, Angelina Jolie, and Brad Pitt), and musicians (Bob Dylan, Dave Matthews). Celebrity wine sales exceeded $50 million in 2015.

• Thanks to the Internet, anyone can become a wine critic or ask the critics questions on eRobertParker.com, *Wine Spectator*'s blog index, *Wine Enthusiast*'s UnReserved, or Dr. Vino, to name a few.

• Wine in a box is becoming more popular, especially among California jug wine producers, to reduce greenhouse emissions and lower carbon footprints by not having to ship glass.

- Exports of American wine went from almost nothing in 1970 to more than $1.5 billion today!

- When I started studying wine, there were only a few hundred wineries in the United States. Today there are more than 10,000!

- The UK's 2016 decision to leave the European Union will create havoc in their wine market, especially with 2015 Bordeaux "en premier" sales . . . but this could be great news for buyers of Bordeaux throughout the rest of the world!

WINE CONSUMERS

Combining better quality, familiar varietals, and expert marketing has given consumers worldwide some of the best wines ever produced at some of the most reasonable prices. Today you have a better selection of wine at all price points than ever before, and it promises to get even better in the future!

Here are my picks for the wine consumer highlights of the last forty years:

- In 2012, the United States became the largest wine market in the world with sales more than $40 billion. Sales in 2016 exceeded more than $53 billion! Americans are drinking more and better wine than ever before. Wine consumption here reached a record in 2015 of 893 million gallons, an increase in more than 626 million gallons since 1970. Per capita wine consumption increased from 1.31 gallons in 1970 to 3.14 gallons in 2015.

- 2015 was the twentieth consecutive year of American wine consumption growth, with total table wine sales reaching more than 769 million gallons.

- The Millennial generation (born between 1980 and 1995, and of legal drinking age as of 2016), 80 million people strong, has shown the largest percentage increase in wine consumption over Generation X (born between 1965 and 1980, 44 million) and Baby Boomers (born between 1945 and 1965, 77 million).

- Direct-to-consumer wine shipments have increased by more than 10 percent.

- Wine events proliferate in the United States, and almost all donate some proceeds to charity. In 2015, Auction Napa Valley raised $15.7 million, and since 2001 the Naples Winter Wine Festival has raised $18.7 million.

- Wine lovers turn increasingly to auctions: Worldwide auction sales totaled $337 million in 2013 compared to $33 million in 1994. United States auction sales in 2013 hit more than $126 million, and Internet auction sales exceeded $38.6 million.

- Fraudulent wines have become more prevalent. Recently, a "wine collector" was found guilty of fraud for selling counterfeit wine. (Recommended reading: *The Billionaire's Vinegar*.)

- The best châteaux of Bordeaux have been priced out of reach for the average consumer. Some 2009 and 2010 Bordeaux sell for more than $3,500 a bottle! You can "thank" China, with its new interest in Bordeaux wines, for these prices.

- Transparency of wine prices worldwide has made it better for the consumer. Internet sites like winesearcher.com will give you the price of a wine around the world.

- In France, Spain, and Italy, wine consumption has dropped more than 50 percent since 1970.

- Since his first review in 1978, American wine critic Robert Parker has become an international icon with his 100-point scoring method. He recently sold the *Wine Advocate* to three investors from Singapore but will continue to write about California.

- Election year 2016: According to the *Journal of Wine Economics*, liberals drink more alcohol.

PRELUDE TO WINE

GRAPES OF THE WORLD ✳ WINE FLAVORS ✳ BOTTLES AND GLASSES ✳ THE PHYSIOLOGY OF SMELL AND TASTE ✳ TASTING WINE ✳ HOW TO READ A WINE LABEL ✳ WINE AROMAS AND FLAVORS TABLE ✳ THE 60-SECOND WINE EXPERT

More than **50 MAJOR WHITE-WINE GRAPE VARIETIES** are grown throughout the world.

OTHER WHITE GRAPES

GRAPES	WHERE THEY GROW BEST
Albariño	Spain
Assyrtiko	Greece
Chenin Blanc	Loire Valley, France; California
Furmint	Hungary
Gewürztraminer, Pinot Blanc, Pinot Gris	Alsace, France
Hárslevelü	Hungary
Grüner Veltliner	Austria
Macabeo	Spain
Moschofilero	Greece
Olaszrizling	Hungary
Pinot Grigio (Pinot Gris)	Italy; California; Oregon; Alsace, France
Roditis	Greece
Sémillon	Bordeaux (Sauternes), France; Australia
Szürkebarát	Hungary
Torrontés Riojano	Argentina
Trebbiano	Italy
Verdejo	Spain
Vidal	Canada; New York
Viognier	Rhône Valley, France; California

GRAPES OF THE WORLD

THE QUESTION STUDENTS most frequently ask is what will help them most in learning about wine. The answer is to understand the major grape varieties and where they grow in the world.

WHITE GRAPES

So let's start with the three major grapes you need to know to understand white wine. More than 90 percent of all quality white wine comes from these three grapes, listed here from lightest style to the fullest:

Riesling   Sauvignon Blanc   Chardonnay

World-class white wine also comes from other grapes, but knowing these three makes for a good start.

TEXTURE	GRAPES	TANNIN LEVEL	WHERE THEY GROW BEST	COLOR LEVEL	AGEABILITY
Light		*Low*		*Lighter*	*Drink young*
	RIESLING		GERMANY; ALSACE, FRANCE; NEW YORK; WASHINGTON		
	SAUVIGNON BLANC		BORDEAUX, FRANCE; LOIRE VALLEY, FRANCE; NEW ZEALAND; CALIFORNIA (FUMÉ BLANC)		
	CHARDONNAY		BURGUNDY, FRANCE; CHAMPAGNE, FRANCE; CALIFORNIA; AUSTRALIA		
Full-bodied		*High*		*Deeper*	*Wine to age*

Other countries grow world-class Rieslings, Sauvignon Blancs, and Chardonnays, but in general the above regions specialize in wines made from these grapes.

RED GRAPES

Here are what I consider to be the major red-wine grapes, ranked from lightest to most full-bodied. This chart and the one on the prior page will give you an idea of the styles of the wines and also a feeling for gradations of weight, color, tannin, and ageability.

TEXTURE	GRAPES	TANNIN LEVEL	WHERE THEY GROW BEST	COLOR LEVEL	AGEABILITY
Light		*Low*		*Lighter*	*Drink young*
	GAMAY		BEAUJOLAIS, FRANCE		
	PINOT NOIR		BURGUNDY, FRANCE; CHAMPAGNE, FRANCE; CALIFORNIA; OREGON		
	TEMPRANILLO		RIOJA, SPAIN		
	SANGIOVESE		TUSCANY, ITALY		
	MERLOT		BORDEAUX, FRANCE; NAPA, CALIFORNIA		
	ZINFANDEL		CALIFORNIA		
	CABERNET SAUVIGNON		BORDEAUX, FRANCE; NAPA, CALIFORNIA; CHILE		
	NEBBIOLO		PIEDMONT, ITALY		
	SYRAH / SHIRAZ		RHÔNE VALLEY, FRANCE; AUSTRALIA; CALIFORNIA		
Full-bodied		*High*		*Deeper*	*Wine to age*

Given all the variables that go into making the many different styles of wine, putting this chart together proved extremely challenging. Exceptions to the rules always exist, just as other countries and wine regions not listed here produce world-class wine from some of the red grapes shown. You'll discover this for yourself if you do your homework and taste a lot of different wines. Good luck!

Hundreds of different red-wine grapes are planted throughout the world. **CALIFORNIA ALONE GROWS MORE THAN 30 DIFFERENT RED-WINE GRAPE VARIETIES.**

OTHER RED GRAPES	
GRAPES	**WHERE THEY GROW BEST**
Agiorgitiko	Greece
Blaufränkisch	Austria
Barbera	Italy; California
Cariñena	Spain
Carménère	Chile
Cinsault	Rhône Valley, France
Concord	United States
Cabernet Franc	Loire Valley and Bordeaux, France
Dolcetto	Italy
Grenache / Garnacha	Rhône Valley, France; Spain
Kadarka	Hungary
Kékfrankos	Hungary
Malbec	Bordeaux and Cahors, France; Argentina
Monastrell	Spain
Petite Syrah	California
Pinot Meunier	Champagne, France
Portugieser	Hungary
St. Laurent	Austria
Xinomavro	Greece

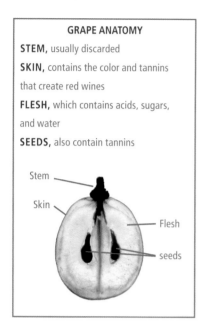
VITIS is Latin for vine.

VINUM is Latin for wine.

A SAMPLING OF THE MAJOR GRAPES:

Vitis vinifera	Chardonnay
	Cabernet Sauvignon
Vitis labrusca	Concord
	Catawba
Hybrids	Seyval Blanc
	Baco Noir

WINE FLAVORS

What causes the tastes and flavors of wine? How does a wine made from grapes smell of cherries, lemongrass, or apples if those aren't added to the fermentation vat and no artificial flavorings are used? Wine's flavors come from three main sources:

Grapes   Fermentation   Maturation and Aging

The biology and chemistry of each of these sources give us the main tastes of wine—sweet, sour, sometimes bitter—and the aroma compounds that we associate with different foods, spices, or minerals. These aroma compounds are often the same as those in actual cherries, lemongrass, or apples, but they form due to the complicated biology of grapes, the metabolic action of yeast, or the many other chemical interactions of the winemaking and aging processes.

Following the winemaking process from grape to bottle will give us a chance to see how flavors form in our wine.

FLAVORS FROM GRAPES

The major wine grapes come from *Vitis vinifera*. All over the world, winemakers use *Vitis vinifera*, which includes many different varieties of grapes—both red and white. However, other grapes are also used for winemaking. The most important native grape species in America is *Vitis labrusca*, which grows widely in New York as well as other East Coast and Midwestern states. Hybrids cross *Vitis vinifera* and native American grape species, such as *Vitis labrusca*.

The grape variety has a huge influence on wine flavor. Varietal character—the usual or expected taste and aroma of a particular grape—is an important concept in winemaking, and each type of grape has typical characteristics. For example, black grapes with thick skins tend to produce wines high in tannin, which equates to bitterness and astringency when a wine is young. Riesling grapes tend to produce wines high in acidity (sourness and tartness), and Muscat grapes produce highly aromatic wines that smell of orange flowers. Many different aspects of varietal character come through in the wine. One of the winemaker's challenges is either to preserve or to tame the distinctive qualities of grapes to create a well-balanced wine.

RED GRAPE VARIETY	GRAPE FLAVORS
CABERNET SAUVIGNON	CASSIS (BLACK CURRANT), BLACKBERRY, VIOLETS
GRENACHE	CHERRY, RASPBERRY, SPICY
MERLOT	BLACKBERRY, BLACK OLIVE, PLUM
NEBBIOLO	PLUM, RASPBERRY, TRUFFLE, ACIDITY
PINOT NOIR	PERFUMED, RASPBERRY, RED CHERRY, ACIDITY
SANGIOVESE	BLACK CHERRY, BLACKBERRY, VIOLET, SPICE
SYRAH / SHIRAZ	SPICY, BLACK FRUIT, BLUEBERRY
TEMPRANILLO	FRUITY, CHERRY
ZINFANDEL	SPICY, RIPE BERRY, CHERRY
WHITE GRAPE VARIETY	GRAPE FLAVORS
CHARDONNAY	APPLE, MELON, PEAR
RIESLING	MINERALITY, CITRUS, TROPICAL FRUIT, ACIDITY
SAUVIGNON BLANC	TOMATO STALK, CUT GRASS, GRAPEFRUIT, CITRUS, AROMATIC

Planting of vineyards for winemaking **BEGAN MORE THAN 8,000 YEARS AGO** near the Black Sea in places such as Georgia.

Winemakers say that **WINEMAKING BEGINS IN THE VINEYARD** with the growing of the grapes.

Vines are planted during their dormant periods, usually in the months of April and May. Most **VINES WILL CONTINUE TO PRODUCE GOOD-QUALITY GRAPES FOR 40 YEARS** or more.

A vine doesn't usually produce grapes suitable for winemaking **UNTIL THE THIRD YEAR**.

The "very French notion of terroir looks at all the natural conditions which influence the biology of the vinestock and thus the composition of the grape itself. The terroir is the coming together of the climate, the soil, and the landscape. It is the combination of an infinite number of factors: temperatures by night and by day, rainfall distribution, hours of sunlight, slope and drainage, to name but a few. All these factors react with each other to form, in part of the vineyard, what French wine growers call a terroir."

—BRUNO PRATS, former proprietor of Château Cos d'Estournel

LOCATION

It matters where grapes are planted. Grapes are agricultural products that require specific growing conditions. Just as you wouldn't grow oranges in Maine, so you wouldn't try to grow grapes at the North Pole. Vines have limitations. Some of these limitations are the growing season, number of days of sunlight, angle of the sun, average temperature, and rainfall. Soil is of primary concern, and adequate drainage is a requisite. The right amount of sun ripens the grapes properly to give them their sugar.

Many grape varieties produce better wines when planted in certain locations. For example, most red grapes need a longer growing season than white grapes, so red grapes usually are planted in warmer locations. In colder northern regions—Germany and northern France, for instance—most vineyards are planted with white grapes. In the warmer regions of Italy, Spain, Portugal, and California's Napa Valley, red grapes thrive.

TERROIR

The concept of terroir can be difficult to grasp because it isn't scientific. It's the "somewhereness" of a particular region or vineyard, including the soil composition and geography; sunlight, weather, and climate; rainfall; plant life of the area; and many other elements. Many winemakers believe that terroir has an impact on the flavor of wine, and the effects on grape quality from certain aspects of terroir, such as sunlight and soil drainage, are measurable.

The "taste" of soil One aspect of terroir widely believed to carry through into the finished wine is soil type. In general terms, this flavor can be described as "minerality." Certain wine regions are famous for the apparent effect of their soil on the wines they producee. German Rieslings may taste of the slate in which they grow; likewise, in Burgundy the Chardonnay grapes, which grow in limestone, may feature aromas of gunflint or wet river pebbles. Grapevines don't absorb soil through their roots, and they take in only trace amounts of minerals available in any soil, making it more likely that minerality results from some other aspect of terroir or regional winemaking processes. Still, proponents of terroir swear by the flavor of the land in wine. The mystery deepens when you consider that a sea brine aroma may manifest in Muscadet, grown at the mouth of the Loire River in France, near the Atlantic Ocean.

The taste of nearby plants On the other hand, the aromas of regional plants in wine likely come from the plants themselves. Eucalyptus aroma in wine has been shown in some cases to come from the transfer of eucalyptus oil from nearby trees to the grapes. The aroma of garrigue, the scrubby mixture of evergreen plants and herbs such as rosemary and wild thyme that grows in the southern Rhône Valley and around the Mediterranean, may find its way into wine in the same way. (Many wine tasters and critics use the expression of a wine smelling of dried herbs and spices.)

THE HARVEST

Grapes are picked when they reach the proper sugar/acid ratio for the style of wine the vintner wants to produce. Go to a vineyard in June, and taste one of the small green grapes. Your mouth will pucker because the grape is so tart and acidic. Return to the same vineyard—even to that same vine—in September or October, and the grapes will taste sweet. All those months of sun have given sugar to the grape as a result of photosynthesis.

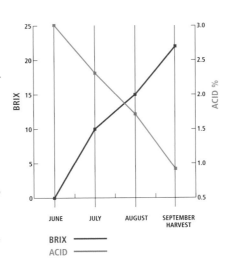

WEATHER

Weather can interfere with the quality of the harvest as well as its quantity. In the spring, as vines emerge from dormancy, a sudden frost may stop the flowering, thereby reducing yields. Even a strong windstorm can affect grapes adversely at this crucial time. Not enough rain, too much rain, or rain at the wrong time also can wreak havoc.

Rain just before the harvest will swell the grapes with water, diluting the juice and making thin, watery wines. Lack of rain will affect the wine's balance by creating a more powerful and concentrated wine but a smaller crop. A severe drop in temperature may affect the vines even outside the

Randall Grahm, owner of Bonny Doon Vineyard in California, performed an admittedly crude **EXPERIMENT IN MINERALITY**: "We simply took interesting rocks, washed them very well, smashed them up, and immersed them in a barrel of wine for a certain period." The result? Changes in the texture of the wine, more intense aroma, and greater complexity.

Don't forget that the **SEASONS IN THE SOUTHERN HEMISPHERE**—which includes Australia, New Zealand, Chile, Argentina, and South Africa—are reversed.

It takes an average of **100 DAYS** between a vine's flowering and the harvest.

BRIX: the winemaker's measure of sugar in grapes.

VINEYARD PRODUCTION:
5 bottles of wine produced annually from one grapevine
720 bottles of wine from a ton of grapes
5,500 bottles of wine produced annually from an acre of grapevines
(Napa Valley Vintners)

growing season. In New York State, the winter of 2003–04 was one of the coldest in 50 years. The result: a major decrease in wine production, with some vineyards losing more than 50 percent of their crop for the 2004 vintage.

But growers have countermeasures. They employ some of these while the grapes are on the vine; others are part of the winemaking process.

PROBLEM	RESULTS	SOLUTIONS
FROST	REDUCED YIELD	WIND MACHINES, SPRINKLER SYSTEMS, FLAMING HEATERS
NOT ENOUGH SUN	UNDERRIPE, GREEN HERBAL, VEGETAL CHARACTER, HIGH ACID, LOW SUGAR	CHAPTALIZATION
TOO MUCH SUN	OVERRIPE, HIGH-ALCOHOL, PRUNE CHARACTER	AMELIORATION (THE ADDITION OF WATER)
TOO MUCH RAIN	THIN, WATERY WINES	PRAY FOR DRIER WEATHER!
MILDEW	ROT	SPRAY WITH COPPER SULFATE
DROUGHT	SCORCHED GRAPES	IRRIGATE OR PRAY FOR RAIN
HIGH ALCOHOL	CHANGE IN THE BALANCE OF THE COMPONENTS	DE-ALCOHOLIZE
HIGH ACIDITY	SOUR, TART WINE	DE-ACIDIFY
PHYLLOXERA	DEAD VINES	GRAFT VINES ONTO RESISTANT ROOTSTOCK

RIPENESS

The concept of vintage—as in "2009 was a great vintage in Bordeaux"—involves all the weather and other events in the vineyard during the growing season, but in the end it comes back to the ripeness of the grapes at harvest. Were the grapes picked at the perfect moment in their development, when acidity, sugars, and flavors had peaked? Did this happen before the first killing frost and before a heavy rain that could dilute the juice or cause rot?

When grapes are ripe, they contain higher sugar levels, which generally translate to higher alcohol at fermentation and fuller body in the final wine. The flavors and aromas of ripe grapes are also fully developed for the possibility of greater richness and complexity in the wine. Green (unripe) grapes may result in wine with high acidity that's out of balance with the wine's flavors and with high tannin from grape skins not yet fully developed. The winemaker also may have trouble achieving an acceptable level of alcohol from fermentation. Measures can be taken in the winery to correct these problems, but often it's not possible to undo the effects of green grapes completely.

VINE AGE

Older grapevines produce fewer bunches of grapes that tend to have smaller berries and concentrated flavors—a greater intensity of aroma and flavor that translates into the wine made from these grapes.

PHYLLOXERA

A grape louse, phylloxera, is one of the grapevine's worst enemies because it eventually kills the entire plant. An epidemic infestation in the 1870s came close to destroying *all* the vineyards of Europe. Luckily, the roots of native American vines have a natural immunity to this louse. After this discovery, all European vines were pulled up and grafted onto phylloxera-resistant American rootstocks.

"NOBLE ROT"

For almost all wines, rot is undesirable and can prove disastrous. But a few of the world's finest sweet wines couldn't be made without the presence of *Botrytis cinerea*, or "noble rot." The classic sweet wines of French Sauternes, German Beerenauslese and Trockenbeerenauslese, and the Hungarian Tokaji Aszú all have a distinctive honeyed flavor due to the presence of this type of rot. This mold punctures the grape skin, allowing water to dissipate and increasing the concentration of the sugar and acid. Wines made from grapes

Although the words "old vines" or "vieilles vignes" on a wine label are not legally regulated, most winemakers agree that vines must be at least **35 YEARS OLD** to qualify.

Grapevines can grow and produce limited quantities of fruit for **MORE THAN 100 YEARS**. The Champagne house Bollinger still harvests vines planted in the mid-1800s.

One of the few countries to **ESCAPE PHYLLOXERA** is Chile. Chilean wine producers imported their vines from France in the 1860s, before phylloxera attacked the French vineyards.

In the early 1980s, phylloxera became a problem in the vineyards of California. Vineyard owners had to to replant their vines at a cost of $15,000 to $25,000 per acre, costing the California wine industry **MORE THAN $1 BILLION.**

with noble rot also have an intensity of flavor not found in conventionally harvested wines. The rot affects grape bunches gradually, so growers have the option of picking when grapes are affected only partially or waiting for a thorough onset. This means it's possible to taste only slight *Botrytis* in a wine or to get the full impact.

FLAVORS FROM FERMENTATION

Fermentation is the process by which grape juice turns into wine. The simple formula for fermentation is:

Sugar + Yeast = Alcohol + Carbon Dioxide

The fermentation process begins when the grapes are crushed and ends when all of the sugar has converted to alcohol or the alcohol level has reached around 15 percent, the point at which the alcohol kills off the yeast. Through photosynthesis, sugar occurs naturally in the ripe grape. Yeast also occurs naturally as the white bloom on the grape skin. However, today's winemakers don't always use this natural yeast. Laboratory strains of pure yeast have been isolated and may often be used, each strain contributing something unique to the style of the wine.

Carbon dioxide dissipates into the air, except in Champagne and other sparkling wines, in which this gas is retained through a special process that we'll discuss in Class Eight.

The winemaking process, in which yeast consumes sugars in the grape must and produces alcohol and carbon dioxide, is also crucial to creating flavors and aromas in wine. Depending on the temperature of the fermentation, it may take less than a week (for red wines) or a few weeks or even months (for white and sweet wines). The temperature—hot fermentation or cold fermentation—also affects the types of flavors created.

Many other factors come into play in creating flavor, such as whether the wine ferments in stainless steel tanks (which, being inert, impart no aroma) or oak vats (which may add a slight oak flavor and tannin to the wine) as well as the type of yeast the winemaker uses for fermentation.

WINEMAKING AND GRAPE-GROWING CATCHPHRASES
Reductive winemaking
Cold soaking of grapes
Phenolic ripening
Green harvesting

For wines sold in the United States, the percentage alcohol listed on the label is allowed a **MARGIN OF 1.5 PERCENT ABOVE OR BELOW THE PERCENTAGE STATED**, up to 14 percent. So, a wine labeled 13.5 percent alcohol could be as low as 12 percent or as high as 15 percent.

MOG: Material Other than Grapes.
MUST: the juice and skin mixture that comes from the grapes.

Pressing of white grape must is a delicate process usually done with **HIGH-TECH EQUIPMENT TO PREVENT A FORCEFUL PRESSING** that will extract bitter tannins from the skins and seeds.

ALCOHOL CONTENT, FLAVORS, AND BODY

The more alcohol in a wine, the more body (weight) it will have. Riper grapes at harvest contain more natural sugar, which gives the yeast more to ferment into alcohol.

"Extract"—the total solid material present in the liquid of wine—also contributes to body. Extract includes tannins, proteins, and other microscopic solids and can be increased by macerating (see page 13) the grapes before or after fermentation and by not filtering the wine. Residual sugar remaining in the wine after fermentation is also part of the extract and contributes greatly to body. Sweet wines, for example, usually have more body than dry wines.

Sparkling wine
8–12% alcohol

Table wine
8–15% alcohol

Fortified wine
17–22% alcohol

THE FERMENTATION PROCESS

The grapes come in from the vineyards, ideally packed carefully in small crates so they don't get crushed and begin fermentation before their time. When making great wine, the fruit is hand-sorted on a conveyor belt to remove sticks, leaves, stones, and other mog.

The first decision of the winemaker is whether to destem the grapes. White grapes almost always go through the destemming machine. For red wine, leaving some or all of the stems intact will add tannin when the juice, skins, and stems are soaked together. The grapes also may be put through a crusher, which breaks the berries.

After the grapes are sorted and destemmed and possibly crushed, red and white winemaking follow different paths, primarily due to the grape skins. All grape skins contain flavor compounds essential to the success of the wine. But skins and seeds also contain tannin, which can cause bitterness and astringency in young wines. Past a certain point, tannin is undesirable in white wines. For this reason, after crushing, the white grape must usually is pressed immediately to separate the juice for fermentation.

Some types of white grapes may be allowed to soak for a certain time with the skins, a process called skin contact. This allows varietal flavors and aromas—those specific to the grape variety—to be extracted from the skins and creates a richer flavor in the wine.

RED GRAPES AND WHITE WINE

The color of wine comes primarily from the grape skins. By removing the skins immediately after picking, no color transfers to the wine, and it will be white. In the Champagne region of France, many of the grapes grown are red, yet most of the resulting wine is white. California's White Zinfandel wine comes from red Zinfandel grapes.

MACERATION

Unlike white skins and juice, which are separated before fermentation, the must of black grapes goes directly to the fermentation vats. There, it may undergo maceration, or soaking, to extract aromas, tannins, and color from the skins. Maceration increases aroma intensity and the wine's mouthfeel—the weight and texture of the wine in your mouth. The winemaker may choose to macerate the must before and/or after fermentation.

CARBONIC MACERATION

Beaujolais, from Burgundy, France, has a particularly light and fruity flavor, with an aroma of fresh crushed strawberries or red raspberries. This comes from a process called carbonic maceration, in which the grape berries are left whole and undergo a type of fermentation inside each berry, without the assistance of yeast. Eventually, normal fermentation takes place, but the initial, whole-berry fermentation gives the wines a brighter color and that distinctive tutti-frutti.

ADDING SUGAR

Sometimes sugar is added to wine before fermentation in regions where this is permitted. The process is called chaptalization (after Jean-Antoine Chaptal, a proponent of the practice in the early 1800s), and it allows sugar to be added to grape must so the yeast generates more alcohol in the final wine. The added sugar compensates for grapes that don't have enough of their own natural sugars to produce a wine of sufficient alcohol—basically, to compensate for underripe grapes. Chaptalization doesn't result in a sweet wine since all of the sugars convert into alcohol.

"Wine makes daily living easier, less hurried, with fewer tensions and more tolerance."

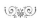

—BENJAMIN FRANKLIN

Some of the natural sugars in ripe grapes remain undigested by yeast after fermentation. This is referred to as **RESIDUAL SUGAR** in the wine, or RS. A wine with no RS, or RS below a certain legal level, is a "dry" wine.

The European Union rules that a wine labeled **"DRY"** can have up to 4 grams of sugar per liter. A wine labeled **"SWEET"** can have 45 grams per liter.

Sur lie, a French term, is used when a wine is left **AGING WITH ITS SEDIMENT**, such as dead yeast cells and grape skins and seeds.

Wild yeast is airborne in vineyards all over the world, and many wineries ferment using only the yeast present on the grape skins at harvest. **SOME WINEMAKERS USE CULTURED YEAST**, however, which can give a more predictable flavor.

THREE HIGH-TANNIN GRAPES

Nebbiolo

Cabernet Sauvignon

Syrah / Shiraz

WALNUTS also contain tannin.

King Tutankhamen, who died in 1327 B.C., apparently preferred the taste of red wine, according to scientists who found **ANCIENT RESIDUES OF RED-WINE COMPOUNDS** (tannins) in jars in his tomb.

FIVE HIGH-ACID GRAPES

Riesling (white)

Chenin Blanc (white)

Nebbiolo (red)

Sangiovese (red)

Pinot Noir (red)

AS SUGAR LEVELS INCREASE, perceived acidity decreases.

DOES THE YEAST HAVE A FLAVOR?

Yeast does have a flavor, as you know if you've ever smelled or eaten freshly baked bread. In winemaking, the yeast always has some impact on the flavor of the wine, but whether it's detectable depends on choices made by the winemaker. A sure way to create a yeasty aroma in wine is lees contact.

Lees are the dead yeast cells and other solids that settle to the bottom of the wine after fermentation. When fermentation takes place in barrels, white wine often will be left in the barrels with the lees for up to a year after fermentation has ended. This lees contact gives the wine a rich mouth-feel and a brioche or bread-roll aroma—the same effect that yeast has in Champagne making. Stirring the lees in the barrels, a process called *bâton-nage*, can increase their influence.

TANNIN

Tannin is a natural preservative and one of the many components that give wine its longevity. It comes from skins, pits, and stems of the grapes. Another source of tannin is wood, such as the oak barrels in which some wines ferment or age. Red wines generally have a higher level of tannin than whites because red grapes usually ferment with their skins.

Think of tannins as "astringent." Especially in young wines, tannin can make the wine taste bitter. Tannin is not a taste, however—it's a tactile sensation.

Tannin is also found in strong tea. What can you add to tea to make it less astringent? Milk—the fat and proteins in milk soften the tannins. So it is with a highly tannic wine. If you take another milk by-product, such as cheese, and have it with wine, it softens the tannin and makes the wine more appealing. Enjoy a beef entrée or one served with a cream sauce and a young, tannic red wine to experience this phenomenon for yourself.

ACIDITY

All wine has a certain amount of acidity. White wines generally have more perceived acidity than reds, though winemakers try to balance the fruit and acid. An overly acidic wine is also described as tart or sour. Acidity is a very important component in the aging of wines.

MALOLACTIC FERMENTATION

Malolactic fermentation ("malo" for short) takes place after the alcoholic fermentation and any lees contact. Almost all red wines undergo malo for increased stability after bottling, but it is used very selectively for whites.

Grapes have a high level of tart malic acid at harvest, the same acidity as in green apples. For most red wines and some whites, the winemaker will allow lactic bacteria naturally present to start a malolactic fermentation and convert some amount of that puckery malic acid into softer lactic acid. Malo is avoided for most white wines, except for some Chardonnays, because tart acidity is often desirable and because malo tends to give wines a buttery flavor. If you've ever had a rich, buttery California Chardonnay, you've tasted the effects of malo.

in general, the **LIGHTER THE COLOR**, the more acidity is perceived.

The word *malic* comes from the **LATIN WORD FOR APPLE**, *malum*.

FLAVORS FROM MATURATION AND AGING

Barrels have been used to ferment, mature, and ship wine for thousands of years. Early in the history of barrel use, winemakers discovered that different kinds of barrels, or even different sizes, used for varying amounts of time imparted certain flavors to wine. These flavors range from woody or cedar to vanilla, clove, or coconut, depending on the source of the barrels and how they were made.

Relatively recent alternatives to barrels, such as cement vats or stainless steel tanks, allow wines to remain free of oak flavors, for a bright, fruity effect. Most wines in the world are made with no oak aging, and it's up to the winemaker to determine the type and amount of oak influence in wine.

RED GRAPE VARIETY	WINEMAKING AND AGING FLAVORS
CABERNET SAUVIGNON	PENCIL SHAVINGS, TOAST, TOBACCO, DEAD LEAF
GRENACHE	CONCENTRATIONS, EXTRACTION
MERLOT	PENCIL SHAVINGS, TOAST
NEBBIOLO	STRONG TEA, NUTMEG, GAMEY
PINOT NOIR	SMOKY, EARTHY
SANGIOVESE	CEDAR, PLUM, VANILLA
SYRAH / SHIRAZ	TOASTY, VANILLA, COFFEE
TEMPRANILLO	OAK (AMERICAN), TOBACCO
ZINFANDEL	SAVORY, TAR, CHOCOLATE
WHITE GRAPE VARIETY	WINEMAKING AND AGING FLAVORS
CHARDONNAY	VANILLA, TOAST, BUTTERSCOTCH
RIESLING	STEELY, GREEN APPLES, PETROL
SAUVIGNON BLANC	COCONUT, SMOKY, VANILLA

Large barrels versus small Barrels range in size from 1,000- or 1,200-liter giants down to fewer than 100 liters. The larger the barrel, the lower the ratio of barrel surface area to volume, meaning that less of the wine by

"I like to think about the life of wine, how it is a living thing. I like to think about what was going on the year the grapes were growing. How the sun was shining, if it rained. I like to think about all the people who tended and picked the grapes. And if it's an old wine, how many of them must be dead by now. I like how wine continues to evolve, like if I opened a bottle of wine today it would taste different than if I'd opened it on any other day, because a bottle of wine is actually alive. And it's constantly evolving and gaining complexity, that is until it peaks, like your '61. And then it begins its steady inevitable decline."

—MAYA, from the movie *Sideways* (2004)

volume will make direct contact with the inner surface of the barrel. The largest barrels have little if any flavor impact on the wine. The barrel size most recognizable to consumers is the 225-liter barrique used in Bordeaux.

Oak flavor The wood cells inside the barrel impart their flavors and tannins when they come into contact with the alcohol in wine, adding an oak flavor. New barrels impart more flavor; as barrels are used again and again, the wine leaches much of the flavor and tannin from the cells, leaving the barrel "neutral." Not only flavor and tannin come from barrels, however—they also allow more oxygen contact with the wine. Barrels used in their first three years to impart flavor may be kept for many more simply to give wines a very slow oxidation. Winemakers often age a percentage of a given wine in new barrels and the rest in neutral barrels, then blend the two to achieve the desired wine style.

Toast When barrels are made, they are held over a heat source (fire) that makes the wood pliable and easier to bend. It also toasts the wood. The more the flame chars the interior, the more of a barrier will exist between the cells of the oak and the wine. This means less tannin and wood flavor will leach into the wine. But the toasting process imparts flavors of its own. Winemakers can order barrels with different degrees of toast depending on what flavors they want. Light toast gives few flavors of its own but still allows the wine access to heavy tannin from the oak cells. Medium toast often gives the wine a vanilla or caramel flavor. Heavy toast can taste like cloves, cinnamon, smoke, or coffee.

American oak, French oak, or Eastern European oak Oak for barrels comes from all over the United States and Europe. American oak barrels are less expensive, but European oak adds a different intensity and flavor to the wine. Winemakers source barrels according to what flavor and tannin profile they want for the wine. Differences in flavor derive from the different species of oak, different grains of the wood, and variations in barrel making.

WHAT DOES "UNFILTERED" MEAN?

After any barrel aging and before bottling, wine may be filtered to remove stray yeast cells or bacteria, microscopic bits of grape material, and other potentially unstable solids. The winemaker can give the wine a light filtration or a heavier one. Heavy filtration can strip out so much of the solid

Alternatives that may be used **TO ACHIEVE A BASIC OAK EFFECT** in less expensive wines: oak sticks or barrel staves, oak pellets, chips, powder, and even oak extract.

The flavor that a barrel gives a wine is different depending on **WHERE THE BARREL CAME FROM.** The United States, France, and Slavonia all make barrels that give a wine distinct but different flavors.

French barriques cost up to $1,200 each, while American oak barrels of the same size **COST ROUGHLY HALF.**

matter that the wine loses flavor and texture. Some winemakers and consumers believe that wine should remain unfiltered, in its more natural state, for a fuller, truer flavor experience. Unfiltered wine may be slightly less clear than filtered wine and have a fuller body and richer mouthfeel, a more intense flavor, and even some sediment on the bottom of the bottle.

VINTAGE

A vintage indicates the year the grapes were harvested, so every year is a vintage year. A vintage chart reflects the weather conditions for various years. Better weather usually results in a better rating for the vintage and therefore a higher likelihood that the wine will age well.

ARE ALL WINES MEANT TO BE AGED?

No. It's a common misconception that all wines improve with age. In fact, more than 90 percent of all wines in the world are made to be consumed within one year, and less than 1 percent of the world's wines are made to be aged for more than five years. Wines change with age. Some get better, but most don't. The good news is that the 1 percent represents more than 350 million bottles of wine every vintage!

AGING AND THE FLAVOR OF RED WINE

Wine is like a living organism, always changing from the moment it comes into being. Even bottled, it ages due to the effects of oxygen and reactions that cause tannins to drop to the bottom of the bottle as grainy sediment, new flavors to develop, and color to change from bright to pale.

The first known reference to a specific vintage was made by Roman scientist Pliny the Elder, who rated the wines of 121 B.C. **"OF THE HIGHEST EXCELLENCE."**

2010 was a great vintage year in **EVERY MAJOR WINE REGION ON EARTH!**

Around 90 percent of wine bought in the United States is consumed **WITHIN 24 HOURS OF PURCHASE.**

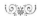
**MY FAVORITE WINES
FOR LONG AGING:**

REDS:

Red Bordeaux

Barolo or Barbaresco

Napa Cabernet Sauvignon

Rhône Valley (Syrah / Grenache)

Vintage Port

WHITES:

White Burgundy from the Côte de
Beaune

Chenin Blanc (Vouvray) from the Loire

German Riesling (Auslese or above)

Tokay from Hungary

White Bordeaux (Sauternes)

As tannins become sediment, the tannin in the wine itself decreases, so the wine tastes gentler, with more fruit, tannin, and acid balance. When wine is young, its fruit flavors are fresh; as it ages, the fruit may taste dried (dried cherries, prunes, dates), and the wine may develop vegetal aromas (mushrooms, canned peas, asparagus). Oxygen also makes itself known in the form of a gradual browning of the wine's color and a gradual nutty flavor.

WHAT MAKES A WINE LAST MORE THAN FIVE YEARS?

The color and the grape Red wines, because of their tannin content, will generally age longer than whites. Certain red grapes, such as Cabernet Sauvignon, tend to have more tannin than, say, Pinot Noir.

The vintage The better the weather conditions in one year, the more likely the wines from that vintage will have a better balance of fruits, acids, and tannins and therefore have the potential to age longer.

Where the wine comes from Certain vineyards have optimum conditions for growing grapes, including soil, weather, drainage, and slope of the land. All of these factors contribute to producing a great wine that will taste better after aging.

How the wine was made (vinification) The longer the wine remains in contact with its skins during fermentation (maceration), and if it is fermented and / or aged in oak, the more of the natural preservative tannin it will have, which can help it age longer. These are just two examples of how winemaking can affect the aging of wine.

Storage conditions Even the best-made wines in the world won't age well if stored improperly. Best storage conditions: 55°F and 75 percent humidity.

BAD FLAVORS

Successful winemaking depends on the cooperation of certain micro-organisms—and equally on the good behavior of others. Occasionally, things go wrong. Here are the five most common wine faults or flaws and what they taste like.

Corked wine This isn't bits of cork floating in the glass. "Corked" describes a musty aroma in wine caused by the organic compound commonly called trichloroanisole (TCA). Many theories explain how TCA affects the cork, but we know that, when TCA in the cork comes into contact with wine in the bottle, it causes a smell similar to wet or mildewed cardboard. This can range in strength from almost undetectable—when it merely dulls the flavor of the wine—to a strong reek that you can smell from across the room.

There's no remedy for corked wine. Because it causes huge losses in the wine industry each year, many winemakers are switching to screw-cap closures instead of natural cork.

Oxidation Just as a cut apple oxidizes when exposed to air, grape juice undergoes a transformation through contact with oxygen. Oxygen begins its interaction with grape juice the moment the grapes are harvested and brought to the winery, and much of winemaking is about carefully protecting the wine from oxygen. Many winemakers, depending on the style of wine they produce, allow controlled oxidation to add an additional layer of flavor in their wine. Accidental overexposure to oxygen results in browning of the wine and a nutty, sherrylike flavor.

Sulfur Sulfur dioxide is a natural antioxidant, preservative, and disinfectant used by most winemakers at various stages of the winemaking process to prevent unwanted oxidation of the grape juice and to inhibit the action of bacteria or wild yeast. If the level of sulfur in the finished wine isn't carefully monitored, you'll know by the smell (burnt matches) that the sulfur was overused. If there's any hint of sulfur dioxide in the wine, that's a flaw.

Brett If you've ever tasted a wine with an aroma of a barnyard—more specifically: sweaty saddle or sweaty horse—you've tasted Brett. Brett is short for *Brettanomyces*, a yeast that may grow in the winery, particularly on equipment or in barrels not carefully cleaned, and will infect wine that comes into contact with it. For some, Brett isn't all that bad: Many tasters think it adds a desirable complexity to the flavor of wine when present at low levels.

Volatile acidity All wines have a certain level of desirable volatile acidity, or VA, but VA becomes a fault when the bacteria *Acetobacter*—used to create vinegar—goes to work. *Acetobacter* creates excess acetic acid in wine, which in high concentrations causes the wine to smell like vinegar.

TCA is present not only in wine but causes **MUSTY ODORS** in some packaged food products as well.

Ten years ago, appoximately 9 percent of all wine **COLORS WERE CONSIDERED BAD.** Today that number has dropped to 3 percent.

To identify the flavor of oxidation in wine, **THINK OF SHERRY,** which is intentionally oxidized during winemaking.

Winemakers can avoid adding sulfur during winemaking, but all wines contain at least a small amount because **YEAST PRODUCES SULFUR** during fermentation.

Sulfur is a **COMMON PRESERVATIVE** in foods such as dried fruit.

—— FURTHER READING ——

The Art and Science of Wine by James Halliday

From Vines to Wine by Jeff Cox

The Vintner's Apprentice by Eric Miller

BOTTLES AND GLASSES

BOTTLES

SIZES AND NAMES

NAME	BOTTLE RATIO	VOLUME
SPLIT	¼	187.5 ML
DEMI / HALF	½	375 ML
STANDARD	1	750 ML
MAGNUM	2	1.5 L
JEROBOAM	4	3 L
REHOBOAM	6	4.5 L
SALMANAZAR	12	9 L
BALTHAZAR	16	12 L
NEBUCHADNEZZAR	20	15 L
MELCHIOR	24	18 L

SHAPES AND WINES

The shape of a bottle can tell you at a glance what kind of wine it likely contains, but the **COLOR ALSO CAN HELP.** Certain German white wines usually come in brown bottles, while others come in green.

From the Jeroboam up, wine bottle sizes take their names from kings in the Old Testament.

Riesling
Flute-style

Cabernet Sauvignon, Merlot
Squared shoulders

Chardonnay, Pinot Noir
Sloping shoulders

Champagne, sparkling wine
Sloping shoulders, thicker glass

Melchior 24 Bottles

Nebuchadnezzar 20 Bottles

Balthazar 16 Bottles

Salmanazar 12 Bottles

Rehoboam 6 Bottles

Jeroboam 4 Bottles

Magnum 2 Bottles

Standard 1 Bottle

Which size bottle do many collectors **PREFER FOR AGING** their wines? See page 293.

Demi / Half   Split

CONTENTS OF A BOTTLE OF WINE

Alcohol

Water

Other:

glycerol   amino acids
acids   esters
phenols   sulfites
minerals   acetaldehyde
sugar

A bottle of wine (750 ml) contains 600–800 grapes (2.4 lbs.) and is on average **86 PERCENT WATER.**

A standard 225 L barrel of wine is **240 BOTTLES.**

Standard bottle (750 ml) = 5 glasses (5 ounces / 150 ml)

GLASSES

WINE GLASSES AND WINE STYLES

These are just some of the specialized glasses that glassmakers have created for various styles of wine. An **ALL-PURPOSE 10–12 OUNCE** wine glass is perfectly appropriate for all still wines.

Bold Red
Example: Cabernet Sauvignon

Light Red
Example: Pinot Noir

Sweet Red
Example: Port

Bold White
Example: Chardonnay

Delicate White
Example:
Sauvignon Blanc

Flute
Example: sparkling

Sweet White
Example: Sauternes

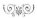

"Wine is the most healthful and most hygienic of beverages."

—LOUIS PASTEUR

THE PHYSIOLOGY OF SMELL AND TASTE

BY KEVIN ZRALY AND WENDY DUBIT

One of the most wonderful things about wine is its ability to bring us to our senses. All of our senses factor into the enjoyment of wine, but none does so as powerfully or pleasurably as olfaction, our sense of smell. Happily, most wine tasters regularly experience what evolving scientific understanding also proves: the importance of smell and its impact on everything from learning and loving to aging and health.

Our love of wine and fascination with olfaction brought Wendy and me together to write this chapter. We hope you enjoy it with a good glass of wine, great memories in mind, and more in the making.

A LETTER FROM KEVIN

The sense of smell has always facinated me. The sweet aroma of chamomile tea brewing on the kitchen woodstove dominates my earliest memories of my grandfather's farm. I grew up in a small town not far from New York City in a house surrounded by a forest of clean, fragrant pines. That memory no doubt led me to build a new house smack in the middle of a pine forest.

When I was a child I practically lived at the local swimming pool, and I smelled of chlorine all summer long. Even as an adult, I find the taste and smell of hot buttered popcorn contributes enormously to how much I enjoy a movie. Of course not everything smells like roses or summons sweet memories. We once had a gingko tree in our front yard that shed foul, nasty-smelling fruit once a year.

As a teenager with hormones skyrocketing, I doused myself in English Leather cologne. To this day, opening a bottle immediately transports me back to the fun-filled days of youth. I'm not sure why, but I stopped wearing cologne when I truly began to smell wine. Is it coincidence, or is it smell?

Nor will I ever forget the smell of downtown New York following the September 11th terrorist attacks. It lingered for months. Even a year later, a

Scent critic Chandler Burr rated the top ten best-smelling cities in the world. My hometown of **PLEASANTVILLE, NEW YORK, CAME IN SECOND** in the world!

sudden whiff caught me by surprise. Fifteen years later, its mephitic cloud still hovers, a smell indelibly etched in my memory.

The smells of wine—grapes, earth, the wine itself—seduced me as a young adult; 40 years later I am still in their thrall. The sexy musk of freshly plowed earth, the fragrant balm of grapes fermenting right after harvest, and the lusty bouquet of new Beaujolais still intoxicate. An old red wine with hints of tobacco, mushrooms, fallen leaves, and the damp-earth smell of my wine cellar still invigorate.

Just as the smell of cooking garlic whets my appetite and the smell of the seashore calms my nerves, so the smell of crisp autumn air reminds me that the harvest is in and my favorite time of year has come to its end.

Smell is critical to the preservation of life and one of our most primitive senses. Yet we humans, having radically reshaped our relationship with the natural world, often take our sense of smell for granted. I continue to examine how smell and taste figure in my life. I hope that you will enjoy exploring the fascinating mysteries of olfaction in this chapter and that it will enrich your daily life and intensify your enjoyment of wine.

A LETTER FROM WENDY

I've always lived fully attuned to each of the five senses, but it's my nose that I've followed most. Doing so has brought me nearly everywhere I want to be—most notably to the wine industry.

From as far back as age eight, I implicitly linked my sense of smell to my love of learning. If my mind tired during studies, I might peel a tangerine or sit nearer a lilac bush or linden tree. By high school, I used this technique

WENDY DUBIT, founder of The Senses Bureau (www.thesensesbureau.com) and Vergant Media (www.vergant.com), served as editor in chief of *Friends of Wine* and *Wine Enthusiast* magazines before starting a number of media entities ranging from record labels to television series. She continues to write and speak on wine, food, and lifestyle and to lead tastings worldwide, including Wine Workout, which uses tasting wine as a way to strengthen the senses, memory, and mind.

more explicitly and began adding color and music for optimal learning and sensory experiences. Concepts and their applications became linked to and triggered by shades and scents of citrus and pine, strands of Vivaldi and Chopin. What I lacked in photographic memory, I could usually compensate for by engaging and summoning my senses.

As a teen, I was invited to the "openings" of my parent's dinner parties, where my dad, who delighted in all things Burgundy and Bordeaux, offered me a small pour of wine and asked for my olfactory impressions. I'll always remember the evening I discovered a marriage of river rocks, wet leather from the underside of a saddle, hay flecked with wildflowers, and golden apples in a single pour.

"Ah," Dad said, nodding in encouragement, "Puligny-Montrachet."

The name itself was as delightfully poetic to my ear as the wine had been to my nose and mouth. Even though those youthful days were rich with honest smells—kitchen, backyard, woods, stream, farm—I'll always remember being most awed by the abundant and complex smells I found in a single glass of wine. A glass of great wine encompasses an entire world of smell, layer upon layer of riches.

Since those early dinner parties, Puligny has become a favorite wine and a symbol of the enduring bond between Dad and me. The last time I saw him was in a hospital—decades later—and I'll always cherish the evening he asked for a glass of Puligny. Surely he knew that the orderlies wouldn't bring a bottle with his dinner, so I talked to him about the wine. I described its beguiling white Burgundian blend of minerals, acidity, crisp fruit, and toasted oak. I recalled our trips to the Côte de Nuits and the Côte de Beaune, detailing the particular pleasures of each bottle of wine we'd brought home. As I was talking, my father became increasingly relaxed. By the time I finished he was utterly calm, with a dramatically improved oxygenation level.

"Thank you," he said, bowing his head. "I just wanted to hear it in your words."

Wine is both training ground and playground for all five of our senses, our memory, and our intellect. Consequently, our enjoyment and under-standing of the full wine-tasting experience improves dramatically if we observe, smell, taste, feel, analyze, and remember more carefully. Good wine demands that we stop and savor each taste to allow its rich, sensuous story to unfold more completely. Every wine deserves the attention of all five senses. But smell, with its ability to evoke memory and feeling, matters most.

Numerous studies have proven the **POWER OF SCENTS TO AFFECT MOOD AND MEMORY.** Lavender has the power to calm. Citrus enhances alertness and now is broadcast in many office buildings in Japan. Shakespeare writes in Hamlet, "There's rosemary, that's for remembrance. Pray thee, love, remember."

The **OLDEST PART OF THE HUMAN BRAIN** is the olfactory region.

As proof of the evolutionary importance of smell, **1–2 PERCENT OF OUR GENES AFFECT OLFACTION**, approximately the same percentage involved in the immune system.

Implicit memories are perceptual, emotional, sensory, and often are encoded and retrieved unconsciously. Explicit memories are factual, episodic, temporal, and require conscious coding and retrieval. **A GOOD WINE, WELL PERCEIVED AND DESCRIBED**, lives on in both forms of memory.

Axel and Buck isolated **10,000 DIFFERENT SMELLS**.

HOW WE SMELL

With each inhalation, we gather essential information about the world around us—its delights, opportunities, and dangers. We can shut our eyes, close our mouths, withdraw our touch, and cover our ears, but the nose, with notable exceptions, is always working, alerting us to potential danger and possible pleasure.

Our sense of smell also enhances learning, evokes memory, promotes healing, cements desire, and inspires us to action. It's so important to the preservation and sustenance of life that the instantaneous information it gathers bypasses the thalamus, which processes other senses, and moves directly to the limbic system. The limbic system controls our emotions, our emotional responses, mood, motivation, and our pain and pleasure sensations, and it's where we analyze olfactory stimuli.

The limbic system is the collective name for structures in the human brain involved in emotion, motivation, and emotional association with memory. It plays its role in the formation of memory by integrating emotional states with stored memories of physical sensations—such as smells.

Memory stored in the limbic system uniquely links emotional state with physical sensation, creating our most important and primitive form of learning: working memory. We remember smell differently than we recall sight, sound, taste, or touch because we may respond to smell the same way we respond to emotion: an increased heart rate, enhanced sensitivity, and faster breathing. It's this emotional connection that gives smell the power to stimulate memory so strongly and why a single smell can transport us instantly back to a particular time and place.

In 2004, Columbia University professor Richard Axel and Fred Hutchinson Cancer Research Center professor Linda B. Buck recieved the

LIMBIC SYSTEM

OLFACTORY BULB

Nobel Prize in Medicine for their breakthrough discoveries in olfaction. Axel and Buck discovered a large family of genes in the cells of the epithelium, or lining, of the upper part of the nose that control production of unique protein receptors, called olfactory receptors. Olfactory receptors specialize in recognizing and then attaching themselves to thousands of specific molecules of incoming odorants. Once attached, the trapped chemical molecules are converted to electrical signals. These signals relay to neurons in the olfactory bulbs (one in each nasal cavity) before traveling along the olfactory nerve to the primary olfactory cortex, part of the brain's limbic system, for analysis and response. By the time the electrical signals of smell reach the limbic system, the component parts of a smell—wet leather, wildflowers, golden apples, and river rocks—already have been identified and translated into electric signals. The limbic system recombines these components for analysis by scanning its vast memory data bank for related matches. With analysis complete, the limbic system triggers an appropriate physiological response. In the case of Puligny wine, the limbic system might recognize it as a pleasant white wine made from Chardonnay grapes. More experienced wine tasters, with a more highly developed memory data bank, connect our wine to other Puligny wines and recognize it as Puligny. Expert tasters might be able to recall the vineyard, maker, and year. The more we taste, test, and study, the better we become at identification and enjoyment.

Scientists and experts agree that smell accounts for up to 90 percent of what many perceive as **TASTE AND MOUTHFEEL.**

SIZE AND SHAPE do matter. Deep, good wineglasses, such as Riedel's lines of stemware, enhance varietal aroma.

THE NOSE KNOWS: Exposure to certain easily recognizable smells while forming memories will link the memory to the smell. So (as Wendy implicitly understood as a young girl) eating tangerines, for example, while studying for a test makes it easier to remember the information by recalling the smell of tangerines while taking the test.

DIFFERENT SMELLS OF WINE come from the grape, the winemaking, and the aging.

THREE AROMATIC GRAPES
Muscat
Gewürztraminer
Torrontés

OLFACTORY PATHWAY FROM BOTTLE TO BRAIN

We can trace the olfactory pathway, of a bottle of Puligny for example, through the following steps:

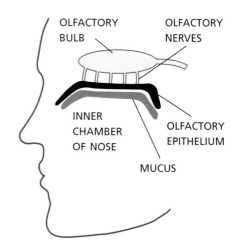

- Open the bottle, in happy anticipation.

- Pour the wine into a proper glass.

- Swirl the glass to release the wine's aromas.

- Inhale the wine's bouquet deeply and repeatedly.

- Chemical components— esters, ethers, aldehydes— swirl upward through the nostrils on currents of air.

- Midway up the nose, millions of olfactory receptor neurons (olfactory epithelia), with their specialized protein receptors, bind the odorants that form the components of the specific wine profile.

- Interaction of the odor molecules matched with the right receptor causes the receptor to change shape.

- This change gives rise to an electrical signal that goes first to the olfactory bulb and then to the areas of the brain that convert the electrical signal to the identification of a smell, or group of smells.

- The brain associates the smell(s) with perception, impressions, emotions, memories, knowledge, and more.

THE BIOLOGY OF SMELL

The septum, made up of cartilage, divides the nose into two separate chambers, or nostrils, each with discretely wired epithelium and olfactory bulbs. Each nostril serves a different function and operates at peak capacity at different times. It is rare for both nostrils, even in the healthiest noses, to work at full capacity simultaneously, and people with a deviated septum often report being able to breathe out of only one nostril. Lyall Watson, author of

Jacobson's Organ and the Remarkable Nature of Smell, reports, "A three-hour cycle of alternation between left and right nostrils goes on night and day. At night it contributes to sleep movements." Watson hypothesizes that by day, when we are conscious, right and left nostrils direct information to accordant parts of the brain—the right being the side that perceives, intuits, encodes, and stores implicitly; the left being the side that explicitly analyzes, names, records, and retrieves. "Ideally, we need both. . . . But if a situation is strange and requires action based more on prediction than precedent, you would be better off facing it with a clear left nostril."

Each nostril can **DETECT DIFFERENT SMELLS**.

HOW WE TASTE

Like smell, taste belongs to our chemical sensing system. Special structures called taste buds detect taste, and we have, on average, between 5,000 and 10,000 of them, mainly on the tongue but with a few at the back of the throat and on the palate. Taste buds are the only sensory cells that are replaced regularly throughout a person's lifetime, with total regeneration taking place approximately every ten days. Scientists are examining this phenomenon, hoping to discover ways to replicate the process, inducing regeneration in damaged sensory and nerve cells.

Clustered within each taste bud, gustatory cells have small gustatory hairs containing gustatory receptors. The gustatory receptors, like the olfactory receptors, sense specific types of dissolved chemicals. Everything we eat and drink must be dissolved—usually by saliva—in order for the gustatory receptors to identify the taste. Once dissolved, the gustatory receptors read then translate a food's chemical structure before converting that information to electrical signals. These electrical signals travel, via the facial and glossopharyngeal nerves, through the nose and on to the brain, where they are decoded and identified as a specific taste.

A well-crafted wine's aroma evolves in the glass and our noses quickly become inured to smell. This is why it's advisable to **REVISIT A WINE'S AROMA A FEW TIMES IN ANY GIVEN TASTING** or flight. Tasters can take a cue from the old perfumer's trick of sniffing their sleeves between the many essences / elixirs they may smell on a given day. In other words, they turn to something completely different—balancing sense with non-sense.

SALIVATION

Saliva is critical not only to the digestion of food and to the maintenance of oral hygiene but also to flavor. Saliva dissolves taste stimuli, allowing their chemistry to reach the gustatory receptor cells.

Remember being told to chew your food slowly so that you would enjoy your meal more? It's true. Taking more time to chew food and savor

TASTING AND CHEWING increase the rate of salivary flow.

beverages allows more of their chemical components to dissolve and more aromas to be released. This result provides more material for the gustatory and olfactory receptors to analyze, sending more complex data to the brain, which enhances perception. Taste and smell intensify.

While the majority of our taste buds are located in the mouth, we also have thousands of additional nerve endings—especially on the moist epithelial surfaces of the mouth, throat, nose, and eyes—that perceive texture, temperature, and assess a variety of factors, recognizing sensations like the prickle of sulfur, the coolness of mint, and the burn of pepper. While humans can detect an estimated 10,000 smells and smell combinations, we can taste just four or five basic flavors—sweet, salty, sour, bitter, and savory (umami). Of these, only sweet, sour, and occasionally bitterness are applicable to wine tasting.

The overall word for what we perceive in food and drink through a combination of smelling, tasting, and feeling is flavor, with smell being so predominant of the three that we believe that wine tasting is actually "wine smelling." Some chemists describe wine as "a tasteless liquid that is deeply fragrant." It is flavor that lets us know whether we are eating an apple or a pear, drinking a Puligny-Montrachet or an Australian Chardonnay. If you doubt the importance of smell in determining taste, hold your nose while eating chocolate or cheese, either of which will tend to taste like chalk.

TASTE PLACE

Some taste maps place concentrated sweet receptors at the tip of the tongue, bitter at the back, and sour at the sides, but taste buds are distributed broadly throughout the mouth. In wine tasting, it's important to let wine aerate once it reaches your mouth so that it will release more aromas and intensify flavor. Do this by rolling the wine over your tongue and allowing it to linger on the tongue. This process also spreads the wine across a wider array of gustatory receptors and gives them more time to analyze its taste. You'll discover that a good wine will reveal a first, middle, and lasting impression, which are determined largely by aroma and mouthfeel.

There is **NO SALT** in wine.

BITTERNESS IN WINE arises from a combination of high alcohol and high tannin.

WHERE DO YOU EXPERIENCE BITTERNESS?

The back of the tongue

On the sides of the mouth

In the throat

Much of **WHAT IS COMMONLY DESCRIBED AS TASTE**—80–90 percent or more—is aroma/bouquet, as sensed and articulated by our olfactory receptors, and mouthfeel and texture as sensed by surrounding organs.

MOUTHFEEL

Mouthfeel is literally how a wine feels in the mouth. These feelings are characterized by sensations that delight, prick, and/or pain our tongue, lips, and cheeks and that often linger in the mouth after swallowing or spitting. They can range from the piquant tingle of Champagne bubbles to the teeth-tightening astringency of tannin; from the cool expansiveness of menthol/eucalyptus to the heat of a high-alcohol red; and from the cloying sweetness of a low-acid white to the velvet coating of a rich Rhône. The physical feel of wine is also important to mouthfeel and includes: body, thin to full; weight, light to heavy; and texture, austere, unctuous, silky, and chewy. Each contributes to wine's overall balance. More than just impressions, these qualities can trigger a physical response—drying, puckering, and salivation—that can have wines literally dancing on the tongue and clinging to the teeth.

WINE TEXTURES
LIGHT: skim milk
MEDIUM: whole milk
FULL: heavy cream

SMELL AND TASTE TOGETHER

Recent research presents additional proof that taste seldom works alone —as wine tasters have known for centuries—and provides the first clear scientific evidence that olfaction is uniquely "dual." We often smell by inhaling through both nose and mouth simultaneously, adding to smell's complexity.

Smells can reach the olfactory receptors by two paths:

Orthonasal stimulation Odor compounds (smells) reach the olfactory bulb via the external nares or nostrils.

Retronasal stimulation Odor compounds reach the olfactory bulb via the internal nares, located inside the mouth (the respiratory tract at the back of the throat). This is why even if you pinch your nose shut, a strong cheese inhaled through the mouth may still smell. Molecules that stimulate the olfactory receptors float around in your mouth, up through your internal nares, and stimulate the olfactory neurons in the olfactory bulb.

According to an article in the journal *Neuron*, researchers reported that the smell of chocolate stimulated different brain regions when introduced into the olfactory system through the nose (orthonasally) than it did when introduced through the mouth (retronasally). The study suggests that sensing odor through the nose may help indicate the availability of food while identification through the mouth may signify receipt of food.

"A wine goes in my mouth, and I just see it. I see it in three dimensions. The textures. The flavors. The smells. They just jump out at me. I can taste with a hundred screaming kids in a room. When I put my nose in a glass, it's like tunnel vision. I move into another world, where everything around me is just gone, and every bit of mental energy is focused on that wine."
—ROBERT M. PARKER JR., author and wine critic, in the *Atlantic Monthly*

Hypergeusia, hypogeusia, and aguesia— **HEIGHTENED TASTE AND PARTIAL AND TOTAL TASTE LOSS,** respectively—are rare and usually reflect a smell loss, which is often confused with a taste loss.

OLFACTORY ABILITIES OVER A LIFETIME

Experts agree that, except in rare instances of brain disease or damage, we are born with relatively equal ability to perceive smell, although our ability to identify and articulate those smells varies widely. In general, women have the advantage over men in perceiving and identifying smells throughout their life cycle. While it's not known why, theories hold that, because women bear the enormous responsibility of conceiving and raising children, a keen sense of smell evolved as an aid to everything from choosing a mate to caring for a family.

Dr. Alan Hirsch of the Smell & Taste Treatment and Research Foundation and experts from the Monell Chemical Senses Center have shed additional light on the evolution and devolution of smell over a lifetime by describing the changes that occur at periods in the life cycle.

Fetus In utero, the fetus acquires its blood supply through the placenta, via which it may receive odorants that help the baby recognize Mom at birth, and which may lead to developing food preferences for what Mom ate or drank.

Lactation Flavors and smells from food and beverage make their way through mother's milk to the infant. As a result, preferences form toward sweet and away from bitter. Any wine or spirits the mother consumes while nursing are measurable in the baby.

Early childhood As a child grows, so does his or her ability to recognize and remember different odors, especially those paired with an emotional event. At this point in their development, children usually have a hard time describing smells in words, but they are forming lifelong positive and negative sensory and emotional impressions. For example, smelling roses in the garden with Mom will have a far different impact on the feeling the scent elicits later in life than if a child first smells roses at the funeral of a loved one.

Elementary school years Boys' and girls' ability to perceive and identify smells continues to develop, becoming more acute, with the ability to distinguish more smells.

Puberty The sense of smell reaches its most acute level in both boys and girls, although girls surge further ahead at the onset of menstruation. This heightened sensitivity to smell will persist throughout their fertile years.

Adulthood Women consistently outscore men in their ability to put names to smells in adulthood, and women give higher ratings on pleasure and intensity, lower ratings on unpleasant aromas. Women's sense of smell is particularly acute at ovulation and during pregnancy.

Midlife Men and women slowly lose their acuity of smell between the ages of 35 and 40, though the ability to identify and remember smells can continue to improve over the course of a lifetime.

Age 65 By age 65, about half the population will experience a decline, on average, of 33 percent in olfactory abilities. A quarter of the population has no ability to smell after 65.

Age 80 A majority of the population will show losses of up to 50 percent in olfactory abilities by age 80.

The Smell & Taste Treatment and Research Foundation published the following lists of the **DIFFERENT SMELLS THAT AROUSE WOMEN AND MEN:**

WOMEN	MEN
Turn-ons	*Turn-ons*
Baby powder	Cinnamon buns
Banana-nut bread	Doughnuts
Chocolate	Lavender
Cucumber	Licorice
Good & Plenty candy	Pumpkin pie
Lavender	
Turn-offs	*Turn-offs*
Charcoal barbecue smoke	None found!
Cherry	
Men's cologne	

(Scripps Howard)

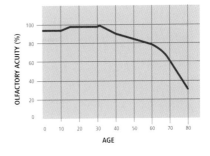

OLFACTORY ACUITY reaches its peak in young adulthood, around 32 years old.

KINDS OF TASTERS

According to Janet Zimmerman, in her article "Science of the Kitchen: Taste and Texture," approximately one-quarter of the population are "non-tasters," half are "tasters," and one-quarter are "super-tasters." Super-tasters have a significantly higher number of taste buds than tasters, and both groups outnumber non-tasters for taste buds. The averages for the three groups are 96 taste buds per square centimeter for non-tasters, 184 for tasters, and a whopping 425 for super-tasters. Non-tasters are far from picky and seem less conscious of and therefore less engaged with what they eat and drink. Tasters, the largest and least homogeneous group, vary in their personal preferences but tend to enjoy the widest array of food and drink and relish the act of eating and drinking the most of the three groups. Super-tasters tend to taste everything more intensely. Sweets are sweeter, bitters are more bitter, and many foods and beverages, including alcohol, taste and feel unpleasantly strong.

ACCOUNTING FOR SMELL AND TASTE

What accounts for ethnic and cultural differences in smell and taste abilities, perceptions, and preferences? According to Monell Chemical Senses Center anthropologist Claudia Damhuis, some odor associations/preferences might be innate (such as an aversion to the odor of rotten food), but the vast majority of them are learned.

THE WAY WE LEARN

The ability to identify and perceive odors, as well as odor preferences, is learned both implicitly and explicitly through a number of variables including environment, culture, custom, context, and a variety of sociocultural factors. Factors that impact cultural differences in odor preferences include:

- Physiological differences, such as the size and presence of glands in different populations
- Differences in hygienic habits
- Acceptability and denial of odors according to cultural norms and etiquette
- Familiarity with specific odors

- The role and function attributed to specific odors
- Cultural differences in food preparations and related olfactory experiences and association
- Precision of language used to express odor perceptions and associations

GENERAL PREFERENCES

Across a great variety of ethnicities, odors can fall into a few general categories of association, which are smells and flavors associated with nature, man, civilization, food and drink, and more.

A worldwide smell survey conducted by *National Geographic* and Monell found universal unpleasantness noted across nine regions for fecal odors, human odors, material in decomposition, and mercaptans (sulfur-containing compounds often added to natural gas as a warning agent). Most odors, however, were rated pleasant, including vegetation, lavender, amyl acetate (banana odor), galaxolide (synthetic musk), and eugenol (synthetic clove oil).

CULTURAL DIFFERENCES

Physiology, environment, diet, and language all play roles in cultural preference. The Asian preference for soy rather than dairy products—which carries through even in the smells and flavors of mothers' milk—might account for Asian cultural aversion to strong cheese smells and flavors. Asian-American communities, families, or individuals may or may not exhibit this aversion, depending on the degree to which they retain native food-and-drink customs or adopt local ones.

Other cultural differences might be environmental, as was suggested by a study of the Serer N'Dut of Senegal, who classify their odors in only five categories—scented, milk-fishy, rotten, urinelike, and acidic—or linguistic, as in a cross-cultural French / Vietnamese / American study in which participants' odor categorization didn't correlate with their linguistic categorization.

IMPLICIT LEARNING IS LARGELY UNCONSCIOUS. Odors are identified and perceived and associations are made mainly in the background, such as the smell of hot dogs in a baseball stadium. EXPLICIT LEARNING IS A CONSCIOUS PROCESS, in which the person is aware of the learning taking place, such as at a wine tasting.

One culture's special foods and beverages, such as chile peppers, can become highly popular and spread quickly to other groups. Others prove less appealing and stay put. Think of Korea's kim-chee; Norway's lutefisk; prairie oysters in the American West; and, in the wine world, Greece's RETSINA, A WINE FLAVORED BY TREE RESIN.

Mercaptans, described as smelling UNCOMFORTABLY SKUNKLIKE, are a natural by-product of fermentation. They can be removed by aeration during the winemaking process.

English wine writers occasionally use gooseberries to describe a wine's aroma, but MOST AMERICANS ARE UNFAMILIAR WITH GOOSEBERRIES and don't know what they smell like.

In *The Emperor of Scent,* Chandler Burr uses A PARTICULARLY PUNGENT BURGUNDIAN CHEESE to illustrate cultural preferences: When they smell Soumaintrain, "Americans think, 'Good God!' The Japanese think, 'I must now commit suicide.' The French think, 'Where's the bread?'"

THINGS THAT CAN AFFECT YOUR SENSE OF SMELL

According to the University of California at San Diego Nasal Dysfunction Clinic, an estimated 1 to 2 percent of the American population suffers from the total loss of the sense of smell.

The primary complaint for the majority of people who seek help for smell loss is that food has lost its flavor. But their lives suffer in other ways, too, from the inability to avoid such dangers as spoiled food and gas leaks to missing out on some of life's greatest and most sensuous pleasures because the sense of smell plays a key role in sexual excitement. Americans may spend an enormous amount of time and money masking body odors and sexual smells, but those smells remain vital to our sense of self and our bonds with others—from the families in which we're born to the families we create.

SMELL AND TASTE DISORDERS

It's extremely rare to be born with chemosensory disorders. Most smell disorders develop after an injury, illness, or in response to irritants or drugs.

An array of injuries, illnesses, and irritants can adversely affect the sense of smell, partially or fully, permanently or temporarily, including head or brain injuries; nose injuries; allergies, colds, and sinusitis; diseases including diabetes, epilepsy, and lupus; and pollutants and toxic chemicals.

Unfortunately, even when an illness is temporary or a chemical irritant is fleeting, damage to nasal plates and passages can be permanent and impair or destroy the sense of smell. While cells in the olfactory epithelium do regenerate normally, severe damage can eliminate their ability to regenerate.

Treatments that can affect the sense of smell adversely include surgery of the head and neck, dental work, chemotherapy and other cancer treatments, many types of medications, and alcohol.

Some medicines can have a positive impact on the sense of smell and taste. Interestingly, groups of medicines used to treat allergies, sinusitis, infection, and inflammation can open nasal passages and therefore have temporary ameliorative effects on smell and taste. They include antihistamines and decongestants, antibiotics, and nasal douches and lubricants.

Cluster headaches, migraines, and Addison's disease temporarily can heighten the sense of smell and taste (sometimes horrifically).

TESTING AND TREATMENT

Professionals and laypeople alike have many interesting ways to test the sense of smell. Dr. Richard Doty, founder of Sensonics, Inc., has developed an array of tests that assess chemosensory function. They range from the scratch-and-sniff University of Pennsylvania smell identification test to the smell threshold test, often used to identify sensory experts and to screen workers involved with potential hazards. The Smell & Taste Treatment and Research Foundation uses these, as well as hedonic testing, to measure how much subjects like what they smell, and memory testing to see what types of memory (short-term, long-term, implicit, explicit) the smells have been committed to. You can find more information on these and other methods of assessing the olfactory sense by consulting the resources list on page 43.

Because smell can be so important to our lives, it's not uncommon to find coexisting mood disorders among people with olfactory disorders. Depending on the cause and severity of the smell disorder, treatment ranges from medications—such as vitamins, steroids, calcium channel blockers, anticonvulsants, and antidepressants—to surgery.

It's important to seek help to identify, assess, treat, and manage these disorders. For those who can, we recommend . . . wine tasting!

TRAINING AND STRENGTHENING

Many animals have a more highly developed sense of smell than we do, but we humans have brains brilliantly designed to preserve, protect, and enrich all aspects of our lives through smell. In our experience, there's no better way to train and strengthen the senses, memory, and mind than through fully and consciously savoring wine.

The best news? Besides investing in some good bottles, proper storage, and proper glassware, we already have all we need to appreciate wine fully, in the form of our five senses. Wine tasters have known innately for ages what evolving scientific understanding and empirical evidence are proving only now: the power and importance of smell. The explicit knowledge of the science of smell is good, but it's not always essential to our implicit experience.

That said, to embrace, apply, articulate, and improve on what we already have, let's open a bottle of vino!

TOWARD A COMMON LANGUAGE OF SMELL AND TASTE

Smell is a relatively inadequate word for our most primitive and powerful sense. It means both the smells that emanate from us (we are what we eat and drink) as well as the smells we perceive. Over time, wine tasters have done much to create a common language and to savor the intersection where enlivened and articulated senses meet memory, anticipation, association, and personal preferences.

Like colors, aroma falls into basic categories that, when combined, yield the rich symphony that is wine. Ann Noble's *Wine Aroma Wheel* (see resources in the margin) categorizes basic fruit aromas as: citrus, berry, tree, tropical, dried (fruit), canned, dried. Other aroma categories include nutty, caramelized, woody, earthy, chemical, pungent, floral, and spicy. See the table on pages 52–53 for a more extensive list of descriptors for wine.

Still, no two people smell or perceive smells alike. It's deeply personal and experiential. Here is our best effort to convey how scent feels and what it means to us:

Wendy says "Puligny" to herself because she loves the word nearly as much as the wine. It serves as a homing signal that brings her to self and center—to a time and a place and a wine she loves and to the kind of bonds that endure.

Kevin goes out on his porch with a glass of some favorite, special vintage and looks into the night sky. Embodied in every sip is all that he treasures and honors about Windows on the World and a reason to look up at the stars.

We hope and trust that you'll find wine and spirits like this and that you'll share words of them with us. In the meantime, here's to your health and happiness, and to savoring wine and life in and with every sense!

SOURCES AND RESOURCES

The Emperor of Scent: A True Story of Perfume and Obsession by Chandler Burr

Jacobson's Organ and the Remarkable Nature of Smell by Lyall Watson

Life's a Smelling Success: Using Scent to Empower Your Memory and Learning by Alan Hirsch, M.D.

Monell Chemical Senses Center, www.monell.org

National Institutes of Health, www.nidcd.nih.gov/health/smelltaste

A Natural History of the Senses by Diane Ackerman

Professional Friends of Wine: A Sensory User's Manual, www.winepros.org/wine101/sensory_guide.htm

Sense of Smell Institute, www.senseofsmell.org

The Senses Bureau, www.thesensesbureau.com

Sensonics, www.sensonics.com

Smell & Taste Treatment and Research Foundation, www.scienceofsmell.com

Tim Jacob Smell Research Laboratory, www.cf.ac.uk/biosi/staff/jacob

University of California San Diego Nasal Dysfunction Clinic, health.ucsd.edu/specialties/surgery/otolaryngology/nasal

Wine Aroma Wheel, by Ann Noble, www.winearomawheel.com

TASTING WINE

Now that you know the basics of how wine is made and how we sense it, you're almost ready to begin the first three classes on white wines.

You can read all the books (and there are plenty) written on wine to become more knowledgeable on the subject, but the best way to enhance your understanding of wine is to taste as many wines as possible. Reading covers the more academic side of wine, while tasting is more enjoyable and practical. A little of each will do you the most good.

Wine tasting breaks down into five basic steps: color, swirl, smell, taste, and savor. You may wish to follow them with a glass of wine in hand.

COLOR

The best way to determine a wine's color is against a white background—a napkin or tablecloth—holding the glass of wine at an angle in front of it. The range of colors depends of course on whether you're tasting a white or red wine. Here are the colors for both, beginning with the youngest wine and moving to an older wine:

WHITE WINE	RED WINE
PALE YELLOW-GREEN	PURPLE
STRAW YELLOW	RUBY
YELLOW-GOLD	RED
GOLD	
OLD GOLD	BRICK RED
YELLOW-BROWN	RED-BROWN
MADERIZED	
BROWN	BROWN

As white wines age, they gain color. Red wines, on the other hand, lose color as they age.

If you can see through a red wine, it's generally ready to drink.

Color tells you a lot about the wine. Since we start with the white wines, let's consider three reasons that a white wine may have more color:

1. It's older.
2. Different grape varieties give different color. (For example, Chardonnay usually gives off a deeper color than does Sauvignon Blanc.)
3. The wine aged in wood.

In my classes, it's not unusual to hear that some believe that a wine is pale yellow-green, while others say it's gold. Everyone begins with the same wine, but color perceptions vary. There are no right or wrong answers because perception is subjective. So you can imagine what happens when we actually taste the wine!

SWIRL

Swirl to allow oxygen to get into the wine. Swirling releases the esters, ethers, and aldehydes that combine with oxygen to yield a wine's bouquet. In other words, swirling aerates the wine and releases more of the bouquet and aroma. Put your hands over the glass of wine when you swirl to create a more powerful bouquet and aroma.

SMELL

This is the most important part of wine tasting. You can perceive just five tastes—sweet, sour, bitter, salty, savory—but the average person can identify more than 2,000 different scents, and wine has more than 200 of its own. Now that you've swirled the wine and released the bouquet, smell the wine at least three times. You may find that the third smell will give you more information than the first smell did. What does the wine smell like? What type of nose does it have? Again, smell is the most important step in the tasting process and most people simply don't spend enough time on it.

Pinpointing the nose of the wine helps you identify certain characteristics. Since I prefer not to use subjective words, I may say that a wine smells like a French white Burgundy. But this description doesn't satisfy the majority of a given class. They want to know more. What do steak and onions smell like? The answer: "Like steak and onions." See what I mean?

The best way to learn your own preferences for styles of wine is to "memorize" the smell of the individual grape varieties. For white, try to memorize the three major grape varieties: Chardonnay, Sauvignon Blanc,

Aroma is the smell of the grapes. **BOUQUET IS THE TOTAL SMELL OF THE WINE.** "Nose" is a word that wine tasters use to describe the bouquet and aroma of the wine.

One of my favorite bouquets comes from older wines usually of 20 years or more. I call it the **"DEAD LEAF" SMELL** when in the fall the air is full of fallen leaves.

and Riesling. Keep smelling them, and smelling them, and smelling them until you can identify the differences, one from the other. For the reds, it's a little more difficult, but you still can take three major grape varieties: Pinot Noir, Merlot, and Cabernet Sauvignon. Try to memorize those smells without using flowery words, and you'll understand what I mean.

For those who remain unconvinced, I have a list of 500 different words commonly used to describe wine. Here is a small excerpt:

acetic	character	legs	seductive
aftertaste	corky	light	short
aroma	developed	maderized	stalky
astringent	earthy	mature	sulfury
austere	finish	metallic	tart
baked-burnt	flat	nose	thin
balanced	fresh	nutty	tired
bitter	grapey	off	vanilla
body	green	oxidized	woody
bouquet	hard	pétillant	yeasty
bright	hot	rich	young

Again, see pages 52–53 for a more extensive list of descriptors.

You're also more likely to recognize some of the defects of a wine through your sense of smell. Following is a list of some of the negative smells in wine:

SMELL	WHY
VINEGAR	TOO MUCH ACETIC ACID IN WINE
SHERRY	OXIDATION
DANK, WET, MOLDY, CELLAR SMELL	WINE ABSORBS THE TASTE OF A DEFECTIVE CORK (REFERRED TO AS "CORKED WINE")
SULFUR (BURNT MATCHES)	TOO MUCH SULFUR DIOXIDE

Oxygen can be the best friend of a wine, but it also can be its worst enemy. A little oxygen helps release the smell of the wine (as with swirling), but prolonged exposure can be harmful, especially to older wines. Authentic Sherry, from Spain, is intentionally made through controlled oxidation.

One of the most difficult challenges in life is to **MATCH A SMELL OR A TASTE** with a word that describes it.

WineSpeak by Bernard Klem includes **36,975 WINE-TASTING DESCRIPTIONS.** Who knew?

Each person has a different threshold for sulfur dioxide, and although most people don't have an adverse reaction, it can prove problematic for individuals with asthma. To protect those prone to bad reactions to sulfites, federal law in the United States requires wineries to label their wines with the warning that the wine contains sulfites. Every wine contains a certain amount of sulfites. They're a natural by-product of fermentation.

TASTE

For many people, tasting wine means taking a sip and swallowing immediately. For me, this isn't tasting. Tasting you do with your taste buds. You have taste buds all over your mouth—on both sides of the tongue, underneath, on the tip, and extending to the back of your throat. If you gulp the wine, you bypass all of those important taste buds. When you taste

The average person has **5,000 TO 10,000 TASTE BUDS.**

Tasting wine is confirming what the **COLOR AND SMELL** are telling you.

wine, leave it in your mouth for three to five seconds before swallowing. The wine warms up, sending signals about the aroma and bouquet up through the nasal passage then on to the olfactory bulb, and then to the limbic system of the brain. Remember, 90 percent of taste is smell.

WHAT TO THINK ABOUT WHEN TASTING WINE

Be aware of the most important sensations of taste and your own personal thresholds of those tastes. Also, pay attention to where they occur on your tongue and in your mouth. As mentioned earlier, you can perceive just five tastes: sweet, sour, bitter, salty, and savory (but there's no salt in wine, so we're down to four). High alcohol and high tannin usually create bitterness in wine. Sweetness occurs only in wines with some residual sugar left over after fermentation. Sour (sometimes called "tart") indicates the acidity in wine.

Sweetness The highest threshold is on the tip of the tongue. If there's any sweetness in a wine whatsoever, you'll get it right away.

Acidity Found at the sides of the tongue, the cheek area, and the back of the throat. White wines and some lighter-style red wines usually contain a higher degree of acidity.

Bitterness Tasted on the back of the tongue.

Tannin The sensation of tannin begins in the middle of the tongue. Tannin frequently exists in red wines or white wines aged in wood. When the wines are too young, tannin dries the palate to excess. If the wine has a lot of tannin, it can coat your whole mouth, blocking the fruit. Remember, tannin is not a taste: it's a tactile sensation.

Fruit and varietal characteristics These aren't tastes but smells. You'll find the weight of the fruit (the "body") in the middle of your tongue.

Aftertaste The overall taste and balance of the components of the wine that lingers in your mouth. How long does the balance last? A long, pleasing aftertaste is usually a sign of a high-quality wine. The taste of many of the great wines lasts anywhere from one to three minutes, with all their components in harmony.

I like my wine bright, rich, mature, developed, **SEDUCTIVE, AND WITH NICE LEGS!**

OTHER SENSATIONS associated with wine include numbing, tingling, drying, cooling, warming, and coating.

"One not only drinks wine, one smells it, observes it, tastes it, sips it, and—one talks about it."

—KING EDWARD VII
of England

BITTER: Think endive or arugula.
TANNIN: Think gritty.

TYPES OF TASTINGS	
HORIZONTAL	Tasting wines from the same vintage
VERTICAL	Comparing wines from different vintages
BLIND	The taster does not have any information about the wines
SEMI-BLIND	The taster knows only the style of wine (grape) or where it comes from

"The key to great wine is balance, and it is the sum of the different parts that make a wine not only delicious but complete and fascinating as well as worthy of aging."

—FIONA MORRISON, M.W.

"The hardest thing to attain . . . is the appreciation of difference without insisting on superiority."

—GEORGE SAINTSBURY,
Notes on a Cellar-Book (1920)

WHAT MAKES A GREAT WINE GREAT?

Varietal character

Balance of components

Complexity

Sense of place

Emotional response

"Great wine is about nuance, surprise, subtlety, expression, qualities that keep you coming back for another taste. Rejecting a wine because it is not big enough is like rejecting a book because it is not long enough, or a piece of music because it is not loud enough."

—KERMIT LYNCH,
Adventures on the Wine Route

—— FURTHER READING ——

Making Sense of Wine by Alan Young

Pocket Guide to Wine Tasting by Michael Broadbent

Vintage Timecharts by Jancis Robinson

SAVOR

After you've had a chance to taste the wine, savor it for a few moments. Think about what you just experienced, and ask yourself the following questions to help focus your impressions.

- Was the wine light, medium, or full-bodied?
- For a white wine: How was the acidity? Very little, just right, or too much?
- For a red wine: Is the tannin in the wine too strong or astringent?
- What is the strongest component (residual sugar, fruit, acid, tannin)?
- How long did the balance of the components last (10 seconds, 60 seconds, etc.)?
- Is the wine ready to drink, or does it need more time to age?
- What kind of food would you enjoy with the wine?
- To your taste, is the wine worth the price?
- Most importantly: Do you like it? Is it your style?

Tasting wine is like visiting an art gallery. You wander from room to room, looking at the paintings. Your first impression tells whether you like something. Once you decide you like a piece of art, you want to know more: Who was the artist? What's the history behind the work? How was it done? So it is with wine. Once oenophiles (wine aficionados) discover a wine that they like, they want to learn everything about it: the winemaker; the grapes; exactly where the vines were planted; the blend, if any; and the history behind the wine.

HOW TO KNOW WHETHER A WINE IS GOOD

The definition of a good wine is one that you enjoy. I cannot emphasize this enough. Trust your own palate, and don't let others dictate taste to you!

WHEN IS A WINE READY TO DRINK?

This is one of the most frequently asked questions. The answer is very simple: when all components of the wine are in balance to your particular taste.

HOW TO READ A WINE LABEL

Labels tell you everything you need to know about the wine—and more. Here are some quick tips you can use when you scan the shelves at your favorite retailer. The Rudd label shown below will serve as an example.

STATE California
COUNTY Sonoma
VITICULTURAL AREA (AVA)
  Russian River Valley
VINEYARD Bacigalupi
WINERY Rudd

The most important piece of information on the label is the producer's name. In this case, the producer is Rudd.

This label shows that the wine is made from the Chardonnay grape. For American wines, if the grape variety appears on the label, a minimum of 75 percent of the wine must come from that grape variety.

If the wine bears a vintage date, 95 percent of the grapes must have been harvested that year.

If the wine is designated "California," then 100 percent of the grapes must have been grown in California.

If the label designates a certain federally recognized viticultural area (AVA), such as the Russian River Valley (as on our sample label), then at least 85 percent of the grapes used to make that wine must have been grown in that location.

The alcohol content is given in percentages. Usually, the higher the percentage of alcohol, the "fuller" the wine will be.

"Produced and bottled by" means that at least 75 percent of the wine was fermented by the winery named on the label.

Some wineries tell you the exact varietal content of the wine, and/or the sugar content of the grapes when they were picked, and/or the amount of residual sugar (to let you know how sweet or dry the wine is).

In America the **LEGAL LIMIT FOR THE ALCOHOL CONTENT OF TABLE WINE IS 7–13.9 PERCENT**, with a 1.5 percent allowance either way—as long as the allowance doesn't go beyond the legal limit. If the alcohol content of a table wine exceeds 14 percent, the label must show that. Sparkling wines may be 10–13.9 percent, with the 1.5 percent allowance.

NEW WORLD VERSUS OLD WORLD
Wines from America, Argentina, Australia, Chile, New Zealand, and South Africa usually list the grape variety on the label. French, Italian, and Spanish wines usually list the region, village, or vineyard where the wine was made—but not the grape.

As you will see, wines can be labeled and named by region, varietal, or proprietary name, and different rules apply in different countries. See "How to Read a German Wine Label," on page 135, for a different example.

WINE AROMAS AND FLAVORS

	FRUITY	FLORAL	CARAMELIZED	NUTTY		VEGETAL		SPICY
TROPICAL	Banana	Acacia	Beeswax	Almond	**FRESH HERBS**	Boxwood	**SWEET SPICES**	Cinnamon
	Guava	Chamomile	Brioche	Biscuit		Dill		Clove
	Honeydew	Geranium	Butterscotch	Hazlenut		Eucalyptus		Vanilla
	Lychee	Hawthorn	Caramel	Walnut		Grass		
	Mango	Hibiscus	Chocolate			Mint	**PUNGENT SPICES**	Anise
	Passion fruit	Honeysuckle	Honey			Thyme		Black pepper
	Pineapple	Iris	Malt		**DRIED HERBS**	Black tea		Ginger
CITRUS	Grapefruit	Jasmine	Molasses			Green tea		Licorice
	Lemon	Lavender	Toffee			Hay		Lovage
	Lime	Lilac	White chocolate			Tobacco		Nutmeg
	Orange	Linden			**FRESH VEGETABLES**	Bell pepper		
TREE FRUITS	Apple	Orange blossom				Green pepper		
	Apricot	Peony				Japaleño		
	Elderberry	Potpurri				Sun-dried tomato		
	Green apple	Rose				Tomato		
	Peach	Violet			**COOKED VEGETABLES**	Artichoke		
	Pear	Yarrow				Asparagus		
RED FRUITS	Cherry					Green bean		
	Raspberry					Canned peas		
	Red currant							
	Strawberry							
BLACK FRUITS	Blackberry							
	Black cherry							
	Black currant							
	Plum							
DRIED	Date							
	Dried apricot							
	Dried fig							
	Fruitcake							
	Prune							
	Raisin							

MINERAL	WOODY		BIOLOGICAL		DAIRY	CHEMICAL	
Flint	Cedar		ANIMAL	Mousy	Butter	PUNGENT	Nail polish remover (ethyl acetate)
Gravel	Moss			Horsey	Cream		
River rocks	Oak			Wet dog			Vinegar (acetic acid)
Slate	Pine			Wet wool			
Stone	Resinous		EARTHY	Cheesy		SULFUR	Burnt match
	Sandalwood			Forest floor			Cooked cabbage
	SMOKY	Bacon		Mushroom			Garlic
		Coffee		Soy sauce			Natural gas (mercaptans)
		Leather	LACTIC	Sauerkraut			Rotten eggs (hydrogen sulfide)
		Tar		Sweaty			Rubber
		Toast		Yogurt			Skunk
			YEASTY	Baker's yeast			Sulfur dioxide
				Bandage		PETROLEUM	Diesel
				Bread			Kerosene
							Plastic

Professional wine tasters use hundreds of words to describe the aroma, bouquet, flavors, and tastes of wine. Some of them might sound crazy, and the descriptors in this table apply to all wines: young or old, white or red. Many wines will feature only, say, three of these, and some of them are faults, so don't look for them all. Nor do you have to know them all, but they offer a taste of the more common ones you're likely to encounter.

THE 60-SECOND WINE EXPERT

I use this "60-second Wine Expert" tasting method in my classes for students to record their impressions. The minute is divided into four sections: 0 to 15 seconds, 15 to 30 seconds, 30 to 45 seconds, and the final 45 to 60 seconds. Try this with your next glass of wine.

STEP ONE Look at the color of the wine.

STEP TWO Smell the wine three times.

STEP THREE Put the wine in your mouth and leave it there for three to five seconds.

STEP FOUR Swallow the wine.

STEP FIVE Wait and concentrate on the wine for 60 seconds before discussing it.

The first taste of wine will shock your taste buds. This comes from the alcohol content, acidity, and sometimes the tannin. The higher the alcohol or acidity, the more of a shock. For the first wine in any tasting, take a sip and swirl it around in your mouth, but don't evaluate it. Wait another 30 seconds, try it again, and then begin the 60-second wine expert tasting.

0 to 15 seconds If there's any residual sugar / sweetness in the wine, you'll experience it now. If there's no sweetness in the wine, the acidity is usually at its strongest sensation in the first 15 seconds. Look for the fruit level of the wine and its balance with the acidity or sweetness.

15 to 30 seconds After the sweetness or acidity, look for great fruit sensation. After all, that's ultimately what you want! By 30 seconds, you want a balance of all the components. By this time, you can identify the weight of the wine. Is it light, medium, or full-bodied? Think about what kind of food to pair with this wine (see pages 285–286).

30 to 45 seconds Start formulating your opinion of the wine. Not all wines need 60 seconds of thought. Lighter-style wines, such as Rieslings, usually show their best at this point. The fruit, acid, and sweetness of a great German Riesling should be in perfect harmony from this point on. For quality red and white wines, acidity should now balance with the fruit of the wine.

45 to 60 seconds Very often wine writers use the term "length" to describe how long the components, balance, and flavor continue in the mouth. Concentrate on the length of the wine in these last 15 seconds. In big, full-bodied red wines from Bordeaux and the Rhône Valley, Cabernets from California, Barolos and Barbarescos from Italy, and even some full-bodied Chardonnays, concentrate on the level of tannin in the wine. Just as the acidity and fruit balance are major concerns in the first 30 seconds, it's now the tannin and fruit balance you want in the last 30 seconds. If the fruit, tannin, and acid all balance at 60 seconds, then the wine is ready to drink. If the tannin overpowers the fruit at the 60-second mark, consider whether to drink the wine now or put it away for more aging.

It's extremely important, if you want to learn the true taste of the wine, that you take at least one minute to concentrate on all of its components. But 60 seconds is the *minimum* time to wait before making a decision about a wine. Many great wines continue to show balance well past 120 seconds. The best wine I ever tasted lasted more than three minutes—that's three minutes of perfect balance of all components!

TASTING NOTES   DATE / /

NAME

VINTAGE   COUNTRY/REGION

PRICE   GRAPES

COLOR   (P. 59)

AROMAS / BOUQUET   (P. 6-7)

FLAVORS   (P. 62)

CHECKLIST

BODY/TEXTURE   FRUIT   RESIDUAL SUGAR   ACID   TANNIN

LIGHT   LOW

MEDIUM   BALANCED

FULL   HIGH

60-SECOND WINE TASTING

0-15 SECONDS

15-30 SECONDS

30-45 SECONDS

45-60 SECONDS

NOTES/FOOD CHOICES

OVERALL RATING

POOR   ACCEPTABLE   GOOD   EXCELLENT   EXCEPTIONAL

This is a tasting page from my *Windows on the World Wine Tasting Notebook,* which includes key information from this book in an easy-to-carry format and also gives you a place to record all your wine tasting notes.

"Wine is the best of all beverages . . . because it is purer than water, safer than milk, plainer than soft drinks, gentler than spirits, nimbler than beer, and ever so much more pleasant to the educated senses of sight, smell, and taste than any of the drinkable liquids known to us."

—ANDRE L. SIMON, author and founder of the Wine & Food Society

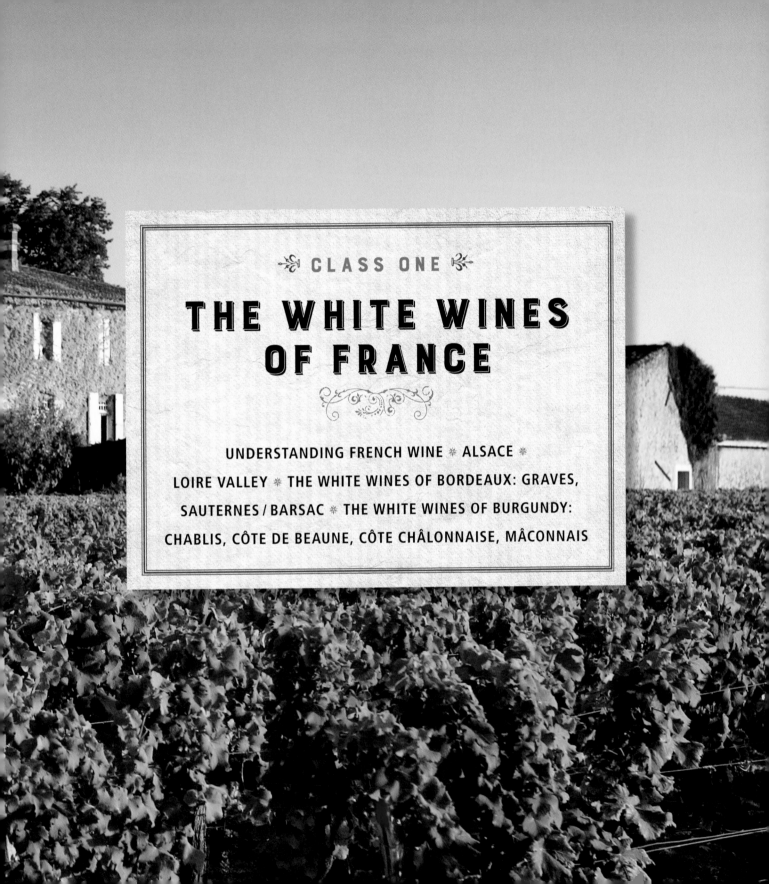

THE WHITE WINES OF FRANCE

UNDERSTANDING FRENCH WINE ✳ ALSACE ✳
LOIRE VALLEY ✳ THE WHITE WINES OF BORDEAUX: GRAVES,
SAUTERNES / BARSAC ✳ THE WHITE WINES OF BURGUNDY:
CHABLIS, CÔTE DE BEAUNE, CÔTE CHÂLONNAISE, MÂCONNAIS

UNDERSTANDING FRENCH WINE

BEFORE WE BEGIN our first class, you should know a few important points about all French wines. First look at the map of France to familiarize yourself with the main wine-producing areas. As we progress, you'll understand why geography is so important.

This table offers a quick rundown of which areas produce which styles of wine:

In 2015, France was the **NUMBER-TWO PRODUCER** of wines in the world.

WINE REGIONS	STYLES	MAJOR GRAPES
ALSACE	MOSTLY WHITE	RIESLING, GEWÜRZTRAMINER
BORDEAUX	RED AND WHITE	SAUVIGNON BLANC, SÉMILLON, MERLOT, CABERNET SAUVIGNON, CABERNET FRANC
BURGUNDY	RED AND WHITE	PINOT NOIR, GAMAY, CHARDONNAY
CHAMPAGNE	SPARKLING WINE	PINOT NOIR, CHARDONNAY
CÔTES DU RHÔNE	MOSTLY RED	SYRAH, GRENACHE
LANGUEDOC / ROUSSILLON	RED AND WHITE	CARIGNAN, GRENACHE, SYRAH, CINSAULT, MOURVÈDRE
LOIRE VALLEY	MOSTLY WHITE	SAUVIGNON BLANC, CHENIN BLANC, CABERNET FRANC
PROVENCE	RED, WHITE, AND ROSÉ	GRENACHE, SYRAH

Five major regions of Languedoc-Rousssillon:

1. Corbières-Boutenac
2. Faugères
3. La Clape
4. Minervois-La Livinière
5. Saint-Chinian

Why would Georges Duboeuf, Louis Latour, and many other famous winemakers start wineries in Languedoc and Roussillon? **THE LAND IS MUCH LESS EXPENSIVE** compared to regions such as Burgundy or Bordeaux, so the winemakers can produce moderately priced wines and still get a good return on their investment.

IN PROVENCE, look for the producers Domaine Tempier, Château Routas, and Château d'Esclans (Whispering Angel).

AMERICANS LOVE FRENCH WINE. We are the number-one export market especially for wine from Champagne, Loire, Burgundy, Rhône, and Bordeaux.

The regions **MOST ACTIVE IN THE PRODUCTION OF** *VIN DE PAYS* varietal wines are Languedoc and Roussillon in southwest France. Called in the past the "wine lake" because of the vast quantities of anonymous wine made there, Languedoc has more than 700,000 acres of vineyards and produces more than 200 million cases a year, about a third of the total French crop.

If you're interested in wine, you're bound to encounter French wine at one time or another. Why? Because of the thousands of years of history and winemaking tradition, because of the great diversity and variety of wines from the many different regions, and because French wines have the reputation for ranking among the best in the world. The reason for this goes back to quality control.

Strict government laws established by the Appellation d'Origine Contrôlée regulate French winemaking. If you don't want to say "Appellation d'Origine Contrôlée" all the time, you can simply say "AOC." This is the first of many wine lingo abbreviations you'll learn in this book.

Vins de pays This category is growing in importance. A 1979 French legal decision liberalized the rules for this category, permitting the use of nontraditional grapes in certain regions and even allowing vintners to label wines with the varietal rather than the regional name. For exporters

FRENCH CONTROL LAWS

Established in the 1930s, the Appellation d'Origine Contrôlée (AOC) laws set minimum requirements for each wine-producing area in France. These laws also can help you decipher French wine labels, since the AOC controls the following:

AOC CONTROLS	EXAMPLE	EXAMPLE
GEOGRAPHIC ORIGIN	Chablis	Pommard
GRAPE VARIETY Which grapes can be planted where	Chardonnay	Pinot Noir
MINIMUM ALCOHOL CONTENT This varies depending upon the particular area where the grapes are grown	10%	10.5%
VINE-GROWING PRACTICES For example, a vintner can produce only so much wine per acre	40 hectoliters/ hectare	35 hectoliters/ hectare

1 HECTOLITER = 26.42 gallons
1 HECTARE = 2.471 acres

ONLY 35 PERCENT of all French wines are worthy of the AOC designation.

There are more than 300 AOC FRENCH WINES.

FAMOUS NON-AOC FRENCH WINES that are available in America include: Moreau, Boucheron, Chantefleur, and René Junot.

to the American market, where consumers are becoming accustomed to buying wines by grape variety—Cabernet Sauvignon or Chardonnay, for example—this change makes their wines much easier to sell.

Vins de table These ordinary table wines represent almost 35 percent of all wines produced in France. Most French wine is meant to be consumed as a simple beverage. Many of the *vins de table* are marketed under proprietary names and are the French equivalent of California jug wines. Don't be surprised if you go into a grocery store in France to buy wine and find it in a plastic wine container with no label on it! You can see the color through the plastic—red, white, or rosé—but the only marking on the container is the alcohol content, ranging from 9 to 14 percent. Choose your wine depending on how sharp you need to feel for the rest of the day!

When you buy wines, keep the distinctions between *vins de pays* and *vins de table* in mind because there's a difference between them not only in quality but also in price.

The major white wine–producing Regions of France are:

Alsace   **Loire Valley**   **Bordeaux**   **Burgundy**

Let's start with Alsace and the Loire Valley because these are the two French regions that specialize in white wines. As you can see from the map at the beginning of this chapter, Alsace, the Loire Valley, and Chablis (a white wine–producing region of Burgundy) all lie in the northern half of France. These areas produce predominantly white wines because of the shorter growing season and cooler climate best suited for growing white grapes.

CHAMPAGNE is another major white-wine producer, but that's for another class.

ALSACE

People often are confused about the difference between wines from Alsace and those from Germany. But the confusion can be justified since, from 1871 to 1919, Alsace belonged to Germany and both wines are sold in tall bottles with tapering necks. To confuse you further, Alsace and Germany grow the same grape varieties. But when you think of Riesling, what are your associations? You'll probably answer "Germany" and "sweetness." That's a very typical response, and that's because German winemakers add a small amount of naturally sweet unfermented grape juice back into the wine to create the distinctive German Riesling. The winemaker from Alsace ferments every bit of the sugar in the grapes, which is why 90 percent of all Alsace wines are totally dry.

Another fundamental difference between wine from Alsace and wine from Germany is the alcohol content. Wine from Alsace has 11 to 12 percent alcohol, while most German wine has a mere 8 to 9 percent.

The four white grapes grown in Alsace you should know are:

22%	19%	15%	7%
Riesling	**Gewürztraminer**	**Pinot Gris**	**Pinot Blanc**

All wines produced in **ALSACE ARE AOC-DESIGNATED** and represent nearly 20 percent of all AOC white wines in France.

THE THREE AOCS OF ALSACE

Alsace 78%
Crémant d'Alsace (sparkling) 18%
Alsace Grand Cru 4%

Alsace produces 9 percent of its red wines from the Pinot Noir grape. These generally are **CONSUMED IN THE REGION** and rarely are exported.

WINE LABELING IN ALSACE differs from the other French regions administered by the AOC because Alsace is one of the few regions that labels its wine exclusively by varietal. All Alsace wines that include the name of the grape on the label must be made entirely from that grape.

TWO GREAT SWEET (LATE HARVEST) WINES from Alsace are Vendange Tardive and Sélection de Grains Nobles.

Alsace

English Channel

Paris ★

ALSACE

TYPES OF WINE PRODUCED IN ALSACE

As mentioned previously, virtually all Alsace wines are dry, and 90 percent of the wines produced are white. Riesling is the major grape planted here, and it's responsible for the highest-quality wines of the region. Alsace is also known for its Gewürztraminer, which stands in a class by itself. Most people either love it or hate it because Gewürztraminer has a very distinctive style. *Gewürz* is the German word for "spice," which aptly describes the wine.

Pinot Blanc and Pinot Gris are becoming increasingly popular among the growers of Alsace.

CHOOSING AN ALSACE WINE

Consider two important factors in choosing a wine from Alsace: the grape variety and the reputation and style of the shipper. Some of the most reliable shippers include:

Domaine Dopff au Moulin

Domaine F. E. Trimbachs

Domaine Hugel & Fils

Domaine Léon Beyer

Domaine Marcel Deiss

Domaine Weinbach

Domaine Zind-Humbrecht

The majority of grape growers (approximately 4,600) in Alsace don't grow enough grapes to make it economically feasible to produce and market their own wine. Instead, they sell their grapes to a shipper who produces, bottles, and markets the wine under its own name. The art of making high-quality Alsace wine lies in the selection of grapes that each shipper makes.

QUALITY LEVELS OF ALSACE WINES

The shipper's reputation determines the quality of Alsace wines rather than any labeling on the bottle. That said, the vast majority of any given Alsace wine is the shipper's varietal. A very small percentage is labeled with a specific vineyard's name, especially in the appellation "Alsace Grand Cru." Some wines are labeled "Réserve" or "Réserve Personelle," terms that aren't legally defined.

38,500 ACRES OF GRAPES are planted in Alsace, but the average plot of land for each grower is only 5 acres.

ALSACE HAS LITTLE RAINFALL, especially during the grape harvest. The town of Colmar—the Alsace wine center—is the second driest in France. That's why they say a "one-shirt harvest" will be a good vintage.

Sometimes you'll see "Grand Cru" on an Alsace label. This wine can be made only from the best grape varieties of Alsace. More than 50 different vineyards are entitled to the Grand Cru label.

SHOULD ALSACE WINES BE AGED?

In general, most Alsace wines are made to be consumed young—from one to five years after they're bottled. As in any fine-wine geographic area, in Alsace a small percentage of great wines is produced that may be aged for ten years or more.

FORTY YEARS LATER IN ALSACE

I am enjoying the same producers, such as Trimbach and Hugel, as I did decades ago. A dry, crisp, acidic Riesling is still one of my favorite wines to have at the beginning of a meal, especially with a fish appetizer. Pinot Blanc is a perfect summer picnic wine or for wine by the glass at a restaurant, and the famous Gewürztraminer is one of the most unique and flavorful wines in the world.

The best part about Alsace wines is that they are still very affordable, of good quality, and available throughout the United States.

– BEST RECENT VINTAGES OF ALSACE –

2005**　2007**　2008**　2009**　2010*
2011*　2012*　2013 **　2014　2015*

* EXCEPTIONAL VINTAGE　** EXTRAORDINARY VINTAGE

WINE AND FOOD

"Alsace wines are not suited only to classic Alsace and other French dishes. For instance, I adore **Riesling** with raw fish specialties such as Japanese sushi and sashimi, while our **Gewürztraminer** is delicious with smoked salmon and brilliant with Chinese, Thai, and Indonesian food.

"**Pinot Blanc** is round, soft, not aggressive . . . an all-purpose wine . . . that can be used as an apéritif, with all kinds of pâté and charcuterie, and also with hamburgers. Perfect for brunch—not too sweet or flowery."

—Étienne Hugel

"**Riesling** with fish—blue trout with a light sauce. **Gewürztraminer** as an apéritif; with foie gras or any pâté at meal's end; or with Muenster cheese or a stronger cheese such as Roquefort."

—Hubert Trimbach

AS THIS LABEL INDICATES, Hugel & Fils began producing wine in 1639.

FOR THE TOURIST

Visit the beautiful wine village of Riquewihr, which has buildings that date from the fifteenth and sixteenth centuries.

FOR THE FOODIE

Alsace is not just about great wine. It has more than 26 Michelin-rated restaurants. Three of them have three stars.

FURTHER READING

Alsace and Its Wine Gardens by S. F. Hallgarten

Alsace Wines and Spirits by Pamela Vandyke Price

Loire Valley

LOIRE VALLEY

Starting at the city of Nantes, a bit upriver from the Atlantic Ocean, the Loire Valley stretches inland for six hundred miles along the Loire River. You should be familiar with two white-grape varieties here:

Sauvignon Blanc   **Chenin Blanc**

Rather than choosing by grape variety and shipper, as you would in Alsace, choose Loire Valley wines by style and vintage. These are the main styles:

Muscadet A light, dry wine, made from 100 percent Melon de Bourgogne grapes. If you see the phrase "sur lie" on a Muscadet wine label, it means that the wine aged on its lees (sediment).

Pouilly-Fumé A dry wine that has the most body and concentration of all the Loire Valley wines. It's made with 100 percent Sauvignon Blanc. The distinct nose, or bouquet, of Pouilly-Fumé comes from a combination of the Sauvignon Blanc grape and the soil of the Loire Valley.

Most Pouilly-Fumé and Sancerre wines are **NOT AGED IN WOOD.**

Sancerre Striking a balance between full-bodied Pouilly-Fumé and light-bodied Muscadet, it's made with 100 percent Sauvignon Blanc.

Vouvray This "chameleon" can be dry, semisweet, or sweet and is made from 100 percent Chenin Blanc.

POUILLY-FUMÉ

Many people ask whether Pouilly-Fumé is smoked because they automatically associate the word *fumé* with smoke. Two of the many theories about the origin of the word come from the white morning mist that blankets the area. As the sun burns off the mist, it looks like smoke rising. Others say it's the "smokelike" bloom on Sauvignon Blanc grapes.

Other Sauvignon Blanc wines from the Loire to **LOOK FOR: MENETOU-SALON AND QUINCY**. For Chenin Blanc try **SAVENNIÈRES**.

WHEN ARE THE WINES READY TO DRINK?

Generally, Loire Valley wines are meant to be consumed young. The exception is a sweet Vouvray, which can be laid down for a longer time.

Here are more specific guidelines:

Muscadet	Sancerre	Pouilly-Fumé
one to two years	two to three years	three to five years

SAUVION

PRODUCE OF FRANCE

Sancerre

APPELLATION SANCERRE CONTRÔLÉE

MIS EN BOUTEILLE PAR SAUVION
LE CLÉRAY · 44194 VALLET · FRANCE

POUILLY-FUMÉ VERSUS POUILLY-FUISSÉ

Students often ask whether these similarly named wines are related. Pouilly-Fumé is made from 100 percent Sauvignon Blanc and comes from the Loire Valley. Pouilly-Fuissé is made from 100 percent Chardonnay and comes from the Mâconnais region of Burgundy (page 72).

FORTY YEARS LATER IN THE LOIRE VALLEY

I am still enamored of the quality and diversity of the white wines of the Loire Valley. Forty years ago, the most important Loire Valley wine was Pouilly-Fumé. Today Sancerre is the most popular Loire wine in America. Both wines come from the same grape variety, 100 percent Sauvignon Blanc, both are medium-bodied with great acidity and fruit balance, and both are perfect food wines. Muscadet continues to be a great value, and Vouvray is still the best example of the quality that the grape Chenin Blanc can achieve. The wines have maintained their style and character, representing great value for the consumer.

> **— BEST RECENT VINTAGES OF THE LOIRE VALLEY —**
> 2005* 2009* 2010* 2011 2012 2013 2014 2015*
> *EXCEPTIONAL VINTAGE*

WINE AND FOOD

"All you have to do is look at the map to see where **Muscadet** is made: by the sea where the main fare is shellfish, clams, and oysters.

"With **Pouilly-Fumé,** smoked salmon; turbot with hollandaise; white meat chicken; veal with cream sauce.

"Shellfish, simple food of the sea because **Sancerre** is drier than Pouilly-Fumé."

—Baron Patrick de Ladoucette

"A nice semidry **Vouvray** with fruit and cheese. **Muscadet** is good with a huge variety of excellent and fresh 'everyday' foods, including all the seafood from the Atlantic Ocean, the fish from the river—pike, for instance—game, poultry, and cheese (mainly goat cheese). Of course, there is a must in the region of Nantes: freshwater fish with the world-famous butter sauce, the beurre blanc, invented at the turn of the century by Clémence, who happened to be the chef at Goulaine."

—Robert, Marquis de Goulaine

THE WHITE WINES OF BORDEAUX

DOESN'T BORDEAUX MEAN RED WINE?

That's a misconception. Two of the five major areas of Bordeaux—Graves and Sauternes—are known for their excellent white wines. Sauternes is world-famous for its sweet white wine. The major white-grape varieties used in both areas are:

Sauvignon Blanc   **Sémillon**

BORDEAUX PRODUCTION

85% red

13% white

2% sweet wine

GRAND CRU CLASSÉ DE GRAVES

Château Olivier

PESSAC-LÉOGNAN
APPELLATION PESSAC-LÉOGNAN CONTROLEE

GROUPEMENT FONCIER AGRICOLE DU CHATEAU OLIVIER
J.-J. DE BETHMANN - PROPRIÉTAIRE
LÉOGNAN - 33850 - GIRONDE - FRANCE

MIS EN BOUTEILLE AU CHATEAU
12,5% vol   PRODUCE OF FRANCE   75 cl

When the original edition of the *Complete Wine Course* came out in 1985, the appellation "Pessac-Léognan" had not yet been established. Since 1987, this **"NEW" APPELLATION IS YOUR GUARANTEE** of the finest dry white wines in Bordeaux.

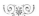

Graves *means "gravel"—the type of soil found in the region.*

GRAVES

White Graves wines are classified by two levels of quality:

Graves   **Pessac-Léognan**

The most basic Graves is called simply Graves. Those labeled "Graves" come from the southern portion of the region surrounding Sauternes. The best wines are produced in Pessac-Léognan, which lies mostly north

CLASSIFIED WHITE CHÂTEAU WINES make up only 3 percent of the total production of white Graves.

of Graves, near the city of Bordeaux. The best wines are known by the name of a particular château, a special vineyard that produces the best-quality grapes. The grapes grown for these wines enjoy better soil and better growing conditions overall. The classified château wines and the regional wines of Graves are always dry.

CHOOSING A GRAVES WINE

Buy a classified château wine. The classified châteaux are:

Château Bouscaut*

Château Carbonnieux*

Château Couhins-Lurton

Domaine de Chevalier

Château Haut-Brion

Château la Louvière*

Château la Tour-Martillac

Château Laville-Haut-Brion

Château Malartic-Lagravière

Château Olivier*

Château Smith-Haut-Lafitte

The largest producers and the easiest to find

FORTY YEARS LATER IN WHITE BORDEAUX

The dry white wines of Bordeaux never were considered equal to the great red châteaux and sweet whites of Sauternes. That has changed over the last 40 years. Winemakers have spent millions of dollars on state-of-the-art equipment, and new vineyard management has created great white-wine production, especially in the Pessac-Léognan.

Few other regions in the world blend Sauvignon Blanc and Sémillon and age them in oak. Winemakers here have been very careful to integrate the fruit and oak together to maintain the freshness and crispness of the wine. Recent vintages have been outstanding.

THE STYLE OF CLASSIFIED white château wines varies according to the ratio of Sauvignon Blanc and Sémillon used. Château Olivier, for example, is made with 65 percent Sémillon, and Château Carbonnieux with 65 percent Sauvignon Blanc.

– BEST RECENT VINTAGES OF WHITE GRAVES –

2000*   2005*   2006   2007*   2008   2009*
2010*   2011   2014*   2015*

EXCEPTIONAL VINTAGE

GRAND VIN DE GRAVES

CHÂTEAU
LA LOUVIÈRE
PESSAC-LÉOGNAN
APPELLATION PESSAC-LÉOGNAN CONTRÔLÉE
PRODUCE OF FRANCE
ANDRÉ LURTON
PROPRIÉTAIRE-VITICULTEUR A LÉOGNAN · GIRONDE · FRANCE

MIS EN BOUTEILLE AU CHÂTEAU

WINE AND FOOD

"Oysters, lobster, Rouget du Bassin d'Arcachon with a **Châteaux Olivier**."

—Jean-Jacques de Bethmann

"With **Château La Louvière Blanc**: grilled sea bass with a beurre blanc, shad roe, or goat cheese soufflé. With **Château Bonnet Blanc**: oysters on the half-shell, fresh crab salad, mussels, and clams."

—Denise Lurton-Moullé

"With a young **Château Carbonnieux Blanc**: chilled lobster consommé, or shellfish, such as oysters, scallops, or grilled shrimp. With an older **Carbonnieux**: a traditional sauced fish course or a goat cheese."

—Anthony Perrin

SAUTERNES/BARSAC

Sauternes is always sweet, meaning that not all the grape sugar has turned into alcohol during fermentation. Dry Sauternes doesn't exist. The Barsac district, adjacent to Sauternes, has the option of using Barsac or Sauternes as its appellation. The main grape varieties in Sauternes are:

Sémillon   Sauvignon Blanc

The two different quality levels in style are

Regional ($)   Classified château ($$$–$$$$)

Sauternes is **EXPENSIVE TO PRODUCE** because several pickings must be completed before the crop is entirely harvested. The harvest can last into November.

THERE ARE MORE SÉMILLON grapes planted in Bordeaux than there are Sauvignon Blanc.

In 2011, **ONE BOTTLE OF CHÂTEAU D'YQUEM 1811 SOLD FOR $117,000**, the most money ever paid for a white wine.

Château d'Yquem makes a dry white wine simply called Y. By law, **DRY WINE MADE IN SAUTERNES CANNOT BE CALLED APPELLATION SAUTERNES**. It can be called only Appellation Bordeaux. Chateau d'Yquem didn't produce a wine in 2012 due to poor weather conditions.

Sauternes is still producing one of the best sweet wines in the world. With the extraordinary vintages of 2005, 2009, 2011, and 2015 you'll be able to find excellent regional Sauternes if you buy from the best shippers. These wines represent a good value for your money, considering the labor involved in production, but they won't have the same intensity of flavor as that of a classified château.

SAUTERNES CLASSIFICATIONS

FIRST GREAT GROWTH—GRAND PREMIER CRU

CHÂTEAU D'YQUEM*

FIRST GROWTH—PREMIERS

CHÂTEAU CLIMENS* (BARSAC)	CHÂTEAU LAFAURIE-PEYRAGUEY*
CHÂTEAU CLOS HAUT-PEYRAGUEY*	CHÂTEAU RABAUD-PROMIS
CHÂTEAU COUTET* (BARSAC)	CHÂTEAU RIEUSSEC*
CHÂTEAU DE RAYNE-VIGNEAU*	CHÂTEAU SIGALAS-RABAUD*
*CHÂTEAU GUIRAUD	CHÂTEAU SUDUIRAUT*
CHÂTEAU LA TOUR BLANCHE*	

SECOND GROWTHS—DEUXIÈMES CRUS

CHÂTEAU D'ARCHE	CHÂTEAU LAMOTHE
CHÂTEAU BROUSTET (BARSAC)	CHÂTEAU LAMOTHE-GUIGNARD
CHÂTEAU CAILLOU (BARSAC)	CHÂTEAU DE MALLE*
CHÂTEAU DOISY-DAËNE (BARSAC)	CHÂTEAU MYRAT (BARSAC)
CHÂTEAU DOISY-DUBROCA (BARSAC)	CHÂTEAU NAIRAC* (BARSAC)
CHÂTEAU DOISY-VÉDRINES* (BARSAC)	CHÂTEAU ROMER DU HAYOT*
CHÂTEAU FILHOT*	CHÂTEAU SUAU (BARSAC)

These châteaux are the most readily available in America.

GRAVES VERSUS SAUTERNES

If the same grapes make dry Graves and sweet Sauternes, why the difference in styles? The best Sauternes is made primarily with the Sémillon grape. Second, to make Sauternes, the winemaker leaves the grapes on the vine longer until a mold called *Botrytis cinerea* ("noble rot") forms. When that happens, the water within them evaporates, and they shrivel. Sugar concentrates as the grapes "raisinate." Then, during the winemaking process, not all the sugar is allowed to ferment into alcohol: hence, the high residual sugar.

CHÂTEAU RIEUSSEC IS OWNED by the same family as Château Lafite-Rothschild.

– BEST VINTAGES OF SAUTERNES –

1986* 1988* 1989* 1990* 1995 1996 1997* 1998
2000 2001* 2002 2003* 2005** 2006* 2007* 2008*
2009** 2010* 2011** 2013* 2014* 2015*

*EXCEPTIONAL VINTAGE   ** EXTRAORDINARY VINTAGE*

SAUTERNES IS A WINE YOU CAN AGE. In fact, the best classified château wines in good vintages easily can age for more than 50 years!

JUST DESSERTS

My students always ask, "What do you serve with **Sauternes**?" Here's a lesson I learned when I first encountered the wines of Sauternes.

Many years ago, I was invited to one of the châteaux of the region for dinner. My group was offered appetizers of foie gras, and, to my surprise, Sauternes was served with it. All the books I had ever read said to serve drier wines first and sweeter wines later, but I thought it best not to question my host's selection.

When we sat down for the first dinner course (fish), once again we were served a Sauternes. This continued through the main course—rack of lamb—when *another* Sauternes was served.

I thought for sure our host would serve a great old red Bordeaux with the cheese course,

but I was wrong again. With the Roquefort cheese came a very old Sauternes.

With dessert on its way, of course I expected another Sauternes and waited with anticipation for the final choice. You can imagine my surprise when a dry red Bordeaux—Château Lafite-Rothschild—accompanied dessert!

Our host's point was that Sauternes doesn't have to be served only with dessert. All the Sauternes went well with the courses because all the sauces complemented the wine and food. In fact, the only wine that didn't go well with dinner was the Château Lafite-Rothschild with dessert, but we drank it anyway!

Hopefully this anecdote will inspire you to serve Sauternes with everything. I prefer to enjoy Sauternes by itself; I'm not a believer in the "dessert wine" category. This dessert wine is dessert in itself.

OTHER SWEET-WINE PRODUCERS in Bordeaux: Ste-Croix-du-Mont and Loupiac.

NOT CLASSIFIED, BUT OF OUTSTANDING QUALITY:

Château Fargues, Château Gilette, and Château Raymond Lafon.

THE WHITE WINES OF BURGUNDY

One of the finest wine-producing areas in the world, Burgundy is one of the major regions that holds an AOC designation in France. However, people often are confused about what a Burgundy really is because the name has been borrowed so freely.

Burgundy is *not* a synonym for red wine, even though the color known as burgundy is obviously named after red wine. Adding to the confusion (especially in the past) is that many red wines around the world were labeled simply "Burgundy" even though they were ordinary table wines. Some wineries, especially in America, continue to label their wines as Burgundy, but these wines bear no resemblance to authentic French Burgundy wines.

The main regions within Burgundy are:

| Chablis | Côte d'Or { | Côte de Nuits |
| | | Côte de Beaune |

| Côte Châlonnaise | Mâconnais | Beaujolais |

Before we explore Burgundy, region by region, it's important to know the types of wine produced there. Take a look at the infographic below, which breaks down the types of wine and tells you the percentage of reds to whites.

68 percent of all Burgundy is red, and 32 percent is white.

| Chablis | Mâconnais | Côte Châlonnaise | Côte de Beaune | Côte de Nuits | Beaujolais |
| 100% | 85% / 15% | 40% / 60% | 30% / 70% | 5% / 90% | 1% / 99% |

THE APÉRITIF KIR, popular from time to time, is a mixture of white wine and crème de cassis liquor made from black currants. It was the favorite drink of the mayor of Dijon, Canon Kir, who added the sweet cassis to balance the high acidity of the local white wine made from the Aligoté grape.

Burgundy is so famous for its red wines that people may forget that some of the finest, most renowned and expensive white wines of France come from there. The three areas in Burgundy that produce world-famous white wines that we'll examine are:

Chablis   **Côte de Beaune**   **Mâconnais**

The largest city in Burgundy is known not for its wines but for **ANOTHER WORLD-FAMOUS PRODUCT.** The city is Dijon, and the product is mustard.

FOR THE TOURIST: My favorite hotels lie in the city of Beaune.

CÔTE D'OR PRODUCTION

78% red

22% white

BURGUNDY

37.5%
44 Villages

53%
23 Regional
Appellations

10%
645 Premier
Cru Vineyards

1.5%
32 Grand Cru
Vineyards

For great value look for **REGIONAL BURGUNDY WINE**, such as Bourgogne Blanc.

The average yield for a Village wine in Burgundy is **360 GALLONS PER ACRE**. For the Grand Cru wines it is 290 gallons per acre, a noticeably higher concentration, which produces a more flavorful wine.

MOST PREMIER CRU WINES give you the name of the vineyard on the label, but others are simply called Premier Cru, which is a blend of different cru vineyards.

There are **ONLY 245 ACRES** planted in Chablis Grand Cru vineyards.

BURGUNDY AND NEW OAK

25%
Village wine

40–70%
Premier Cru

80–100%
Grand Cru

You need to know only one white-grape variety: Chardonnay. All the great white Burgundies are made from 100 percent Chardonnay. Although Chardonnay is used to make all the best white Burgundy wines, the three areas produce many different styles. Much of this difference has to do with where the grapes grow and the vinification procedures. For example, the northern climate of Chablis produces wines with more acidity than those in the southern region of Mâconnais.

As for vinification procedures, after the grapes are harvested in the Chablis and Mâconnais areas, most are fermented and aged in stainless steel tanks. In the Côte de Beaune, after the grapes are harvested, a good percentage of the wines ferment in small oak barrels and also age in oak barrels. The wood adds complexity, depth, body, flavor, and longevity to the wines.

White Burgundies are dry.

BURGUNDY CLASSIFICATIONS

The type of soil and the angle and direction of the slope primarily determine quality, divided into the following levels:

Regional Appellations $

Village wine Bears the name of a specific village. $$

Premier Cru From a specific vineyard with special characteristics, within one of the named villages. Usually a Premier Cru wine will list on the label the village first and the vineyard second. $$$

Grand Cru From a specific vineyard that possesses the best soil and slope in the area and meets or exceeds all other requirements. In most areas of Burgundy, the village doesn't appear on the label—only the Grand Cru vineyard name is used. $$$$+

A NOTE ON THE USE OF WOOD

Each wine region in the world has its own way of producing wines. Wine was always fermented and aged in wood—until the introduction of cement tanks, glass-lined tanks, and, most recently, stainless steel tanks. Despite these technological improvements, many winemakers prefer to use the more traditional methods. For example, some of the wines from Louis Jadot ferment in wood as follows:

- One-third of the wine ferments in new wood.
- One-third ferments in year-old wood.
- One-third ferments in older wood.

Jadot's philosophy holds that the better the vintage, the newer the wood: Younger wood imparts more flavor and tannin, which might overpower wines of lesser vintage. Thus, younger woods generally are reserved for aging the better vintages.

CHABLIS

Chablis lies in the northernmost area in Burgundy, and it produces only white wine. All french Chablis is made of 100 percent Chardonnay grapes. The name "Chablis" suffers from the same misinterpretation and overuse as the name "Burgundy." Because the French didn't take the necessary legal precautions to protect the use of the name, "Chablis" now randomly applies to many ordinary bulk wines from other countries. As a result, Chablis has developed associations with some very undistinguished wines, but this isn't the case with French Chablis. In fact, the French take their Chablis very seriously. These are classifications and quality levels for Chablis:

Petit Chablis The most ordinary Chablis; rarely seen in America.

Chablis This wine comes from grapes grown anywhere in the Chablis district, also known as a Village wine.

Chablis Premier Cru Good quality Chablis that comes from specific high-quality vineyards.

Chablis Grand Cru The highest classification of Chablis and the most expensive because of its limited production. Only seven vineyards in Chablis can be called Grand Cru.

There are more than 250 GRAPE GROWERS IN CHABLIS, but only a handful age their wine in wood.

CHABLIS VILLAGE $

CHABLIS PREMIER CRU $$

CHABLIS GRAND CRU $$$$

DOMAINE LAROCHE USES SCREW CAPS
on all their wines, including the Grand Crus.

The **WINTER TEMPERATURES** in some parts of Chablis can match those of Norway.

Of these quality levels, the best value is a Chablis Premier Cru.

If you're interested in only the best Chablis, here are the seven Grands Crus and the most important Premier Cru vineyards:

THE SEVEN GRAND CRU VINEYARDS OF CHABLIS	
BLANCHOTS	PREUSES
BOUGROS	VALMUR
GRENOUILLES	VAUDÉSIR
LES CLOS	

SOME OF THE TOP PREMIER CRU VINEYARDS OF CHABLIS	
CÔTE DE VAULORENT	MONTMAINS
FOURCHAUME	MONTS DE MILIEU
LECHET	VAILLON
MONTÉE DE TONNERRE	

CHOOSING A CHABLIS

The two major aspects to look for in Chablis are the shipper and the vintage. The most important shippers of Chablis to the United States include:

A. Regnard & Fils	Joseph Drouhin	Albert Pic & Fils
La Chablisienne	Domaine Laroche	Louis Jadot
François Raveneau	Louis Michel	Guy Robin
René Dauvissat	J. Moreau & Fils	Robert Vocoret
Jean Dauvissat	Simmonet-Febvre	William Fèvre

WHEN TO DRINK CHABLIS

Chablis	Premier Cru	Grand Cru
within two years of the vintage	between two and four years of the vintage	between three and eight years of the vintage

– BEST RECENT VINTAGES OF CHABLIS –

2006* 2007* 2008* 2009* 2010* 2011* 2012* 2013* 2014 2015*

* EXCEPTIONAL VINTAGE

CÔTE DE BEAUNE

This is one of the two major areas of the Côte d'Or. The wines produced here are some of the finest examples of dry white Chardonnay produced in the world and serve as a benchmark for winemakers everywhere.

The three most important white wine–producing villages of the Côte de Beaune are:

Meursault   **Puligny-Montrachet**   **Chassagne-Montrachet**

All three produce their white wine from the same grape—100 percent Chardonnay. These are my favorite white wine–producing villages and vineyards in the Côte de Beaune.

CÔTE DE BEAUNE

VILLAGE	PREMIER CRU VINEYARDS	GRAND CRU VINEYARDS
ALOXE-CORTON		CORTON-CHARLEMAGNE CHARLEMAGNE
BEAUNE	CLOS DES MOUCHES	
CHASSAGNE-MONTRACHET	LES RUCHOTTES MORGEOT	BÂTARD-MONTRACHET* CRIOTS-BÂTARD-MONTRACHET MONTRACHET*
MEURSAULT	BLAGNY LA GOUTTE D'OR LES CHARMES LES GENEVRIÈRES LES PERRIÈRES PORUZOTS	
PULIGNY-MONTRACHET	CLAVOILLONS LES CAILLERETS LES CHAMPS GAIN LES COMBETTES LES FOLATIÈRES LES PUCELLES LES REFERTS	BÂTARD-MONTRACHET* BIENVENUE-BÂTARD MONTRACHET CHEVALIER-MONTRACHET MONTRACHET*-

* The vineyards of Montrachet and Bâtard-Montrachet overlap between the villages of Puligny-Montrachet and Chassagne-Montrachet.

The **LARGEST GRAND CRU**, in terms of production, is Corton-Charlemagne, which represents more than 50 percent of all white Grand Cru wines.

THE CÔTE DE NUIT is primarily a red wine–producing region, but the villages of Vougeot and Musigny make some exceptional white wines.

NAME OF VILLAGE $

Puligny-Montrachet

APPELLATION CONTROLÉE

Louis Latour

MIS EN BOUTEILLE PAR LOUIS LATOUR
NÉGOCIANT A BEAUNE (COTE-D'OR)

NAME OF VILLAGE + PREMIER CRU VINEYARD $$

Puligny-Montrachet

LES REFERTS
APPELLATION CONTROLÉE

Louis Latour

MIS EN BOUTEILLE PAR LOUIS LATOUR
NÉGOCIANT A BEAUNE (COTE-D'OR), FRANCE

NAME OF GRAND CRU VINEYARD $$$

Montrachet

APPELLATION CONTROLÉE

MIS EN BOUTEILLE PAR
LOUIS LATOUR NÉGOCIANT A BEAUNE (COTE-D'OR), FRANCE

WHAT MAKES EACH BURGUNDY WINE DIFFERENT?

In Burgundy, one of the most important factors in making a good wine is soil. The quality of the soil is the main reason that there are three levels and price points between a Village, a Premier Cru, and a Grand Cru wine. "The difference between the Village wine, Puligny-Montrachet, and the Grand Cru Montrachet is not in the type of wood used in aging or how long the wine is aged in wood. The primary difference is in the location of the vineyards, i.e. the soil and the slope of the land," says Robert Drouhin of Maison Joseph Drouhin.

Another major factor that differentiates each wine is the vinification procedure, the "recipe" the winemaker uses. It's the same as if you were to compare chefs at three different restaurants: They may start out with the same ingredients, but what they do with those ingredients matters.

> **FROM ST. AUBIN, try** the great Chardonnays of Pierre-Yves Colin-Morey, Philippe Colin, Alain Chavy, and Maroslavac-Leger.

– BEST RECENT VINTAGES OF CÔTE DE BEAUNE WHITE –
2002* 2005* 2006* 2007* 2008* 2009* 2010*
2011 2012* 2013* 2014 2015*

* EXCEPTIONAL VINTAGE

CÔTE CHÂLONNAISE

This is is the least known of the major wine districts of Burgundy. Although the Châlonnaise produces such red wines as Givry and Mercurey (see Class Four, "The Red Wines of Burgundy and the Rhône Valley"), it also produces some very good white wines that not many people know, which means value for you—specifically the wines of Montagny and Rully. These wines are of the highest quality produced in the area, similar to the white wines of the Côte d'Or but less costly.

Look for the wines of Antonin Rodet, Faiveley, Louis Latour, Moillard, Olivier Leflaive, Jacques Dury, Chartron & Trébuchet, Marc Morey, and Vincent Girardin.

MÂCONNAIS

The southernmost white wine–producing area in Burgundy, the Mâconnais, has a climate warmer than that of the Côte d'Or and Chablis. Mâcon wines are, in general, pleasant, light, uncomplicated, reliable, and a great value. From basic to best, here are the different quality levels of Mâconnais wines:

1. Mâcon Blanc
2. Mâcon Supérieur
3. Mâcon-Villages
4. St-Véran
5. Pouilly-Vinzelles
6. Pouilly-Fuissé

Of all Mâcon wines, Pouilly-Fuissé is unquestionably one of the most popular. It ranks among the highest-quality Mâconnais wines, fashionable to drink in the United States long before most Americans discovered the splendors of wine. As wine consumption increased here, Pouilly-Fuissé and other famous areas such as Pommard, Nuits-St.-Georges, and Chablis became synonymous with the best wines of France and frequently appeared on restaurants' wine lists.

Mâcon-Villages is the best value. Why pay more for Pouilly-Fuissé—sometimes three times as much—when a simple Mâcon will do just as nicely?

— BEST RECENT VINTAGES OF MÂCON WHITE —

2009** 2010* 2011 2012* 2013* 2014 2015*

*EXCEPTIONAL VINTAGE ** EXTRAORDINARY VINTAGE*

More than **FOUR-FIFTHS OF THE WINES** from the Mâconnais are white.

There is a **VILLAGE NAMED CHARDONNAY** in the Mâconnais area, where the grape's name is said to have originated.

Since **MÂCON WINES ARE USUALLY NOT AGED IN OAK,** they are ready to drink as soon as they are released.

IF YOU'RE TAKING A CLIENT OUT on a limited expense account, a safe wine to order is Mâcon. If the sky's the limit, go for the Meursault!

ESTATE-BOTTLED WINE is made, produced, and bottled by the owner of the vineyard.

DOMAINE LEFLAIVE'S WINES ARE NAMED FOR CHARACTERS AND PLACES IN A LOCAL MEDIEVAL TALE. The chevalier of Puligny-Montrachet, missing his son who was off fighting in the Crusades, amused himself in the ravinelike vineyards (Les Combettes) with a local maiden (Pucelle), only to welcome the arrival of another son (Bâtard-Montrachet) nine months later.

BURGUNDY REVIEW

Now that you're familiar with the many different white wines of Burgundy, how to choose the right one? First look for the vintage. With Burgundy, it's especially important to buy a good year. After that, your choice becomes a matter of taste and cost. If price is no object, aren't you lucky?

Also, after some trial and error, you may find that you prefer the wines of one shipper over another. Here are some of the shippers to look for when buying white Burgundy:

Bouchard Père & Fils	Louis Latour
Chanson	Olivier Leflaive Frères
Joseph Drouhin	Prosper Maufoux
Labouré-Roi	Ropiteau Frères
Louis Jadot	

Although 80 percent of Burgundy wines sell through shippers, some fine estate-bottled wines are available in limited quantities in America. The better ones include:

Château Fuissé	Pouilly-Fuissé
Domaine Bachelet-Ramonet	Chassagne-Montrachet
Domaine Boillot	Meursault
Domaine Bonneau du Martray	Corton-Charlemagne
Domaine Coche-Dury	Meursault, Puligny-Montrachet
Domaine Des Comtes Lafon	Meursault
Domaine Étienne Sauzet	Puligny-Montrachet
Domaine Lucien le Moine	Corton-Charlemagne
Domaine Leflaive	Meursault, Puligny-Montrachet
Domaine Matrot	Meursault
Domaine Philippe Colin	Chassagne-Montrachet
Domaine Vincent Girardin	Chassagne-Montrachet
Tollot-Beaut	Corton-Charlemagne

5 BEST VALUE WHITE WINES OF FRANCE UNDER $30

Pascal Jolivet Sancerre • Trimbach Riesling • William Fèvre Chablis • Château Larrivet-Haut-Brion • Louis Jadot Mâcon

See page 311 for a complete list.

FORTY YEARS LATER IN WHITE BURGUNDY

If you're looking for pure unoaked Chardonnay at its best, the crisp flavorful Chablis region of France will satisfy your tastes. Over the last 40 years, these wines have only improved. Through enhanced frost protection, the region has increased its vineyard acreage from 4,000 to 12,000 acres since the late 1950s without losing its quality. Great news for the consumer.

The white wines of the Mâconnais and Châlonnaise represent some of the great value wines made from 100 percent Chardonnay, yet most usually are priced under $20 a bottle. Wines labeled "Bourgogne Blanc" are fantastic values.

One of the big changes, especially in Mâcon, is the inclusion of the grape variety on the label. With increased competition from new-world Chardonnay producers, the French government finally has realized that Americans and other countries buy wines by grape variety.

The great white wines of the Côte d'Or have achieved greatness in the last 40 years. For me, these are the best white wines in the world! The new generation of winemakers has studied around the world, leading to more control in the vineyards and in the cellars, plantings of new clones, and picking lower yields. Chaptalization, the once prevalent addition of sugar to the fermenting juice to increase the alcohol content, rarely happens today, which means the wines have a better natural balance.

TEST YOUR KNOWLEDGE of the white wines of France by trying the quiz on page 329.

—————— **FURTHER READING** ——————

Burgundy by Anthony Hanson

Burgundy by Robert M. Parker Jr.

Making Sense of Burgundy by Matt Kramer

Côte D'Or: A Celebration of the Great Wines of Burgundy by Clive Coates

The Wines of Burgundy by Clive Coates

WINE AND FOOD

When you choose a white Burgundy, you have a gamut of wonderful food possibilities. Mâconnais wines are suitable for picnics as well as for formal dinners—you might select one of the fuller-bodied Côte de Beaune wines or an all-purpose Chablis.

"Drink young **Chablis** or **St-Véran** with shellfish. Fine **Côte d'Or** wines match well with any fish or light white meat, such as veal or sweetbreads."

—Robert Drouhin

"A basic **Village Chablis** is good as an apéritif and with hors d'oeuvre and salads. A great **Premier Cru** or **Grand Cru Chablis** needs something more special, such as lobster. It's an especially beautiful match if the wine has been aged a few years."

—Christian Moreau

"My favorite food combination with white **Burgundy** wine is, without doubt, homard grillé Breton [blue lobster.] Only harmonious, powerful, and delicate wines are able to go with the subtle, thin flesh and very fine taste of the Breton lobster. **Chablis** is a great match for oysters, snails, and shellfish, but a **Grand Cru Chablis** should be had with trout. With Village wines of the **Côte de Beaune**, which should be had at the beginning of the meal, try a light fish or quenelles [light dumplings]. **Premier Cru** and **Grand Cru** wines can stand up to heavier fish and shellfish such as lobster—but with a wine such as **Corton-Charlemagne**, smoked Scottish salmon is a tasty choice."

—Pierre Henry Gagey

"**Chablis** with oysters and fish. With **Corton-Charlemagne**, filet of sole in a light Florentine sauce. Otherwise, the **Chardonnays** of Burgundy complement roast chicken, seafood, and light-flavored goat cheese particularly well."

—Louis Latour

⚜ GUIDED TASTING ⚜

Start with a lighter-styled Riesling from Alsace, and end with a sweet Sauternes from Bordeaux. Remember to use the *Windows on the World Wine Tasting Notebook* when tasting these wines. Pay attention to the balance of fruit and acid, and note that some high-acid wines taste better with food, especially shellfish.

THE WINES

Riesling

One Riesling, tasted alone:

    1. Alsace Riesling

Melon and Sauvignon Blanc

Two wines from the Loire Valley, compared:

    2. Muscadet

    3. Pouilly-Fumé

Sauvignon Blanc and Sémillon

One Bordeaux, tasted alone:

    4. Château from Graves or Pessac-Leognan

Chardonnay

Four wines from Burgundy, compared:

    5. Unoaked Mâcon-Villages

    6. Oaked Chablis Premier Cru

    7. Village wine, such as Meursault

    8. Premier Cru, such as Puligny-Montrachet Les Combettes

Gewürztraminer

One Alsace wine, tasted alone:

    9. Gewürztraminer

Sémillon

One Sauternes, tasted alone:

    10. Bordeaux, Château from Sauternes

AMERICAN WINE & THE WHITE WINES OF CALIFORNIA

AMERICAN WINEMAKING ❊ CALIFORNIA WINEMAKING ❊
THE WHITE WINES OF CALIFORNIA ❊ THE WINES OF WASHINGTON,
NEW YORK, AND OREGON ❊ THE WINES OF THE SOUTH ❊
THE WINES OF THE GREAT LAKES

Upon discovering North America, **LEIF ERIKSSON NAMED IT VINELAND.** More species of native grapes exist in North America than on any other continent.

French Huguenots established colonies in Jacksonville, Florida, in 1562 and produced wine using the wild Scuppernong grape. Evidence points to a flourishing wine industry in 1609 at the site of the early Jamestown settlements. In 2004 an **OLD WINE CELLAR WAS DISCOVERED IN JAMESTOWN** with an empty bottle dating back to the seventeenth century.

AMERICAN WINEMAKING

WINE DRINKING HAS jumped by more than a third in the United States over the last 20 years, according to Gallup, with about 30 percent of Americans drinking at least one glass of wine a week. Americans prefer domestic wines: More than three-quarters of all wines consumed by Americans are produced in the United States. Meanwhile, the number of American wineries has doubled in the last two decades—to more than 6,000—and, for the first time in American history, all 50 states produce wine.

Because American wines so dominate the United States market, it makes sense to take a detailed look at winemaking here. We often think of the wine industry as "young" in America, but its roots go back some 400 years.

THE EARLY DAYS

Shortly after arriving in America, the Pilgrims and early pioneers, accustomed to drinking wine with meals, delighted in finding grapevines growing wild. These thrifty, self-reliant colonists thought they had found in this species (primarily *Vitis labrusca*) a means of producing their own wine, thereby ending their dependency on costly wine from Europe. They cultivated the existing local grapevines, harvested the grapes, and made their first American wine. The new vintage possessed an entirely different—and disappointing—flavor when compared to wine made from European grapes. They ordered cuttings of the *Vitis vinifera* vine from Europe, which for centuries had produced the finest wines in the world. Soon ships arrived bearing the tender cuttings, and the colonists, having paid scarce, hard-earned money for these new vines, planted and tended them with great care. They were eager to taste their first wine made from European grapes grown in American soil.

Despite their efforts, few of the European vines thrived. Many died, and those that survived produced few grapes. That meager yield resulted in very poor-quality wine. Early settlers blamed the cold climate, but today we know that their European vines lacked immunity to the New World's plant diseases and pests. For the next 200 years every attempt at establishing varieties of *vinifera*—either intact or through crossbreeding with native vines—failed. Left with no choice, growers throughout the Northeast and Midwest returned to planting *Vitis labrusca*, North America's vine, and a small wine industry managed to survive.

European wine remained the preferred, though high-priced, choice. The failures of these early attempts to establish a wine industry in the United States, along with the high cost of imported wines, resulted in decreasing demand for wine. Gradually American tastes changed, and wine served at mealtimes marked only special occasions. Beer and whiskey had conquered wine's traditional place in American homes.

The major varieties of wine produced in the United States are made from these species:

American *Vitis labrusca*, such as the Concord, Catawba, and Delaware; and *Vitis rotundifolia*, commonly called Scuppernong

European *Vitis vinifera*, such as Riesling, Sauvignon Blanc, Chardonnay, Pinot Noir, Merlot, Cabernet Sauvignon, Zinfandel, and Syrah

Hybrids A cross between *vinifera* and a native American species, such as Seyval Blanc, Vidal Blanc, Baco Noir, or Chancellor

WINE IN THE WEST

Wine production in the West began with the Spanish. As Spanish settlers pushed northward from Mexico, the Catholic Church followed, and a great era of mission-building began. Early missions amounted to more than just churches, though; they contained entire communities conceived as

Early German immigrants imported Riesling grapes and called their finished wine **HOCK**; the French called their wine **BURGUNDY** or **BORDEAUX**; and the Italians borrowed the name "**CHIANTI**" for theirs.

VITIS LABRUSCA, the "slip-skinned" grape, is native to both the Northeast and the Midwest and produces a unique flavor. It is used in making grape juice—the bottled kind you'll find on supermarket shelves. Wine produced from *labrusca* grapes tastes, well, more "grapey" (also described as "foxy") than European wines.

Benmarl
WINERY

Hudson River Region
BACO NOIR
NEW YORK
2006

EARLY MISSIONARIES established wineries in the southern parts of California. The first commercial winery was established in what is today Los Angeles.

The grape variety the missionaries used to make their sacramental wine was called **THE MISSION GRAPE.** Unfortunately, it didn't have the potential to produce a great wine.

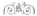

First Lady Mary Todd Lincoln served American wines in the White House in 1861.

When **ROBERT LOUIS STEVENSON** honeymooned in the Napa Valley in 1880, he described the efforts of local vintners to match soil and climate with the best possible varietals. "One corner of land after another . . . this is a failure, that is better, this is best. So bit by bit, they grope about for their Clos de Vougeot and Lafite . . . and **THE WINE IS BOTTLED POETRY."**

Welch's grape juice has been around since the late 1800s. It originally was produced by staunch Prohibitionists and labeled "**DR. WELCH'S UNFERMENTED WINE."** In 1892 they renamed it "Welch's Grape Juice" and successfully launched it at the Columbian Exposition in Chicago in 1893.

self-sufficient fortifications protecting Spanish colonial interests throughout the Southwest and along the Pacific Coast. Besides growing their own food and making their own clothing, those early settlers also made their own wine, produced primarily for use in the Church. The demand for wine led Father Junípero Serra to bring *Vitis vinifera* vines—brought to Mexico by the Spaniards—from Mexico to California in 1769. These vines took root, thriving in California's moderate climate. The first true California wine industry had begun, albeit on a small scale.

Two events occurred in the mid-1800s that resulted in an explosive growth of quality wine production. The 1849 California Gold Rush brought immigrants from Europe and the East Coast along with their winemaking traditions. They cultivated the vines and soon were producing good-quality commercial wine.

The second critical event occurred in 1861, when Governor Downey of California, understanding the importance of viticulture to the state's growing economy, commissioned Agoston Haraszthy to select and import classic *Vitis vinifera* cuttings—such as Riesling, Zinfandel, Cabernet Sauvignon, and Chardonnay—from Europe. Haraszthy traveled to Europe, returning with more than 100,000 carefully selected vines. Not only did these grape varieties thrive in California's climate, but they also produced good-quality wine! Serious California winemaking began in earnest.

In 1863, while California wines were flourishing, European vineyards were in trouble. Phylloxera—an aphid pest native to the East Coast of the U.S. and very destructive to grape crops—began attacking European vineyards. This infestation, which arrived in Europe on cuttings from native American vines exported for experimental purposes, proved devastating. Over the next two decades, the phylloxera blight destroyed thousands of acres of European vines, severely diminishing European wine production just as demand was growing rapidly.

California became virtually the only area in the world producing wine made from European grapes. Demand for its wines skyrocketed. This helped develop, almost overnight, two huge markets for California wine. The first market clamored for good, inexpensive, yet drinkable wine produced on a mass scale. The second market sought higher-quality wines. California growers responded to both demands, and by 1876 California was producing more than 2.3 million gallons of wine per year, some of remarkable quality. California had become, for the moment, the new center of global winemaking.

Unfortunately, in that same year, phylloxera arrived in California and began attacking those vineyards. Once there, it spread as rapidly as it had in Europe. With thousands of vines dying, the California wine industry faced financial ruin. To this day, the phylloxera blight remains one of the most destructive crop epidemics of all time.

Luckily, other states had continued producing wine made from *labrusca* vines, and American wine production didn't grind to a complete halt. Meanwhile, after years of research, European winemakers finally found a defense against the pernicious phylloxera aphid. They successfully grafted *Vitis vinifera* vines onto the rootstock of *labrusca* vines, immune to the phylloxera, rescuing their wine industry.

Americans followed, and the California wine industry not only recovered but began producing better-quality wines than ever before. By the late 1800s, California wines were winning medals in international competitions, gaining the respect and admiration of the world. It took only 300 years!

Forty different **AMERICAN WINERIES WON MEDALS AT THE 1900 PARIS EXPOSITION**, including those from California, New Jersey, New York, Ohio, and Virginia.

PROHIBITION

In 1920, the Eighteenth Amendment to the U.S. Constitution created yet another setback for the American wine industry. The National Prohibition Act, also known as the Volstead Act, prohibited the manufacture, sale, transportation, importation, exportation, delivery, or possession of intoxicating liquors for beverage purposes. Prohibition, which continued for 13 years, nearly destroyed what had become a thriving and national industry.

"PROHIBITION IS BETTER THAN NO LIQUOR AT ALL."
—Will Rogers

IN 1920 THERE WERE MORE THAN 700 WINERIES IN CALIFORNIA. By the end of Prohibition there were 160.

But one of the loopholes in the Volstead Act allowed for the manufacture and sale of sacramental wine, medicinal wines for sale by pharmacists with a doctor's prescription, and medicinal wine tonics (fortified wines) sold without prescription. Perhaps more importantly, Prohibition allowed anyone to produce up to 200 gallons yearly of fruit juice or cider. The fruit juice, sometimes made into concentrate, proved ideal for making wine. People bought grape concentrate from California and had it shipped to the East Coast. The top of the containers warned: CAUTION: DO NOT ADD SUGAR OR YEAST OR ELSE FERMENTATION WILL TAKE PLACE! Some of this yield found its way to bootleggers throughout America who did just that. But not for long. The government banned the sale of grape

"Once, during Prohibition, I was forced to live for days on nothing but food and water."

—W. C. FIELDS

juice, preventing illegal wine production. Growers stopped planting, and the American wine industry came to a halt.

Fortified wine, or medicinal wine tonic—containing about 20 percent alcohol, which makes it more like a distilled spirit than regular wine—was still available and became America's number-one wine. American wine soon became popular more for its effect than its taste; in fact, the word "wino" came into use during the Depression from the name given to those unfortunate souls who turned to fortified wine to forget their troubles.

Prohibition ended in 1933, but its impact reverberated for decades. By its end, Americans had lost interest in quality wine. During Prohibition, thousands of acres of valuable grapes around the country had been plowed under. Wineries nationwide shut down, and the winemaking industry dwindled to a handful of survivors, mostly in California and New York. Many growers on the East Coast returned to producing grape juice—the ideal use for the American *labrusca* grape. From 1933 to 1968, grape growers and winemakers had little more than personal incentive to produce any wine of quality. Jug wines, named for the containers in which they were bottled, were inexpensive, nondescript, and mass produced. A few wineries, notably in California, were producing some good wines, but the majority of American wines produced during this period were ordinary.

Although Prohibition proved devastating to the majority of American wine producers, some endured by making sacramental wines. Beringer, Beaulieu, and the Christian Brothers managed to survive this dry time in that way. Since these wineries didn't have to interrupt production during Prohibition, they had a jump on those that had to start all over.

In repealing Prohibition, the federal government empowered states to legislate the sale and transportation of alcohol. Some states handed control to counties and, occasionally, even municipalities—a tradition that continues today, varying from state to state and often from county to county.

THE RENAISSANCE OF AMERICAN WINE

It's hard to say exactly when the American wine renaissance began, but let's start in 1968, when, for the first time since Prohibition, table wines—wines with alcohol content between 7 and 14 percent—outsold fortified wines, which have an alcohol content between 17 and 22 percent. Although American wines were improving, consumers still believed the best wines came from Europe, especially France.

In the mid-sixties and early seventies, a small group of dedicated California winemakers began concentrating on making high-quality wine to equal Europe's best. Their early wines demonstrated potential and began attracting the attention of astute wine writers and wine enthusiasts around the country.

As they continued to improve their product, these same winemakers realized that they had to find a way to differentiate their quality wines from California's mass-produced wines—which had generic names: Burgundy, Chablis, or Chianti—and to ally their wines, at least in the minds of wine buyers and consumers, with European wines. Their solution was brilliant: They labeled their best wines by varietal.

Varietal designation calls the wine by the name of the predominant grape used to produce it: Cabernet Sauvignon, Chardonnay, Pinot Noir, etc. The savvy consumer learned that a wine labeled "Chardonnay" had the general characteristics of any wine made from that grape. Wine buying became easier for both buyers and sellers.

Varietal labeling quickly spread throughout the industry and became so successful that, in the 1980s, varietal designation became an American industry standard, forcing the federal government to revise its labeling regulations.

Today, varietal labeling is the norm for the highest-quality American wines. Many other countries have adopted the practice which has helped bring worldwide attention to California wine. California still produces 90 percent of American wine, but its success has inspired winemakers in other areas of the country to refocus on producing high-quality wines—as we'll see.

—— FURTHER READING ——
Last Call: The Rise and Fall of Prohibition by Daniel Okrent

THE BEST-KNOWN WINERIES OF CALIFORNIA IN THE 1960s AND 1970s:

Almaden	Korbel
Beaulieu	Louis Martini
Beringer	Mirassou
Buena Vista	Parducci
Charles Krug	Paul Masson
Concannon	Sebastiani
Hanzell	Simi
Inglenook	Wente

In the early 1970s, **CHENIN BLANC** was the best-selling white wine and **ZINFANDEL** the best-selling red.

THREE MAJOR GRAPES CONSUMED BY AMERICANS ARE:
1. Chardonnay
2. Cabernet Sauvignon
3. Merlot

TOP AMERICAN MARKETS FOR WINE:
1. New York
2. Los Angeles
3. Chicago
4. Boston
5. San Francisco

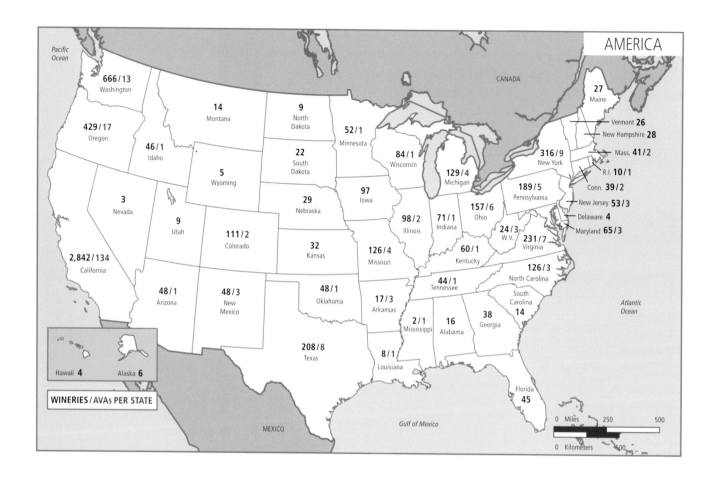

AMERICA

Pacific
Ocean

666/13
Washington

14
Montana

9
North
Dakota

52/1
Minnesota

CANADA

27
Maine

Vermont 26
New Hampshire 28

429/17
Oregon

46/1
Idaho

22
South
Dakota

84/1
Wisconsin

129/4
Michigan

316/9
New York

Mass. 41/2
R.I. 10/1
Conn. 39/2

5
Wyoming

97
Iowa

189/5
Pennsylvania

New Jersey 53/3

3
Nevada

29
Nebraska

157/6
Ohio

24/3
W.V.

Delaware 4
Maryland 65/3

9
Utah

111/2
Colorado

98/2
Illinois

71/1
Indiana

231/7
Virginia

2,842/134
California

32
Kansas

126/4
Missouri

60/1
Kentucky

126/3
North Carolina

Atlantic
Ocean

48/1
Arizona

48/3
New
Mexico

48/1
Oklahoma

44/1
Tennessee

South
Carolina
14

17/3
Arkansas

2/1
Mississippi

16
Alabama

38
Georgia

208/8
Texas

8/1
Louisiana

Florida
45

Hawaii 4   Alaska 6

WINERIES / AVAs PER STATE

MEXICO

Gulf of Mexico

0 Miles   250   500

0 Kilometers   500

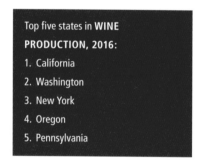

Top five states in **WINE
PRODUCTION, 2016:**

1. California
2. Washington
3. New York
4. Oregon
5. Pennsylvania

America has **MORE THAN 230
VITICULTURAL AREAS,** 134 of which
are located in California.

(WineInstitute.org)

QUALITY AMERICAN WINES

To buy American wines intelligently means having knowledge about and familiarity with each state as well as the regions within the state. Some states—or even regions within a state—may specialize in white wine, others in red; some regions even specialize in wine made from a specific grape variety. Therefore, it's helpful to know the defined grape-growing areas within each state or region, the American Viticultural Areas (AVAs).

An AVA is a specific grape-growing area recognized by and registered with the federal government. Styled after the European regional system, AVA designation began in the 1980s. In France, Bordeaux and Burgundy are strictly enforced regional appellations (marked "Appellation d'Origine Contrôlée," or AOC); in Italy, Tuscany and Piedmont are recognized as zones (marked "Denominazione di Origine Controllata," or DOC). So is

Napa Valley a defined viticultural area in California. Columbia Valley is an AVA in Washington; both Oregon's Willamette Valley and New York's Finger Lakes district are similarly identified.

Vintners are discovering, as their European counterparts did years ago, which grapes grow best in which particular soils and climatic conditions. AVA is important to wine buying and will continue to be as individual AVAs become known for certain grape varieties or wine styles. If an AVA appears on the label, at least 85 percent of the grapes must come from that region.

Let's look at the Napa Valley, the best-known AVA in the United States, renowned for its Cabernet Sauvignon. Within Napa exists a smaller, inner district called Carneros, which has a cooler climate. Chardonnay and Pinot Noir need a cooler growing season to mature properly, so these grape varieties are suited especially to that AVA. New York's Finger Lakes region is noted for its Riesling, and if you've seen the movie *Sideways*, you know that Santa Barbara is a great place for Pinot Noir.

Although not necessarily a guarantee of quality, an AVA designation identifies a specific area well known and established for its wine. It's a geographic point of reference for winemakers and consumers about its provenance. The more knowledge you have about a wine's origin by region and grape, the easier it is to buy even unknown brands with confidence. As you learn more about the characteristics of major grapes and styles of wine, and which you prefer, you'll be able to identify the AVAs that produce wines you're most likely to enjoy.

But there is more: The most recent worldwide trend is to ignore all existing standards by giving the highest-quality wines a proprietary name, which helps high-end wineries differentiate their best wines from other wines from the same AVA, from similar varietals, and even from their own other offerings. In the United States, many of these proprietary wines fall under the category of Meritage (see page 190). Examples of American proprietary wines include Dominus, Opus One, and Rubicon.

Because of federal laws governing standards and labels, select wineries increasingly are using proprietary names. Federal law mandates, for example, that if a label lists a varietal, at least 75 percent of the grapes used to make the wine must come from that varietal.

SOME OF THE BEST KNOWN CALIFORNIA AVAS:

Alexander Valley	Los Carneros
Anderson Valley	Napa Valley
Chalk Hill	Paso Robles
Dry Creek Valley	Russian River Valley
Edna Valley	Santa Cruz Mountain
Fiddletown	Sonoma Valley
Howell Mountain	Stag's Leap
Livermore Valley	

In 2016, there were **MORE THAN 6,810 BONDED WINERIES** in the United States, up from fewer than 500 in 1970. Of them, 99 percent are small and family owned.

Wineries in the United States are opening at the rate of **300 PER YEAR.**

U.S. wine exports have increased from nothing in 1970 to more than $1.5 billion in 2016. The **TOP EXPORT MARKETS** are: Canada, United Kingdom, Hong Kong, Japan, Italy.

AMERICAN WINE SALES hit $38 billion in 2015.

——— FURTHER READING ———

American Vintage by Paul Lukacs

American Wine by Jancis Robinson and Linda Murphy

The Oxford Companion to the Wines of North America by Bruce Cass and Jancis Robinson

Imagine a talented, innovative winemaker in the Columbia Valley of Washington. He or she wants to produce an outstanding, full-bodied Bordeaux-style wine consisting of 60 percent Cabernet Sauvignon blended with several other grapes. Our ambitious winemaker has invested considerable time and labor to produce a really great wine, suitable for aging, that will be ready to drink in five years—and even better in ten.

But how to distinguish this wine, how to attract buyers willing to pay a premium price for an unknown wine? It can't be labeled "Cabernet Sauvignon" because fewer than 75 percent of the grapes used are of that type. For this reason, many producers of fine wine use proprietary names. It's indicative of the healthy state of the American wine industry as well. More and more winemakers are turning out better and better wines, and the very best is yet to come!

THE FUTURE OF AMERICAN WINES

Americans are drinking American wine! More than 75 percent of wines consumed in the United States come from this country—and not just from the top four states: California, Washington, New York, and Oregon. When I began studying wine in 1970, two-thirds of the states had no wineries at all. Now all 50 states are producing wine.

Plenty of books are available on French, Italian, Spanish wines, etc., but comparatively few cover American wines. In the last 20 years, the remarkable rise in the quality of wine production has prompted an increase in wine consumption in America. These two trends keep reinforcing each other, so we can continue to expect great things in American winemaking for many years to come.

American wine also has an enormous "fun factor." Studying and tasting the wines from around this country are exciting! It's a lesson in U.S. geography, history, agriculture, and the passion of American grape growers and winemakers. Wineries here have become major tourist attractions. Wine trails have sprung up all across the country in combination with other historical landmarks in those particular regions. Wine definitely has gone mainstream in America. Our time has arrived. Thanks to the conviction and determination of American producers and the demands of American consumers, I can say proudly that many of the best wines in the world are produced in the United States of America.

CALIFORNIA WINEMAKING

No wine-growing area in the world has come so far so quickly as California. Americans historically have had little interest in wine, but from the moment we first became "wine conscious," winemakers in California rose to the challenge. Forty years ago we were asking if California wines measured up to European wines. Now California wines are available worldwide: Exports have increased dramatically in recent years to countries such as Japan, Germany, and Britain. California produces more than 90 percent of United States wine. If the state were a nation, it would be the fourth leading wine producer in the world!

AN INTRODUCTION TO CALIFORNIA WINES

The map on this page will help familiarize you with the winemaking regions. It's easier to remember them if you divide them into four groups:

THE MAIN VITICULTURAL AREAS

REGION	COUNTY	BEST WINES
NORTH COAST	NAPA SONOMA MENDOCINO LAKE	CABERNET SAUVIGNON CHARDONNAY MERLOT SAUVIGNON BLANC ZINFANDEL
SAN JOAQUIN VALLEY		INEXPENSIVE JUG WINES
NORTH CENTRAL COAST	MONTEREY SANTA CLARA LIVERMORE	CHARDONNAY GRENACHE MARSANNE ROUSSANE SYRAH VIOGNIER
SOUTH CENTRAL COAST	SAN LUIS OBISPO SANTA BARBARA	CHARDONNAY PINOT NOIR SAUVIGNON BLANC SYRAH

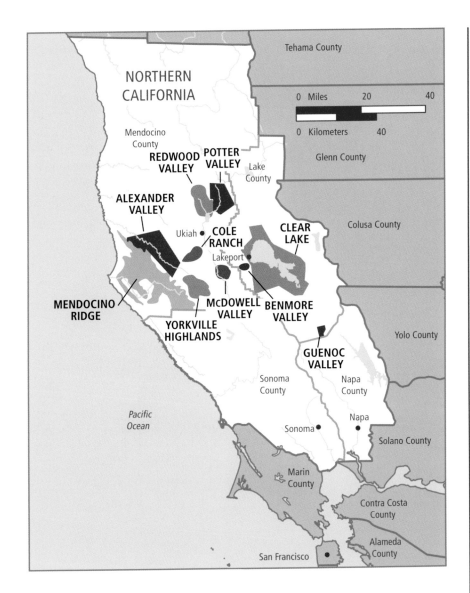

NORTHERN CALIFORNIA

Tehama County

0 Miles 20 40
0 Kilometers 40

Mendocino County

Glenn County

REDWOOD VALLEY

POTTER VALLEY

Lake County

ALEXANDER VALLEY

Ukiah

COLE RANCH

CLEAR LAKE

Colusa County

Lakeport

MENDOCINO RIDGE

McDOWELL VALLEY

BENMORE VALLEY

Yolo County

YORKVILLE HIGHLANDS

GUENOC VALLEY

Sonoma County

Napa County

Pacific Ocean

Napa

Sonoma

Solano County

Marin County

Contra Costa County

Alameda County

San Francisco

If an **INDIVIDUAL VINEYARD** is noted on the label, 95 percent of the grapes must come from the named vineyard, which must lie within an approved AVA.

More than 60,000 wine labels are registered in California.

Although you may be most familiar with Napa and Sonoma, fewer than 10 percent of all California wine comes from these two regions combined. Even so, Napa alone accounts for more than 30 percent of dollar sales of California wines. Wine from the San Joaquin Valley accounts for 58 percent of the wine grapes planted, much of it jug wine. Maybe that doesn't seem too exciting— that the production of jug wine dominates California winemaking history—but Americans aren't atypical in this preference. In France, AOC wines account for only 35 percent of all French wines; the rest are everyday table wines.

NAPA VALLEY, PAST AND PRESENT
1970: 27 wineries
2016: 400+ wineries

ACRES OF WINE GRAPES planted in Napa: 44,398

TOP GRAPES PLANTED IN NAPA
1. Cabernet Sauvignon (19,894 acres)
2. Chardonnay (7,238 acres)
3. Merlot (5,734 acres)

EARLY EUROPEAN WINEMAKERS:

FRANCE
Paul Masson: 1852
Étienne Thée and Charles LeFranc
    (Almaden): 1852
Pierre Mirassou: 1854
Georges de Latour (Beaulieu): 1900

GERMANY
Beringer Brothers: 1876
Carl Wente: 1883

ITALY
Giuseppe and Pietro Simi: 1876
John Foppiano: 1895
Samuele Sebastiani: 1904
Louis Martini: 1922
Adolph Parducci: 1932

FINLAND
Gustave Niebaum (Inglenook): 1879

IRELAND
James Concannon: 1883

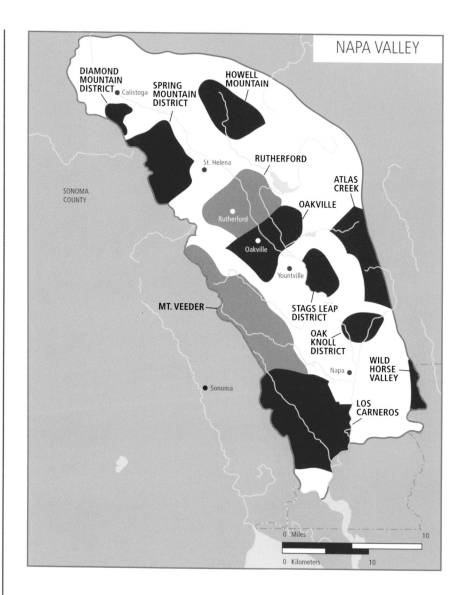

JUG WINES AND VARIETALS

Jug wine refers to simple, uncomplicated, everyday drinking wine. These wines sometimes are labeled with a generic name, such as Chablis or Burgundy. Inexpensive and well made, they originally were bottled in jugs, rather than conventional bottles, hence the name. They are very popular and account for the largest volume of California wine sold in the United States.

Ernest and Julio Gallo, who began their winery in 1933, are the major producers of jug wines in California. Many people credit the Gallo brothers

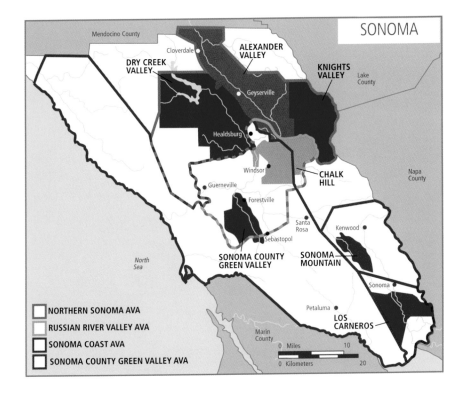

SONOMA

Mendocino County
Cloverdale
ALEXANDER VALLEY
DRY CREEK VALLEY
KNIGHTS VALLEY
Lake County
Geyserville
Healdsburg
Windsor
Napa County
CHALK HILL
Guerneville
Forestville
Santa Rosa
Kenwood
Sebastopol
North Sea
SONOMA COUNTY GREEN VALLEY
SONOMA MOUNTAIN
Sonoma
Petaluma
LOS CARNEROS
Marin County

NORTHERN SONOMA AVA
RUSSIAN RIVER VALLEY AVA
SONOMA COAST AVA
SONOMA COUNTY GREEN VALLEY AVA

0 Miles 10
0 Kilometers 20

Acres of wine grapes **PLANTED IN SONOMA**: more than 60,000

TOP GRAPES PLANTED IN SONOMA
1. Chardonnay (15,639 acres)
2. Pinot Noir (11,644 acres)
3. Cabernet Sauvignon (11,335 acres)

As of 2016, Sonoma had **MORE THAN 450 WINERIES**.

with converting American drinking habits from spirits to wine. The best jug wines in the world come from California. They maintain both consistency and quality from year to year.

As early as the 1940s, Frank Schoonmaker—an importer, writer, and one of the first American wine experts—convinced some California winery owners to market their best wines using varietal labels.

Robert Mondavi may be one of the best examples of a winemaker who concentrated solely on varietal wine production. In 1966, Mondavi left his family's Charles Krug Winery and started the Robert Mondavi Winery. His role was important to the evolution of varietal labeling of California wines. He was among the first major winemakers to make the total switch that led to higher-quality winemaking. Robert Mondavi was also a great promoter for the California wine industry. "He was able to prove to the public what the people within the industry already knew—that California could produce world-class wines," said California vintner Eric Wente.

Almaden, Gallo, and Paul Masson still produce **JUG WINES**.

E & J Gallo Winery owns **MORE THAN 20,000 ACRES** in California. Gallo produces 67 million cases of wine annually and is the largest winery in the world.

Early California winemakers sent their children to **STUDY OENOLOGY** at Geisenheim in Germany or Bordeaux in France. Today, many European winemakers send their children to the University of California at Davis and to Fresno State University.

In 2016, more than 21 million people visited California wine-growing areas. Vineyards and wineries are the **SECOND-MOST POPULAR CALIFORNIA TOURIST DESTINATIONS** after Disneyland!

Wine is **CALIFORNIA'S MOST VALUABLE FINISHED AGRICULTURAL PRODUCT,** with a $52 billion economic impact. (The film industry: $30 billion.)

THE UNIVERSITY OF CALIFORNIA AT DAVIS graduated only five students from its viticulture and enology department in 1966. Today it has a waiting list of students from all over the world.

WORLD-CLASS IN 40 YEARS

Many reasons account for California's winemaking success, including:

Location Napa and Sonoma counties, two of the major quality-wine regions, both lie less than a two-hour drive from San Francisco. That proximity encourages residents and tourists to visit the wineries in the two counties, most of which offer tastings and sell their wines in their own shops.

Weather Abundant sunshine, warm daytime temperatures, cool evenings, and a long growing season all add up to good conditions for growing many grape varieties. California is subject to sudden changes in weather, but a fickle climate isn't a major worry.

The University of California at Davis and Fresno State University Both schools have trained many young California winemakers, and their curricula concentrate on the scientific study of wine, viticulture, and, most important, technology. Their research—focused on soil, strains of yeast, hybridization, temperature-controlled fermentation, and other viticultural techniques—has revolutionized the wine industry worldwide.

Money and Marketing Strategy Marketing may not make the wine, but it certainly helps sell it. As more and more winemakers concentrated on making the best wine they could, American consumers responded with appreciation. They were willing to buy and pay more as quality improved. In order to keep up with consumer expectations, winemakers needed more research, development, and working capital. The wine industry turned to investors, both corporate and individual.

Since 1967, when the now defunct National Distillers bought Almaden, multinational corporations have recognized the profit potential of large-scale winemaking and have entered the wine business aggressively. They've brought huge financial resources and expertise in advertising and promotion that have helped advance American wines domestically and internationally. Other early corporate participants included Pillsbury and Coca-Cola.

On the other side of the investor scale stand the individual investor / growers drawn to the business by their love of wine and their desire to live the winemaking lifestyle. These individuals focus more on producing quality wines.

By the 1990s both corporate and individual investors had helped California fine-tune its wine industry, which today produces not only delicious and reliable wines in great quantity but also truly outstanding wines, many with investment potential.

EARLY PIONEERS

Some of the pioneers of the back-to-the-land movement:

"FARMER"	ORIGINAL PROFESSION	WINERY
JAMES BARRETT	ATTORNEY	CHATEAU MONTELENA
TOM BURGESS	AIR FORCE PILOT	BURGESS
BROOKS FIRESTONE	TAKE A GUESS!	FIRESTONE
JESS JACKSON	ATTORNEY	KENDALL-JACKSON
TOM JORDAN	GEOLOGIST	JORDAN
DAVID STARE	CIVIL ENGINEER	DRY CREEK
ROBERT TRAVERS	INVESTMENT BANKER	MAYACAMAS
WARREN WINIARSKI	COLLEGE PROFESSOR	STAG'S LEAP

Clonal selection, wind machines, drip irrigation, biodynamic vineyards, and mechanical harvesting are some **NEW TECHNIQUES** in vineyard management.

The majority of California wines retail from **$9 TO $20.**

In 1970 the average price per acre in Napa was $2,000–$4,000. Today, **ONE PRIME ACRE IN THE NAPA VALLEY COSTS BETWEEN $150,000 AND $400,000** unplanted, and it takes an additional $100,000 per acre to plant. This per-acre investment sees no return for three to five years. To this, add the cost of building the winery, buying the equipment, and hiring the winemaker.

HOLLYWOOD AND VINE
Many movie actors, directors, and producers have invested in vineyards and wineries throughout California, including Francis Ford Coppola.

KENDALL-JACKSON

CHARDONNAY
CALIFORNIA 2003

FOR MORE THAN TWO DECADES, MY FAMILY HAS SOURCED FRUIT FROM MOUNTAIN AND HILLSIDE VINEYARDS TO BRING YOU FLAVORFUL WINES.

VINTNER'S RESERVE

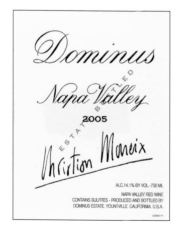

CALIFORNIA VERSUS EUROPEAN WINEMAKING

European winemaking has established traditions that have remained essentially unchanged for hundreds of years. These practices involve the ways grapes are grown and harvested and in some cases include winemaking and aging procedures.

California maintains few traditions, and winemakers can take full advantage of modern technology. Furthermore, they have the freedom to experiment and create new products. European wine-control laws prohibit some of the experimenting that California winemakers undertake, such as combining different grape varieties to make new styles of wine. Californians thus have greater opportunity to try many new ideas.

Another way in which California winemaking differs is that many California wineries carry an entire line of wines. Many of the larger houses produce more than 20 different labels. In Bordeaux, most châteaux produce only one or two wines.

Nor can you ignore the fundamentals of wine-growing: California's rainfall, weather patterns, and soil differ from those of Europe. The greater abundance of sunshine in California can result in wines with greater alcohol content, ranging on average from 13.5 percent to 14.5 percent, compared to 12 percent to 13 percent in Europe. This higher alcohol content changes the balance and taste of the wines.

That said, many well-known and highly respected European winemakers have invested in California vineyards to make their own wine. European, Canadian, and Japanese companies own more than 45 California wineries. For example:

- Baron Philippe de Rothschild, then owner of Château Mouton-Rothschild in Bordeaux, and Robert Mondavi, joined forces to produce a wine called Opus One, one of the most influential joint ventures.

- The Moueix family, the owners of Château Pétrus in Bordeaux, have vineyards in California. Their wine is a Bordeaux-style blend called Dominus.

- Moët & Chandon, part of Moët-Hennessy, owns Domaine Chandon in the Napa Valley.

- Roederer grows grapes in Mendocino County and produces Roederer Estate.

- Mumm produces a sparkling wine called Mumm Cuvée Napa.

- Taittinger has its own sparkling wine called Domaine Carneros.

- Spanish sparkling-wine house Codorníu owns a winery called Artesa.
- Freixenet owns land in Sonoma County and produces a wine called Gloria Ferrer.
- The Torres family of Spain owns a winery called Marimar Torres Estate in Sonoma County.
- Until recently, frenchman Robert Skalli (maker of the Fortant de France wines) owned more than 6,000 acres in the Napa Valley and the winery St. Supery.
- Tuscan wine producer Piero Antinori owns Antica winery in Napa.

CALIFORNIA WINE STYLES

"Style" refers to the characteristics of the grapes and wine. It's the trademark of the individual winemaker, an artist who tries different techniques to explore the fullest potential of the grapes.

Most winemakers will tell you that 95 percent of winemaking lies in the quality of the grapes. The other 5 percent comes from the winemaker's personal touch. Here are just a few of the hundreds of decisions a winemaker must make when developing his or her style of wine:

- When should the grapes be harvested?
- What varieties of grapes should be blended, and in what proportion?
- Should the juice be fermented in stainless steel tanks or oak barrels? How long should it ferment? At what temperature?
- Should the wine age at all? If so, how long? In oak? What kind of oak— American, French?
- How long should the wine age in the bottle before being sold?

The list goes on. Because winemaking has so many variables, producers can create many styles of wine from the same grape variety—so you can choose the style that suits your taste. With the relative freedom of winemaking in the United States, the style of California wines continues to be diversity.

But that diversity can cause confusion. The renaissance of the California wine industry began only about 40 years ago. Within that short period of time, some 2,100 new wineries have been established in California. Today, more than 2,800 wineries operate there, most of them making more than

California wine has **NO CLASSIFICATION SYSTEM** that resembles the European equivalent.

"You are never going to stylize the California wines the same way that European wines have been stylized, because we have more freedom to experiment. I value my freedom to make the style of wine I want more than the security of the AOC laws. Laws discourage experimentation."
—Louis Martini

STAINLESS STEEL tanks are temperature controlled, allowing winemakers to control the temperature at which the wine ferments. For example, a winemaker could ferment wines at a low temperature to retain fruitiness and delicacy, while preventing browning and oxidation.

Ambassador Zellerbach, who created Hanzell Winery, was one of the first California winemakers to use **SMALL FRENCH OAK AGING BARRELS** because he wanted to recreate a Burgundian style.

OVERHEARD AT A RESTAURANT in Yountville, Napa Valley: "How do you make a small fortune in the wine business?" "Start with a large fortune and buy a winery."

FAMOUS INDIVIDUAL VINEYARDS OF CALIFORNIA

Bacigalupi	Hyde
Bancroft Ranch	Martha's Vineyard
Beckstoffer	McCrea
Bien Nacido	Monte Rosso
Durell	Robert Young
Dutton Ranch	S.L.V.
Gravelly Meadow	To-Kalon
Hudson	

Kistler

Sonoma Mountain

Los Vestres

N 15805   2003

In the 2014 vintage, Kistler Vineyards produced **CHARDONNAYS FROM TEN SPECIFIC VINEYARDS!**

---

one wine. The variety of styles reflects the price differences. Cabernet Sauvignons range from Two Buck Chuck to Harlan Estate at more than $500 a bottle—so how do you choose? The constant changes in the wine industry keep California winemaking in a state of flux.

You can't necessarily equate quality with price, though. Some excellent varietal wines produced in California fall well within the budget of the average consumer. On the other hand, some varietals—primarily Chardonnay and Cabernet Sauvignon—may be quite expensive.

As in any market, supply and demand mainly determine price. However, new wineries have start-up costs, which sometimes affect the price of the wine. Older, established wineries, which long ago amortized their investments, can keep prices low when the supply/demand ratio calls for it. Remember, when buying California wine, price doesn't always reflect quality.

PHYLLOXERA REDUX

In the 1980s, phylloxera destroyed a good part of the vineyards of California, costing more than $1 billion in new plantings. But it also proved that good can come from bad.

What's the good news? This time, vineyard owners didn't have to wait to discover a solution; they already knew what to do to replace the dead vines—replant with a different rootstock resistant to phylloxera. The short-term effects were terribly expensive, but the long-term effect should be better-quality wine. Why?

In the early days of California grape-growing, little thought went into where a specific grape would grow best. Many Chardonnays were planted in climates that were too warm, and Cabernet Sauvignons in climates too cold. With the onset of phylloxera, vineyard owners had a chance to rectify those errors; when replanting, they matched the climate and soil with the best grape variety. Grape growers also had the opportunity to plant different grape clones. But the biggest change happened to the planting density of the vines themselves. Traditional spacing used by most wineries fell somewhere between 400 and 500 vines per acre. Today, with the new replanting, it's not uncommon to have more than 1,000 vines per acre, and many vineyards have planted more than 2,000 per acre.

The bottom line: If you like California wines now, you'll love them more with time. The quality is already better and the costs are lower—making it a win-win situation for everyone.

THE WHITE WINES OF CALIFORNIA

CHARDONNAY

The most important white-wine grape grown in California is Chardonnay. The major regions for California Chardonnay are:

Carneros   **Napa**   **Santa Barbara**   **Sonoma**

This green-skinned grape (*Vitis vinifera*) often ranks as the finest white-grape variety in the world. It's responsible for all the great French white Burgundies, such as Meursault, Chablis, and Puligny-Montrachet. In California, as the most successful white grape, it has yielded a wine of tremendous character and magnificent flavor. In the vineyard, yields are fairly low, and the grapes command high prices. The wines often age in small oak barrels, increasing their complexity. Chardonnay is always dry and benefits from aging more than any other American white wine. Superior examples can keep and develop well in the bottle for five years or longer.

The best wineries age these wines in wood, sometimes for more than a year. French oak barrels have doubled in price over the last five years,

California has more **CHARDONNAY** planted than any country **IN THE WORLD!**

More than 24 different varieties of white-wine grapes grow in California.

The **TWO LEADING** premium white grapes planted in California in 2016:
1. Chardonnay (97,826 acres)
2. Sauvignon Blanc (15,248 acres)

A THIRD OF ALL GRAPES grown in Sonoma are Chardonnay.

MONTEREY COUNTY HAS THE MOST
Chardonnay in California with 17,164 acres.

averaging $1,000 per barrel. Add to this the cost of the grapes and the length of time before the wine is actually sold, and you can see why the best California Chardonnays cost more than $25.

NOT ALL CALIFORNIA CHARDONNAYS ARE CREATED EQUAL

Put it this way: Grocery stores sell many brands of ice cream. The brands use similar ingredients, but there's only one Ben & Jerry's. The same holds true for wine. Among the many points to consider: Where do the grapes come from? Was the wine barrel fermented? Did it undergo malolactic fermentation? Is the wine aged in wood or stainless steel? If wood, what type of oak? How long does it remain in the barrel?

MY FAVORITE CALIFORNIA CHARDONNAYS

Acacia	Flowers	Peter Michael
Arrowood	Grgich Hills	Phelps
Au Bon Climat	Hanzell	Ramey
Aubert	Kistler	Robert Mondavi
Beringer	Kongsgaard	Rudd Winery
Brewer-Clifton	Landmark	Saintsbury
Cakebread	Lewis	Sbragia Family
Chalk Hill	Littorai	Shafer
Chateau Montelena	Marcassin	Silverado
Chateau St. Jean	Martinelli	Talbott
Diatom	Mount Eden	Testarossa
Dutton Goldfield	Paul Hobbs	Tor
Ferrari-Carano		

– **BEST RECENT VINTAGES OF CALIFORNIA CHARDONNAY** –

CARNEROS: 2004* 2007** 2008 2009* 2010 2011 2012* 2013* 2014* 2015*

NAPA: 2007* 2008* 2009** 2010* 2011 2012* 2013* 2014*

SONOMA: 2004** 2005** 2006* 2007** 2008* 2009** 2010* 2011 2012* 2013* 2014* 2015*

SANTA BARBARA: 2007* 2008 2009* 2010 2011 2012 2013* 2014* 2015*

* EXCEPTIONAL VINTAGE ** EXTRAORDINARY VINTAGE

OTHER MAJOR CALIFORNIA WHITE-WINE GRAPES

Sauvignon Blanc Sometimes labeled "Fumé Blanc," this is one of the grapes used in making the dry white wines of the Graves region of Bordeaux and the white wines of Sancerre and Pouilly-Fumé in the Loire Valley of France as well as New Zealand. California Sauvignon Blanc makes one of the best dry white wines in the world. It's sometimes aged in small oak barrels and occasionally blended with the Sémillon grape.

Chenin Blanc In California, the grape—one of the most widely planted in the Loire Valley—yields a very attractive, soft, light-bodied wine. It's usually made very dry or semisweet; it's a perfect apéritif wine, simple and fruity.

Viognier One of the major white grapes from France's Rhône Valley, Viognier thrives in warmer and sunny climates, so it's a perfect grape for the weather conditions in certain areas of California. It has a distinct fragrant bouquet. Not as full-bodied as most Chardonnays, nor as light as most Sauvignon Blancs, it's an excellent food wine.

MY FAVORITE CALIFORNIA SAUVIGNON BLANCS

Brander	Grey Stack	Orin Swift
Caymus	Honig	Quintessa
Chalk Hill	Joseph Phelps	Robert Mondavi
Chateau St. Jean	Kenwood	Silverado
Dry Creek	Mason	Simi
Ferrari-Carano	Matanzas Creek	Vogelzang
Girard	Merry Edwards	

CALIFORNIA WINE TRENDS

The 1960s saw expansion and development. The 1970s brought growth, especially in the number of wineries established in California and the corporations and individuals that became involved. The 1980s and 1990s fostered experimentation in grape-growing as well as in winemaking and marketing techniques.

Over the past 20 or so years, winemakers finally had a chance to step back and fine-tune their wine. Today, they're producing wines with tremendous

Robert Mondavi realized that no one was buying Sauvignon Blanc, so he changed its name to **FUMÉ BLANC.** Strictly a marketing maneuver—it was still the same wine. Result: sales took off. Mondavi decided not to trademark the name, allowing anyone to use it (and many producers do).

ROBERT MONDAVI WINERY

2007

FUMÉ BLANC

Napa Valley

JOSEPH PHELPS
VINEYARDS
Viognier
NAPA VALLEY
VINTAGE 2006

CALIFORNIA TRENDS THROUGH THE DECADES

1960s and 1970s: **JUG WINES** (Chablis, Burgundy)

1980s: **VARIETAL WINES** (Chardonnay, Cabernet Sauvignon)

1990s: **VARIETAL LOCATION** (Cabernet Sauvignon—Napa, Pinot Noir—Santa Barbara)

2000s: **SPECIFIC VINEYARDS** for varietals

Today: **CONSISTENTLY GREAT WINES** from all regions

—— **FURTHER READING** ——

The Far Side of Eden and Napa by James Conaway

Making Sense of California Wine by Matt Kramer

The New California Wine by Jon Bonné

Wine Atlas of California by James Halliday

The Wine Atlas of California and the Pacific Northwest by Bob Thompson

Wine Spectator's California Wine by James Laube

Wines of California, Deluxe Edition by Mike DeSimone and Jeff Jenssen

structure, finesse, and elegance that many lacked in the early years of the California winemaking renaissance. They also are making wines that can give pleasure when young and great wines that I hope I will be around to share with my grandchildren. The benchmark for quality has increased to such a level that the best wineries have improved, but more important to the consumer is that even the wines under $20 are better than ever before.

Another trend has pushed wineries toward specializing in particular grape varieties. Forty years ago, I would have talked about which wineries in California were best overall. Today, I'm more likely to talk about which AVA, winery, or individual vineyard makes the best Chardonnay or which winery makes the best Sauvignon Blanc.

Chardonnay remains the major white-grape variety by far in California. Sauvignon Blancs / Fumé Blancs have improved greatly, and they're easier to consume young. Although they still don't have the cachet of a Chardonnay, they pair better with most foods. Other white-grape varieties, such as Riesling and Chenin Blanc, aren't meeting with the same success, and they're harder to sell. Still, to keep it interesting, some winemakers are planting more European varietals, including Viognier and Pinot Gris.

WINE AND FOOD

"With **Chardonnay**: oysters, lobster, a more complex fish with beurre blanc, pheasant salad with truffles. With **Sauvignon Blanc**: traditional white meat or fish course, sautéed or grilled fish (as long as it isn't an oily fish)."

—Margrit Biever and Robert Mondavi

"With **Chardonnay**: fresh boiled Dungeness crab cooked in Zatarain's crab boil, a New Orleans–style boil. Serve this with melted butter and a large loaf of sourdough French bread. With **Sauvignon Blanc**, "I like fresh salmon cooked in almost any manner. Personally, I like to take a whole fresh salmon or salmon steaks and cook them over the barbecue in an aluminum foil pocket. Place the salmon, onion slices, lemon slices, copious quantities of fresh dill, salt, and pepper on aluminum foil and make a pocket. Cook over the barbecue until barely done. Place the salmon in the oven to keep it warm while you take the juices from the aluminum pocket, reduce the juices, strain, and whisk in some plain yogurt. Enjoy!"

—David Stare, Dry Creek

"With **Chardonnay**: ceviche, shellfish, salmon with a light hollandaise sauce."

—Warren Winiarski, Stag's Leap Wine Cellars

"With **Chardonnay**: barbecued whole salmon in a sorrel sauce. With **White Riesling**: sautéed bay scallops with julienne vegetables."

—Janet Trefethen

"With **Chardonnay**: Sonoma Coast Dungeness crab right from the crab pot, with fennel butter as a dipping sauce."

—Richard Arrowood

"With **Chardonnay**: salmon, trout, or abalone, barbecued with olive oil and lemon leaf and slices."

—Bo Barrett, Chateau Montelena Winery

"With my Cakebread Cellars Napa Valley **Chardonnay**: bruschetta with wild mushrooms, leek-and-mushroom-stuffed chicken breast, and halibut with caramelized endive and chanterelles."

—Jack Cakebread

"With **Chardonnay**: lobster or salmon with lots of butter."

—Ed Sbragia, Sbragia Family Vineyards

2015	
CALIFORNIA	NEW YORK
469,000 acres	37,000 acres
2,842 wineries	316 wineries
WASHINGTON	OREGON
44,000 acres	20,400 acres
666 wineries	429 wineries

THE PACIFIC NORTHWEST WINE-GROWING REGION includes Washington, Oregon, and Idaho in America and British Columbia in Canada.

WASHINGTON IS THE SECOND LARGEST wine-producing state.

WASHINGTON, PAST AND PRESENT
1970: 10 wineries (9 acres)
2015: 666 wineries (44,000 acres)

WASHINGTON'S WINE PRODUCTION

50% white   50% red

THE WINES OF WASHINGTON

Washington's wine industry has matured considerably in the last 40 years, and the state has some of the best wine regions of the world. It has taken people a while to understand and appreciate these wines for many reasons, not the least of which is weather. Ask the average wine drinker about winemaking in this region of the United States, and one of the most common responses you'll get is, "How do you make great wine in a rainy climate like Seattle's?"

The Cascade Mountains—which include two active volcanoes, Mount Rainier and Mount St. Helens—split Washington State into two regions: the east and the west. On the eastern side of this mountain range, geologic cataclysms—dramatic lava flows from 15 million years ago and monstrous floods during the last Ice Age—created soil conditions ideal for growing superior grapes and making high-quality wine. An enormous difference exists between Washington's west coast maritime climate and its eastern continental climate: 60 inches of annual rainfall along the Pacific versus just 8 in eastern Washington, where wine grapes thrive in its arid, hot summers. The eastern wine-growing region also has an ideal irrigation system

Artist Series #15   *Tyrell Collins*

WOODWARD CANYON
2006
Washington State Cabernet Sauvignon

ALC 14.5% BY VOL

Chateau Ste. Michelle is the **WORLD'S LARGEST RIESLING PRODUCER** and formed a winemaking partnership with the famous German wine producer Dr. Loosen to produce a Riesling wine called Eroica.

In 2012, Washington had its **LARGEST HARVEST** and in 2013 it had the warmest vintage since 2003.

—— **FURTHER READING** ——

Washington Wines & Wineries by Paul Gregutt

The Wine Project by Ron Irvine

partly deriving from the Columbia River, which helps produce perfectly ripe grapes.

Unlike California, Washington's winemaking history is all about the present and future. Only 10 wineries were operating here in 1970; today there are almost 700. It was wheat to grapes, orchards to vineyards, and Rieslings to reds (think Cabernet Sauvignon, Merlot, and Syrah). Still, Washington remains the number-one American producer of Riesling, and its Chardonnays, with their balance, great fruit, and lively acidity, are some of the best in the country.

The major white grapes grown in Washington are:

Chardonnay	Riesling
(7,654 acres)	(6,320 acres)

The major red grapes are:

Cabernet Sauvignon	Merlot
(10,293 acres)	(8,235 acres)

MY FAVORITE WASHINGTON PRODUCERS

Andrew Will	Doyenne	Owen Roe
Betz Family	Fidelitas	Pepper Bridge
Canoe Ridge	Gramercy Cellars	Quilceda Creek
Cayuse	Hogue Cellars	Reynvaan
Charles Smith	Januik	Seven Hills
Chateau Ste. Michelle	L'Ecole No. 41	Spring Valley
Columbia Crest	Leonetti Cellar	Woodward Canyon
Columbia Winery	Long Shadows	Winery
DiStefano	McCrea Cellars	

> **– BEST RECENT VINTAGES OF WASHINGTON WINES –**
> 2005*   2006*   2007*   2008**   2009*   2010*   2011
> 2012**   2013*   2014   2015
> ** EXCEPTIONAL VINTAGE   ** EXTRAORDINARY VINTAGE*

THE WINES OF NEW YORK

New York is the third largest wine-producing state in America, with nine AVAs. The three main wine regions in New York are:

Finger Lakes with the largest wine production east of California
Hudson Valley concentrating on premium farm wineries
Long Island New York's red-wine region

The three main categories of grapes grown here are:

Native American	European	French-American
Vitis labrusca	*Vitis vinifera*	hybrids

New york's Hudson Valley is one of America's oldest wine-growing regions. French Huguenots planted the grapevines here in the 1600s. The Hudson Valley also boasts the oldest active winery in America: Brotherhood, which recorded its first vintage in 1839. Alex and Louisa Hargrave started the first winery on Long Island in 1973.

In 2015 *Wine Enthusiast* magazine chose New York as the wine region of the year, beating out Champagne, Chianti, Sonoma, and Washington.

There are **316 WINERIES IN NEW YORK,** up from fewer than 10 in 1970.

From 2001 to 2013, **MORE THAN 200 WINERIES** have opened in New York.

In the **THREE MAJOR REGIONS,** the Finger Lakes region has 128 wineries, the Hudson Valley has 60, and Long Island has 72.

The climate on Long Island has more than 200 days of sunshine and a longer growing season, making it perfect for **MERLOT AND BORDEAUX-STYLE WINES.**

The Finger Lakes wineries **PRODUCE 85 PERCENT** of New York's wine.

NATIVE AMERICAN VARIETIES

Vitis labrusca vines are popular among grape growers in New York because they are hardy and can withstand cold winters. Among the most familiar grapes of the *Vitis labrusca* family are Concord, Catawba, and Delaware. Until the last decade, these were the grapes used to make most New York wines. Words such as "foxy," "grapey," "Welch's," and "Manischewitz" often describe these wines—a sure sign of *Vitis labrusca*.

EUROPEAN VARIETIES

Forty years ago, some New York wineries began to experiment with the traditional European (*Vitis vinifera*) grapes. Dr. Konstantin Frank, a Russian viticulturist skilled in cold-climate grape growing, came to America and catalyzed efforts to grow *Vitis vinifera* in New York. This was unheard of—and laughed at—back then. Other vintners predicted that he'd fail, that it was impossible to grow *vinifera* in New York's cold and capricious climate.

"What do you mean?" Frank replied. "I'm from Russia—it's even colder there."

Most people remained skeptical, but Charles Fournier of Gold Seal Vineyards gave Frank a chance to prove his theory. Sure enough, Frank succeeded with *vinifera* and has produced some world-class wines, especially his Riesling and Chardonnay. So have many other New York wineries, thanks to the vision and courage of Frank and Fournier.

FRENCH-AMERICAN VARIETIES

Some New York and East Coast winemakers have planted French-American hybrid varieties, which combine European taste characteristics with American vine hardiness to withstand the cold winters in the Northeast. French viticulturists originally developed these varieties in the nineteenth century. Seyval Blanc and Vidal are the most prominent white-wine varieties; Baco Noir and Chancellor are the most common reds.

The most significant developments in New York wine are taking place on Long Island and in the Finger Lakes region. Both have experienced tremendous growth of new vineyards. Since 1973, grape-growing acreage on Long Island has increased from 100 acres to more than 4,000 acres, with more expansion expected in the future.

The wines of the Finger Lakes region continue to improve as the winemakers work with grapes that thrive in the cooler climate, including European varieties such as Riesling, Chardonnay, and Pinot Noir.

The predominant use of *Vitis vinifera* varieties allows Long Island wineries to compete more effectively in the world market, and Long Island's longer growing season offers greater potential for red grapes.

The Millbrook Winery in the Hudson Valley has shown that this region can produce world-class wines—not only white, but red too, from grapes such as Pinot Noir and Cabernet Franc.

> **– BEST RECENT VINTAGES OF NEW YORK WINES –**
> 2010   2012   2013*   2014   2015
> *EXCEPTIONAL VINTAGE*

More than 70 percent of Oregon
wineries are located in the
WILLAMETTE VALLEY.

The Columbia Valley and Walla Walla
Valley AVAs encompass parts of Oregon
as well as Washington.

Both the **WILLAMETTE VALLEY AND
BURGUNDY, FRANCE,** are located at 45
degrees North latitude.

Willamette Valley is pronounced Wil-AM-it,
DAMN IT!

*More than half of
Oregon's vineyards
are planted with
Pinot Noir.*

OREGON STATE LAW requires that a
wine labeled "Pinot Noir" must contain
100 percent Pinot Noir.

THE WINES OF OREGON

Although grapes were planted and wine was made as early as 1847, Oregon's modern viticultural era began roughly 40 years ago with a handful of intrepid wine pioneers, including David Lett (Erie winery) Dick Erath (Erath winery), and Dick Ponzi (Ponzi winery). This new breed of grape growers and winemakers believed that cool-climate varietals such as Pinot Noir, Chardonnay, and Pinot Gris not only would grow in Oregon but would produce world-class wines—and they have! What separated Oregon winemaking from its neighbors in California and Washington was the importation of French clones from Burgundy and Alsace.

Most Oregon wineries are small, family-owned, artisanal producers. Their proximity to the city of Portland and Oregon's beautiful coastline make this a must-visit wine region.

The major grapes grown in Oregon are:

Pinot Noir	Pinot Gris
(12,560 acres)	(2,590 acres)

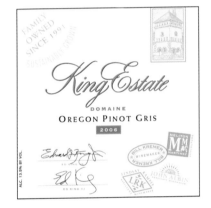

The **KING ESTATE** in Oregon is the largest producer of Pinot Gris in the United States.

MY FAVORITE OREGON WINES

A to Z	Brick House	King Estate
Adelsheim	Chehalem	Penner-Ash
Alexana	Cristom	Ponzi
Archery Summit	Domaine Drouhin	Rex Hill
Argyle	Domaine Serene	Shea
Artisanal	Elk Cove	Sokol Blosser
Beaux Frères	Erath	Soter
Benton Lane	Evening Lands	St. Innocent
Bergström	Eyrie	Tualatin
Bethel Heights	Ken Wright	

– **BEST RECENT VINTAGES OF OREGON WINES** –

2005*   2006*   2008**   2009*   2010**   2011
2012**   2013   2014   2015

* EXCEPTIONAL VINTAGE   ** EXTRAORDINARY VINTAGE

——— **FURTHER READING** ———

The Northwest Wine Guide by Andy Perdue

Wines of the Pacific Northwest by Lisa Shara Hall

WINES OF THE SOUTH

VIRGINIA

Records from Jamestown show that vineyards were planted and wine was made in the Virginia colony in 1609. Before he became the third president, Thomas Jefferson served as minister to France and imported some of the great wines from France, planting his own vineyard in Virginia. It was as challenging back then as it is today. George Washington was unsuccessful with his vineyard. Even in 1979, Virginia only had six wineries.

The number-one grape is Chardonnay, but Viognier has become an increasingly popular white grape. Norton, a native grape, has a strong following, and beautiful red blends have also succeeded. Northern Virginia has seen the most growth in the last seven to ten years and has produced tremendous wines. Outside the big four, Virginia is one of the fastest-growing wine regions in the country.

VIRGINIA RANKS FIFTH in the U.S. with 231 wineries and 2,974 acres of vines.

WELL-KNOWN VIRGINIA WINERIES

AmRhein Wine Cellars

Barboursville Vineyards

Boxwood Winery

Château Morrisette

Fabbioli Cellars

Horton Vineyards

Jefferson Vineyards

Keswick Vineyards

King Family Vineyards

Rappahannock Cellars

Trump Winery

White Hall Vineyards

The Winery at La Grange

TEXAS

Missionaries planted the first vineyard in Texas in 1662. Texas's oldest winery, Val Verde Winery, has been in operation since 1883. You might not think the climate would make for good wine, but the wineries of Texas are committed to growing primarily Cabernet Sauvignon and Chardonnay. Recent plantings of Malbec and Viognier point to an interesting future. The state has eight AVAs. The largest, Texas Hill Country, has more than 600 acres and 70 wineries.

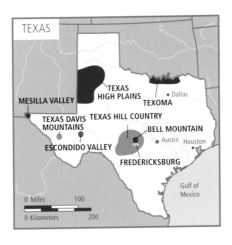

MISSOURI

Grapes were first planted in Missouri in the early 1800s. At one time Missouri ranked second in production, just behind New York (before California started making wine). The oldest winery is Stone Hill Winery, established in 1847. Many German immigrants settled in Hermann, Missouri, in 1837 because of its resemblance to the Rhine Valley in Germany, planting vineyards on both sides of the Missouri River. Hermann held its first Weinfest in the fall of 1848, a tradition that continues in today's Octoberfest celebrations. Augusta became the first federally recognized AVA in 1980.

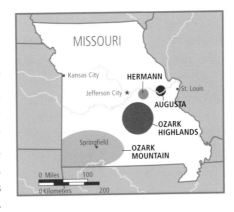

Today, Missouri grows a combination of *Vitis labrusca* (Concord) as well as French hybrids (Vignoles), but its most important grape is Norton, which produces a pleasant dry-style red wine. Norton originated in Virginia, but today it's Missouri's official grape.

The **GRAPE VARIETY NORTON** is sometimes referred to as the grape Cynthiana.

The Heck family, **CREATORS OF KORBEL**, began their winemaking careers in Missouri.

WELL-KNOWN NORTH CAROLINA WINERIES

Biltmore Winery

Childress Vineyards

Duplin Wine Cellars

RagApple Lassie Vineyards

RayLen Vineyards

Shelton Vineyards

Westbend Vineyards

NORTH CAROLINA

French explorer Giovanni de Verrazano receives credit for discovering the Scuppernong grape in the Cape Fear River Valley in 1524. Sir Walter Raleigh explored the Carolinas in the late 1500s and wrote that the land overflowed with grapes. This was the first grape cultivated in America and is to this day the official fruit of North Carolina.

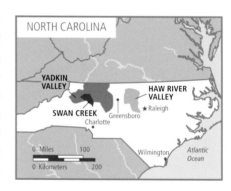

Medoc vineyard, in Brinkleyville, Halifax County, was the state's first commercial winery, established in 1835, and once led the country in wine production. Since 2001 the number of wineries has more than quadrupled with a new focus on European-style *vinifera* grapes such as Cabernet Sauvignon, Chardonnay, and Merlot. Most of the *vinifera* is planted in the northwestern and Piedmont regions of the state. The most important is grape-growing area is the Yadkin Valley, North Carolina's first AVA, recognized in 2003. It includes more than 30 wineries and 400 acres devoted to vineyards.

BILTMORE ESTATE in Asheville receives more than 1.4 million visitors annually.

THE WINES OF THE GREAT LAKES

PENNSYLVANIA

William Penn planted the first vineyard in Pennsylvania in 1683, and Pennsylvania is the site of America's first commercial vineyard—the Pennsylvania Vine Company, established in 1793. Pennsylvania is a "control state," meaning that all the wines are purchased by the state and sold through their stores. Pennsylvania is one of the largest

single buyers of wines in the U.S. It is also the fifth largest wine-grape producer in the nation.

Like New York, Pennsylvania produces wines from Native American grapes, such as Concord and Niagara; *vinifera* grapes, such as Cabernet Sauvignon and Chardonnay; and also hybrids such as, Seyval Blanc and Chambourcin. Most of Pennsylvania's wineries lie in the warmer, southeastern portion of the state, such as York, Bucks, Chester, and Lancaster Counties.

OHIO

The first vineyards were planted here in 1823, and by 1842 there were 1,200 acres. The oldest and largest winery in Ohio is Meier's Winery, established in 1856. In the 1860s Ohio was the largest producer of wine in the country. Most of the vineyards were planted with Native American grapes, and Ohio became famous for its Sparkling Catawba. Unfortunately the

PENNSYLVANIA RANKS SEVENTH in the U.S. with 189 wineries and 13,600 acres of vines.

WELL-KNOWN PENNSYLVANIA WINERIES

Allegro Vineyards

Arrowhead Wine Cellars

Blue Mountain

Chaddsford Winery

J. Maki

Manatawny Creek

Pinnacle Ridge Winery

VaLa Vineyards

OHIO RANKS EIGHTH in the U.S. with 157 wineries and 1,900 acres of vines.

At the turn of the twentieth century, dozens of wineries were located on the islands of Lake Erie, and thousands of gallons of wine were produced. It became known as the **"LAKE ERIE GRAPE BELT."**

MICHIGAN RANKS NINTH in the U.S. with 129 wineries and 14,200 acres of vines.

Château Grand Traverse first produced **ICE WINE** in 1983.

majority of the vines died from disease, and Prohibition severely curtailed the wine industry.

More than 30 different grapes are planted in Ohio, a blend of *Vitis labrusca*, hybrids such as Seyval Blanc and Chambourcin, and more recently *Vitis vinifera* such as Riesling and Cabernet Franc. Through the efforts of the Ohio State Viticultural and Enology programs, the quality of the wines has improved dramatically.

MICHIGAN

Of the 14,200 acres of grapes in Michigan, only 2,600 are used for producing wine. But the Riesling grape is thriving in the cool climate, and plantings have increased substantially over the last ten years.

The maritime climate greatly influences Michigan winemaking. The Leelanau Peninsula, home to more than 50 percent of Michigan's wineries, benefits from the Lake Effect in many ways. The snow insulates the vines during winter, slowing the bud break in spring and preventing damaging frost, making the growing season last much longer. The Michigan Grape Council is testing other areas in the state to find the best grape-growing land and to increase production, which will mean more quality wines from Michigan.

ILLINOIS

In 1778, french settlers in La Ville de Maillet (now Peoria) brought the winemaking expertise of their homeland to Illinois. The village featured a winepress and an underground wine vault. In the 1850s, farmers started planting the Concord grape. Emile Baxter and Sons opened a winery in Nauvoo in 1857, along the banks of the Mississippi River. Baxter's Vineyards remains Illinois's oldest operating winery, run by a fifth generation of Baxters. More recently, the Illinois wine industry has exploded, growing from just 12 wineries in 1997 to more than 90 today. Acreage devoted to grape production also has grown at a tremendous rate, and today Illinois consistently ranks among the top twelve wine-producing states.

ILLINOIS RANKS TWELFTH in the U.S. with 98 wineries and 1,083 acres of vines.

WELL-KNOWN ILLINOIS WINERIES

Alto Vineyards

Baxter's Vineyards

Fox Valley Winery

Galena Cellars

Hickory Ridge Vineyard

Lynfred Winery

Mary Michelle Winery & Vineyard

Owl Creek Vineyard

Spirit Knob Winery and Winery

Vahling Vineyards

---

5 BEST VALUE WHITE WINES OF AMERICA UNDER $30

Chateau St. Jean Chardonnay • Columbia Crest Sémillon-Chardonnay • Dr. Konstantin Frank Riesling • Frog's Leap Sauvignon Blanc • King Estate Pinot Gris

See pages 306–307 for a complete list.

TEST YOUR KNOWLEDGE of American wines by trying the quiz on page 331.

❧ GUIDED TASTING ☙

Follow the same wine styles as with France, but this time use American white wines. Start with an unoaked, low-alcohol Riesling, which will leave the palate refreshingly light. Then move on to some food-friendly Sauvignon Blancs, and work your way through some great Chardonnays.

THE WINES

American Riesling
One Riesling, tasted alone:
1. *Finger Lakes, New York, Riesling*

American Sauvignon Blanc
Two Sauvignon Blancs, compared:
2. *Sonoma County Sauvignon Blanc*
3. *Napa Valley Sauvignon Blanc*

American Chardonnay
One Chardonnay, tasted alone:
4. *Unoaked California Chardonnay*

Two Chardonnays, compared (blind tastings):
5. *Blind Tasting 1:*
Unoaked California Chardonnay versus Heavily Oaked California Chardonnay
OR
Sonoma Valley Chardonnay versus Napa Valley Chardonnay

6. *Blind Tasting 2:*
White Burgundy versus Napa or Sonoma Valley Chardonnay
OR
New York Chardonnay versus California Chardonnay
OR
Australian Chardonnay versus California Chardonnay
In both blind tastings, to be fair, both wines should be of the same quality, vintages within a year of each other, and in the same price range.

Four Chardonnays, compared, from four different AVAs:
7. *Sonoma County Chardonnay*
8. *Santa Barbara Chardonnay*
9. *Monterey Chardonnay*
10. *Carneros Chardonnay*

Aged Chardonnay (more than five years old), tasted alone:
11. *Napa, aged Chardonnay*

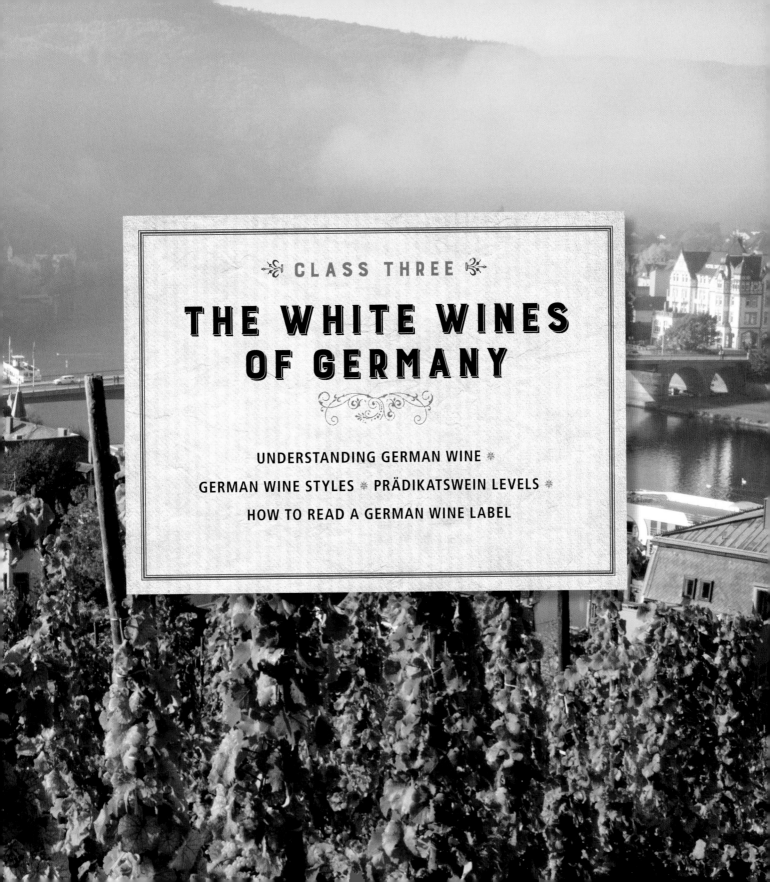

CLASS THREE

THE WHITE WINES OF GERMANY

UNDERSTANDING GERMAN WINE ✳

GERMAN WINE STYLES ✳ PRÄDIKATSWEIN LEVELS ✳

HOW TO READ A GERMAN WINE LABEL

In Germany, 100,000 grape growers cultivate nearly 270,000 acres of vines, meaning **THE AVERAGE HOLDING PER GROWER IS 2.7 ACRES.**

WHO'S VINEYARD IS IT?
PIESPORTER GOLDTRÖPFCHEN:
350 owners
WEHLENER SONNENUHR:
250 owners
BRAUNEBERGER JUFFE:
180 owners

On a globe, put your finger on Germany, and then spin it westward into North America. You're pointing to **NEWFOUNDLAND, CANADA.**

One mechanical harvester can do the **WORK OF 60 PEOPLE.**

UNDERSTANDING GERMAN WINE

Today Germany—a minor player on the world wine stage—features more than 1,400 wine villages and 2,600-plus vineyards. No problem, right? But if you had to study German wines before 1971, you would have had 30,000 different names to remember! A large assortment of people used to own very small parcels of land, which is why there were so many names. Then, in an effort to reduce confusion, the West German government passed a law in 1971, mandating that a vineyard consist of at least twelve and a half acres of land. That legislation cut the list of vineyard names considerably, but it increased the number of owners.

Germany produces only 2 or 3 percent of the world's wines. (The national beverage is beer, remember.) What wines it does produce depend largely on the weather. Why? Germany is the northernmost country in which vines can grow, and 80 percent of the quality vineyards lie on hilly slopes—which means forget about mechanical harvesting!

The following graphic will give you a better idea of the hilly conditions vintners face in order to grow grapes that produce the highest-quality wines in Germany.

10°
14% Flat Land

45°
14% Hillsides

60°
66% Steep Hillsides

North Sea

GERMANY

Hamburg

Berlin ★

SAALE-UNSTRUT

SAXONY

Rhein River

AHR

Bonn

MITTELRHEIN
RHEINGAU
HESSISCHE BERGSTRASSE

MOSEL

Frankfurt

NAHE

FRANCONIA

Mosel River

RHEINHESSEN

PFALZ

BADEN WÜRTTEMBERG

Munich

0 Miles 100 200

0 Kilometers 200

GERMANY, PAST AND PRESENT
1970: 77,372 hectares of vineyards
2015: 102,186 hectares of vineyards

85%

85 percent of the wines Germany produces are white.

If a wine label gives the grape variety—Riesling, for example—85 percent of the wine must be made from the Riesling grape.

If a German wine shows a vintage on the label, 85 percent of the grapes used must be from that year. Top German wine producers use 100 percent of the varietal and the vintage on the label.

Germany has been growing the **RIESLING GRAPE SINCE 1435.**

Fifty years ago, most German wines were dry and very acidic. Even in the finer restaurants, you'd be offered **A SPOONFUL OF SUGAR** with a German wine **TO BALANCE THE ACIDITY**.

Germany has more than **50,000 ACRES OF RIESLING,** and no other country comes close. More than 60 percent of the world's Riesling is grown in Germany. Australia is next, with 10,000 acres, France has 8,000, and Washington has 632 acres.

The most important grape varieties are:

Riesling This is the most widely planted and the best grape variety produced in Germany. If you don't see "Riesling" on the label, the wine probably has little if any Riesling grape. Remember, if the label gives the grape variety, the wine must contain at least 85 percent of that grape, according to German law. Of the grapes planted in Germany, 21 percent are Riesling.

Müller Thurgau A cross between Riesling and Chasselas, it accounts for 13.5 percent of Germany's wines.

Silvaner This grape variety accounts for just 5 percent of Germany's wines.

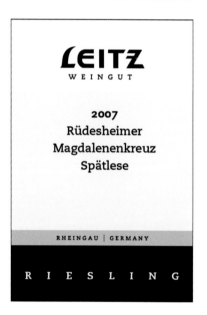

THE WINEMAKING REGIONS OF GERMANY

Germany has 13 official winemaking regions, but just four of them produce the best German wines. They are:

Rheinhessen	Rheingau	Mosel	Pfalz
		(Mosel-Saar-Ruwer until 2007)	(Rheinpfalz until 1992)

Rhein wines generally have more body than Mosels, which usually have higher acidity and lower alcohol levels than Rheins. Mosels show more autumn fruits like apples, pears, and quince, while Rhein wines show more summer fruits like apricots, peaches, and nectarines.

Some important villages to look for in each of the four chief regions:

Rheinhessen Oppenheim, Nackenheim, Nierstein

Rheingau Eltville, Erbach, Rüdesheim, Rauenthal, Hochheim, Johannisberg

Mosel Erden, Piesport, Bernkastel, Graach, Ürzig, Brauneberg, Wehlen

Pfalz Deidesheim, Forst, Wachenheim, Ruppertsberg, Dürkheimer

GERMAN WINE STYLES

Simply put, German wine balances sweetness with acidity and low alcohol. Remember the equation:

$$Sugar + Yeast = Alcohol + Carbon\ Dioxide$$

The sugar ultimately comes from the sun. If your vines are growing on a southerly slope and you have a good year, you'll get a lot of sun and therefore the right amount of sugar to produce a good wine. Many times, however, German winemakers aren't so fortunate, and they don't get enough sun to ripen the grapes properly. The result: higher acidity and lower alcohol. To compensate, some winemakers add sugar to the must before fermentation to increase the amount of alcohol. This process is called chaptalization, which is verboten for higher-quality German wines.

The three basic styles of German wine are:

Trocken	Halbtrocken	Fruity
Dry	Medium-dry	Semidry to very sweet

But those designations don't take into account the ripeness levels of the wine, which matters!

SÜSSRESERVE

A common misconception about German wine holds that, after fermentation is halted, the remaining residual sugar gives the wine its sweetness naturally. On the contrary, some wines are fermented dry. Many German winemakers withhold a certain percentage of unfermented grape juice from the same vineyards, varietal, and sweetness level. This Süssreserve contains all the natural sugar, which winemakers add back to the wine after fermentation. The finest estates don't use the Süssreserve method but do rely on stopping the fermentation to achieve their style.

RIPENESS LEVELS

As a result of the 1971 legislation, German wine falls into two main categories: Tafelwein and Qualitätswein.

Tafelwein Literally, table wine. The lowest designation given to a wine grown in Germany, it never carries the vineyard name and rarely leaves the country.

Qualitätswein Literally, quality wine, which in turn also falls into two types.
1. ***Qualitätswein bestimmter Anbaugebiete*** QbA indicates a quality wine that comes from 1 of the 13 specified regions.
2. ***Prädikatswein*** This is a quality wine with distinction—the good stuff, in other words. These wines may not be chaptalized.

Given good weather, the longer the grapes remain on the vine, **THE SWEETER THEY BECOME**—but the winemaker takes a risk when doing this because all could be lost in the event of bad weather.

TYPICAL VINTAGE YEAR IN GERMANY

Prädikatswein 44.5%

Tafelwein 5.8%

QbA 49.7%

All Qualitätswein and Prädikatswein must **PASS A TEST BY AN OFFICIAL LABORATORY** and tasting panel to be given an official number, prior to the wine's release.

The story goes that, at the **VINEYARDS OF SCHLOSS JOHANNISBERG,** the monks couldn't pick the grapes until the abbot of Fulda gave his permission. During the harvest of 1775, the abbot was away attending a synod. That year the grapes were ripening early, and some had started to rot on the vine. The concerned monks dispatched a rider to ask the abbot's permission to pick the grapes. By the time the rider returned with the official assent, the monks despaired but went ahead with the harvest anyway. To their amazement, the wine was one of the best they had ever tasted. That was the beginning of Spätlese-style wines.

In **1921,** the first Trockenbeerenauslese was made in the Mosel region.

Today, most German wines, including Beerenauslese and Trockenbeerenauslese, are bottled in spring and early summer. Many no longer receive additional cask or tank maturation because it has been discovered that this extra **BARREL AGING DESTROYS THE FRUIT.**

PRÄDIKATSWEIN LEVELS

In increasing order of quality, price, and ripeness at harvest, here are the six Prädikatswein levels:

Kabinett Light semidry wines made from normally ripened grapes.

Spätlese "Late-picking," meaning that this medium-style wine comes from grapes picked after the normal harvest. The extra days of sun give the wine more body and a more intense flavor.

Auslese "Out-picked," meaning that the grapes come from particularly ripe bunches, which yield a medium-to-fuller-style wine. If you've ever grown fruit, you've probably done the same by picking the especially ripe ones, leaving the others on the vine.

Beerenauslese "Berry picking," which simply signifies that individual grapes are selected. These luscious grapes go into the rich dessert wines for which Germany is renowned. Beerenauslese is made usually only two or three times every decade.

Trockenbeerenauslese A step above the Beerenauslese, and don't let the big words scare you. These grapes are dried (trocken), so they're more like raisins. These raisinated grapes produce the richest, sweetest, and most expensive honeylike wine.

Eiswein A very rare, sweet, concentrated wine made from frozen grapes left on the vine and pressed while still frozen. According to law, this wine must be made from grapes at least ripe enough to make a Beerenauslese.

EDELFÄULE

Botrytis cinerea—called *Edelfäule* in German—is a mold that attacks grapes, as we saw in the section on Sauternes. It's also instrumental in the production of Beerenausleses and Trockenbeerenausleses. Noble rot occurs late in the growing season when nights are cool and heavy with dew, mornings are foggy, and days are warm. When noble rot attacks the grapes, they shrivel, and their water content evaporates, leaving concentrated sugar. Grapes affected by this mold may not look very appealing, but don't let looks deceive you: The proof is in the wine!

CHOOSING A GERMAN WINE

Make sure it comes from one of the four major regions. Next, see if the wine comes from the Riesling grape. Riesling shows the best-tasting characteristics and denotes a quality wine. Also be aware of the vintage. It's especially important with German wines to know whether the wine was made in a good year. The final and most important consideration is to buy from a reputable grower or producer.

So what's the difference between a $100 Beerenauslese and a $200 Beerenauslese—besides a hundred bucks? The major difference is the grapes. The $100 bottle probably comes from Müller-Thurgau grapes or Silvaner, while the $200 bottle no doubt comes from Riesling. The wine region also

Germany produces red wines, too, but only about 15 percent of their wines. **RED GRAPES SIMPLY DON'T GROW AS WELL** in Germany's northerly climate.

partially determines quality. Traditionally, the best Beerenausleses and Trockenbeerenausleses come from the Rhein or the Mosel.

Quality is higher in wine when:
- The grapes come from great vineyards.
- The grapes were grown in a great climate or are from a great vintage.
- The wine is produced from low yields.
- The wine is produced by great winemakers.

MY FAVORITE GERMAN WINE PRODUCERS

MOSEL

C. von Schubert	Friedrich-Wilhelm-	Meulenhof
Dr. H. Thanisch	Gymnasium	Rheinhold Haart
Dr. Loosen	Fritz Haag	S. A. Prum
Dr. Pauly-Bergweiler	J. J. Prum	Schloss Leiser
Egon Müller	Joh. Jos. Christoffel Erben	Selbach-Oster
	Kesselstatt	St. Urbans-Hof

RHEINHESSEN

Keller	Strub

RHEINGAU

Josef Leitz	Robert Weil	Schloss Vollrads
Kessler	Schloss Johannisberg	

PFALZ

Basserman-Jordan	Dr. Bürklin Wolf	Lingenfelder
Darting	Dr. Deinhard	Muller-Catoir

HOW TO READ A GERMAN WINE LABEL

German wine labels give you plenty of information. For example, take a look at the label below.

Joh. Jos. Christoffel Erben is the producer.

Mosel is the region (one of the main four).

2001 is the year in which the grapes were harvested.

Ürzig is the town and ***Würzgarten*** is the vineyard from which the grapes originate. (Just as a person from New York is a New Yorker, the Germans add the suffix "-er" to Ürzig to make Ürziger.)

Riesling is the grape variety, which means this wine contains at least 85 percent Riesling.

Auslese is the ripeness level, in this case from bunches of overripe grapes.

Qualitätswein mit Prädikat is the quality level of the wine.

A.P. Nr. 2 602 041 008 02 is the official testing number, which shows that a panel of tasters tasted that wine and that it passed the government's strict quality standards.

Gutsabfüllung means "estate-bottled."

A.P. Nr. 2 602 041 008 02

2 = The government referral office or testing station

602 = Location code of bottler

041 = Bottler ID number

008 = Bottle lot

02 = The year the wine was tasted by the board

RECENT TRENDS

Germany is producing higher-quality wines than ever before, and international interest in these wines has increased. Lighter-style Trockens (dry), Halbtrockens (medium-dry), Kabinetts, and even Spätleses easily can serve as apéritifs or accompany light or grilled food—spicy or Pacific Rim cuisines in particular. If you haven't had a German wine ever or in a long time, the vintages from 2001 through 2006 show the greatness of what German white wines are all about. Plus, with more modern designs, those old hard-to-read Gothic script wine labels have become more user-friendly.

The **2010 VINTAGE** in Germany was one of the smallest harvests in 30 years.

– **BEST RECENT VINTAGES OF GERMAN WHITE WINES** –

2001** 2002* 2003* 2004* 2005** 2006* 2007**
2008* 2009** 2010* 2011** 2012 2013 2014 2015**

*EXCEPTIONAL VINTAGE ** EXTRAORDINARY VINTAGE*

5 BEST VALUE WHITE WINES OF GERMANY UNDER $30

Dr. Loosen Riesling • J. J. Prüm Wehlener Sonnenuhr Spätlese • Josef Lietz
Rüdesheimer Klosterlay Riesling Kabinett • Selbach-Oster Zeltinger
Sonnenuhr Riesling Kabinett • Strub Niersteiner Olberg Kabinett or Spätlese

See page 312 for a complete list.

WINE AND FOOD

With **Riesling Spätlese Halbtrocken**: "We have a tradition of cooking freshwater fish that come from a number of small creeks in the Palatinate Forest, so my personal choice would be trout, either herbed with thyme, basil, parsley, and onion and cooked in wine; or smoked with a bit of horseradish. We find it to be a very versatile wine, a very good match with a whole range of white meat. Pork is traditional in the Palatinate region, as are chicken and goose dishes."

—Rainer Lingenfelder of Weingut Lingenfelder Estate, Pfalz

"There's a wide variety of food that goes very well with—and this is the key—a fruity, only moderately sweet, well-balanced **Riesling Spätlese**. Start with mild curries and sesame- or ginger-flavored, not-too-spicy dishes. Or try either gravlax or smoked salmon. You can even have Riesling Spätlese with a green salad in a balsamic vinaigrette, preferably with a touch of raspberry, as long as the dressing is not too vinegary. Many people avoid pairing wine with a salad, but it works beautifully.

"For haute cuisine, fresh duck or goose liver lightly sautéed in its own juice, or veal sweetbreads in a rich sauce. Also salads with fresh greens, fresh fruit, and fresh seafood marinated in lime or lemon juice or balsamic vinegar.

"With an old, ripe **Spätlese**: roast venison, dishes with cream sauces, and any white-meat dish stuffed with or accompanied by fruit. It is also delicious with fresh fruit itself or as an apéritif."

With **Riesling Spätlese Halbtrocken**: "This is a food-friendly wine, but the first thing that comes to mind is fresh seafood and fresh fish. Also wonderful with salads with a mild vinaigrette, and with a course that's often difficult to match: cream soups. If we don't know exactly what to drink with a particular food, Spätlese Halbtrocken is usually the safe bet.

"It may be too obvious to say foie gras with **Eiswein**, but it is a classic."

—Johannes Selbach of Selbach-Oster, Mosel

SELBACH-OSTER HAS PARTNERED with veteran California winemaker Paul Hobbs and planted a Riesling vineyard in the Finger Lakes region of New York.

TEST YOUR KNOWLEDGE of the white wines of Germany by trying the quiz on page 333.

—— **FURTHER READING** ——

The Gault-Millau Guide to German Wines by Armin Diel and Joel Payne

GUIDED TASTING

People don't know or understand German white wines as well as French or Californian wines and often dismiss them for being light-bodied and having higher levels of residual sugar. Don't make that mistake. Learn the main regions, villages, vineyards, classifications, and a little German pronunciation, and you'll find it easy to understand and enjoy the charm and elegance of these great German white wines.

THE WINES

Quality German Wine
One wine, tasted alone:
    1. Any Qualitätswein from Germany

Kabinett
Two Kabinetts, compared:
    2. Mosel Riesling Kabinett
    3. Rheinhessen Riesling Kabinett

Spätlese
Two Spätleses, compared:
    4. Mosel Riesling Spätlese
    5. Pfalz Riesling Spätlese

Auslese
Two Ausleses, compared:
    6. Mosel Riesling Auslese
    7. Rheingau Riesling Auslese

THE RED WINES OF BURGUNDY AND THE RHÔNE VALLEY

UNDERSTANDING THE RED WINES OF BURGUNDY ✳ BEAUJOLAIS ✳
CÔTE CHÂLONNAISE ✳ CÔTE D'OR ✳ THE RHÔNE VALLEY

UNDERSTANDING THE RED WINES OF BURGUNDY

Burgundy's reputation for winemaking dates as far back as 51 B.C.

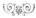

You must memorize **MORE THAN 1,000 NAMES** and more than 110 appellations to become a Burgundy wine expert.

T HE FLAVORS, NUANCES, and length of taste in red wines evoke a sense of excitement, and we tend to concentrate more when we taste them. In white wines, we were looking mainly for the balance of acid and fruit, but now we're looking for additional characteristics, such as tannin levels, as we sense more components in the wines and more levels of complexity.

Before we continue, though, you need to know: There are no shortcuts! Burgundy represents one of the most difficult subjects in the study of wines. People may say, "There's *so much* to know," and "It looks so hard." If you're having trouble understanding these wines, don't feel like you're alone. After the French Revolution in 1789, all the vineyards were sold off in small parcels. Then the Napoleonic Code instituted equal inheritance among heirs, which fragmented vineyards further. Burgundy has many villages and vineyards, and, yes, they're all important. I'm going to help you decode the mysteries—regions, names, labels—but to understand, enjoy, and speak about Burgundy wines intelligently, you really need to know only 15 to 25 names.

The main red wine–producing regions are:

Beaujolais   Côte Châlonnaise   Côte d'Or { Côte de Nuits / Côte de Beaune

The two major grape varieties are:

Pinot Noir   Gamay

Under AOC laws, all red Burgundies must come from the Pinot Noir grape, except Beaujolais, which comes from the Gamay grape.

THE IMPORTANCE OF SOIL

Any producer of quality Burgundy will say that soil represents the most important element in making those wines. Terroir—consisting of soil composition, together with the slope of the land and climatic conditions—determines whether a wine ranks as a Village, Premier Cru, or Grand Cru. On a trip I took to Burgundy, it rained for five straight days. On the sixth day, workers gathered at the bottom of the vineyard slopes with pails and shovels, collecting the soil that had run down the hillside to return it to the vineyard. That's how important soil is to Burgundy wines.

THE MAGNIFICENT AND DIFFICULT PINOT NOIR

Pinot Noir's fame originates in Burgundy. It's difficult to make this thin-skinned grape into a great wine. It's susceptible to many diseases, and too much sunlight (heat) during the growing season kills the chances of a balanced wine. But if a grower proves both passionate and patient, a great Pinot Noir offers less tannin, less extraction of color, and less body. The best Pinot Noirs from Burgundy don't flex dense muscle but rather display an elegant finesse.

BEAUJOLAIS

Made from 100 percent Gamay grapes, Beaujolais typically tastes light and fruity, is meant to be consumed young, and can be chilled. Most bottles cost between $8 and $20, although price varies with quality. Beaujolais reigns as the best-selling Burgundy in America probably because there's so much of it, it's so easy to drink, and it's affordable.

All grapes in the Beaujolais region are **PICKED BY HAND.**

Beaujolais has three different quality levels:

Beaujolais This basic Beaujolais accounts for the majority produced. Cost: $.

Beaujolais-Villages This classification comes from certain villages, and 35 of them produce consistently better wines. Most Beaujolais-Villages contain a blend of wines from these villages, and the label usually doesn't feature a particular village name. Cost: $$.

Cru Named for the village that produces this highest quality of Beaujolais. Cost $$$$.

There are ten crus (villages):

Brouilly	**Fleurie**	**Moulin-à-Vent**
Chénas	**Juliénas**	**Régnié**
Chiroubles	**Morgon**	**Saint-Amour**
Côte de Brouilly		

Also look for these shippers / producers:

Bouchard   **Drouhin**   **Duboeuf**   **Jadot**

How long you keep a Beaujolais depends on the quality level and the vintage. Beaujolais and Beaujolais-Villages will last between one and three years. Crus can last longer because they have more fruit and tannin. Some Beaujolais Crus maintain their excellence after more than ten years. But these prove the exception rather than the rule.

Beaujolais Nouveau releases **THE THIRD THURSDAY IN NOVEMBER** amid great hoopla. Restaurants and retailers all vie to offer the new Beaujolais to their customers first.

BEAUJOLAIS NOUVEAU

Beaujolais Nouveau tastes even lighter and fruitier than your basic Beaujolais. This "new" Beaujolais undergoes fermentation and bottling and appears on retailer shelves in a matter of weeks, giving the winemaker a virtually instant return. Like a movie trailer, it also offers an indication of the quality of the vintage and style that the winemaker will produce for the regular Beaujolais the following spring. Drink Beaujolais Nouveau young, within six months of bottling. If you're holding a bottle significantly older than that . . . well, now's the time to give it to your "friends."

As a young wine student, I visited the Beaujolais region. In one village, I ordered a glass of Beaujolais, and the waiter brought me a chilled glass of wine. Every book I'd read always said to serve red wines at room temperature, but when it comes to Beaujolais Nouveau, Beaujolais, and Beaujolais-Villages, **CHILL THEM SLIGHTLY TO BRING OUT THE FRUIT AND ACIDITY.** Try a chilled Beaujolais in the summer, and you'll see what I mean. Beaujolais Crus have more fruit and tannin, though, and taste better at room temperature.

"Beaujolais is one of the very few red wines that can be drunk as a white. Beaujolais is my daily drink. And sometimes I blend one-half water to the wine. It is the most refreshing drink in the world."

—Didier Mommessin

– BEST RECENT VINTAGES OF BEAUJOLAIS –

2009**   2010*   2011   2012*   2013   2014*   2015**

* EXCEPTIONAL VINTAGE   ** EXTRAORDINARY VINTAGE

If you see the word "monopole" on a Burgundy label, it has **JUST ONE OWNER.**

WINE AND FOOD

Beaujolais goes well with light, simple meals and cheeses that don't overpower. Try to match Beaujolais with veal, fish, or fowl, and take note of what some of the experts say:

"A lot of dishes can be eaten with **Beaujolais.** What you choose depends on the appellation and vintage. With charcuteries and pâtés, you can serve a young **Beaujolais or Beaujolais-** **Villages**. With grilled meat, more generous and fleshy wines, such as **Juliénas** and **Morgon crus,** can be served. With meats cooked in a sauce—for example, coq au vin— I would suggest a **Moulin-à-Vent cru** from a good vintage."

—Georges Duboeuf

"**Beaujolais** with simple meals, light cheeses, grilled meat—everything except sweets."

—André Gagey of Louis Jadot

CÔTE CHÂLONNAISE

These classic Pinot Noir wines offer tremendous value, and you should know three villages from this area:

Mercurey	Givry	Rully
95% red	90% red	50% red

Of these, Mercurey (rhymes with ray) is most important, producing wines of high quality. Because they're not well known in America, Mercurey wines often make for a very good value. Look for these shippers/producers when buying Côte Châlonnaise wines:

Mercurey	**Château de Chamirey**
	Domaine de Suremain
	Faiveley
	Michel Juillot
Givry	**Chofflet-Valdenaire**
	Domaine Jablot
	Domaine Thenard
	Louis Latour
Rully	**Antonin Rodet**

CÔTE D'OR

This is the beating heart of Burgundy. The Côte d'Or—pronounced "coat door"—means "gold coast." One theory holds that the region takes its name from autumnal foliage . . . as well as the income it brings to winemakers. Because the area is very small, its best wines rank among the priciest in the world. If you want a $9.99 bottle, look elsewhere!

As with the white wines of the same region, these reds also have quality levels: regional, Village, Premier Cru, and Grand Cru. Scant Grand Cru wine is produced, but it has the highest quality and is extremely expensive. Regional wine, on the other hand, is more readily available, but very few rate as outstanding.

The Côte d'Or consists of two regions:

The highest-quality red Burgundy wines come from the Côte de Nuits. To understand the wines of the Côte d'Or, familiarize yourself with the most important villages, some of the Premier Cru vineyards, and of course the Grand Cru vineyards.

CÔTE D'OR

DIJON
GEVREY-CHAMBERTIN — FIXIN
CHAMBOLLE-MUSIGNY — MOREY-ST-DENIS
— VOUGEOT
CÔTE DE NUITS — VOSNE-ROMANÉE
NUITS-ST-GEORGES
— ALOXE-CORTON
— BEAUNE
CÔTE DE BEAUNE — POMMARD
VOLNAY
— MEURSAULT
PULIGNY-MONTRACHET
CHASSAGNE-MONTRACHET
SANTENAY

0 Miles   5   10   15
0 Kilometers   10   15

GENERIC WINES ARE LABELED SIMPLY "BURGUNDY" OR "BOURGOGNE." A higher level of generic wines will say "Côte de Beaune Villages" or "Côte de Nuits Villages," being a blend of different Village wines.

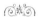

Burgundy has more than 500 Premier Cru vineyards.

The Cote d'Or has **32 GRAND CRU VINEYARDS**.

By far the most-produced red Grand Cru is **CORTON,** representing about 25 percent of all Grand Cru red wines.

CÔTE DE BEAUNE

MOST IMPORTANT VILLAGES	MY FAVORITE PREMIER CRU VINEYARDS	GRAND CRU VINEYARDS
ALOXE-CORTON	CHAILLOTS FOURNIÈRES	CORTON CORTON BRESSANDES CORTON CLOS DU ROI CORTON MARÉCHAUDE CORTON RENARDES
BEAUNE	BRESSANDES CLOS DES MOUCHES FÈVES GRÈVES MARCONNETS	
POMMARD	ÉPENOTS RUGIENS	
VOLNAY	CAILLERETS CLOS DES CHÊNES SANTENOTS TAILLEPIEDS	

CÔTE DE NUITS

If you haven't been paying close attention to geography, start now. The majority of Grand Cru vineyards lie in this area.

MOST IMPORTANT VILLAGES	MY FAVORITE PREMIER CRU VINEYARDS	GRAND CRU VINEYARDS
CHAMBOLLE-MUSIGNY	CHARMES LES AMOUREUSES	BONNES MARES (PARTIAL) MUSIGNY
FLAGEY-ÉCHÉZEAUX		ÉCHÉZEAUX GRANDS-ÉCHÉZEAUX
GEVREY-CHAMBERTIN	AUX COMBOTTES CLOS ST-JACQUES LES CAZETIERS	CHAMBERTIN CHAMBERTIN CLOS DE BÈZE CHAPELLE-CHAMBERTIN CHARMES-CHAMBERTIN GRIOTTE-CHAMBERTIN LATRICIÈRES-CHAMBERTIN MAZIS-CHAMBERTIN MAZOYÈRES-CHAMBERTIN RUCHOTTES-CHAMBERTIN
MOREY-ST-DENIS	CLOS DES ORMES LES GENEVRIÈRES RUCHOTS	BONNES MARES (PARTIAL) CLOS DE LA ROCHE CLOS DE TART CLOS DES LAMBRAYS CLOS ST-DENIS
NUITS-ST-GEORGES	LES ST-GEORGES PORETS VAUCRAINS	
VOSNE-ROMANÉE	BEAUX-MONTS	LA GRANDE-RUE LA ROMANÉE LA TÂCHE MALCONSORTS RICHEBOURG ROMANÉE-CONTI ROMANÉE-ST-VIVANT
VOUGEOT		CLOS DE VOUGEOT

The **FOUR SMALLEST FRENCH APPELLATIONS** lie in the Côte de Nuits:

Griotte Chambertin, 2.63 acres

La Grande Rue, 1.65 acres

La Romanée Conti, 1.63 acres

La Romanée, 0.85 acres

CHAMBERTIN CLOS DE BÈZE was Napoléon's favorite wine, of which he reportedly said: "Nothing makes the future look so rosy as to contemplate it through a glass of Chambertin." Perhaps he ran out at Waterloo!

In the 1800s, some villages in Burgundy added the name of their most famous **VINEYARD TO THE NAME OF THE VILLAGE.** Gevrey became Gevrey-Chambertin, and Puligny became Puligny-Montrachet. Can you name the others?

Tucked between the Grands Crus La Tâche and Romanée-Conti in Vosne-Romanée, La Grande-Rue ascended from being a Premier Cru **TO THE GRAND CRU LEVEL.**

Clos de Vougeot is Burgundy's largest Grand Cru vineyard, at 125 acres and with more than 80 owners. Each owner makes his or her own winemaking decisions, such as when to pick the grapes, fermentation style, and how long to age the wine in oak. **ALL CLOS DE VOUGEOT IS NOT CREATED EQUAL.**

VILLAGE ONLY = VILLAGE WINE $

VILLAGE + VINEYARD = PREMIER CRU $$

VINEYARD ONLY = GRAND CRU $$$$

Beginning with the 1990 vintage, all Grand Cru Burgundies must include the words **"GRAND CRU" ON THE LABEL.**

THE IMPORTANCE OF GEOGRAPHY

Geography helps make you a smart buyer. If you know the key villages and vineyards, you're more likely to make a better purchase. You don't have to memorize all the villages and vineyards, though. A label often contains all the information you need. Take a look at this one, and follow along:

Where is the wine from? France

What type of wine is it? Burgundy

Which region is it from? Côte d'Or

Which area? Côte de Nuits

Which village? Chambolle-Musigny

Anything else? Yes, the wine comes from Musigny, one of the 32 Grand Cru vineyards.

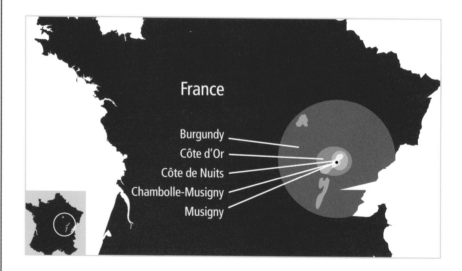

The more you zoom in, the better the quality of the wine, and the more it likely will cost. Why? Supply and demand. The growers and shippers of the Côte d'Or have a problem that all businesspeople envy: not enough supply to meet the demand. This has been the case for years and will continue because Burgundy is a small region that produces a limited amount of wine. (Bordeaux, by comparison, produces three times as much wine as Burgundy.)

BURGUNDY WINE HARVEST IN CASES	
REGIONAL APPELLATIONS	2,136,674
BEAUJOLAIS	11,503,617
CHABLIS	755,188
CÔTE CHÂLONNAISE	357,539
CÔTE D'OR: CÔTE DE NUITS	511,594
CÔTE D'OR: CÔTE DE BEAUNE	1,391,168
MÂCONNAIS	2,136,674
OTHER APPELLATIONS	339,710
TOTAL HARVEST	**19,132,164**

(average number of cases over a five-year period for red and white)

In the 1960s, Burgundy wines were fermented and vatted for up to three weeks. Today's Burgundy wines are usually **FERMENTED AND VATTED FOR 6 TO 12 DAYS.**

BURGUNDY, PAST AND PRESENT
1970s: 15 percent Domaine-bottled
2016: 60 percent Domaine-bottled

KNOW YOUR VINTAGES, and— because of the delicacy of the Pinot Noir grape—buy from a merchant who handles Burgundy wines with care.

FORTY YEARS LATER IN BURGUNDY

The red wines of Burgundy still stand as the benchmark for Pinot Noir throughout the world. Over the last 40 years, the great wines of Burgundy have improved—and of course become more expensive! The good wines have become more consistent and increased in quality. Both the shippers (*négociants*) and the estate-bottled producers are making the best wines that Burgundy has ever known. Better clonal selection, vineyard management, and a new generation of winemakers will continue this greatness for decades.

VALUE BURGUNDIES: Chorey-les-Beaune from Tollot-Beaut, Alex Gambal, Arnoux, and Champy.

Many wine writers and Burgundy lovers describe the taste of Pinot Noir as **SEDUCTIVE AND SMOOTH.**

—— **FURTHER READING** ——

Burgundy by Anthony Hanson

Burgundy by Robert M. Parker Jr.

The Great Domaines of Burgundy by Remington Norman

Making Sense of Burgundy by Matt Kramer

The Original Grand Crus of Burgundy by Charles Curtis

The Wines of Burgundy by Clive Coates

Look for these shippers / producers:

Bouchard Père et Fils	Jaffelin	Joseph Drouhin
Chanson	Louis Jadot	

Some fine estate-bottled wines are available in limited quantities in America. Look for the following:

Armand Rousseau	Henri Lamarche	Parent
Clerget	Jayer	Pierre Damoy
Comte de Voguë	Jean Grivot	Pierre Gelin
Daniel Rion	Leroy	Potel
Denis Mortet	Louis Trapet	Pousse d'Or
Dujac	Lucien Le Moine	Prince de Mérode
Faiveley	Marquis d'Angerville	Romanée-Conti
Georges Roumier	Méo Camuzet	Tollot-Beaut
Groffier	Michel Gros	Vincent Girardin
Henri Gouges	Mongeard-Mugneret	

– BEST RECENT VINTAGES OF CÔTE D'OR –

1999* 2002** 2003* 2005** 2006 2007 2008*
2009** 2010** 2011 2012* 2013* 2014 * 2015**

* EXCEPTIONAL VINTAGE ** EXTRAORDINARY VINTAGE

WINE AND FOOD

"White wine is never a good accompaniment to red meat, but a light red **Burgundy** can match a fish course (not shellfish). Otherwise, for light red Burgundies, white meat—not too many spices; partridge, pheasant, and rabbit. For heavier-style wines, lamb and steak are good choices."

—Robert Drouhin

"With red **Beaujolais** wines, such as Moulin-à-Vent Château des Jacques, for example, a piece of pork like an andouillette from Fleury is beautiful. A **Gamay**, more fruity and fleshy than Pinot Noir, goes perfectly with this typical meal from our terroir. My favorite food combination with a red **Burgundy** wine is poulet de bresse demi d'oeil. The very thin flesh of this truffle-filled chicken and the elegance and delicacy from the great **Pinot Noir**, which comes from the best terroir, go together beautifully."

—Pierre Henry Gagey of Louis Jadot

"With **Château Corton Grancey**, filet of duck in a red-wine sauce. Otherwise, **Pinot Noir** is good with roast chicken, venison, and beef. Mature wines are a perfect combination for our local cheeses, Chambertin and Citeaux."

—Louis Latour

THE RHÔNE VALLEY

Typically bigger and fuller than Burgundies, Rhône wine usually has a higher alcohol content, and the reason goes back to geography. The Rhône Valley lies in southeastern France, south of Burgundy, where the climate runs sunny and hot. The sun gives the grapes more sugar, which boosts the alcohol level. The rocks in the soil also retain the intense summer heat, both day and night. By law, Rhône Valley winemakers must create wines containing a specified amount of alcohol. For example, AOC regulations require a 10.5 percent minimum for Côtes du Rhône and 12.5 percent for Châteauneuf-du-Pape. A simple Côtes du Rhône parallels a Beaujolais, except the Côtes du Rhône has more body and alcohol. (A Beaujolais must contain a minimum of just 9 percent alcohol.)

The winemaking regions of the Rhône Valley fall into two distinct areas: northern and southern. The most famous reds from the northern region include:

Crozes-Hermitage	Côte Rôtie	Hermitage
(3,000+ acres)	(555 acres)	(324 acres)

Also look for St-Joseph and Cornas.

The most famous reds from the southern region are:

Châteauneuf-du-Pape	Gigondas
(7,822 acres)	(3,036 acres)

The two major grape varieties in the Rhône Valley are:

Grenache	Syrah

From the North, the Côte Rôtie, Crozes-Hermitage, and Hermitage come primarily from the Syrah grape. These are the region's biggest and fullest wines. From the South, Châteauneuf-du-Pape can contain a blend of as many as 13 different grape varieties, but the best producers use a higher percentage of Grenache and Syrah in the blend.

The two most famous white wines of the Rhône Valley, Condrieu and Château Grillet, are both made from the Viognier grape. There's a white Châteauneuf-du-Pape as well as a white Hermitage, but only a few thousand cases are produced each year.

Some of the oldest vineyards in France lie in the Rhône Valley. Hermitage, for example, has been in existence for **MORE THAN 2,000 YEARS.**

RHÔNE VALLEY

LEADING ACREAGE OF GRENACHE / GARNACHA
France (96,000 hectares)
Spain (83,000 hectares)
California (7,700 hectares)
Australia (4,000 hectares)

TWO OTHER IMPORTANT RED GRAPES that grow in the Rhône Valley are Cinsault and Mourvèdre.

Côtes du Rhône wine can come from grapes grown in either or both of the two Rhône regions, but **MORE THAN 90 PERCENT OF ALL CÔTES DU RHÔNE** wines come from the southern region.

THE 13 CRUS OF THE RHÔNE VALLEY

North	South
Château-Grillet (white)	Châteauneuf-du-Pape
Condrieu (white)	Gigondas
	Lirac
Cornas	Tavel (rosé)
Côte-Rôtie	Vacqueyras
Crozes-Hermitage	
Hermitage	
St-Joseph	
St-Pera	

REGION	HOURS OF SUNSHINE PER YEAR
Burgundy	2,000
Bordeaux	2,050
Châteauneuf-du-Pape	2,750

The medieval **PAPAL COAT OF ARMS** appears on some Châteauneuf-du-Pape bottles. Only owners of vineyards can use this coat of arms on their labels.

Rhône Valley wines have no official classification system, but the different quality levels are:

8% Côtes du Rhône Villages $$

Crus 10% (specific regions) $$$$

24% Other appellations

Côtes du Rhône $ 58%

CHÂTEAUNEUF-DU-PAPE

Châteauneuf-du-Pape means "the pope's new castle," so named for the Avignon palace in which Pope Clement V resided in the fourteenth century, heralding the nearly 70-year Avignon Papacy. As mentioned, winemakers can use 13 different grapes for Châteauneuf-du-Pape. Those who use more of the best grapes—like a chef cooking only with the finest, organic ingredients, for example—produce the best-tasting and the most expensive wines. A $25 bottle of Châteauneuf-du-Pape may contain only 20 percent of top-quality grapes (Grenache, Mourvèdre, Syrah, and Cinsault). A $75 bottle may contain 90 percent of those top-quality grapes.

THE 13 GRAPES ALLOWED IN CHÂTEAUNEUF-DU-PAPE

Grenache	Muscardin
Syrah	Vaccarèse
Mourvèdre	Picardin
Cinsault	Clairette
Picpoul	Roussanne
Terret	Bourboulenc
Counoise	

The first 4 grapes represent 92 percent of the grapes used, with Grenache by far the most.

TAVEL

This rosé stands apart from most others because of its unusual dryness. It comes primarily from the Grenache grape, although nine grape varieties can go into the blend. At heart, Tavel is just like a red wine, with all the same components but less color. How does that happen? It's all about the vatting process.

With short-vatted wines, the grape skins ferment with the must for a short time, only long enough to impart that rosé color. With long-vatted wines—such as Châteauneuf-du-Pape or Hermitage—the skins ferment longer with the must, giving a rich, ruby color to the wine.

WINES MADE IN THE RHÔNE VALLEY

Red 91%

White 3%

Rosé 6%

CÔTES DU VENTOUX IS A GOOD VALUE.
One of the most widely available wines to look for in this category is La Vieille Ferme.

The Rhône Valley wines prove that **NOT ALL GREAT WINES NEED AGE.** An exception to the aging rule, Hermitage is the best and **THE LONGEST-LIVED OF THE RHÔNE WINES.** In a great vintage, Hermitage wines can last for 50 years.

CHOOSING A RED RHÔNE WINE

First decide whether you prefer a light Côtes du Rhône or a bigger, more flavorful one, such as an Hermitage. Then consider the vintage and the producer. Two of the oldest and best-known firms are M. Chapoutier and Paul Jaboulet Aîné.

Here are some of the best producers:

NORTHERN RHÔNE

Delas	Jean-Louis Chave	M. Chapoutier
E. Guigal	Jean-Luc-Colombo	Paul Jaboulet Aîné

SOUTHERN RHÔNE, CHÂTEAUNEUF-DU-PAPE

Beaucastel	Domaine de la Janasse	Domaine St.-Préfert
Bosquet des Papes	Domaine du Pégü	Domaine Vacheron-
Château Rayas	Domaine du Vieux	Pouizin
Clos des Papes	Télégraphe	Mont Redon
	Domaine Giraud	Roger Sabon & Fils

SOUTHERN RHÔNE, GIGONDAS

Château de St.-Cosme	Notre Dame des	Pierre-Henri Morel
Domaine La	Paillières	Tardieu-Laurent
Bouissièrel	Olivier Ravoire	

Rhône Valley wines prove that not all great wines need age. Here's when to drink them:

Tavel Within two years

Côtes du Rhône Within three years

Crozes-Hermitage Within five years

Châteauneuf-du-Pape After five years, but higher quality Châteauneuf-du-Pape tastes better after ten

Hermitage Within seven to eight years, but a great vintage tastes best after fifteen

FORTY YEARS LATER IN THE RHÔNE VALLEY

Four decades ago, the red wines of Burgundy and Bordeaux overshadowed Rhône Valley wines. Today all three are equals, except the best quality value wines come from the Rhône. The region also has benefited from great weather over the last decade, especially in the south. All of which makes for superb wines at a reasonable cost.

OLDER GREAT VINTAGES
NORTH: 1983, 1985, 1988, 1989, 1990, 1991
SOUTH: 1985, 1988, 1989, 1990

– BEST VINTAGES OF RED RHÔNE VALLEY WINES –

NORTH: 1995 1996 1997 1998 1999* 2000 2001 2003* 2004 2005* 2006* 2007* 2009** 2010** 2011* 2012* 2013* 2014 2015**

SOUTH: 1995 1998* 1999 2000* 2001* 2003* 2004* 2005** 2006* 2007** 2009* 2010** 2011* 2012* 2013 2014 2015**

* EXCEPTIONAL VINTAGE ** EXTRAORDINARY VINTAGE

RHÔNE VALLEY VINTAGES CAN BE TRICKY: a good year in the North may be a bad year in the South, and vice versa.

---

5 BEST VALUE RED WINES OF BURGUNDY AND THE RHÔNE VALLEY UNDER $30

Château Cabrières Côte du Rhône • Côtes-de-Nuits-Village, Joseph Drouhin • Georges Duboeuf Morgon "Caves Jean Ernest Descombes" • Jean-Maurice Raffault Chinon

See pages 310–311 for a complete list.

UNITED STATES IMPORTS of Rhône wines have risen more than 200 percent in the last five years.

WINE AND FOOD

"Red Rhône wines achieve their perfection from ten years and beyond, and are best when combined with game and other meats with a strong flavor. A good dinner could be wild mushroom soup and truffles with a white Beaucastel, and stew of wild hare à la royale [with foie gras and truffles] served with a red **Château de Beaucastel**."

—Jean Pierre and François Perrin
of Château de Beaucastel

"My granddad drinks a bottle of Côtes du Rhône a day, and he's in his eighties. It's good for youth. It goes with everything except old fish! Hermitage is good with wild boar and mushrooms. A Crozes Hermitage complements venison or roast rabbit in a cream sauce, but you have to be very careful with the sauce and the weight of the wine. Beef ribs and rice go well with a **Côtes du Rhône**, as does a game bird like roast quail. Tavel, slightly chilled, is refreshing with a summer salad. **Muscat de Beaumes-de-Venise** is a beautiful match with foie gras."

—Frédéric Jaboulet

With a **Côtes du Rhône**, Michel Chapoutier recommends poultry, light meats, and cheese. **Côte Rôtie** goes well with white meats and small game. **Châteauneuf-du-Pape** complements the ripest of cheese, the richest venison, and the most lavish civet of wild boar. An **Hermitage** is suitable with beef, game, and any full-flavored cheese.

If you **PREFER SWEET WINES**, try Beaumes-de-Venise, made from the Muscat grape.

TEST YOUR KNOWLEDGE of the red wines of Burgundy and the Rhône Valley by trying the quiz on page 335.

—— **FURTHER READING** ——
The Wines of the Rhône Valley by Robert M. Parker Jr.

❧ GUIDED TASTING ❧

In order of importance, the three points to know about red Burgundy wines are the producer, vintage, and quality ranking. Take note of these details after tasting each wine in this flight. Whether it's a simple, medium-bodied Côtes du Rhône; a spicy Crozes-Hermitage; or a voluptuous, high-alcohol Châteauneuf-du-Pape, these are some of the greatest wines in the world and still offer some of the best values.

THE WINES

Beaujolais
Two Beaujolais wines, compared:
1. *Beaujolais Villages*
2. *Beaujolais Cru*

Côte Châlonnaise
One wine, tasted alone:
3. *A wine from Côte Châlonnaise*

Côte d'Or
Two Côte de Beaune wines, compared:
4. *Village wine*
5. *Premier Cru*
Two Côte de Nuits wines compared
6. *Village wine*
7. *Premier Cru*

Côtes du Rhône
Three Côtes du Rhône wines, compared:
8. *Côtes du Rhône*
9. *Crozes-Hermitage*
10. *Châteauneuf-du-Pape*

CLASS FIVE

THE RED WINES OF BORDEAUX

UNDERSTANDING THE RED WINES OF BORDEAUX ❋ MÉDOC ❋
GRAVES ❋ POMEROL ❋ ST-ÉMILION ❋
BORDEAUX VINTAGES ❋ CHOOSING A RED BORDEAUX

Bordeaux regularly produced **MORE WHITE WINE THAN RED UNTIL 1970.**

BORDEAUX WINE PRODUCTION

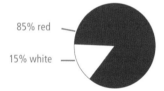

85% red

15% white

BORDEAUX HAS some 172,000 acres of Merlot, 72,000 acres of Cabernet Sauvignon, and 33,000 acres of Cabernet Franc.

UNDERSTANDING THE RED WINES OF BORDEAUX

THIS PROVINCE OF France teems with excitement and history, and its wines speak for themselves. You'll find this region much easier to understand than Burgundy because fewer landholders own bigger plots of land, and, as the wine-loving author Samuel Johnson once said, "He who aspires to be a serious wine drinker must drink claret"—the old word for the dry red table wine known as Bordeaux.

Some 57 wine regions in Bordeaux produce high-quality wines that can carry the Bordeaux name on the label according to AOC rules. Of those, four stand out for red wine:

Médoc	Graves / Pessac-Léognan	Pomerol	St-Émilion
40,676 acres	12,849 acres	1,986 acres	23,062 acres
(only red)	(red and dry white)	(only red)	(only red)

The Médoc has seven important communes, or subsidiary appellations, that you should know:

Haut Médoc	Margaux	Pauillac	St-Julien
Listrac	Moulis	St-Estèphe	

The three major grapes are:

Merlot   Cabernet Franc   Cabernet Sauvignon

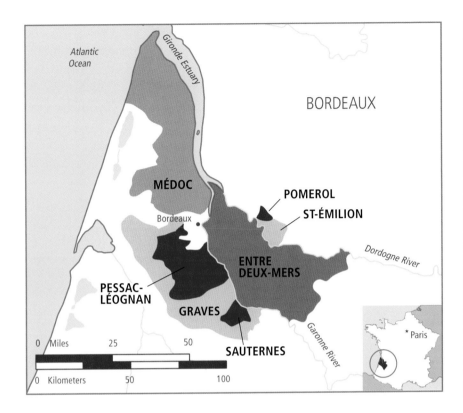

Atlantic
Ocean

Gironde Estuary

MÉDOC

Bordeaux

POMEROL

ST-ÉMILION

Dordogne River

ENTRE
DEUX-MERS

PESSAC-
LÉOGNAN

GRAVES

SAUTERNES

Garonne River

*Paris

0 Miles 25 50

0 Kilometers 50 100

Two other grapes that sometimes go into Bordeaux wines are **PETIT VERDOT AND MALBEC.**

PROPRIETARY WINES YOU MAY KNOW:

Baron Philippe   Michel Lynch

Lacour Pavillon   Mouton-Cadet

Lauretan

MAJOR SHIPPERS OF REGIONAL WINES FROM BORDEAUX INCLUDE:

Baron Philippe de Rothschild

Barton & Guestier (B & G)

Borie-Manoux

Cordier

Dourthe Kressmann

Dulong

Eschenauer

Ets J-P Moueix

Sichel

Yvon Mau

Unlike Burgundy, where winemakers must use 100 percent Pinot Noir to make most red wines (and 100 percent Gamay for Beaujolais), the red wines of Bordeaux almost always come from a blend of grapes. As a rule of thumb, the regions and villages to the west, or left, of the Garonne, use primarily the Cabernet Sauvignon grape, and those to the right, or east, of the Dordogne use mostly Merlot.

27 PERCENT of France's AOC wines come from the Bordeaux region.

The three different quality levels of Bordeaux wine are:

Bordeaux This lowest AOC level consists of nice, inexpensive, consistent "drinking" wines. Sometimes these proprietary wines go by a kind of brand name, such as Mouton-Cadet, rather than by the sub-region or vineyard. Cost: $.

Region Only grapes and wines made in the specified 57 areas can go by their regional names: Pauillac and St-Émilion, for example. These are more expensive than those labeled simply "Bordeaux." Cost: $$.

PROPRIETARY BORDEAUX
Appellation Bordeaux Contrôlée

REGIONAL
Appellation Pauillac Contrôlée

CHÂTEAU
Appellation Pauillac Contrôlée
with château name

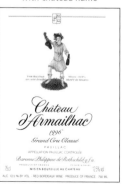

Region + Château Château wines come from individual vineyards, and Bordeaux has more than 7,000. As far back as 1855, Bordeaux officially classified the quality levels of some of its châteaux. Hundreds have received official recognition for their quality. In the Médoc, for example, the 61 highest-level châteaux are called Grands Crus Classés. The Médoc level below that, Cru Bourgeois, has 246 châteaux. Other areas have their own classification systems. Cost: $$–$$$$.

Wines priced between $8 and $25 account for 80 percent of all Bordeaux wines.

MAJOR RED BORDEAUX CLASSIFICATIONS

REGION	CLASSIFICATION	YEAR ESTABLISHED	CLASSIFIED CHÂTEAUX
GRAVES	GRANDS CRUS CLASSÉS	1959	12
MÉDOC	GRANDS CRUS CLASSÉS	1855	61
MÉDOC	CRUS BOURGEOIS	1920 (REVISED 1932, 1978, 2003, 2010)	246
POMEROL	NO OFFICIAL CLASSIFICATION		
ST-ÉMILION	PREMIERS GRANDS CRUS CLASSÉS	1955 (REVISED 1996, 2006, 2012)	18
ST-ÉMILION	GRANDS CRUS CLASSÉS	1955 (REVISED 1996, 2006, 2012)	85

CHÂTEAUX

When most people think of châteaux, they picture grandiose homes filled with valuable art and antiques, surrounded by rolling vineyards—but most châteaux aren't like that at all. A château could be a mansion on a large estate, yes, but it also could be a modest home with a two-car garage. The best quality and therefore the most expensive wines of Bordeaux come from châteaux, and some of the best known Grands Crus Classés command the highest wine prices in the world! No one wants to memorize the names of thousands of châteaux, though, so let's take a closer look at the most important classification in Bordeaux.

MÉDOC

GRAND CRU CLASSÉ

For the International Exposition of 1855, Emperor Napoleon III asked wine brokers to select the best wines to represent France. The brokers agreed to create the classification with the proviso that it never become official. They ranked the top Médoc wines according to price, which at the time directly correlated with quality. According to this system, the top four (now five) vineyards, or *crus*, produced "first-growth" wines; the next fourteen best made second-growth; and so on until the fifth-growth producers, thereby creating what became—*voilà*!—the Official Classification of 1855, on the next page.

Grands Crus Classés represent LESS THAN 5 PERCENT of Bordeaux wines.

TYPICAL MÉDOC BLEND

10%–20% Cabernet Franc —

25%–40% Merlot —

60%–80% Cabernet Sauvignon —

"For a given vintage there is quite a consistent ratio between the prices of the different classes, which is of considerable help to the trade. So a fifth growth would always sell at about half the price of a second. The thirds and fourths would get prices halfway between the seconds and the fifths. The first growths are getting about 25 percent over the second growths."

—Ch. Cocks, *Bordeaux et Ses Vins*, 1868

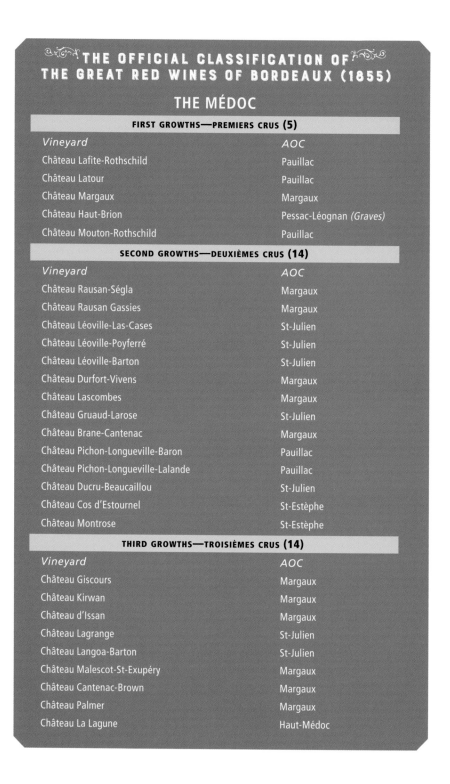

THE OFFICIAL CLASSIFICATION OF THE GREAT RED WINES OF BORDEAUX (1855)

THE MÉDOC

FIRST GROWTHS—PREMIERS CRUS (5)

Vineyard	AOC
Château Lafite-Rothschild	Pauillac
Château Latour	Pauillac
Château Margaux	Margaux
Château Haut-Brion	Pessac-Léognan *(Graves)*
Château Mouton-Rothschild	Pauillac

SECOND GROWTHS—DEUXIÈMES CRUS (14)

Vineyard	AOC
Château Rausan-Ségla	Margaux
Château Rausan Gassies	Margaux
Château Léoville-Las-Cases	St-Julien
Château Léoville-Poyferré	St-Julien
Château Léoville-Barton	St-Julien
Château Durfort-Vivens	Margaux
Château Lascombes	Margaux
Château Gruaud-Larose	St-Julien
Château Brane-Cantenac	Margaux
Château Pichon-Longueville-Baron	Pauillac
Château Pichon-Longueville-Lalande	Pauillac
Château Ducru-Beaucaillou	St-Julien
Château Cos d'Estournel	St-Estèphe
Château Montrose	St-Estèphe

THIRD GROWTHS—TROISIÈMES CRUS (14)

Vineyard	AOC
Château Giscours	Margaux
Château Kirwan	Margaux
Château d'Issan	Margaux
Château Lagrange	St-Julien
Château Langoa-Barton	St-Julien
Château Malescot-St-Exupéry	Margaux
Château Cantenac-Brown	Margaux
Château Palmer	Margaux
Château La Lagune	Haut-Médoc

Château Desmirail	Margaux
Château Calon-Ségur	St-Estèphe
Château Ferrière	Margaux
Château d'Alesme (formerly Marquis d'Alesme)	Margaux
Château Boyd-Cantenac	Margaux

FOURTH GROWTHS—QUATRIÈMES CRUS (10)	
Vineyard	*AOC*
Château St-Pierre	St-Julien
Château Branaire-Ducru	St-Julien
Château Talbot	St-Julien
Château Duhart-Milon-Rothschild	Pauillac
Château Pouget	Margaux
Château La Tour-Carnet	Haut-Médoc
Château Lafon-Rochet	St-Estèphe
Château Beychevelle	St-Julien
Château Prieuré-Lichine	Margaux
Château Marquis de Terme	Margaux

FIFTH GROWTHS—CINQUIÈMES CRUS (18)	
Vineyard	*AOC*
Château Pontet-Canet	Pauillac
Château Batailley	Pauillac
Château Grand-Puy-Lacoste	Pauillac
Château Grand-Puy-Ducasse	Pauillac
Château Haut-Batailley	Pauillac
Château Lynch-Bages	Pauillac
Château Lynch-Moussas	Pauillac
Château Dauzac	Haut-Médoc
Château d'Armailhac (called Château Mouton-Baron-Philippe from 1956 to 1988)	Pauillac
Château du Tertre	Margaux
Château Haut-Bages-Libéral	Pauillac
Château Pédesclaux	Pauillac
Château Belgrave	Haut-Médoc
Château Camensac	Haut-Médoc
Château Cos Labory	St-Estèphe
Château Clerc-Milon-Rothschild	Pauillac
Château Croizet Bages	Pauillac
Château Cantemerle	Haut-Médoc

"*The classified growths are divided in five classes and the price difference from one class to another is about 12 percent.*"

—William Frank,
Traité sur les Vins du Médoc, 1855

UNDERSTANDING THE 1855 CLASSIFICATION

As you can see, the 1855 classification can look a little cumbersome, so I've separated the classification into growths, communes, and the number of vineyards in each. My table shows which communes have the most first growths—all the way down to fifth growths. It also shows which commune corners the market on all growths. A quick glance offers some instant facts to guide you when you buying a Médoc Bordeaux: Pauillac has the most first-growths and the most fifth-growths. Margaux sweeps the third growths and the overall châteaux count, and only Margaux has a château in each category. St-Julien has no first- or fifth-growths but its strengths lie in second- and fourth-growths.

BOX SCORE OF THE 1855 CLASSIFICATION

COMMUNE	1ST	2ND	3RD	4TH	5TH	TOTAL
MARGAUX	1	5	10	3	2	21
PAUILLAC	3	2	0	1	12	18
ST-JULIEN	0	5	2	4	0	11
ST-ESTÈPHE	0	2	1	1	1	5
HAUT-MÉDOC	0	0	1	1	3	5
GRAVES	1	0	0	0	0	1
CHÂTEAUX	5	14	14	10	18	61

THE HISTORY OF THE 1855 CLASSIFICATION

Much has changed over the last century and a half. Some vineyards have doubled or tripled production by buying neighboring land; the châteaux have seen many changes of ownership; and, like all businesses, the wine industry in Bordeaux has seen good times and bad. The 1855 classification has remained stable, but both it and its relative meaning have changed slightly over the years. Here are three examples.

In 1920, Baron Philippe de Rothschild assumed control of the family vineyard, but he refused to accept that in 1855 the brokers had ranked the château a second-growth (two years after his great-grandfather, an

Englishman, bought it). Baron Philippe felt it should have been classified a first-growth from the beginning, and he fought for years to change the designation. When that change finally came in 1973, the château's motto changed from

> *Premier ne puis, second ne daigne, Mouton suis.*
> First, I cannot be. Second, I do not deign to be. Mouton I am.

to

> *Premier je suis, Second je fus, Mouton ne change.*
> First, I am. Second, I used to be. Mouton doesn't change.

In the early 1970s, Château Margaux and all Bordeaux wines were having a difficult time, even at the highest level. The family who owned Château Margaux then was struggling financially and didn't put enough time or money into running the vineyard, so the quality of the wine fell from its traditional excellence. Then, in 1977, the Franco-Greek Mentzelopoulos family bought the château for $16 million, and since then the quality of the wine has risen even beyond its first-growth standards.

The cru bourgeois Château Larose-Trintaudon is **THE LARGEST VINEYARD IN THE MÉDOC** area, making nearly 100,000 cases of wine per year.

Château Gloria, which lies in the commune of St-Julien, didn't exist in 1855. Starting in the 1940s, Henri Martin, the mayor of St-Julien, bought parcels of second-growth vineyards. As a result, the château he founded now produces top-quality wine not included in the 1855 classification.

Also keep in mind that the techniques that winemakers use today differ from those used in 1855 and make for better wine. Some of the châteaux in the 1855 classification deserve a lesser ranking, and others deserve a better one, but, even after more than 150 years, the classification still offers a valid and useful guide to both quality and price.

CRU BOURGEOIS

The Crus Bourgeois are châteaux originally classified in 1920. Rather than remaining fixed like the Official Classification, the Crus Bourgeois designation varies over time. In 1932 it featured 444 properties, but in 1962 it listed only 94. The latest classification of Crus Bourgeois of the Médoc and Haut-Médoc took place in 2010 and has 246 châteaux. Because of the high quality of the 2000, 2003, 2005, 2009, 2010, and 2015 vintages, you'll find some of today's best values in the Cru Bourgeois classification.

Look for these producers:

Château Chasse-Spleen	Château Les Ormes-Sorbet
Château Coufran	Château Marbuzet
Château d'Angludet	Château Meyney
Château de Lamarque	Château Monbrison
Château de Pez	Château Patache d'Aux
Château Fourcas-Hosten	Château Phélan-Ségur
Château Greysac	Château Pibran
Château Haut-Marbuzet	Château Pontensac
Château Labégorce-Zédé	Château Poujeaux
Château La Cardonne	Château Siran
Château Larose-Trintaudon	Château Sociando-Mallet
Château Les Ormes-de-Pez	Château Vieux Robin

GRAVES WINE PRODUCTION

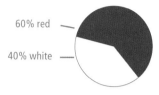

60% red

40% white

In 1987, the northern Graves region established the **PESSAC-LÉOGNAN** (for both reds and whites) communal appellation.

Guests at an exclusive hotel in the vineyards of Château Smith-Haut-Lafitte can enjoy **TREATMENTS FEATURING GRAPEVINE EXTRACT,** crushed grape seeds, and grapeseed oil.

MERLOT IS THE MAJOR GRAPE used to produce wine in the Pomerol region. Very little Cabernet Sauvignon goes into these wines.

Château Pétrus makes as much wine in one year as Gallo makes in **SIX MINUTES.**

GRAVES

The most famous château here, which we saw in the 1855 classification, is Château Haut-Brion. Other good red Graves classified in 1959 as Grands Crus Classés include:

Château Bouscaut
Château Carbonnieux
Château de Fieuzal
Château Haut-Bailly
Château La Mission-Haut-Brion
Château La Tour-Martillac

Château Malartic-Lagravière
Château Olivier
Château Pape-Clément
Château Smith-Haut-Lafitte
Domaine de Chevalier

POMEROL

The smallest of the top red-wine regions in Bordeaux, Pomerol produces only 15 percent as much wine as St-Émilion, so Pomerol wines are relatively scarce and, if you do find them, expensive. The red wines of Pomerol tend to be softer, fruitier, and ready to drink sooner than Médoc wines. No official classification exists, but here are some of the finest Pomerols on the market:

Château Beauregard
Château Bourgneuf
Château Clinet
Château Gazin
Château La Conseillante
Château La Fleur-Pétrus
Château La Pointe
Château Lafleur
Château Latour-à-Pomerol

Château L'Église Clinet
Château L'Évangile
Château Le Pin
Château Nénin
Château Petit-Village
Château Pétrus
Château Plince
Château Trotanoy
Vieux Château-Certan

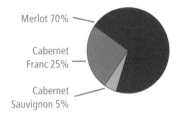

GRAPE VARIETIES OF ST-ÉMILION

Merlot 70%

Cabernet Franc 25%

Cabernet Sauvignon 5%

ST-ÉMILION

One of the most beautiful villages in France, St-Émilion produces about two-thirds as much wine as the Médoc. A century after the Médoc classification came the St-Émilion classification, which features 18 first growths comparable to the Médoc's Grand Cru Classé wines.

PREMIERS GRANDS CRUS CLASSÉS

HIGHEST LEVEL

Château Angélus

Château Ausone

Château Chevâl Blanc

Château Pavie

Château Beau-Séjour-Bécot

Château Beauséjour-
   Duffau-Lagarrosse

Château Belair-Monange

Château Canon

Château Canon-La-Gaffelière

Château Figeac

Château La Gaffelière

Château La Mondotte

Château Larcis Ducasse

Château Pavie Macquin

Château Troplong Mondot

Château Trottevieille

Château Valandraud

Clos Fourtet

Below that level, here are the important Grands Crus Classés and other St-Émilion wines generally available in America:

Château Bellevue

Château Dassault

Château de Ferrand

Château Faugères

Château Fombrauge

Château Grand-Corbin

Château Haut-Corbin

Château La Tour-Figeac

Château Monbousquet

Château Pavie Decesse

Château Tertre Daugax

Clos des Jacobins

OTHER RED BORDEAUX REGIONS TO LOOK FOR:

Côtes de Blaye

Côtes de Bourg

Fronsac

The earliest harvest since 1893 was 2003. **THAT VINTAGE SUFFERED** summer heat waves, fierce storms, and hail, reducing production to the lowest since 1991.

Many experts consider the decade of 2000–2010 **THE BEST IN THE HISTORY OF BORDEAUX.**

Drink your lighter vintages, such as 2011 and 2012, while you **WAIT PATIENTLY** for your great vintages such as 2009, 2010, and 2015 to mature.

Bordeaux produces **60–70 MILLION CASES** (720–840 million bottles) of wine for each vintage.

"Great vintages take time to mature. Lesser wines mature faster than the greater ones. . . . Patience is needed for great vintages, hence the usefulness and enjoyment of lesser vintages. . . . Often vintages which have a poorer rating—if young—will give a greater enjoyment than a better-rated vintage—if young."

—Alexis Lichine

BORDEAUX VINTAGES

Now that you know the greatest red-wine regions of Bordeaux, here are some of their best vintages.

– LEFT BANK OF THE GARONNE RIVER –
MÉDOC, ST-JULIEN, MARGAUX, PAUILLAC, ST-ESTÈPHE, GRAVES

GREAT OLDER VINTAGES	GREAT VINTAGES	GOOD VINTAGES
1982	1990	1994
1985	1995	1997
1986	1996	1998
1989	2000	1999
	2003	2001
	2005	2002
	2009	2004
	2010	2006
	2015	2007
		2008
		2011
		2012
		2013
		2014

– RIGHT BANK OF THE DORDOGNE RIVER –
ST-ÉMILION, POMEROL

GREAT OLDER VINTAGES	GREAT VINTAGES	GOOD VINTAGES
1982	1990	1995
1989	1998	1996
	2000	1997
	2001	1999
	2005	2002
	2009	2003
	2010	2004
	2015	2006
		2007
		2008
		2011
		2012
		2013
		2014

CHOOSING A RED BORDEAUX

Remember, Bordeaux wines are blends. Do you want a Merlot-style Bordeaux, such as St-Émilion or Pomerol, or a Cabernet style, such as Médoc or Graves? Keep in mind that Merlot is more accessible and easier to drink when young.

Next, do you want to drink the wine now or age it? A great château Bordeaux in a great vintage needs a minimum of ten years to age. Down a level, a Cru Bourgeois or a second label of a great château in a great vintage needs at least five years. Drink a regional wine within two or three years of the vintage, and a wine labeled simply "Appellation Bordeaux Contrôlée" as soon as it hits store shelves.

Then select the right vintage for what you want. If you're looking for a wine to age, you need a great vintage. If you want a wine ready to drink now and from a greater château, choose a lesser vintage. If you want a wine ready to drink now and a great vintage, look for a lesser château.

As we've seen, not all Bordeaux wines are very expensive. They all have different price ranges, so don't let cost expectations prevent you from finding and enjoying a good value. Some red Bordeaux do cost much more than others, however. These factors separate a $30 bottle from a $300 bottle:

- Where the grapes grew
- Age of the vines (usually the older the vine, the better the wine)
- Yield of the vine (lower yield = higher quality)
- Winemaking technique (how long aged in wood, etc.)
- Vintage

The best way to get the best value for your money is to use the pyramid method. Let's say you like Château Lafite-Rothschild—top of the pyramid in the margin—but you can't afford it. What to do? Look for the region, which is Pauillac. Now you have a choice: Go back to the 1855 classification and look for a fifth-growth wine from Pauillac that represents the region at a lower price. Still too pricey? Drop another level on the pyramid and go for a Cru Bourgeois from Pauillac, or buy a regional wine labeled "Pauillac."

I've never memorized the 7,000 châteaux. If at a wine store I find a château I don't know, I look at the region. If it comes from Pauillac and from a good vintage and it costs $20 to $25, I buy it—because chances are good that the wine will be good, and everything in wine is about hedging your bets.

- Château Lafite-Rothschild $$$$
- Fifth-Growth Pauillac $$$
- Cru Bourgeois Pauillac $$
- Regional Pauillac $

The first growths Château Margaux, Château Latour, Château Lafite-Rothschild, and Château Mouton-Rothschild use less than 40 percent of the crop for their wines. **THE REST GOES INTO THEIR SECOND LABELS**.

In 2011, **ROBERT PARKER CONDUCTED A BORDEAUX TASTING.** He selected the following châteaux: Château Angelus, Château Brane-Cantenac, Château Clos Fourtet, Château Cos d'Estournel, Château Haut Bailly, Château La Conseillante, Château La Fleur Pétrus, Château Le Gay, Château Léoville Las Cases, Château Léoville Poyferré, Château Lynch Bages, Château Malescot St. Exupéry, Château Palmer, Château Pape Clément, Château Pichon Baron, Château Pichon Lalande, Château Pontet-Canet, Château Rauzan Ségla, Château Smith Haut Lafitte, and Château Trotanoy.

Another good way to avoid sky-high Bordeaux prices is to take the time to look for second-label wines. These wines come from the youngest parts of a vineyard, making them lighter in style, quicker to mature, and less expensive than first-label wines.

CHÂTEAU	EXAMPLES OF SECOND-LABELS
CHÂTEAU HAUT-BRION	LE CLARENCE DE HAUT-BRION
CHÂTEAU LAFITE-ROTHSCHILD	CARRUADES DE LAFITE
CHÂTEAU LATOUR	LES FORTS DE LATOUR
CHÂTEAU LÉOVILLE-BARTON	LA RÉSERVE LÉOVILLE-BARTON
CHÂTEAU LÉOVILLE-LAS-CASES	LE PETIT LION
CHÂTEAU LYNCH-BAGES	ECHO DE LYNCH-BAGES
CHÂTEAU MARGAUX	PAVILLON ROUGE DU CHÂTEAU MARGAUX
CHÂTEAU MOUTON-ROTHSCHILD	LE PETIT MOUTON
CHÂTEAU PALMER	ALTER EGO
CHÂTEAU PICHON LALANDE	RÉSERVE DE LA COMTESSE
CHÂTEAU PICHON-LONGUEVILLE	LES TOURELLES DE LONGUEVILLE
DOMAINE DE CHEVALIER	L'ESPIRIT DE CHEVALIER

FORTY YEARS LATER IN BORDEAUX

The most dramatic change in the entire wine world in the last four decades has been the worldwide demand for the best châteaux of Bordeaux. In 1985, the most important market for Bordeaux was the UK. In the 1980s and 1990s, interest in Bordeaux shifted to the Americans and Japanese. Today, Asia has become the new and growing market, particularly Hong Kong, South Korea, and China. All of which means increasingly higher prices for the best Bordeaux. In a way, it's the end of an era. As a young man, my first "eureka" wine moment came when I discovered that a 20-year-old Bordeaux cost less than $25—a lot of money for a college student but worth it. Few people today, young or otherwise, can afford the $2,000 price tag for one bottle of Château Latour 2005, which probably won't be ready to drink for another decade! The great châteaux have become wines of prestige reserved to the wealthy.

That said, we common folk can still find some excellent values from the other 7,000 châteaux. Since 1990, quality has filtered down to the entire region, which is making the best wines in Bordeaux history, especially in the Médoc, St-Émilion, Graves, Côtes de Bourg, and Côtes de Blaye.

5 BEST VALUE RED WINES OF BORDEAUX UNDER $30

Château Cantemerle • Château Greysac • Château La Cardonne
• Château Larose-Trintaudon • Confidences de Prieure Lichine

See pags 310–311 for a complete list.

WINE AND FOOD

"With **Château La Louvière Rouge**: roast leg of lamb or grilled duck breast."
—Denise Lurton-Moulle of Château La Louvière, Château Bonnet

"For **Bordeaux red**, simple and classic is best! Red meat, such as beef and particularly lamb, as we love it in Pauillac. If you can grill the meat on vine cuttings, you are in heaven."
—Jean-Michel Cazes of Château Lynch-Bages and Château Les Ormes-de-Pez

"Sunday lunches at Le Pin include lots of local oysters with chilled white Bordeaux followed by thick entrecôte steaks on the barbecue with shallots and a selection of the family's **Pomerols, Margaux, or Côtes de France red Bordeaux.**
—Jacques and Fiona Thienpont of Château Le Pin

"With **red Bordeaux**: duck breast with wild mushrooms or guinea hen with grapes."
—Antony Perrin of Château Carbonnieux

"With red Bordeaux, especially **Pomerol** wine, lamb is a must."
—Christian Moueix

NIXON'S FAVORITE WINE WAS CHÂTEAU MARGAUX. He always had a bottle of his favorite vintage waiting at his table from the cellar of the famous "21" Club in New York.

When the **FOUR SEASONS RESTAURANT IN NEW YORK** opened in 1959, they served 1918 Château Lafite-Rothschild for $18, or a 1934 Château Latour for $16. They also offered a 1945 Château Cos d'Estournel for $9.50.

TEST YOUR KNOWLEDGE of the red wines of Bordeaux by trying the quiz on page 337.

—— **FURTHER READING** ——

Bordeaux by Oz Clarke

Bordeaux by Robert M. Parker Jr.

The Bordeaux Atlas and Encyclopedia of Chateaux by Hubrecht Duijker and Michael Broadbent

Bordeaux Legends by Jane Anson

The Complete Bordeaux by Stephen Brook

The Finest Wines of Bordeaux by James Lawther

Grands Vins by Clive Coates

GUIDED TASTING

Bordeaux wines have a reputation of being expensive and requiring long aging, which isn't entirely true: 80 percent of all Bordeaux wines retail between $8 and $25, and you can drink most of those either when you buy them or within two years of purchase. The two important points to consider as you taste these wines are the various hierarchies—quality classifications, growths, and labels—and the effects of the aging process.

THE WINES

Bordeaux

Four wines, tasted together:

1. *Appellation Bordeaux Contrôlée*
2. *Appellation Region Controlée*
3. *Château: Cru Bourgeois*
4. *Château: Grand Cru Classé*

Second Labels

Two wines, from the same producer, tasted together:

5. *Second-label Château wine*
6. *First-label Château wine*

The Bordeaux Growth Hierarchy

Three wines, tasted together, each wine from the same vintage:

7. *Château: Cru Bourgeois*
8. *Château: Third, Fourth, or Fifth Growth*
9. *Château: Second Growth*

The Aging Process

One wine, tasted alone:

10. *Aged Bordeaux (at least ten years old)*

CLASS SIX

THE RED WINES OF CALIFORNIA

MORE ABOUT CALIFORNIA WINES ✳ THE MAJOR RED GRAPES
OF CALIFORNIA: CABERNET SAUVIGNON, PINOT NOIR,
ZINFANDEL, MERLOT, AND SYRAH ✳ THE RED-GRAPE BOOM

MORE ABOUT CALIFORNIA WINES

WE COVERED THE history and geography of California in Class Two, so let's review the Golden State's main viticultural areas (in the margin) before continuing with the red wines of California.

Now let's look at the question that faces everyone who wants to enjoy a delicious glass of wine.

RED OR WHITE?

The infographic below represents overall wine consumption in America over the last 40+ years. In 1970, people drank much more red wine than white. From the mid-1970s into the mid-1990s, tastes shifted to white wine. Since then, the pendulum has swung back to red.

1970	1980	1990	2000	2015
24%	53%	70%	55%	40%
76%	47%	30%	45%	60%

The 1980s obsession with health and fitness urged many people to switch from eating meat and potatoes regularly to fish and vegetables, and that lighter diet called more for white wine than red. "Chardonnay" became the new buzzword, replacing the call for just a glass of white wine. Bars that never stocked wine—nothing decent, anyway—started carrying a fine assortment by the glass, and Chardonnay outsold them all. Today, Cabernet Sauvignon, Merlot, and Pinot Noir have become the new buzzwords. The so-called French Paradox and the power of the media also played a key role in the shift. More on that below.

Perhaps the most important reason that red-wine consumption has increased in America is that California is producing better quality red wine than ever before. Remember the phylloxera epidemic that hit the state in the 1980s? (See page 104 for a quick refresher.) Vineyard owners replanted their vines, which allowed for increased red-grape production. Growers then implemented the knowledge they had gained over the years about climate, microclimate, soil, trellising, and other viticultural practices.

Bottom line: California reds are some of the greatest in the world, with more and better yet to come.

THE FRENCH PARADOX

In the early 1990s, the *60 Minutes* news show twice aired a report on a phenomenon known as the French Paradox: The French have a lower rate of heart disease than Americans despite a diet higher in fat. Red wine stood out as one item that the American diet lacks when compared to the French diet, so researchers went looking for a link between the consumption of red wine and a decreased rate of heart disease. In the year following the news of this report, Americans increased their purchases of red wines by 39 percent!

Besides tannin, **RED WINE CONTAINS RESVERATROL**, which in medical studies has been associated with anticancer properties.

Alcohol, **WHEN CONSUMED IN MODERATION**, will increase HDL (good cholesterol) and decrease LDL (bad cholesterol).

Wine is **FAT-FREE** and contains no cholesterol.

THE MAJOR RED GRAPES OF CALIFORNIA

More than 30 different wine grape varieties grow in California, but these 5 are the most important: Cabernet Sauvignon, Pinot Noir, Zinfandel, Merlot, and Syrah.

CABERNET SAUVIGNON

The most successful red grape in California yields some of the greatest red wines in the world. Remember, Cabernet Sauvignon is the predominant variety in the finest red Bordeaux wines, such as Château Lafite-Rothschild and Château Latour. Almost all California Cabernets are dry, and, depending on producer and vintage, they range in style from light and ready to drink to extremely full-bodied and long-lived.

My favorite California Cabernet Sauvignons include:

Araujo	Dunn Howell	Peter Michael
Arrowood	Mountain	Pine Ridge
Beaulieu Private	Frank Family	Plump Jack
Reserve	Gallo of Sonoma	Pride Mountain
Beringer Private	Estate	Ridge Monte
Reserve	Groth Reserve	Bello
Bevan	Harlan Estate	Robert Mondavi
Bond	Heitz	Sbragia Family
Brand	Hess Collection	Vineyards
Bryant Family	Hewitt	Schrader
Cakebread	Hundred Acre	Screaming Eagle
Caymus	Jordan	Shafer Hillside
Chappellet	Joseph Phelps	Select
Chateau Montelena	Kongsgaard	Silver Oak
Chateau St. Jean,	La Jota	Spottswoode
Cinq Cépages	Laurel Glen	Stag's Leap Cask
Clos du Val	Lewis	Staglin
Colgin	Mondavi Reserve	Tor
Dalla Valle	Opus One	Trefethen
Diamond Creek	Paul Hobbs	Whitehall Lane
Duckhorn		

– BEST VINTAGES OF NAPA VALLEY CABERNET SAUVIGNON –

1994* 1995* 1996* 1997* 1999* 2001** 2002** 2003
2004 2005* 2006** 2007** 2008** 2009** 2010**
2011 2012** 2013** 2014 2015*

*EXCEPTIONAL VINTAGE   **EXTRAORDINARY VINTAGE*

"Reserve" on an American wine label has **NO LEGAL MEANING,** but some wineries, such as Beaulieu Vineyards and Robert Mondavi Winery, use it to designate special wines. BV's Reserve comes from a particular vineyard, and Mondavi's Reserve comes from a special blend of grapes. Other vague terms include "cask" wines, "special selections," and "proprietor's reserve."

MOST CABERNET SAUVIGNONS ARE BLENDED with other grapes, primarily Merlot. To name the grape variety on the label, the winemaker must use at least 75 percent Cabernet Sauvignon.

More than 1,000 different **CABERNET SAUVIGNONS** from California are available to the consumer.

GREAT OLDER VINTAGES:
1985, 1986, 1987, 1990, and 1991

"Pinot is James Joyce, while Cabernet is Dickens perhaps. Both sell well, but one is easier to understand."

—*Decanter* magazine

"It's a hard grape to know, as you know. Right? It's, uh, it's thin-skinned, temperamental, ripens early. It's, you know, it's not a survivor like Cabernet, which can just grow anywhere and, uh, thrive even when it's neglected."

—Miles from *Sideways*

PINOT NOIR

Sometimes known not so affectionately as the "headache" grape because of its fragile quality, Pinot Noir is temperamental, high maintenance, expensive, and difficult to grow and make into wine. This great grape of the Burgundy region of France—responsible for the famous Pommard, Nuits-St-Georges, and Gevrey-Chambertin wines—is also one of the principal grapes in Champagne. Many years of experimentation have taken place in California to find the right location to plant Pinot Noir and to perfect fermentation techniques, elevating some of the wines to the level of greatness. Pinot Noir is usually less tannic than Cabernet Sauvignon and matures more quickly, generally within two to five years. Because of the extra growing expenses, the best California Pinot Noirs usually cost more than other varietals.

The three top counties for Pinot Noir are:

Sonoma	Monterey	Santa Barbara
(11,000 acres)	(6,204 acres)	(3,401 acres)

My favorite California Pinot Noirs include:

Acacia	Gary Farrell	Patz & Hall
Artesa	Goldeneye	Paul Hobbs
Au Bon Climat	J. Rochioli	Pisoni
Brewer-Clifton	Kosta Browne	Robert Sinskey
Byron	Littorai	Rochioli
Calera	Lucia	Saintsbury
Dehlinger	Marcassin	Sanford
Donum	Melville	Sea Smoke
Etude	Merry Edwards	Siduri
Flowers	Morgan	Talley
Foxen	Papapietro-Perry	Williams Selyem

– BEST RECENT VINTAGES OF CALIFORNIA PINOT NOIR –

SONOMA: 2007* 2008 2009** 2010** 2011 2012* 2013** 2014* 2015*

CARNEROS: 2008* 2009* 2010 2011 2012* 2013** 2014* 2015*

SANTA BARBARA: 2008 2009* 2010** 2011 2012* 2013* 2014* 2015

MONTEREY: 2008* 2009** 2010* 2011* 2012* 2013* 2014**

* EXCEPTIONAL VINTAGE ** EXTRAORDINARY VINTAGE

ZINFANDEL

This historic grape of California made generic or jug wines in the early years of California winemaking. Over the past 30 years, however, it has developed into one of the best red varietal grapes. The only problem with choosing a Zinfandel wine is that winemakers produce so many different styles. They can range from light and fruity to big, rich, ripe, high-alcohol, spicy, smoky, concentrated, intensely flavored, and with substantial tannin. To say nothing of white Zinfandel!

My favorite Zinfandels include:

Bedrock	Martinelli	Roshambo
Carlisle	Mazzocco	Sbragia
Cline	Merry Edwards	Seghesio
Dehlinger	Rafanelli	Signorello
Dry Creek Winery	Ravenswood	St. Francis
Hartford Family	Ridge	Turley
J. Rochioli	Rosenblum	

– BEST VINTAGES OF NORTH COAST ZINFANDEL –

2003*   2005   2006*   2007*   2008**   2009*
2010*   2011   2012*   2013*   2014**   2015**

*EXCEPTIONAL VINTAGE   **EXTRAORDINARY VINTAGE*

Some California Zinfandel vines are more than **150 years old** and still producing wine.

Some Zinfandels have more than **16 PERCENT ALCOHOL.**

Rosenblum makes more than **10 DIFFERENT ZINFANDELS A YEAR.**

Recent DNA studies have shown that Zinfandel is **THE SAME GRAPE AS PRIMITIVO** in Italy.

WHITE ZINFANDEL outsells red 6:1 in the United States.

GREAT CALIFORNIA ROSÉS
Bonny Doon Vin Gris de Cigare
Etude Pinot Noir Rosé
Frog's Leap La Grenouille
Rouganté
SoloRosa

All of California had just **TWO ACRES OF MERLOT** in 1960. Today it has almost 45,000.

MERLOT

Because Merlot's tannins feel softer and its texture more supple, for many years California winemakers used it only in blends with Cabernet Sauvignon, but Merlot has achieved its own identity as a superpremium varietal. Of all red varietals in California, Merlot has seen the fastest rate of new plantings over the last 20 years. It produces a soft, round wine that generally doesn't need the same aging as a Cabernet Sauvignon. Its early maturation and compatibility with food also make it a top seller at restaurants.

My favorite North Coast Merlots include:

Beringer	Hourglass	Pine Ridge
Carter	Lewis Cellars	Plumpjack
Chimney Rock	Luna	Pride
Clos du Bois	Markham	Provenance
Duckhorn	Matanzas Creek	Shafer
Franciscan	Newton	St. Francis
Havens	Palamo	Whitehall Lane

— BEST VINTAGES OF NORTH COAST MERLOT —
2002* 2004* 2005* 2007* 2008 2009** 2011
2012* 2013* 2014* 2015

*EXCEPTIONAL VINTAGE **EXTRAORDINARY VINTAGE*

SYRAH

One of the major grapes of France's Rhône Valley, Syrah makes for some of the best and most long-lived wines in the world. Called Shiraz when it hails from Australia, this spicy, robust grape has seen phenomenal sales in America, where it thrives in California's sunny, warm weather.

My favorite Syrahs include:

Alban	Epoch	Peay
Bonny Doon	Fess Parker	Phelps
Cakebread	Foxen	Qupe
Clos du Bois	Justin	Saxum
Copain	Lagier Meredith	Sine Qua Non
Dehlinger	Lewis	Tablas Creek
Dumol	Neyers	Viader
Edmunds St. John	Ojai	Wild Horse
Enfield	Pax	Zaca Mesa

> As in the Rhône Valley, Syrah is **OFTEN BLENDED WITH GRENACHE** and other international grapes.

SAN LUIS OBISPO and Sonoma counties have the most acreage of Syrah grapes in California.

— BEST VINTAGES OF CALIFORNIA SYRAH —

SOUTH CENTRAL COAST: 2006* 2007* 2008** 2009** 2010** 2011 2012 2013* 2014*

NORTH COAST: 2004** 2006** 2007** 2008* 2009** 2010* 2011 2012* 2013* 2014*

* EXCEPTIONAL VINTAGE   ** EXTRAORDINARY VINTAGE

THE RED-GRAPE BOOM

The table below tracks the number of acres of California's major red grapes and how those numbers have increased. Note the rapid expansion of the California wine industry!

CALIFORNIA RED-WINE GRAPES

GRAPE	1970	1980	1990	2015
CABERNET SAUVIGNON	3,200	21,800	24,100	87,972
MERLOT	100	2,600	4,000	44,460
PINOT NOIR	2,100	9,200	8,600	42,812
SYRAH	0	0	400	18,476
ZINFANDEL	19,200	27,700	28,000	47,827

MERITAGE WINES

Meritage (rhymes with heritage) is the name for red or white wines made in America from a blend of the classic Bordeaux grapes. Winemakers felt stifled by the legally required 75 percent minimum of a grape that had to go into a bottle for it to carry the name of that variety, so they created this new category because they knew they could make a better wine with a blend of, say, 60 percent of the major grape and 40 percent secondary grapes. Blending gives Meritage producers the same freedom that Bordeaux winemakers have in making their wines.

For red wine, the varieties include:

Cabernet Sauvignon   **Merlot**   **Cabernet Franc**   **Petit Verdot**   **Malbec**

For white wine, the varieties include:

Sauvignon Blanc   **Sémillon**

STYLES OF CALIFORNIA RED WINE

When you buy a Cabernet Sauvignon, Pinot Noir, Zinfandel, Merlot, Syrah, or Meritage wine from California, there's really no good way to know the

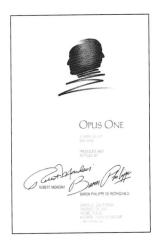

style of the wine just by looking at the label. Unless you know a particular vineyard well, you're stuck with trial-and-error tastings. Just knowing that the same grape can make drastically different styles puts you ahead in the game, though.

California has more than 2,800 wineries, and more than half of them produce red wines, so it's virtually impossible to keep up with the ever-changing styles they produce. Thankfully, more wineries are improving their labeling practices by adding important information, such as whether a wine should be aged, when it's ready to drink, and food pairing suggestions. To avoid unpleasant surprises, find the right retailer who understands both the wine world and your specific tastes.

NAPA VALLEY, PAST AND PRESENT
1970: $2,000–$4,000 per acre
2016: $150,000–$400,000 per acre

Recently, some of the **GREAT WINERIES IN CALIFORNIA WERE SOLD,** including: Mayacamas, Clos Pegase, Qupe, and Araujo.

TEST YOUR KNOWLEDGE of the red wines of California by trying the quiz on page 337.

——— FURTHER READING ———

Making Sense of California Wine by Matt Kramer

The New California Wine by Jon Bonné

Wine Atlas of California by James Halliday

The Wine Atlas of California and the Pacific Northwest by Bob Thompson

Wine Spectator's California Wine by James Laube

Wines of California, Deluxe Edition by Mike DeSimone and Jeff Jenssen

AGING CALIFORNIA RED WINES

California wines generally taste more accessible when younger than, say, a properly aged Bordeaux. That's one reason that California wines sell so well, especially in restaurants.

That said, red wines from California do age well, especially those from the best wineries producing Cabernet Sauvignon and Zinfandel. Some Cabernet Sauvignons from the 1930s, 1940s, and 1950s for the most part still drink well, and some of them taste outstanding, proving the wine's longevity. Zinfandels and Cabernet Sauvignons from the best wineries in great vintages need a minimum of five years before you drink them, and they'll improve over the following ten. That's at least fifteen years of great enjoyment!

FORTY YEARS LATER IN CALIFORNIA

Specific grape varieties now have associations with particular AVAs and even individual vineyards. Go to Napa Valley for Cabernet Sauvignon and Merlot; Anderson Valley, Carneros, Monterey, Santa Barbara, and Sonoma, for Pinot Noir; and the South Central Coast, particularly San Luis Obispo, for Syrah.

California winemaking innovation has settled down, but winemakers haven't given up experimentation altogether. Continuing the trend toward diversity, many new grape varieties are coming from California these days. Expect to see more wines made from Barbera, Grenache, Mourvèdre, and especially Syrah.

Alcohol levels also have changed over the past 40 years, especially in the red wines. Most wines around the world have increased in alcohol content but not to the extent that they have in California. Many winemakers are producing wines with more 15 percent alcohol! That high level changes the balance of a wine as overpowering alcohol replaces elegance and varietal characteristics.

5 BEST VALUE RED WINES OF CALIFORNIA UNDER $30

Beaulieu Cabernet Sauvignon • Bonny Doon "Le Cigare Volant" • Frog's Leap Merlot • Louis M. Martini Cabernet Sauvignon • Ridge Sonoma Zinfandel

See page 304–306 for a complete list.

WINE AND FOOD

"With **Cabernet Sauvignon**, lamb, or wild game such as grouse and caribou. With **Pinot Noir**, pork loin, milder game such as domestic pheasant, and coq au vin."

—Margrit Biever and Robert Mondavi

"Roast lamb is wonderful with the flavor and complexity of **Cabernet Sauvignon**. The wine also pairs nicely with sliced breast of duck, and grilled squab with wild mushrooms. For a cheese course with mature Cabernet, milder cheeses such as young goat cheeses, St. André and Taleggio, are best so the subtle flavors of the wine can be enjoyed."

—Tom Jordan

"With a young **Merlot**, we recommend lamb shanks with crispy polenta or grilled duck with wild rice in Port sauce. One of our favorites is barbecued leg of lamb with a mild, spicy, fruit-based sauce. With older Merlots at the end of the meal, we like to serve Cambazzola cheese and warm walnuts."

—Margaret and Dan Duckhorn

DUCKHORN VINEYARDS

2005
NAPA VALLEY
MERLOT

14.5% ALC/VOL

"With **Cabernet Sauvignon**, prime cut of well-aged grilled beef; also—believe it or not—with chocolate and chocolate-chip cookies. With **Pinot Noir**, roasted quail stuffed with peeled kiwi fruit in a Madeira sauce. Also with pork tenderloin in a fruity sauce."

—Janet Trefethen

"With **Zinfandel**, a well-made risotto of Petaluma duck. With aged **Cabernet Sauvignon**, Moroccan lamb with figs."

—Paul Draper of Ridge Vineyards

"With **Cabernet Sauvignon**, lamb or veal with a light sauce."

—Warren Winiarski of Stag's Leap Wine Cellars

"**Pinot Noir** is so versatile, but I like it best with fowl of all sorts—chicken, turkey, duck, pheasant, and quail, preferably roasted or mesquite-grilled. It's also great with fish such as salmon, tuna, and snapper."

—Josh Jensen of Calera Wine Co.

"With **Cabernet Sauvignon**, Sonoma County spring lamb or lamb chops prepared in a rosemary herb sauce."

—Richard Arrowood

"My favorite food combination with **Zinfandel** is marinated, butterflied leg of lamb. Have the butcher butterfly the leg, then place it in a plastic bag. Pour in half a bottle of Dry Creek Zinfandel, a cup of olive oil, six mashed garlic cloves, salt and pepper to taste. Marinate for several hours or overnight in the refrigerator. Barbecue until medium rare. While the lamb is cooking, take the marinade, reduce it, and whisk in several pats of butter for thickness. Yummy!"

—David Stare of Dry Creek Vineyard

"With **Cabernet Sauvignon**, a good rib eye, barbecued with a teriyaki-soy-ginger-sesame marinade; venison or even roast beef prepared with olive oil and tapenade with rosemary, or even lamb. But when it comes to a good Cabernet Sauvignon: nothing at all—just a good book."

—Bo Barrett of Chateau Montelena Winery

"With **Cabernet Sauvignon**, try a rich risotto topped with wild mushrooms."

—Patrick Campbell of Laurel Glen Vineyard

"**Cakebread Cellars Napa Valley Cabernet Sauvignon** with salmon in a crispy potato crust or an herb-crusted Napa Valley rack of lamb, with mashed potatoes and a red-wine sauce."

—Jack Cakebread

"I like my **Cabernet Sauvignon** with rack of lamb, beef, or rare duck."

—Ed Sbragia of Sbragia Family Vineyards

"With **St. Francis Merlot** Sonoma County, Dungeness crab cakes, rack of lamb, pork roast, or tortellini. With St. Francis Merlot Reserve, hearty minestrone or lentil soup, venison, or filet mignon, or even a Caesar salad."

—Tom Mackey of St. Francis

❧ GUIDED TASTING ☙

Pour the first six wines at the same time so you clearly can see the difference in color among the Pinot Noirs, Zinfandels, and Merlots. After you taste these first six wines, choose the grape variety that best suits your personality. That's your eureka moment!

THE WINES

American Pinot Noir
Two Pinot Noirs, from the same vintage:
  1. *Carneros Pinot Noir*
  2. *Oregon Pinot Noir*

California Zinfandel
Two Zinfandels, from the same vintage:
  3. *Sonoma Zinfandel*
  4. *Napa Zinfandel*

American Merlot
Two Merlots, compared, from the same vintage:
  5. *Washington State Merlot*
  6. *Napa Merlot*

California Cabernet Sauvignon
One wine, tasted alone:
7. *Napa Valley Cabernet Sauvignon* (medium style and medium price)

California Cabernet Sauvignons
Three wines, compared (blind tasting):
  8, 9, 10. *Three different vintages, three different price ranges, or three different California wine regions*

Aged Cabernet Sauvignon
One wine (more than 8 years old), tasted alone:
  11. *Napa Valley Cabernet Sauvignon*

THE WINES OF SPAIN & ITALY

UNDERSTANDING THE WINES OF SPAIN ❋ RIOJA ❋ RIBERA DEL DUERO ❋ PENEDÈS ❋ PRIORAT ❋ THE WHITE WINES OF SPAIN ❋ UNDERSTANDING THE RED WINES OF ITALY ❋ TUSCANY ❋ PIEDMONT ❋ VENETO ❋ OTHER IMPORTANT ITALIAN REGIONS

UNDERSTANDING THE WINES OF SPAIN

S PAIN HAS THOUSANDS of years of grape growing and winemaking history and ranks as the world's third largest producer of wine, after France and Italy, but Spain also has more acres of grapevines than any other country on earth—nearly 3 million!

Since joining the European Union in 1986, Spain has benefited from an infusion of capital into its vineyards and wineries. Modern technology, including stainless steel fermenters and new trellis systems, has helped create outstanding wines from all of its wine regions. To offset the dry climate and frequent droughts, especially in the center and south of the country, irrigating grapevines became legal in 1996, which has increased both the quality and volume of Spain's wine production.

Spain has nearly **800 DIFFERENT WINERIES**, but about 80 percent of the production comes from just a handful of companies.

AALTO
2005   RIBERA DEL DUERO
DENOMINACIÓN DE ORIGEN

OTHER WINE-PRODUCING AREAS OF SPAIN INCLUDE

Bierzo

Castilla-La Mancha

Jumilla

Navarra

Toro

***GRENACHE* IS THE FRENCH NAME** of Garnacha, a Spanish grape brought to France during the Avignon Papacy.

FINCA means "estate" or "farm."

Vinos de Pagos means that the wine comes from **A SINGLE ESTATE.**

The word *joven* occasionally appears on a wine label, indicating that the wine is unoaked or slightly oaked and should be **DRUNK "YOUNG."**

More than 600 grape varieties grow here, but you'll most likely find these in a wine store or restaurant:

NATIVE VARIETIES		INTERNATIONAL VARIETIES	
WHITE	RED	WHITE	RED
ALBARIÑO VERDEJO MACABEO (VIURA)	TEMPRANILLO (TINTO FINO) GARNACHA MONASTRELL CARIÑENA	CHARDONNAY SAUVIGNON BLANC	CABERNET SAUVIGNON MERLOT SYRAH

Spain established its Denominación de Origen (DO) laws in 1970 and revised them in 1982. Similar to the AOC laws of France and Italy's DOC, Spain's DO laws control a region's boundaries, grape varieties, winemaking practices, yield per acre, and most importantly the aging of the wine before it can be released. Today Spain has 69 DO regions, including 2 higher-level Denominación de Origen Calificada (DOC) regions, Rioja and Priorat.

Here are the most important regions along with the most important grapes grown there:

REGION	VARIETY
RIOJA	TEMPRANILLO
RIBERA DEL DUERO	TINTO FINO
PENEDÈS	MACABEO, CABERNET SAUVIGNON, CARIÑENA, GARNACHA
PRIORAT	GARNACHA, CARIÑENA
RUEDA	VERDEJO
RÍAS BAIXAS	ALBARIÑO
JEREZ (SHERRY)	PALOMINO

You'll become a Sherry expert in the next class, so we'll set aside Jerez for now and start with Rioja, which lies in northern Spain, not far from the French border.

RIOJA

Rioja lies fewer than 200 miles to the southwest of Bordeaux, which has influenced Rioja winemaking since the 1800s. During the 1870s, the phylloxera blight, traveling from north to south, arrived in Bordeaux and nearly destroyed the wine industry there. Many Bordeaux landowners and winemakers relocated to Rioja, still blight-free, for the similar climate and growing conditions. As they established their own vineyards and wineries, they affected how Spaniards made Rioja, an influence still apparent today.

Despite a surge in diverse and interesting wines from elsewhere in Spain, Rioja still reigns as the country's principal red wine region, offering both quality and quantity to match the world's best. Today the region has more than 150,000 acres of grapevines, 41 percent of those planted over the last ten years. Rioja continues to innovate within its traditional style and offers a tremendous range of quality at price points appealing to both beginners and collectors. The new, emerging style is bigger and more concentrated. Wineries making this style include Allende, Palacios, Remelluri, Remirez de Ganuza, and Remondo.

The primary red grapes used in Rioja wines are

Tempranillo   Garnacha

but the grape variety doesn't always appear on wine labels. There's no official classification system for Rioja; the three quality levels are:

Crianza   Released after two years of aging, at least one in oak. Cost: $.

Reserva   Released after three years of aging, at least one in oak. Cost: $$.

Gran Reserva   Released after five to seven years of aging, at least two in oak. Cost: $$$.

CRIANZA

RESERVA

GRAN RESERVA

Bodegas Dinastia Vivanco in Briones, Rioja, is the world's **BEST WINE MUSEUM.** If you go, spend the day—it's that good!

CHOOSING A RIOJA WINE

All you need to know is the quality level you want and the reputation of the Rioja winemaker or shipper. That's it! You may also know a Rioja wine by its proprietary name. Look for these bodegas, or wineries, along with some of their better-known proprietary names.

Baron de Ley

Bodegas Bretón

Bodegas Dinastía Vivanco

Bodegas Lan

Bodegas Montecillo

Bodegas Muga (Muga Reserva, Prado Enea, Torre Muga)

Bodegas Remírez de Ganuza

Bodegas Riojanas (Monte Real, Viña Albina)

Bodegas Roda

Bodegas Tobía

Contino

CVNE (Imperial, Viña Real)

El Coto

Finca Allende

Finca Valpiedra

La Rioja Alta (Viña Alberdi, Viña Ardanza)

López de Heredía

Marqués de Cáceres

Marqués de Murrieta

Marqués de Riscal

Martínez Bujanda
  (Conde de Valdemar)

Palacios Remondo

Remelluri

Señorio de San Vicente

Ysios

Three of the best American importers of Spanish wine are Steve Metzler (Classical Wines), Jorge Ordoñez (Fine Estates from Spain), and Eric Solomon (European Cellars).

– BEST VINTAGES OF RIOJA –

| 1994* | 1995* | 2001** | 2004** | 2005** | 2006 | 2008 |
| 2009* | 2010** | 2011* | 2012* | 2013 | 2014 | 2015 |

* EXCEPTIONAL VINTAGE   ** EXTRAORDINARY VINTAGE

Former winemaker at Vega Sicilia Mariano Garcia and his business partner, Javier Zaccagnini, founded Aalto in 1999 and make just two wines: Aalto and Aalto PS. **ADD BOTH TO YOUR WINE CELLAR.**

The word *cosecha*, which means "harvest" or "vintage," appears on some labels. It also can indicate a wine that has little barrel aging. Producers often use it for their **MODERN-STYLE WINES.**

RIBERA DEL DUERO

The major wine grapes used in Ribera del Duero are

Cabernet Sauvignon	Merlot
Garnacha	Tempranillo
Malbec	

When I wrote the first edition of this book, cooperatives made most Ribera del Duero wines—except Spain's most famous winery, Bodegas Vega Sicilia, which has been making wine since the 1860s. But one wine does not a region make. Then, in the 1980s, Pesquera wine received great reviews from the wine press, helping to stimulate quality wine production in the region and setting the stage for astounding growth. Today Ribera del Duero has more than 270 wineries, covering nearly 50,000 acres, and a new generation of quality winemakers is emerging. Aging requirements are the same here as in Rioja (Crianza, Reserva, Gran Reserva).

These are my favorite Ribera del Duero producers:

Aalto	Bodegas Matarromera	Montecastro
Abadía Retuerta	Condado de Haza	Pago de los
Alejandro Fernandez	Dominio de Pingus	Capellanes
Arzuaga	García Figuero	Pesquera
Bodegas Emilio Moro	Hacienda Monasterio	Vega Sicilia
Bodegas Felix Callejo	Legaris	Viña Mayo
Bodegas Los Astrales		

> **– BEST VINTAGES OF RIBERA DEL DUERO –**
> 1996* 2001** 2004** 2005** 2009*
> 2010** 2011 2012** 2013* 2014 2015*
> *EXCEPTIONAL VINTAGE **EXTRAORDINARY VINTAGE

PENEDÈS

Just outside Barcelona, the Penedès region produces the famous sparkling wine called Cava, protected—like Champagne in France—under its own DO.

These are the major grapes used in wines from Penedès:

CAVA	RED	WHITE
CHARDONNAY	CABERNET SAUVIGNON	CHARDONNAY
MACABEO	GARNACHA	MACABEO
PARELLADA	MERLOT	PARELLADA
XAREL-LO	TEMPRANILLO	RIESLING GEWÜRZTRAMINER

The best-known Spanish sparkling wines in America are Freixenet and Codorníu, two of the biggest producers of bottle-fermented sparkling wines in the world. (The Ferrer family, who own Freixenet, also make Segura Viudas Cava, which you also may have seen in wine stores.) For traditional-method sparkling wines, these are very reasonably priced.

Penedès also has a reputation for high-quality table wine. The most famous wine from the Torres family, a name synonymous with quality, is Gran Coronas Black Label, made with 100 percent Cabernet Sauvignon. It's rare and expensive, but they also produce a full range of fine wines in all price categories.

My favorite Penedès producers include:

Albet i Noya   Marques de Monistrol
Jean Leon   Torres (Mas La Plana)

PRIORAT, PAST AND PRESENT
1995: 16 wineries
2016: 102 wineries

One of Spain's wine mavericks, Alvaro Palacios started at his family's winery in Rioja and has expanded into the Priorat and Bierzo, two regions that he helped revitalize. His L'Ermita Priorat is **ONE OF SPAIN'S MOST HIGHLY RATED AND EXPENSIVE WINES.** For better value, try the Finca Dofi. For the best value, Les Terrasses.

Priorat wines must have a minimum of **13.5 PERCENT ALCOHOL.**

PRIORAT

South of Penedès lies Priorat, a region that epitomizes the Spanish wine renaissance. Carthusian monks farmed vineyards here for more than 800 years until the government auctioned their land to local farmers in the early 1800s. In the late 1800s, phylloxera forced most farmers to stop planting grapes, and many began cultivating hazelnuts and almonds instead. By 1910, cooperatives were making most of the wine here, and until about 25 years ago Priorat was known mostly for producing sacramental wine.

In the late 1980s, some of the most well-known Spanish wine producers, including René Barbier and Alvaro Palacios, revived the old Carthusian vineyards. Today Priorat produces some of the best red wine in Spain, as attested by the Spanish government, which awarded Priorat the highest status of DO in 2003. Priorat vineyards lie between an altitude of 1,000 and 3,000 feet above sea level. Most are too steep to maneuver mechanical equipment, so growers use mules—just like the old days!

These are the grapes used to make red Priorat wines:

NATIVE VARIETIES	INTERNATIONAL VARIETIES
GARNACHA CARIÑENA	CABERNET SAUVIGNON MERLOT SYRAH

Because of extremely low yields and demand, it's hard to find an inexpensive Priorat. The best bottles easily sell for more than $100 each.

These are my favorite Priorat producers:

Alvaro Palacios	Clos Martinet	Mas La Mola
Clos Daphne	Clos Mogador	Pasanau
Clos de L'Obac	La Conreria D'Scala Dei	Vall Llach
Clos Erasmus	Mas Igneus	

– BEST VINTAGES OF PRIORAT –
2001** 2004** 2005** 2006* 2007 2008
2009* 2010** 2011 2012 2013 2014 2015*
*EXCEPTIONAL VINTAGE **EXTRAORDINARY VINTAGE*

THE WHITE WINES OF SPAIN

RUEDA

The wines of Rueda, northwest of Madrid, have been well known for centuries, but until the 1970s Ruedas were made with the Palomino grape and fortified in a style similar to Sherry. The new style of Rueda white wine comes from Verdejo, Viura, and occasionally Sauvignon Blanc grapes and tastes dry, fruity, and fresh.

RÍAS BAIXAS

Near Santiago de Compostela in Galicia (north of Portugal), Rías Baixas also began making outstanding white wines in the 1980s. More than 90 percent of Rías Baixas wine comes from the Albariño grape.

5 BEST VALUE RED WINES OF SPAIN UNDER $30

Alvaro Palacios Camins del Priorat • Bodegas Monticello Reserva • El Coto Crianza • Pesquera Tinto Crianza • Marqués de Cáceres Crianza

See page 316–317 for a complete list.

TEST YOUR KNOWLEDGE of the wines of Spain by trying the quiz on page 339.

——— **FURTHER READING** ———

The New and Classical Wines of Spain by Jeremy Watson

The New Spain by John Radford

The Peñín Guide to Spanish Wine (annual) edited by José Peñín

Rioja and Northwest Spain by Jesus Barquin, Luis Gutierrez, and Victor de la Serna

UNDERSTANDING THE RED WINES OF ITALY

More than **ONE MILLION GROWERS** own the 2 million acres of vineyards in Italy.

MY FAVORITE WINE-PRODUCING REGIONS IN ITALY INCLUDE

Veneto (17.7%)

Piedmont (17.1%)

Tuscany (10.7%)

MORE THAN 300 DOC WINES account for 20 percent of Italy's total wine production.

Of all Italian DOC wines, **60 PERCENT ARE RED.**

ITALY HAS BEEN making wine for more than 3,000 years, and today it ranks as one of the world's largest producers. (France and Italy vie every year for the distinction of largest.) Grapevines grow everywhere here. As one retailer of fine Italian wine once told me, "There is no country. Italy is one vast vineyard from north to south."

From serious tasting to everyday drinking, Italian wines are good for any occasion. The country has 20 wine regions, 96 provinces, and more than 2,000 different grape varieties. But don't worry. To master the basics, concentrate on the 3 major regions below, along with their major red-grape varieties, and you'll soon have Italy in the palm of your hand.

REGION	TUSCANY	PIEDMONT	VENETO
VARIETY	SANGIOVESE	NEBBIOLO	CORVINA

Like the French AOC, the Denominazione di Origine Controllata (DOC) defines numerous aspects of Italian wine production, but the biggest difference between the two is that Italy's DOC mandates aging requirements. The DOC laws went into effect in 1963 and govern:

- regional boundaries
- allowable grape varieties
- grape percentages
- wine produced per acre
- alcohol content
- aging requirements

ITALY

TRENTINO-ALTO ADIGE

FRIULI-VENEZIA GIULIA

LOMBARDY

VENETO

PIEDMONT

TUSCANY

UMBRIA

Adriatic Sea

ABRUZZI

Rome

Tyrrhenian Sea

CAMPANIA

Mediterranean Sea

SICILY

Ionian Sea

| 0 | Miles | 100 | 200 |

| 0 | Kilometers | 200 |

DOCG WINES

TUSCANY

Brunello di Montalcino

Carmignano

Chianti

Chianti Classico

Elba Aleatico Passito

Montecucco Sangiovese

Morellino di Scansano
Vernaccia di San Gimignano

Vino Nobile di Montepulciano

PIEDMONT

Acqui or Brachetto d'Acqui

Alta Langa

Barbera d'Asti

Barbera del Monteferrato Superiore

Barbaresco

Barolo

Dolcetta Diano d'Alba

Dolcetto di Dogliani Superiore

Dolcetto di Ovada Superiore

Erbaluce di Caluso

Gattinara

Gavi or Cortese di Gavi

Ghemme

Moscato d'Asti / Alba

Roero

Ruche di Castagnole Monferrato

VENETO

Amarone della Valpolicella

Bardolino Superiore

Conegliano Valdobbiadene-Prosecco

Recioto della Valpolicella

Recioto di Gambellara

Recioto di Soave

Soave Superiore

During the 1980s, the Ministry of Agriculture took quality control a step further by adding the higher-ranking DOCG. The G stands for *Garantita* and means that tasting-control boards guarantee the stylistic authenticity of a wine. A third classification, Indicazione Geografica Tipica (IGT) indicates that a wine doesn't meet DOC requirements, but many of these wines drink at a higher level than DOC table wine.

ITALIAN WINE QUALITY LEVELS

DOCG (73 denominations)

DOC (352 denominations)

} 37% of Italian wine

IGT (118 denominations) } 33% of Italian wine

Vino da Tavola (table wine) } 30% of Italian wine

As a comparison, 30 years ago table wine represented 90 percent of all Italian wine.

ITALIAN WINE NAMES

For Bordeaux, most often you see the name of a château, and you look for the grape variety on California bottles. But in Italy, different winemaking regions have different ways of naming their wines: by grape variety, district or village, or a proprietary name. Note the examples below.

EXAMPLES OF GRAPE VARIETY	EXAMPLES OF DISTRICT OR VILLAGE	EXAMPLES OF PROPRIETARY NAMES
BARBERA	CHIANTI	TIGNANELLO
NEBBIOLO	BAROLO	SASSICAIA
PINOT GRIGIO	BARBARESCO	ORNELLAIA
SANGIOVESE	MONTALCINO	SUMMUS

TUSCANY

Tuscan winemaking has a long history, dating back nearly 3,000 years to the Etruscans, who lived here in pre-Roman times. Chianti is a wine region of Tuscany and also the most well known of all its wines. The name "Chianti" first appears in records from A.D. 700. Brolio, a major producer, has been making it since 1141. More than 30 generations of the family have tended to the vineyards and made the wine.

CHIANTI

Current DOCG rules require winemakers to use at least 80 percent Sangiovese to produce Chianti, but the rules also encourage the use of other grapes by allowing an unprecedented 20 percent of nontraditional grapes (Cabernet Sauvignon, Merlot, Syrah, etc.). Over the last quarter century, this shift and better vineyard development and winemaking techniques have improved the quality and reputation of Chianti greatly.

ONLY ONE-FIFTH of all Chianti is Chianti Classico Riserva.

The different levels of Chianti are:

Chianti   The basic level. Cost: $.

Chianti Classico   From the inner historic district of Chianti. Cost: $$.

Chianti Classico Riserva   From a Classico area and aged at least two years and three months. Cost: $$$$.

Separate DOCG requirements pertain to Chianti Classico and Classico Riserva, and many producers of these wines use 100 percent Sangiovese to set themselves apart.

CLASSICO: All the vineyards lie in the historic part of the region.

SUPERIORE: Higher levels of alcohol and longer aging.

RUFFINO

RISERVA DUCALE®

Chianti Classico

DENOMINAZIONE DI ORIGINE CONTROLLATA E GARANTITA

Riserva

RUFFINO

CHOOSING A CHIANTI

Chianti varies considerably in style—depending on the blend of grapes—so first find the style that you like best. Then always buy from a shipper or producer with a good, reliable reputation.

Some quality Chianti producers include:

Antinori	Castello di Ama	Montepeloso
Antinori Tenuta Belvedere	Castello di Bossi	Nozzole
Badia a Coltibuono	Fattoria di Magliano	Petra
Belguardo	Fattoria le Pupille	Podere
Brolio	Fontodi	Grattamacco
Capannelle	Frescobaldi	Querciabella
Castello Banfi	Le Macchiole	Ricasoli
Castello del Terriccio	Melini	Ruffino
	Michele Satta	Tenuta San Guid
	Monsanto	

OTHER TUSCAN WINES

Tuscany produces many other types of wine, but you should know Brunello di Montalcino, Vino Nobile di Montepulciano, Carmignano, and the Super Tuscans from Bolgeri in Maremma. The first three are DOCG, and, as we'll see, the last isn't—for an interesting reason.

BRUNELLO DI MONTALCINO

The stunningly beautiful village of Montalcino sits atop a hill surrounded by 5,000 acres of vineyards. The wines come from 100 percent Brunello grapes (Sangiovese) and rank among the best in the world. This is one of my absolute favorite red wines. Brunello di Montalcino received DOCG status in 1980. Beginning with the 1995 vintage, Brunellos must age in oak for at least two years, instead of the previous three. The result? A fruitier, more accessible wine. In 2008, Brunello winemakers voted to maintain 100 percent Sangiovese for their wines, not blending it with any other varieties. If you buy a good Brunello, keep in mind that it probably needs five to ten

Because of its limited supply, Brunello di Montalcino is sometimes very expensive. For **ONE OF THE BEST VALUES IN TUSCAN RED WINE,** look for Rosso di Montalcino and Rosso di Montepulciano, especially in great years.

WINERIES		ACRES
964	Chianti Classico	18,000
208	Brunello de Montalcino	5,189
75	Vino Nobile di Montepulciano	3,025

years of additional aging before it reaches peak drinkability. More than 150 producers grow Brunello, and my favorites include:

Altesino	Col d'Orcia	Marchesi de
Barbi	Collosorbo	Frescobaldi
Capanna	Constanti	Poggio Antico
Caparzo	Gaja	Poggio il Castellare
Carpineto	La Fuga	Soldera
Castelgiocondo	La Poderina	Uccelliera
Castello Banfi	Lisini	
Ciacci Piccolomini	Livio Sassetti	
d'Aragona		

VINO NOBILE DI MONTEPULCIANO

This "noble wine from Montepulciano" village comes primarily (at least 70 percent) from the Sangiovese varietal known as *Prugnolo gentile*. Like Montalcino, Montepulciano is a must-visit town for wine-loving tourists. The region has more than 75 wineries and more than 3,000 acres of vines. My favorite producers include:

Avignonesi	Fassati	Poggio alla Sala
Bindella	Fattoria del Cerro	Poliziano
Boscarelli	Icario	Salcheto
Dei	La Braccesca	

CARMIGNANO

This smaller region has been producing great wines since Roman times, but it has become increasingly popular in the last 20 years. DOCG regulations hold that Carmignano must contain at least 50 percent Sangiovese, 10–20 percent Cabernet Sauvignon or Cabernet Franc, plus other indigenous grapes. The wine also must age for at least 3 years. For Carmignano, look for:

Artimino	Poggiolo	Villa di Capezzana

Many wine producers in Italy are now making wines from **CABERNET SAUVIGNON, MERLOT, AND CHARDONNAY.**

THE SUPER TUSCANS

Sometimes called the Wild West because of its landscapes and winemaking, the Maremma wine region lies in southern Tuscany, and Bolgheri is one of Maremma's principal wine villages. Bolgheri's vineyards cover more than 400 acres. Grapes have grown here since the nineteenth century, but, like Carmignano, Bolgheri has risen to international prominence in the last 30 years. Unlike Brunello and Vino Nobile, Bolgheri wines can be made with red Bordeaux grapes, such as Cabernet Sauvignon, Cabernet Franc, and Merlot. Sometimes it also includes Syrah, Petit Verdot, and of course the traditional Sangiovese.

Decades ago, the DOC didn't allow the use of certain grapes, such as Cabernet Sauvignon, and in the 1970s, as was the case in Bordeaux, the market for Chianti wines was suffering. To skirt DOC regulations and make better wines—as we saw California winemakers do—Italian vintners created their own style of wine simply called *vino da tavola*, or table wine. Today these wines have a world-class reputation and have become known as the Super Tuscans that you've probably seen on wine lists at good Italian restaurants.

My favorite producers of Bolgheri / Maremma include:

Ca' Marcanda	Le Macchiole	Petra
Cabreo Il Borgo	Luce	Sassicaia
Castello del Terriccio	Masseto	Solaia
Excelsus	Montepeloso	Summus
Fattoria le Pupille	Olmaia	Tignanello
	Ornellaia	Tua Rita

```
– BEST RECENT VINTAGES OF CHIANTI CLASSICO –
    2006**  2007**  2008   2009   2010**  2011*
       2012*   2013*   2014   2015*

– BEST RECENT VINTAGES OF BRUNELLO DI MONTALCINO –
    2004**  2005   2006**  2007**  2008   2010**
       2011*   2012*   2013   2014   2015*

– BEST RECENT VINTAGES OF BOLGHERI MAREMMA –
    2006**  2007**  2008**  2009   2010**  2011*
       2012*   2013*   2014   2015*

        * EXCEPTIONAL VINTAGE   ** EXTRAORDINARY VINTAGE
```

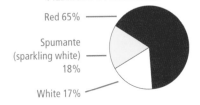

BRICCO: a hillside vineyard.

PIEDMONT'S PRODUCTION

Red 65%

Spumante
(sparkling white)
18%

White 17%

PIEDMONT

Some of the biggest and best red wines in the world come from Piedmont. The major grapes that grow there are:

Barbera	Dolcetto	Nebbiolo
(41,000 acres)	(16,000 acres)	(9,000 acres)

Two of the best DOCG Tuscan wines come from the villages of Barbaresco and Barolo. These "heavyweight" wines come from the Nebbiolo variety and have the fullest style and a high alcohol content. Be careful when you try to match young vintages of these wines with your dinner because they may overpower the food.

	BARBARESCO versus BAROLO	
GRAPE	NEBBIOLO	NEBBIOLO
MINIMUM ALCOHOL CONTENT	12.5%	12.5%
STYLE	LIGHTER, BUT FINE AND ELEGANT	MORE COMPLEX, MORE BODY
MINIMUM AGING	TWO YEARS, ONE IN WOOD	THREE YEARS, ONE IN WOOD
DEFINITION OF "RISERVA"	AGED FOUR YEARS	AGED FIVE YEARS

The entire production of Barolo and Barbaresco (11 million bottles a year) equals **ONE MEDIUM-SIZE CALIFORNIA WINERY!**

The United Nations added nine Piedmont villages to the list of **UNESCO WORLD HERTIAGE SITES,** including Barolo and Barbaresco.

Another great Piedmont wine is called **GATTINARA.** Look for the Antoniolo Reservas.

Three reasons to visit **PIEDMONT IN THE FALL:** the harvest, the food, and the white truffles.

GREAT OLDER VINTAGES of Piedmont: 1982, 1985, 1988, 1989, 1990

My favorite Piedmont producers include:

A. Conterno	G. Conterno	Pio Cesare
Antonio Vallana	Gaja	Pira
B. Giacosa	La Spinetta	Produttori del
Borgogno	Luciano Sandrone	Barbaresco
C. Rinaldi	M. Chiarlo	Prunotto
Ceretto	Marcarini	Renato Ratti
Conterno Fantino	Marchesi di Barolo	Roberto Voerzio
Domenico Clerico	Marchesi di Gresy	Schiavenza
Erbaluce di Caluso	Mascarello e Figlio	Vietti
Fontanafredda	Paolo Scavino	

For aging, Giuseppe Colla of Prunotto advises that, for a good vintage, you set aside a Barbaresco for at least four years and a Barolo for six before drinking. In a great vintage, age a Barbaresco for six and a Barolo for eight. Patience is a virtue—especially with wine. Also keep in mind that many Piedmont wines have changed over the last decade. Past wines were more tannic and difficult to appreciate when young, but many today are much easier to drink.

```
– BEST VINTAGES OF PIEDMONT WINES –
      1996**  1997*  1998*  1999*  2000**
2001**  2004**  2005*  2006*  2007*  2008*  2009*
   2010   2011   2012*  2013*  2014   2015*
      * EXCEPTIONAL VINTAGE   ** EXTRAORDINARY VINTAGE
```

VENETO

This is one of Italy's largest wine-producing regions. Even if you don't recognize the name immediately, you've probably had a Venetian wine at some point, such as a Valpolicella, Bardolino, or Soave. All three are consistent, easy to drink, and don't need aging. They don't match the quality of a Brunello di Montalcino or a Barolo, but they're very good table wines that fit everyone's budget. The best of the three is Valpolicella. Look for Valpolicella Superiore made using the *ripasso* method, which adds the grape skins from Amarone wine back to Valpolicella, giving it more alcohol and flavor. Easy-to-find Veneto producers are:

Allegrini	Folonari	Santa Sofia
Anselmi	Quintarelli	Zenato
Bolla		

AMARONE

The word "Amarone" derives from *amaro*, meaning "bitter," and *-one* (OH-nay), meaning "big." It's a type of Valpolicella wine made by allowing the ripest grapes (Corvina, Rondinella, and Molinara) from the top of each bunch to raisinate on straw mats—a process similar to making French Sauternes or German Trockenbeerenauslese. A key difference, though, is that Amarone makers ferment most of the sugar, bringing the alcohol content to 14–16 percent.

My favorite producers of Amarone include:

Allegrini	Nicolis	Tommasi
Bertani	Quintarelli	Zenato
Masi	Tedeschi	

– BEST VINTAGES OF AMARONE –

1990* 1993 1995* 1996 1997* 1998 2000* 2001
2002* 2003* 2004 2005 2006 2008* 2009 2010
2011 2012* 2013* 2014 2015*

* EXCEPTIONAL VINTAGE

OTHER IMPORTANT ITALIAN REGIONS

All 20 of Italy's wine regions produce good or great wine, so it's worth taking a quick look at the lesser-known regions, which I've broken down into the predominant grapes that grow there, the best wines to try, and some of my favorite producers that make them.

REGION	GRAPE	WINE	PRODUCERS
ABRUZZI	MONTEPULCIANO	MONTEPULCIANO D'ABRUZZO	ELIO MONTI EMIDIO PEPE LA VALENTINA MASCIARELLI
CAMPANIA	AGLIANICO FIANO GRECO SANGIOVESE	GRECO DI TUFO FIANO DI AVELLINO TAURASI	FEUDI DI SAN GREGORIO MASTRO- BERARDINO MOLETTIERA MONTEVETRANO MUSTILLI VILLA MATILDE
FRIULI-VENEZIA GIULIA	PINOT BIANCO PINOT GRIGIO CHARDONNAY SAUVIGNON BLANC		LIVIO FELLUGA MARCO FELLUGA MARIO SCHIOPETTO VIE DI ROMANS
LOMBARDY	NEBBIOLO, TREBBIANO	FRANCIACORTA (SPARKLING) LUGANA	**SPARKLING PRODUCERS:** BELLAVISTA CA' DEL BOSCO
		VALTELLINA (GRUMELLO, SASSELLA, INFERNO, VALGELLA)	**VALTELLINA PRODUCERS:** CONTI SERTOLI FAY NINO NEGRI RAINOLDI

REGION	GRAPE	WINE	PRODUCERS
SICILY	**RED GRAPES:** CABERNET SAUVIGNON MERLOT NERO D'AVOLA (CALABRESE) SYRAH **WHITE GRAPES:** CATARRATTO CHARDONNAY GRECANICO INZOLIA MALVASIA MOSCATO	MARSALA MOSCATO DI PANTELLERIA NERO D'AVOLA	DE BARTOLI, DUCA DI SALAPARUTA (DUCA ENRICO) GULFI MORGANTE PALARI PLANETA RAPITALÀ REGALEALI (ROSSO DEL CONTE) SANTA ANASTASIA
TRENTINO-ALTO ADIGE	**WHITE GRAPES:** PINOT BIANCO PINOT GRIGIO CHARDONNAY SAUVIGNON GEWÜRZTRAMINER **RED GRAPES:** CABERNET FRANC CABERNET SAUVIGNON LAGREIN MERLOT		ALOIS LAGEDE CANTINA DI TERLANO COLTERENZIO FERRARI FORADORI H. LUN ROTALIANO TEROLDEGO TIEFENBRUNNER TRAMIN
UMBRIA	TREBBIANO SAGRANTINO SANGIOVESE MERLOT	ORVIETO SAGRANTINO DI MONTEFALCO TORGIANO ROSSO RISERVA	ARNALDO CAPRAI CASTELLO DELLE REGINE LUNGAROTTI PAOLO BEA

TRI-VENETO, which includes Trentino, Alto-Adige, and Friuli. Some of the best white wines of Italy come from those regions.

La Friuli-Venezia Giulia and Trentino-Alto Adige, the wines are **IDENTIFIED BY PRODUCER AND GRAPE VARIETY** rather than a specific wine name.

PINOT GRIGIO is a white-grape variety found in Alsace, France, where it's called Pinot Gris. It also grows with success in Oregon and California.

The most planted white varietal in Piedmont is **MOSCATO** (25,000 acres).

In Italy, consumption of bottled water and beer are both increasing, while **WINE CONSUMPTION IS DECREASING**.

ITALIAN WHITES

You'll notice that I don't discuss Italian white wines in this class. Why? Take a look at the most popular white wines: Soave, Frascati, and Pinot Grigio. Most of them retail for less than $15, and most Italian whites simply don't match the quality of Italian reds. That said, plantings of international white varieties, such as Chardonnay and Sauvignon Blanc, along with some of the better indigenous grapes, are starting to elevate the quality of Italian white wines. For great Italian whites, try Gavi from Piedmont and wines from the Friuli region.

FORTY YEARS LATER IN ITALY

For the Italians, wine used to be an everyday affair, like salt and pepper, to enhance the taste of food. Since then, winemaking has become a business, and Italian winemakers have shifted from making casual-drinking wines to better-made wines that prove much more marketable internationally. They've done so by using modern technology, updated vineyard management, and modern vinification procedures. They also have experimented with non-traditional grape varieties, such as Cabernet Sauvignon and Merlot. Remember, we're not talking about California; Italy has literally *thousands* of years of traditions that are changing. Vintners there have had to unlearn winemaking techniques that go back dozens of generations in order to make better wines for the export market.

The prices of Italian wines have increased tremendously as well over the last 25 years—not good news for consumers. Some of the wines from Italy have become among the most expensive in the world. Many certainly are worth it, but the value to the consumer isn't the same as it was 40 years ago.

SINGLE-VINEYARD LABELING is one of the newest trends in Italy.

5 BEST VALUE ITALIAN WINES UNDER $30

Allegrini Valpolicella Classico • Castello Banfi Toscana Centine • Michele Chiarlo Barbera d'Asti • Morgante Nero d'Avola • Taurino Salice Salentino

See page 313–314 for a complete list.

WINE AND FOOD

In Italy, wine is made to go with food. No meal is served without it. Take it from these experts.

"**Chianti** with prosciutto, chicken, pasta, and of course pizza. Pair a **Chianti Classico Riserva** with a hearty prime-rib dinner or a steak."

—Ambrogio Folonari of Ruffino

"A **Chianti** is good with all meat dishes, but I save the **Brunello** for 'stronger' dishes, such as steak, wild boar, pheasant, and other game, as well as Pecorino Toscano cheese."

—Ezio Rivella of Castello Banfi

"**Barbaresco** with meat and veal, and also with mature cheeses that are not too strong, such as Emmenthaler and Fontina. Avoid Parmesan and goat cheese when you have a Barbaresco. If you're having a **Barolo**, my favorite is roast lamb."

—Angelo Gaja

"I enjoy light-style **Dolcetto** with all first courses and all white meat—chicken and veal especially—but not fish. The wine doesn't stand up well to spicy sauce, but it's great with tomato sauce and pasta."

—Giuseppe Colla of Prunotto

"**Barbera** and **Dolcetto** are good with chicken and lighter foods. However, **Barolo** and **Barbaresco** need to be served with heavier dishes. Better yet, brasato al Barolo—wine-braised meat, such as pheasant, duck, or wild rabbit. For a special dish, try risotto al Barolo (rice cooked with Barolo). When serving wine with dessert, strawberries or peaches with **Dolcetto**."

—Renato Ratti

"With young **Chianti**, roast chicken, squab, or pasta with meat sauce. To complement an older **Chianti**, a wide pasta with meat braised in Chianti, pheasant or other game, wild boar, or roast beef.

—Lorenza de'Medici of
Badia a Coltibuono

"I enjoy **Chianti** with the grilled foods for which Tuscany is famous, especially its bistecca alla Fiorentina, but also poultry and even hamburgers. With **Chianti Classico Riserva**, wild boar and fine aged Parmesan cheese. The wine is a perfect match for roast-beef, roast turkey, lamb, or veal."

—Piero Antinori

"Piedmontese wines show better with food than in a tasting."
—Angelo Gaja

"When you're having Italian wines, you must not taste the wine alone. You must have them with food."
—Giuseppe Colla of Prunotto

When **DRINKING THE RED WINES OF PIEDMONT**, start with the lighter-style Barbera and Dolcetto, move to the fuller-bodied Barbaresco, and then you can appreciate a Barolo fully. As vintner Renato Ratti said, "Barolo is the wine of arrival."

TEST YOUR KNOWLEDGE of the wines of Italy by trying the quiz on page 339.

—— **FURTHER READING** ——

Italian Wine by Victor Hazan

Italian Wines for Dummies by Mary Ewing Mulligan and Ed McCarthy

The Simon & Schuster Pocket Guide to Italian Wines by Burton Anderson

Vino Italiano by Joseph Bastianich and David Lynch

Wine Atlas of Italy by Burton Anderson

❦ GUIDED TASTING ❧

Many people know something about French or American wines but very little about Italian or Spanish wines, so this tasting is all about discovery and finding new wine styles made from grapes, such as Sangiovese, Nebbiolo, and Tempranillo. For the Piedmont tasting, following the advice of Renato Ratti, you'll start with the lighter-style Barbera, move to the fuller-bodied Barbaresco, and then you will appreciate a Barolo fully as well as the Amarone.

THE WINES

Rioja
Three wines, compared:
1. *Crianza*
2. *Reserva*
3. *Gran Reserva*

Tuscany
Three wines, compared:
4. *Chianti Classico Riserva*
5. *Vino Nobile di Montelpulciano*
6. *Brunello di Montalcino*

Piedmont
Three wines, compared:
7. *Barbera or Dolcetto*
8. *Barbaresco*
9. *Barolo*

Veneto
One wine, tasted alone:
10. *Amarone*

CHAMPAGNE, SHERRY & PORT

UNDERSTANDING SPARKLING AND FORTIFIED WINES ✳
CHAMPAGNE ✳ SHERRY ✳ PORT

UNDERSTANDING SPARKLING AND FORTIFIED WINES

HERE THE WINE school ends—on a happy note! What better way to celebrate than with Champagne?

Why group Champagne, Sherry, and Port together? They're all blended wines, and, as diverse as they are, you buy them by the reputation and reliability of the shipper, often known as a house, which takes responsibility for all phases of production. Moët & Chandon, for example, is one of the most well-known houses for Champagne; Pedro Domecq for Sherry; and Sandeman for Port.

Until around 1850, all Champagne was **SWEET**.

The balance of the fruit and acidity, together with the bubbles, makes **GOOD CHAMPAGNE.**

CHAMPAGNE

Champagne is a sparkling wine that everyone drinks on New Year's Eve, but it's so much more than that. It's France's northernmost winemaking region, an hour and a half northeast of Paris. That location is important because, in cooler, more northerly climates, including that of the Champagne region, grapes have a higher acidity than in most other regions. That's one reason that Champagne has its distinct taste. Acidity in Champagne not only imparts freshness to the wines, but it also increases their longevity.

The region consists of four main areas:

Marne Valley   **Côte des Blancs**   **Reims Mountain**   **Aube**

which together have 43,680 acres of vineyards. More than 20,000 growers sell to around 250 *négociants*, or shippers. Winemakers can use three grapes to produce Champagne:

Chardonnay 27%

Pinot Meunier 35%

Pinot Noir 38 %

In France, only sparkling wines from the Champagne region may be called Champagne. Some American producers use the name on their sparkling wine labels, but don't be fooled—or compare them with proper Champagnes.

The three major types of Champagne are:

Nonvintage/multiple vintage A blend of two or more harvests, 60 to 80 percent from current harvest and 20 to 40 percent from previous vintages.

Vintage From a single vintage.

"Prestige" cuvée From a single vintage with longer aging requirements.

Unlike most of the rest of the wine industry, each individual house decides whether to declare a vintage year, so not every year is a vintage. (See the end of this section for the best vintages.) Prestige Champagnes usually meet the following requirements to receive that designation:

- Best grapes from the highest-rated villages
- Made from only the first pressing of the grapes
- More bottle aging than nonvintage Champagnes
- From vintage years only
- Small quantities

MÉTHODE CHAMPENOISE

Champagne is made by a process called *méthode champenoise*. Outside Champagne, that method is called *méthode traditionnelle, método tradicional*, classic method, etc. The EU doesn't allow the designation of *méthode champenoise* for sparkling wines from outside the Champagne region. This is the process:

Harvest This usually takes place in late September or early October.

Pressing AOC regulations allow only two pressings of the grapes. Prestige cuvée Champagnes usually come exclusively from the first pressing. The taille, or second pressing, often is blended with the cuvée to make vintage and nonvintage Champagnes.

First fermentation In this step, the must becomes wine. Remember the formula:

Sugar + Yeast = Alcohol + Carbon Dioxide

More than 80 percent of the Champagnes produced are **NOT VINTAGE DATED.** This means they are blends of several years' wines.

Nonvintage Champagne is more typical of the **HOUSE STYLE** than vintage Champagne.

Vintage champagne **MUST CONTAIN 100 PERCENT** of that vintage year's harvest.

In 2011, Champagne had its **EARLIEST HARVEST** since 1822.

COMMON CHAMPAGNE AROMAS	
Apple	Yeast (bread dough)
Toast	Hazelnuts
Citrus	Walnuts

Most Champagnes ferment first in stainless steel tanks. The first fermentation takes two to three weeks and, because the carbon dioxide dissipates, produces still wines.

Blending This is the most important step in Champagne production. Each of the still wines comes from a single grape variety from a single village. Here the winemaker has many decisions to make, the three most important being:

1. Which of the three grapes to blend and in what proportions?
2. From which vineyards?
3. Which years or vintages to blend? Should the blend come from the wines of only the current harvest, or should several vintages be blended together?

Liqueur de tirage After blending, the winemaker adds this mixture of sugar and yeast, which begins the second fermentation. Then the wine goes into the bottle with a temporary cap.

Second fermentation In this fermentation, the carbon dioxide remains in the bottle, creating the bubbles. The second fermentation also creates natural sediment.

Aging The amount of time that the wine ages on its sediment largely determines its quality. Nonvintage champagnes must age for at least 15 months after bottling. Vintage Champagnes must age for at least three years after bottling.

Riddling The wine bottles now go into A-frame racks, necks down. The *remueur*, or riddler, goes through the racks, bottle by bottle, slightly turning each and gradually tipping it farther downward. After six to eight weeks, the bottle stands almost completely upside down, the sediment resting in the neck of the bottle. (Barbe-Nicole Ponsardin, widow—*veuve* in French—of François Clicquot, invented this process in 1816.)

Disgorging The top of the bottle goes into a supercooled brine solution to freeze it. A *dégorgeur* removes the temporary bottle cap, and, propelled by the carbon dioxide, out flies the frozen sediment.

DOM PÉRIGNON ages for six to eight years before releasing to market.

The Moët-Hennessy Group, responsible for the production of Dom Pérignon in France also, owns Domaine Chandon. In fact, **THE SAME WINEMAKER** flies to California to help make the Domaine Chandon blend.

CHAMPAGNE
BOLLINGER
R.D. 1985

Elaboré par Bollinger, Ay, France
Produce of France

alc.12% by vol.   EXTRA BRUT   750 ml
NM-121-001

"R.D." on a Champagne wine label means that the wine was **RECENTLY DISGORGED**.

Dosage Pronounced doh-SAZH, this mixture of wine and sugar, goes into the bottle after disgorging. At this point, the winemaker determines whether he or she wants a sweeter or a drier Champagne. These are the sweetness levels of Champagnes:

Brut nature	Extra brut	Brut	Extra sec/dry	Sec	Demi-sec	Doux
No sugar added	Very dry	Dry	Semidry	Semisweet	Sweet	Very sweet

Recorking A real cork replaces the temporary bottle cap. After that, a protective wire cage, called a *muselet*, goes around the neck of the bottle and holds a metal cap atop the cork.

As you can see, this method is laborious, intensive, and expensive, which is why Champagne frequently costs more than other quality wines, sparkling or otherwise. Because the contents are pressurized, the bottles also must be thicker and stronger than ordinary wine bottles, another additional cost.

DIFFERENT STYLES OF CHAMPAGNE

The general rule: The more white grapes in the blend, the lighter the style; the more red grapes, the fuller the style. Blanc de blanc Champagne comes from 100 percent Chardonnay grapes. Blanc de noir comes from 100 percent Pinot Noir. Some producers ferment their wines in wood. Bollinger ferments some of its portfolio this way, and Krug ferments all of its wines in this manner, which gives their Champagne fuller body and bouquet than if fermented in stainless steel.

New Champagne bottles are lighter by 7 percent and **MORE ENVIRONMENTALLY FRIENDLY.** Two big changes: The bottles are slimmer, and the punt at the bottom is deeper and wider.

How many bubbles does a bottle of
Champagne have? According to scientist Bill
Lembeck, **49 MILLION!**

*"It's not a Burgundy; it's not a
Bordeaux; it's a white wine; it's a
sparkling wine that should be kept
no longer than two to three years. It
should be consumed young."*
—Claude Taittinger

CHOOSING A CHAMPAGNE

First, determine the style you prefer, light-bodied to full, and the sweetness level, from brut nature to doux. Then buy your Champagne from a reliable shipper / producer. Champagne has more than 4,000 producers, and each takes pride in its house style and strives for a consistent blend, year after year. It's not a hard and fast rule, but the styles of these nationally distributed houses generally conform to the categories below. Also keep in mind that supply and demand largely dictate the prices of prestige cuvée Champagnes.

LIGHT, DELICATE	LIGHT TO MEDIUM	MEDIUM	MEDIUM TO FULL	FULL, RICH
A. CHARBAUT ET FILS JACQUESSON LANSON	BILLECART-SALMON BRUNO PAILLARD DEUTZ G. H. MUMM LAURENT-PERRIER NICOLAS FEUILLATTE PERRIER-JOUËT POMMERY RUINART PÈRE & FILS TAITTINGER	CHARLES HEIDSIECK MOËT & CHANDON PIPER-HEIDSIECK POL ROGER SALON	HENRIOT LOUIS ROEDERER	A. GRATIEN BOLLINGER KRUG VEUVE CLICQUOT

To evaluate a Champagne, look at the bubbles, an integral part of the wine that creates texture and mouthfeel. The better wines have smaller bubbles and more of them. In a good Champagne, the bubbles last longer.

AGING

As a rule, Champagne is ready to drink as soon as you buy it, but in some cases you can age it. Drink nonvintage Champagnes within two to three years and vintage and prestige cuvée Champagnes within ten to fifteen years. If you're still saving that bottle of Dom Pérignon from fifteen years ago, don't wait any longer. Open it!

"My dear girl, there are some things that just aren't done, such as drinking Dom Perignon '53 above the temperature of 38° Fahrenheit. That's just as bad as listening to the Beatles without earmuffs!"

—Sean Connery as James Bond, in *Goldfinger* (1964)

OPENING A BOTTLE OF CHAMPAGNE

Sabering a bottle makes for a fun—if hazardous—party trick best left to the experts, but everyone should know how to open a bottle of Champagne properly because even doing it manually can prove dangerous. The pressure inside is around 6 atmospheres, or nearly 90 pounds per square inch. That's three times the pressure in a car tire! At all steps below, point the bottle away from yourself, others, or anything fragile.

1. Chill the bottle well.
2. Remove the foil from the top of the bottle.
3. Place your hand on top of the cork and keep it there until you're done. This may seem awkward during some of the subsequent steps, but you'll understand the importance of this step if you've ever seen or had a cork blast off unexpectedly in the middle of the process.
4. Untwist the wire tab to release the cage. You can either remove the cage—carefully—or leave it on top of the cork.
5. Gently place a cloth napkin over the cork. (If the cork suddenly pops, the napkin will absorb the force.)
6. Grasp the napkin-wrapped cork with your dominant hand and the body of the bottle with the other. Twist the bottle in one direction and the cork in the other, easing it out slowly and gently, until it releases. Don't launch it with a loud pop and a lot of wasted foam.

Popping the cork may be fun, but that allows carbon dioxide to escape, and that's what gives Champagne its signature sparkle. If you open a bottle of Champagne properly, as above, it can sit for hours with very little loss of carbonation.

America is the top importer of champagne.

Champagne houses market about two-thirds of Champagne's wines, but they own **LESS THAN 10 PERCENT OF THE VINEYARDS.**

Two methods of making **ROSÉ CHAMPAGNE**: 1) add red wine to the blend; 2) leave the red grape skins in contact with the must for a short period of time.

GLASSWARE

No matter which Champagne you decide to drink, you should serve it in the proper glass. One story holds that the modern coupe—a footed glass with a shallow cup widening toward the rim—derives from the shape of the breast of Helen of Troy. The Ancient Greeks did drink wine from a breast-shaped cup (a *mastos*), but most surviving examples have handles but no stem or foot. Another story, centuries later, holds that the coupe was molded from the left breast of Marie Antoinette, queen of France—also unlikely. Either way, the larger surface area of a coupe means that Champagne loses its bubbles more quickly, so today it's served in a flute or tulip glass, which also helps enhance the aromas of the wine in the glass.

CHAMPAGNE VERSUS SPARKLING WINE

Champagne is made using the *méthode champenoise*; it comes from the Champagne region of France; and in my opinion it's the world's best sparkling wine because that region has the ideal combination of elements necessary for producing excellent sparkling wine. The area has fine chalk soil; the grapes used for sparkling wine grow here best; and the climate of the location is perfect for this style.

Many different regions all over the world produce sparkling wines, but quality varies widely. Spain produces excellent Cava, made using the *método tradicional*. Germany has Sekt, and Italy has Spumante, which means "sparkling," and from Veneto the increasingly popular Prosecco. In America, California and New York are the main producers. California yields many fine examples, including Domaine Carneros, Domaine Chandon, Iron Horse, J, Korbel, Mumm Cuvée Napa, Piper-Sonoma, Roederer Estate, Scharffenberger, and Schramsberg. Many of the larger California wineries also market their own sparkling wines. New York is known for Gold Seal, Great Western, and Taylor.

Most sparkling wines not made using the classic method are made with secondary fermentation taking place in steel tanks, called the Charmat-Martinotti method, as with Prosecco. (A bottle of sparkling wine that costs $9.99 probably was made this way.) Some of the tanks used in this method can produce 100,000 bottles of sparkling wine in one batch!

PROSECCO SALES in America increased 35 percent last year.

PROSECCO WAS ORIGINALLY THE NAME OF THE GRAPE and, in 2008, became the name of the region. The best Prosecco is designated DOCG. The style is medium weight, aromatic, and fresh. It has high acidity, elegance, balance, and low alcohol (11.5–12%).

40 percent of all sparkling wines consumed in America are **IMPORTED**, and about 20 percent of the sparkling wines made here use **THE CLASSIC METHOD**.

IRON HORSE *Russian Cuvée*

— **BEST VINTAGES OF CHAMPAGNE** —

1995**	1996**	1998	1999	2000	2002**	2003
2004**	2005	2006**	2008	2009*	2012**	2013*

* EXCEPTIONAL VINTAGE ** EXTRAORDINARY VINTAGE

WINE AND FOOD

Champagne is one of the most versatile wines that you can drink with a number of foods, from apéritif to dessert. Try these expert-recommended combinations.

"Never with sweets. A **Comtes de Champagne Blanc de Blancs** with seafood, caviar, or pâté of pheasant. Also never with cheese because the bubbles do not go well."

—Claude Taittinger

"With **brut nonvintage**: a light hors d'oeuvre, such as mousse of pike. With **vintage Champagne**: pheasant, lobster or other seafood. With a **rosé Champagne** a strawberry dessert."

—Christian Pol Roger

Serve **BRUT AND EXTRA DRY** as apéritifs or throughout the meal. **SERVE SEC AND DEMI-SEC** with desserts and wedding cake.

TEST YOUR KNOWLEDGE of Champagne by trying the quiz on page 341.

OTHER FORTIFIED WINES that you might know include **VERMOUTH**, from Italy and France, **MARSALA** from Italy, and **MADEIRA**, from Portugal. Not as popular as it once was, Madeira wine was probably the first wine imported into America. The colonists, including George Washington, had a taste for it and used it to toast the signing of the Declaration of Independence.

Sherry accounts for **LESS THAN 3 PERCENT OF SPANISH WINE** production.

The neutral brandy raises the **ALCOHOL CONTENT** of the wine to 15–20 percent.

CHRISTOPHER COLUMBUS'S SHIPS were built in Puerto de Santa María, and the arrangements with Queen Isabella for his journey of discovery were made there as well.

SHERRY

The world's two greatest fortified wines are Sherry and Port. They have much in common, but the end result is two very different styles. Fortified wine is made by the addition of a neutral brandy (distilled wine) to raise the alcohol content. What separates Port from Sherry is when the winemaker adds the brandy. For Port, it's added during fermentation. The extra alcohol kills the yeast and halts fermentation, which is why Port tastes so sweet. For Sherry, the brandy is added after fermentation. Port usually has 20 percent alcohol. Sherry, by comparison, usually has around 18 percent. Let's start with Sherry, produced in sunny southwestern Spain.

The area within these three towns makes up the Sherry triangle:

Jerez de la Frontera   **Puerto de Santa María**   **Sanlúcar de Barrameda**

and it's the English pronunciation of Xeres, the old spelling of the first town's name, that gives us the name of the wine in English.

PALOMINO accounts for 90 percent of the planted vineyards in Jerez.

In the Sherry world, PX stands for the Pedro Ximénez grape. Cream Sherry is a **BLEND OF PX AND OLOROSO.**

The two main grape varieties used to make Sherry are:

Palomino   Pedro Ximénez

The different types of Sherry are:

Manzanilla	Fino	Amontillado	Oloroso	Cream
dry	dry	dry to medium-dry	dry to medium-dry	sweet

CONTROLLED OXIDATION

Normally vintners carefully guard against letting air into wine during the winemaking process, but that's exactly what transforms wine into Sherry. To do so, winemakers place the wine in barrels, about two-thirds full, and place the bung, or stopper, loosely in the barrel to admit air. They store the barrels in a bodega, in this case an aboveground storage structure. During the process, some wine evaporates—at least 3 percent a year (called the Angels' Share). Now you know why the people of Jerez are so happy all the time. They're breathing in Sherry!

In today's Sherry, the wine ages only in **AMERICAN OAK.**

Some Soleras can contain a blend of **10 TO 20 DIFFERENT HARVESTS.**

To clarify the Sherry and remove the sediment, winemakers add **BEATEN EGG WHITES** to the wine. The sediment attaches to the egg whites and drops to the bottom of the barrel. But what do they do with all the yolks? Ever hear of flan? It's the quintessential Spanish custard dessert made from all the yolks. In Jerez, it's called tocino de cielo, "the fat of heaven."

TEST YOUR KNOWLEDGE of Sherry by trying the quiz on page 341.

──── **FURTHER READING** ────

Sherry by Julian Jeffs

Sherry by Talia Baiocchi

THE SOLERA METHOD

The next step in making Sherry is called fractional blending, achieved through the Solera method. In this process, aging and maturation take place by means of the continuous blending of several vintages. At the bottling stage, wine is drawn from the barrels—never more than a third of the barrel's content—to make room for the new vintage. This blending maintains the house style by using the "mother" wine as a base and refreshing it with younger wines.

CHOOSING A SHERRY

Your best guide is the producer, who buys the grapes and does the blending. Ten producers account for 60 percent of the export market, and the top producers include:

Croft	**Hidalgo**	**Sandeman**
Emilio Lustau	**Osborne**	**Savory and James**
González Byass	**Pedro Domecq**	**Williams & Humbert**
Harveys		

STORAGE

After opening, Sherry lasts longer than a regular table wine because of its higher alcohol content, which acts as a preservative. But once opened, it will begin to lose its freshness. To drink Sherry at its best, finish the bottle within two weeks of opening and refrigerate the opened bottle. Treat Manzanilla and Fino Sherry as white wines, and drink them within a day or two.

WINE AND FOOD

"Very old and rare **Sherry** should be served with cheese. **Fino** and **Manzanilla** can be served as an apéritif or with light grilled or fried fish or even smoked salmon. You get the taste of the smoke better than if you have it with a white wine. **Amontillado** should be served with light cheese, chorizo, ham, or shish kebab. It is a perfect complement to turtle soup or consommé. With **Cream Sherry**, cookies, pastries, and cakes. **Pedro Ximénez**, however, is better as a topping for vanilla ice cream or as a dessert wine before coffee and brandy."

—José Ignacio Domecq

"**Fino** should always be served well chilled. I enjoy having Fino as an apéritif with tapas, but I also like to complement practically any fish meal with the wine—clams, shellfish, lobster, prawns, langoustines, fish soup, or a light fish, such as salmon."

—Mauricio González

PORT

Port comes from the Douro region in northern Portugal. In recent years, to avoid misuse of the name, authentic Port wine has been renamed Porto, after Oporto, the city from which it ships. Remember, neutral brandy is added to Port during fermentation, which halts the process and leaves from 9 to 11 percent residual sugar. This is why Port tastes sweet.

These are the two types of Port and their various styles:

CASK-AGED

RUBY PORT	DARK AND FRUITY, BLENDED FROM YOUNG NONVINTAGE WINES. COST: $.
TAWNY PORT	LIGHTER AND MORE DELICATE, BLENDED FROM MANY VINTAGES. COST: $$.
AGED TAWNY	AGED IN CASKS, SOMETIMES FOR FORTY YEARS OR MORE. COST: $$–$$$.
COLHEITA	FROM A SINGLE VINTAGE AND WOOD-AGED AT LEAST SEVEN YEARS. COST: $$–$$$$.

BOTTLE-AGED

LATE BOTTLED VINTAGE (LBV)	FROM A SINGLE VINTAGE, BOTTLED FOUR TO SIX YEARS AFTER HARVEST, AND SIMILAR TO VINTAGE PORT BUT LIGHTER AND READY TO DRINK ON RELEASE WITH NO DECANTING. COST: $$$
VINTAGE CHARACTER	SIMILAR TO LBV BUT MADE FROM A BLEND OF THE BETTER VINTAGES. COST: $$.
QUINTA	FROM A SINGLE VINEYARD. COST: $$$–$$$$.
VINTAGE PORT	AGED TWO YEARS IN WOOD AND WILL MATURE IN THE BOTTLE OVER TIME. COST: $$$$.

The Portuguese have been shipping Port wine to England **SINCE THE 1670s.** During the 1800s, to help preserve it for the long trip, shippers fortified it with brandy, resulting in Port as we know it today.

PORT PRODUCTION PER YEAR

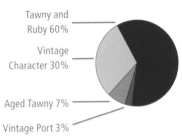

Tawny and Ruby 60%

Vintage Character 30%

Aged Tawny 7%

Vintage Port 3%

IT'S NOT JUST ABOUT PORT. Over the last ten years, Portugal has shifted its focus to dry reds and whites. My favorites include: Douro—Real Companhia Velha, Quinta Castro, Quinta du Passadouro, Rozes, and Durum; and Alentejo—Luis Duarte Vinhos, Susana Esteban.

Cask-aged Ports are ready to drink as soon as they're bottled and won't improve with age. Bottle-aged Ports improve as they mature in the bottle. As with Champagne houses, Port vintages vary from shipper to shipper. For example, in 2003, 2007, and 2011, most producers declared a vintage, but many didn't in the intervening years. Depending on the quality of the vintage, a great Vintage Port will be ready to drink 15 to 30 years after the vintage year! See below for the best vintages.

CHOOSING A PORT

As with Sherry, the grape variety shouldn't dictate your choice. Determine the style and the blend you prefer, and look for the most reliable producers. The most important that are available in America include:

A. A. Ferreira	Fonseca	Robertson's
C. da Silva	Harveys of Bristol	Sandeman
Churchill	Niepoort & Co., Ltd.	Taylor Fladgate
Cockburn	Quinta do Noval	W. & J. Graham
Croft	Quinto Do Vesuvio	Warre's & Co.
Dow	Ramos Pinto	

ENJOYING PORT

Because a bottle of Port likely contains sediment, decant the wine before serving, which will enhance your enjoyment of it (see page 292). As with Sherry, an opened bottle of Port also lasts longer than table wine because of its higher alcohol content. To drink Port at its prime, consume the contents of an opened bottle within one week.

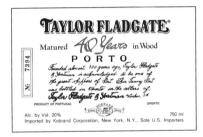

THE BRITISH LOVE PORT. Traditionally, on the birth of a baby, parents buy bottles of Port to put away until the child's 21st birthday—the age of maturity for a child and also a fine Port!

THE FIRST VINTAGE PORT was recorded in 1765.

TEST YOUR KNOWLEDGE of Port by trying the quiz on page 341.

—— **FURTHER READING** ——

The Port Companion by Godfrey Spence

Vintage Port by James Suckling

> **– BEST VINTAGES OF PORT –**
> 1963*   1970**   1977*   1983*   1985   1991*   1992
> 1994**   1995*   1997**   2000**   2003**   2004
> 2007**   2008   2009*   2011**   2012   2013
> *EXCEPTIONAL VINTAGE   **EXTRAORDINARY VINTAGE*

❧ GUIDED TASTING ❧

There's no better way to celebrate your graduation from the Windows on the World Wine School than with Champagne. Taste your way through the major sparkling wines of Europe, then try two American sparkling wines, before raising three glasses of Champagne. End the tasting by comparing the three different quality levels of Port: Ruby, Tawny, and Vintage.

THE WINES

European Sparkling Wine
Two sparkling wines, compared:
  1. *Prosecco*
  2. *Cava Brut*

California Sparkling Wines
Two sparkling wines, compared:
  3. *Sparkling wine from Anderson Valley*
  4. *Sparkling wine from Napa Valley*

Champagne
Two Champagnes, compared:
  5. *Nonvintage Champagne*
  6. *Vintage Champagne*

Port
Three Port wines, compared:
  7. *Ruby Port*
  8. *Tawny Port, 10 Years Old*
  9. *Vintage Port*

WINES OF THE WORLD

CHILE ✻ ARGENTINA ✻ AUSTRALIA ✻

NEW ZEALAND ✻ SOUTH AFRICA ✻ CANADA ✻

AUSTRIA ✻ HUNGARY ✻ GREECE

THE WINES OF CHILE

ON AVERAGE, CHILE stretches just 109 miles wide, but it has more than 2,500 miles of Pacific coastline and many different climates, from desertlike conditions in the north to glaciers in the south. In the middle of the country, within 150 miles of Santiago, the capital, lies the perfect Mediterranean-style climate for growing outstanding wine grapes: warm days, cool nights, and ocean winds. The majestic snow-capped Andes—more than 13,000 feet above sea level on average and the world's longest mountain range—supply all the water necessary for growing grapes through both flood and drip irrigation.

The Spanish first planted grapes here in 1551 and produced the first wine in 1555. In the mid-1800s, vineyard owners imported French varietals, such as Cabernet Sauvignon and Merlot, but not until the phylloxera epic ravaged Europe and America starting in the 1870s did Chilean wines develop a meaningful export market. Industry growth ground to a halt in 1938, however, when the government banned the planting of new vineyards, a prohibition that lasted until 1974 and severely damaged the country's wine quality. In 1979, Torres, the Spanish wine family, introduced modern technology, such as stainless steel fermenting vats, sparking Chile's modern wine industry. In the 1990s, Chile stood on the verge of producing world-class wine, primarily reds and specifically Cabernet Sauvignon. In those days, the industry was still a work in progress, but what a difference 20 years can make—and not

CHILE, PAST AND PRESENT
1995: 12 wineries
2016: more than 100

After a long day of tasting Chilean wines, it's a tradition to end with the national drink—a **PISCO SOUR**: a brandy mixed with lemon and /or lime juice, simple syrup, egg white, and a dash of Angostura bitters. The longer the day, the more Pisco you must have!

just in better wines! Chile's new and improving infrastructure has transformed the country into a destination for both tourists and investors.

FOREIGN INVESTMENT

FOREIGN WINERY	COUNTRY	CHILEAN WINERY
ANTINORI	ITALY	ALBIS
DAN ODFJELL	NORWAY	ODFJELL VINEYARDS
O. FOURNIER	SPAIN	O. FOURNIER
QUINTESSA	USA / CALIFORNIA	VERAMONTE
TORRES WINERY	SPAIN	MIGUEL TORRES WINERY

THE FRENCH CONNECTION

FRENCH INVESTOR	CHILEAN WINERY
BARON PHILIPPE DE ROTHSCHILD	ALMAVIVA
BRUNO PRATS & PAUL PONTALLIER	AQUITANIA
CHÂTEAU LAFITE-ROTHSCHILD	LOS VASCOS
CHÂTEAU LAROSE-TRINTAUDON	CASAS DEL TOQUI
GRAND MARNIER	CASA LAPOSTOLLE
WILLIAM FÈVRE	FÈVRE

Chile is the **FOURTH LARGEST EXPORTER** of wine to America.

THE TOP FIVE CHILEAN WINE BRANDS IN THE AMERICA

Concha y Toro

Walnut Crest

San Pedro

Santa Rita

Santa Carolina

(Impact Databank)

Chilean wineries adhere to EU label requirements, so a wine must contain 85 percent of the grape variety, vintage, or domaine of origin (DO) that appears on the label. Today winemakers have a lot of freedom: Old traditions, such as aging wines in French oak barrels; new technologies, including stainless steel fermentors; and better vineyard management, including drip irrigation, have combined to produce better wines. Even though Chile's winemaking industry is still learning, experimenting, and growing, *its red wines are the best values in the world* in the $15 to $25 range!

The major white grapes are:

Chardonnay

Sauvignon Blanc

The major red grapes are:

Cabernet Sauvignon   **Carménèr**   **Merlot**   **Syrah**

and new plantings of Malbec, Carignan, Pinot Noir, and Cinsault are adding diversity to the Chilean landscape.

Identifying the major winemaking regions can prove tricky in a country so narrow. The best way to look at Chile is west-east and north-south. From west to east, three different climatic conditions exist:

Coastal   cool climate

Central valley   warm climate

Andes Mountains   cool or warm climate

From north to south, the most important regions are:

Casablanca Valley   **Maipo Valley**   **Rapel Valley / Colchagua**

CARMÉNÈRE

Bordeaux heavily influenced Chile's wine industry in its early days, which is why Cabernet Sauvignon ranks as the country's number-one red varietal. In the 1850s, Chileans planted other Bordeaux grapes, including Merlot and Cabernet Franc. Then, in 1994, DNA analysis revealed that a substantial amount of grapes produced and sold as Merlot were actually another Bordeaux grape, Carménère, a thick-skinned grape that has soft, sweet tannins and low acidity.

The potential marketing disaster quickly became a positive opportunity. Carménère has become one of the top varietals in Chile, which remains the only country in the world to produce it as a single varietal. But even in 1997, Carménère lacked consistency from winery to winery; most tasted green and herbaceous. Over the last ten years, the quality has increased dramatically. To make a great wine from the Carménère varietal:

- It must be planted in claylike, well-drained soil.
- Older vines make for better wine.
- Because it ripens late, it needs good weather.
- At the end of the harvest, growers must remove the vines' leaves and expose the grapes to maximum sunlight.

CABERNET SAUVIGNON accounts for 32 percent of the total acreage of premium grapes planted in Chile.

OTHER REGIONS AND THEIR WINES INCLUDE

Aconcagua: Cabernet Sauvignon

Bío Bío: Pinot Noir

Cachapoal: Cabernet Sauvignon

Curicó: Cabernet Sauvignon, Sauvignon Blanc

Limari: Cabernet Sauvignon

Maule: Cabernet Sauvignon

San Antonio: Chardonnay

- It's better blended with Cabernet Sauvignon or Syrah.
- Oak aging is necessary for at least twelve months to integrate the fruit, tannins, and acidity.

You can enjoy this wine young—three to seven years—and the best will cost you $20 or more . . . still a great value!

MY FAVORITE CHILEAN PRODUCERS INCLUDE

Almaviva	Leyda
Anakena (Ona)	Matetic (EQ)
Aquitania	Miguel Torres
Arboleda	Montes (Alpha M, Folly)
Caliterra (Cenit)	Morandé
Carmen (Grande Vidure)	O. Fournier (Centauri)
Casa Lapostolle	Odfjell
(Cuvée Alexandre, Clos Apalta)	Santa Carolina
Casa Silva	(Viña Casa blanca)
Chadwick	Santa Rita (Casa Real)
Concha y Toro (Don Melchor)	Seña
Cono Sur (Ocio)	Tarapaca (Reserva Privada)
Cousiño Macul (Finis Terrae,	Undurraga (Altazor)
Antiguas Reservas, Lota)	Valdivieso (Caballo Loco, Eclat)
De Martino	Los Vascos
Echeverria	(Le Dix de Los Vascos)
Emiliana Orgánico	Veramonte (Primus)
Errazuriz (Don Maximiano)	Viña Koyle

– BEST RECENT VINTAGES OF CHILE –
CASABLANCA: 2011   2012   2013*   2014   2015

MAIPO: 2005** 2006* 2007** 2008* 2009 2010* 2011*
2012   2013*   2014   2015

COLCHAGUA: 2005*   2007*   2009   2010   2011   2012
2013*   2014   2015   2016*

*EXCEPTIONAL VINTAGE **EXTRAORDINARY VINTAGE*

5 BEST VALUE WINES OF CHILE UNDER $30
Arboleda Carmenère • Casa Lapostolle "Cuvée Alexandre" Merlot • Concha y Toro
Puente Alto Cabernet • Montes Cabernet Sauvignon • Veramonte Sauvignon Blanc

See page 309 for a complete list.

THE SEVEN LARGEST WINERIES IN CHILE

WINERY	DATE FOUNDED
San Pedro	1865
Concha y Toro	1883
Errazuriz	1870
Santa Carolina	1875
Santa Rita	1880
Undurraga	1885
Canepa	1930

More than 40 percent of all winemakers in Chile are **WOMEN**.

TEST YOUR KNOWLEDGE of the wines of Chile by trying the quiz on page 343.

—— **FURTHER READING** ——
The Wines of Chile by Peter Richards

THE WINES OF ARGENTINA

The second largest country in South America, Argentina has great climatic conditions and soil, especially for red wines. Because the country receives 300 days of sunshine and just eight inches of rain annually, the Argentineans have established an elaborate network of canals and dams to irrigate their vineyards.

The wine tradition here dates back to Spanish colonization. As with many of the great wine producing countries in the Americas, missionaries first planted and cultivated vines. In this case, Jesuits did so in 1544 in Mendoza and to the north in San Juan. Because its wines were well made and inexpensive, Argentina never exported them; they were consumed domestically. But much has changed in the last 20 years, including a tremendous amount of new investment, not just financial but also in terms of world-renowned experts owning their own vineyards and wineries here.

Argentina has more than 1,000 wineries, more than 600 in Mendoza.

FOREIGN INVESTMENT

With an average price of $30,000 per acre, it's no wonder that so many influential companies have invested in Argentina in recent years.

FOREIGN WINERY	COUNTRY	ARGENTINEAN WINERY
CHANDON	FRANCE	BODEGAS CHANDON
CONCHA Y TORO	CHILE	TRIVENTO, SAN MARTIN
CORDORNÍU	SPAIN	SÉPTIMA WINERY
HESS	SWITZERLAND	COLOMÉ WINERY
O. FOURNIER	SPAIN	O. FOURNIER
PAUL HOBBS	USA	VIÑA COBOS
PERNOD RICARD	FRANCE	ETCHART WINERY
SOGRAPE VINHOS	PORTUGAL	FINCA FLICHMAN

THE BORDEAUX CONNECTION

BORDEAUX WINERY	REGION	ARGENTINEAN WINERY
CHÂTEAU CHEVAL BLANC	FRANCE	CHEVAL DES ANDES
CHÂTEAU LE BON PASTEUR	POMEROL	CLOS DE LOS SIETE
CHÂTEAU LE GAY	POMEROL	MONTEVIEJO
CHÂTEAU LÉOVILLE POYFERRE	ST-JULIEN	CUVELIER LOS ANDES
CHÂTEAU MALARTIC-LAGRAVIERE	PESSAC-LÉOGNAN	BODEGAS DIAMANDES
CHÂTEAUX CLARKE, DASSAULT, AND LISTRAC	ST-ÉMILION	FLECHAS DE LOS ANDES
LURTON	FRANCE	FRANÇOIS LURTON

Argentineans consume about half a pound of beef per person per day, and many of the wineries have **EXCEPTIONAL RESTAURANTS,** from Francis Mallman 1884 to Urban at O. Fournier.

Take the family to **PATAGONIA,** where the most dinosaur fossils in the world are located.

In the 1980s and '90s, annual domestic consumption dropped from 20-plus gallons of wine per person per year to just 8. When the value of the peso collapsed in the Argentine Great Depression (1998–2002), exporting became more profitable. With foreign investment and winemaking consultants already in place, Argentina seized the perfect time to enter the world market, using the Malbec grape to establish its national identity. Today Argentina ranks as the largest producer of wines in South America, fifth largest in the world, and sixth largest consumer of wines in the world. With thousands of acres that still can be planted, it's the up-and-coming country to watch for new wines and regions, and the quality-to-price ratio remains one of the world's best. Look for more and better wines over the next 20 years.

The major white grape varieties are:

Sauvignon Blanc   **Torrontés Riojano**

The major red grape varieties are:

Cabernet Sauvignon   **Merlot**   **Tempranillo**
Malbec   **Syrah**

All Argentinean wines contain 100 percent of the grape varietal named on the label.

From north to south, the most important regions and their best wines are:

NORTH
Salta: Torrontés Riojano, Cabernet Sauvignon
Cafayate: Malbec, Cabernet Sauvignon, Tannat, Torrontés Riojano

CUYO
Mendoza: Malbec, Tempranillo, Cabernet Sauvignon
Uco Valley: Sémillon, Malbec

PATAGONIA
San Juan: Bonarda, Syrah
Río Negro: Pinot Noir, Torrontés Riojano
Neuquén: Sauvignon Blanc, Merlot, Pinot Noir, Malbec

MALBEC is also known as Cot and makes some full-bodied wines in the Cahors region of France.

The blending grape of Argentina is **BARNARDO**. Some 45,500 acres grow in Argentina but, because of its low tannins, it's usually blended with Malbec and Cabernet Sauvignon, rarely appeareing as a single variety.

Michel Rolland, **THE MOST FAMOUS WINE CONSULTANT IN THE WORLD,** has invested his winemaking expertise into an estate of five wineries called Clos de los Siete, all within eyesight of one another. His partners include top winemakers and viticulturists. *Wine Advocate* wrote of the 2007 vintage that "there may be no finer red wine value in Argentina." The four other wineries involved in the group are Monteviejo, Flechas de los Andes, Cuvelier los Andes, and Diamandes.

TEST YOUR KNOWLEDGE of the wines of Argentina by trying the quiz on page 343.

—— **FURTHER READING** ——
Wines of Argentina by Michel Rolland and Enrique Chrabolowsky

More than 70 percent of the country's 500,000 vineyard acres lie in Mendoza, but, of these seven, keep your eye on Salta.

MY FAVORITE ARGENTINEAN PRODUCERS

Achaval Ferrer
(Finca Mirador)
Alta Vista (Alto)
Bodega Noemìa
de Patagonia
Bodega Norton (Perdriel
Single Vineyard)
Catena Zapata
(Adrianna Vineyard)
Cheval des Andes
Clos de los Siete
Cuvelier los Andes
(Grand Malbec)
Enrique Foster
(Malbec Firmado)
Etchart
Finca Flichman
Finca Sophenia
Francois Lurton
(Chacayes)

Kaiken
Luca (Nico by Luca)
Luigi Bosca (Icono)
Mendel
(Finca Remota)
O. Fournier
(Alfa Crux Malbec)
Salentein
(Primum Malbec)
Septima
Susana Balbo
Terrazas
(Malbec Afincado)
Tikal (Locura)
Trapiche
Val de Flores
Viña Cobos
(Marchiori Vineyard)
Weinert

– BEST RECENT VINTAGES OF MENDOZA MALBEC –
2005* 2006** 2007 2008 2009* 2010* 2011*
2012* 2013** 2014 2015 2016*
* EXCEPTIONAL VINTAGE ** EXTRAORDINARY VINTAGE

5 BEST VALUE WINES OF ARGENTINA UNDER $30
Alamos Chardonnay • Catena Malbec • Clos de los Siete Malbec •
Salentein Malbec • Susana Balboa Cabernet Sauvignon

See page 307 for a complete list

THE WINES OF AUSTRALIA

After the British lost the colonies in the American War of Independence (as they call it), they looked to other colonial opportunities, founding Sydney in New South Wales in 1788. The wine industry there began that same year. At first, the country produced mostly fortified wines. Cabernet Sauvignon vine cuttings from Château Haut-Brion in Bordeaux were planted near Melbourne in the 1830s. James Busby brought Syrah cuttings from the Chapoutier vineyards in the Rhône Valley in 1832 and planted them in Hunter Valley. Many of the largest or most prestigious wine companies—Henschke, Lindemans, Orlando, Penfolds, Seppelt—were founded in the nineteenth century and produce excellent wines today.

Once better known for kangaroos and surfing, today Australia ranks as the world's sixth largest wine producer. The shift to quality varietals began in the 1970s and has continued with tremendous speed. From 1988 to 2008, exports of Australian wines increased nearly 100 percent, and now exports exceed $3 billion!

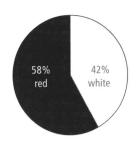

AUSTRALIA, PAST AND PRESENT

1970: 50,561 hectares

2016: 160,000 hectares

AUSTRALIAN WINE EXPORTS TO AMERICA

1990: 578,000 cases

2015: 19,800,000 cases

THE AUSTRALIAN GRAPE HARVEST

58% red

42% white

In 2016, Australia had more than **2,500 WINERIES.**

Australia is now the third largest exporter of wine to America, and **YELLOW TAIL** is the top imported wine. Sales rocketed from 200,000 cases in 2001 to nearly 8 million cases in 2016.

Australia has some of the oldest Shiraz (Syrah) grape vines in the world, many more than **100 YEARS OLD**.

TASMANIA is known for sparkling wines, and **RUTHERGLEN** for fortified wines

More than 100 different grape varieties grow in Australia, but none of them is indigenous. The main white grape varieties are:

Sauvignon Blanc	Chardonnay
Merlot	Riesling

and the main red varietals are:

Shiraz / Syrah	Cabernet Sauvignon
Sémillon	Pinot Noir

The country has more than 60 wine-growing regions, called Geographical Indications. You don't need to know them all, but you should familiarize yourself with the best regions and their best wines:

SOUTH AUSTRALIA
   Adelaide Hills: Chardonnay, Sauvignon Blanc
   Barossa Valle: Shiraz, Grenache
   Clare Valley: Riesling
   Coonawarra: Cabernet Sauvignon
   McLaren Vale: Shiraz, Grenache
NEW SOUTH WALES
   Hunter Valley: Sémillon
VICTORIA
   Yarra Valley: Chardonnay, Pinot Noir
WESTERN AUSTRALIA
   Margaret River: Cabernet Sauvignon, Chardonnay, Sauvignon Blanc / Sémillon

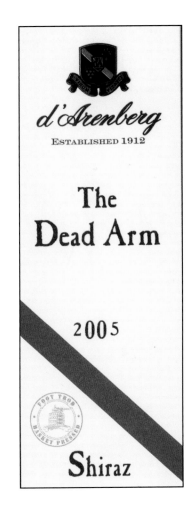

South Australia produces almost half of the country's wines. It also remains one of the few wine regions in the world never to have succumbed to phylloxera, so many growers here still plant using the vines' own rootstock.

The Australian wine industry's Label Integrity Program (LIP) took effect with the 1990 vintage. It doesn't govern as many aspects of wine production as France's AOC laws, but the LIP does regulate and oversee vintage, varietal, and Geographical Indication regulations. To conform to the LIP and the Australian Food Standards Code, Australian wine labels must provide a great deal of information. Take a look at the label below. The producer is Penfolds. For blends that list varieties, labels must show the percentages of each varietal, and the first grape must have the highest percentage. If the label specifies a Geographical Indication—Clare Valley here—at least 85 percent of the wine must originate there. If a vintage appears, 95 percent of the wine must come from that vintage.

Since 1994, Australia and most other wine countries have conformed to an EU wine agreement that calls for an end to the use of borrowed generic names, such as Burgundy, Champagne, Port, and Sherry. One of Australia's most famous wines is Penfolds Grange Hermitage, so, to conform to the agreement, Penfolds dropped "Hermitage," a wine produced in France's Rhône Valley. Even with its "new" name, Penfolds Grange remains one of Australia's greatest wines.

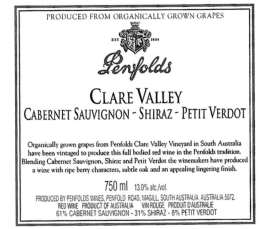

More than 75 percent of Australian wine is now bottled with a **SCREW CAP**.

Australia's most coveted **WINE AWARD**, established in 1962, takes its name from wine-bar owner Jimmy Watson and goes to the best one-year-old red wine each year. The first 15 went to wines labeled "Burgundy type" or "Claret type." Only in 1976 did a wine labeled as a varietal win the trophy.

2006 had the **LATEST HARVEST** ever. 2013 had the **EARLIEST HARVEST** ever.

The vintage in Australia occurs in **THE FIRST HALF OF THE YEAR.** Grapes are harvested from February to May.

MARGARET RIVER WINES had a great vintage in 2013.

TEST YOUR KNOWLEDGE of the wines of Australia by trying the quiz on page 343.

—— **FURTHER READING** ——
Australian Wine Companion by James Halliday

MY FAVORITE AUSTRALIAN PRODUCERS

Cape Mentelle (Cabernet Sauvignon)
Clarendon Hills (Hickinbotham Grenache)
Cullen Wines (Diana Madeline)
d'Arenberg (The Dead Arm Shiraz)
De Bortoli (Noble One)
Grant Burge (Meshach Shiraz)
Hardy's (Chateau Reynella Cellar No. One Shiraz)
Henschke (Cyril Cabernet Sauvignon, Hill of Grace)
Jamshead
Jim Barry
Kaesler
Katnook (Odyssey Cabernet Sauvignon)
Leeuwin Estate (Art Series Chardonnay or Cabernet Sauvignon)
Mollydooker Shiraz (Velvet Glove)
Mount Mary (Quintet)
Penfolds (Grange, Bin 707 Cabernet Sauvignon)
Petaluma (Adelaide Hills Shiraz)

Peter Lehmann (Reserve Riesling or Semillon)
Shaw & Smith (M3 Vineyard Adelaide Hills Chardonnay)
Tahbilk (Eric Stevens Purbrick Shiraz or Cabernet Sauvignon)
Torbreck Vintners (Run Rig)
Tournon
Turkey Flat (Barossa Valley Shiraz)
Two Hands Shiraz (Bella's Garden)
Vasse Felix (Margaret River Chardonnay and Sémillon)
Voyager (Margaret River Sauvignon Blanc/Sémillon)
Wirra Wirra (RSW Shiraz and Angelus Cabernet Sauvignon)
Wolf Blass (Black Label Shiraz)
Yalumba (The Menzies Coonawarra Cabernet Sauvignon)
Yering Station (Shiraz Viognier)

— **BEST RECENT VINTAGES OF WINES** —
FROM BAROSSA, COONAWARRA, AND MCLAREN VALE:

2004** 2005** 2006* 2008* 2009 2010**
2012** 2013* 2014 2015

*EXCEPTIONAL VINTAGE **EXTRAORDINARY VINTAGE

5 BEST VALUE WINES OF AUSTRAILIA UNDER $30

Jacob's Creek Shiraz Cabernet • Leeuwin Estate Siblings Shiraz •
Lindeman's Chardonnay Bin 65 • Penfolds "Bin 28 Kalimna" Shiraz •
Rosemount Estate Shiraz Cabernet (Diamond Label)

See page 308 for a complete list

THE WINES OF NEW ZEALAND

New Zealand features beautiful coastlines, rolling hills, magnificent mountains, and outstanding weather. It's also the home of bungee jumping, which accurately captures the vitality and exuberance of its wine industry. The country recorded its first vintage in 1836 and by 1985 had approximately 15,000 acres of vines. The majority—mostly Müller Thurgau—produced large volumes of low-end wine, however. Vintners produced so much wine that they created a huge surplus, and as a result the government offered cash to any grower who agreed to uproot a quarter of his or her vineyard, an event known as the Vine Pull. This massive purge of inferior wine grapes led to a resurgence of interest in high-quality wine and to widespread plantings of Sauvignon Blanc, Pinot Noir, and Chardonnay. This shift marked the New Zealand wine industry's new beginning. Over

**NEW ZEALAND,
PAST AND PRESENT:**
1985: 100 wineries
2016: 692 wineries

95 percent of New Zealand's population lives within **30 MILES** of the ocean.

93 percent of New Zealand wines are
SEALED WITH SCREW CAPS.

TOTAL ACRES OF GRAPES BY YEAR

1985	15,000 acres
1986	11,000 acres (Vine Pull)
2016	80,000 acres

NEW ZEALAND'S WINE PRODUCTION

80% white

20% red

DOG POINT
VINEYARD
2014
Sauvignon Blanc
Marlborough

New Zealand had in 1996 only 1,000 acres of **PINOT NOIR**. In 2016 there were more than 11,000 acres planted.

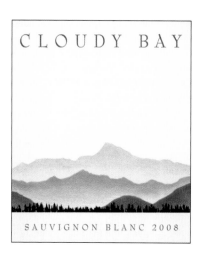

the last 30 years, the vineyards and wines here have grown by leaps and bounds, and the international wine community recognizes New Zealand's Sauvignon Blanc and Pinot Noir wines as world-class.

The frenzy has calmed somewhat, but the wines are still evolving. With more than 25 different grape varieties at their disposal, winemakers are just beginning to understand the full potential of New Zealand's soil and weather. Think of the winemakers and vineyard owners here as the new kids on the block, and you'll have a good sense of the potential that this country has to produce even more world-class wines. The New Zealand public relations theme, "The best is yet to be discovered," pretty much says it all.

The main grape varieties are:

Sauvignon Blanc   Pinot Noir   Chardonnay

Look for Pinot Gris and Syrah in the coming years.

The two islands, North and South, that comprise the country have ten wine regions between them. The five most important and their best wines are:

NORTH ISLAND
Gisborne: Chardonnay
Hawke's Bay: Bordeaux blends, Chardonnay, Syrah
Martinborough/Wairarapa: Pinot Noir
SOUTH ISLAND
Marlborough: Sauvignon Banc, Pinot Noir
Central Otago: Pinot Noir

The most southerly grapes harvested in the world come from Central Otago.

MARLBOROUGH SAUVIGNON BLANC

Sauvignon Blanc accounted for less than 4 percent of New Zealand's total grape crop 30 years ago. Marlborough contains more than half of the country's vineyards and produces 90 percent of its Sauvignon Blanc today. As such, New Zealand touts itself as the Sauvignon Blanc capital of the world, but the terroir here differs significantly from France. Wine writers describe the wine as having crisp, mineral, acidic flavors of grapefruit, lime, or other tropical fruit and assertive, herbaceous, pungent, racy, vibrant aromas—sometimes even like cat pee! What's not to like?

MY FAVORITE NEW ZEALAND WINERIES

Amisfield	Esk Valley	Palliser
Ata Rangi	Felton Road	Quartz Reevf
Babich	Forrest	Sacred Hill
Bell Hill	Greywacke	Saint Clair
Brancott (Montana)	Kim Crawford	Seresin
Cloudy Bay	Kumeu River	Spy Valley
Craggy Range	Matua Valley	Te Mata
Dog Point	Mud House	Trinity Hill
Dry River	Nautilus	Villa Maria

— BEST RECENT VINTAGES OF NEW ZEALAND WINES —
NORTH ISLAND / HAWKE'S BAY AND MARTINBOROUGH:

2006 2007* 2010** 2011* 2012 2013** 2014* 2015*

SOUTH ISLAND / CENTRAL OTAGO AND MARLBOROUGH:

2009* 2010* 2011* 2012 2013** 2014* 2015*

*EXCEPTIONAL VINTAGE   **EXTRAORDINARY VINTAGE

5 BEST VALUE WINES OF NEW ZEALAND UNDER $30

Brancott Estate Pinot Noir Reserve • Cloudy Bay "Te Koko" • Kim Crawford Sauvignon Blanc Stoneleigh Pinot Noir • Te Awa Syrah •

See page 315 for a complete list

Besides wine, New Zealand is famous for its dairy products and wool. Wineries let **SHEEP GRAZE FREELY THROUGHOUT THE VINEYARDS** during the winter to keep the fields clear of grass and weeds.

70 percent of New Zealand vines are **10 YEARS OLD** or younger.

New Zealand had a **RECORD LEVEL OF PRODUCTION** in 2014.

TEST YOUR KNOWLEDGE of the wines of New Zealand by trying the quiz on page 343.

——— FURTHER READING ———

Buyer's Guide to New Zealand Wines by Michael Cooper

THE WINES OF SOUTH AFRICA

South Africa has the world's oldest wine-growing geology. Dutch settlers founded Cape Town in 1652, and the first grape harvest took place there seven years later. Their descendants and those of the French Huguenots who also settled there have grown grapes and made wine for some 350 years, establishing the world-renowned Constantia wine estate in 1685. Until recently, most of the country's wine sold domestically or in Europe and wasn't available in America. Before 1990, a few producers made good wine, but for the most part large cooperatives focused on fortified wines and brandy, basing output on a quota system that valued quantity over quality. In 1994, the dismantling of apartheid and the democratic election of Nelson Mandela as president ended South Africa's economic isolation, allowing its wines to reach the world's markets.

SOUTH AFRICA, PAST AND PRESENT
1970: 88,770 hectares
270 million liters
2016: 110,041 hectares
958 million liters

SOUTH AFRICA'S WINE PRODUCTION

50% white

50% red

Most Western Cape wine regions lie within a two-hour drive of **CAPE TOWN.**

FOREIGN INVESTMENT

INVESTOR	FOREIGN WINERY	REGION / COUNTRY	SOUTH AFRICAN WINERY
ANNE COINTREAU-HUCHON		FRANCE	MORGENHOF
BRUNO PRATS	CHÂTEAU COS D'ESTOURNEL	BORDEAUX	ANWILKA
DONALD HESS		CALIFORNIA, ARGENTINA, AUSTRALIA	GLEN CARLOU
HUBERT DE BOÜARD	CHÂTEAU ANGÉLUS	BORDEAUX	ANWILKA
MAY DE LENCQUESAING	CHÂTEAU PICHON-LALANDE	BORDEAUX	GLENELLY
MICHEL LAROCHE		CHABLIS	L'AVENIR
PHIL FREESE	FORMERLY MONDAVI	CALIFORNIA	VILAFONTÉ
PIERRE LURTON	CHÂTEAU CHEVAL BLANC	BORDEAUX	MORGENSTER
ZELMA LONG	FORMERLY SIMI	CALIFORNIA	VILAFONTÉ

Over the last 20 years, South African wines have improved dramatically. Many now share center stage with some of the world's best. Winemakers are making up for lost time, and the best is yet to come. South Africa now has more than 600 wineries, and a third of the country's vineyards have been replanted since 1994—a key point to know, given that vine age plays a decisive role in the quality of the wine produced.

The country has a wide diversity of terrain and weather conditions. Vineyards lie at altitudes from 300 feet above sea level to 1,300. Some vineyards have cool, coastal climates, while in others summer days exceed 100 degrees Fahrenheit. It's a land of contrast, alive with possibilities.

The major white grape varieties that grow here are:

Chardonnay   **Chenin Blanc (Steen)**   **Sauvignon Blanc**

It remains unclear whether Chenin Blanc or Sauvignon Blanc will become South Africa's benchmark white wine. Historically Chenin Blanc has held that position, and some of those vines are more than 100 years

The world's **BEST CHENIN BLANCS** come from either South Africa or the Loire Valley in France.

MY FAVORITE SOUTH AFRICAN CHENIN BLANCS INCLUDE

Cederberg

De Trafford

Groote Post

Iona

Kanu

Rudera

old. Some producers age it in oak, others age it unoaked, and several winemakers employ both methods.

The major red varieties are:

Bordeaux blends   **Shiraz / Syrah**   **Cabernet Sauvignon**   **Pinotage**
(Cabernet Sauvignon,
Merlot, and Cabernet Franc)

South Africa consists of two main geographic areas, the Western Cape, which produces 97 percent of the country's wine, and the Northern Cape. These break down further into regions, districts, and wards; the most important region is the Coastal Region. The three most historically important Wines of Origin (WO) within the Coastal Region and the best varietals of each are:

Constantia: Sauvignon Blanc, Muscat
Stellenbosch: Chardonnay, Cabernet Sauvignon, Pinotage, Bordeaux blends
Paarl: Chardonnay, Syrah, Chenin Blanc

The country's other important areas and their best wines include:

Darling: Sauvignon Blanc
Durbanville: Sauvignon Blanc, Merlot
Elgin: Riesling, Sauvignon Blanc, Pinot Noir
Franschhoek: Cabernet Sauvignon, Syrah, Semillon
Robertson: Chardonnay, Shiraz
Swartland: Shiraz, Pinotage, Rhône-style blends
Walker Bay: Chardonnay, Pinot Noir

Implemented in 1973, WO regulations strictly control labeling. If a region, district, or ward appears on the label, 100 percent of the grapes must come from that place of origin. If a wine label specifies that it is estate-bottled, 100 percent of the grapes must come from that estate. A vintage designation means that 85 percent of the grapes come from the stated vintage, and a varietal designation means that the wine contains at least 85 percent of the named varietal. The WO doesn't control yield per hectare or irrigation.

PINOTAGE

A viticulturist from Stellenbosch University created this variety in 1925 by crossing Pinot Noir and Cinsault. Unfortunately, it has never had a single flavor profile. Pinotage can produce a light, somewhat insipid wine smelling of acetate, banana, or spray paint, with a strong, acrid aftertaste. It also can make a big, full-bodied, luscious, well-balanced wine with tremendous fruit extraction and a long graceful finish and can age for 20 or more years. The best producers of Pinotage follow a similar formula:

- Vines planted in cooler climates and at least 15 years old
- Low per-acre crop yield
- Long skin contact and maceration in open fermentors
- At least two years of oak aging
- Blending with Cabernet Sauvignon
- At least ten years of bottle aging

My favorite producers of Pinotage include:

L'Avenir   Kanonkop   Fairview   Simonsig

SOUTH AFRICAN DESSERT WINES

Long before vintners in Bordeaux were producing Sauternes or winemakers in Germany were making Trockenbeerenauslese, South Africa produced one of the world's greatest sweet wines. Constantia has been producing fragrant, aromatic wines from the Muscat grape since the 1700s. The Klein Constantia estate still produces wines in this original style, raisinating the grapes rather than botrytizing them.

In 2016 Sout Africa experienced the **DRIEST WEATHER** on record.

TEST YOUR KNOWLEDGE of the wines of South Africa by trying the quiz on page 345.

——— **FURTHER READING** ———
Wines of the New South Africa by Tim James

MY FAVORITE SOUTH AFRICAN WINE PRODUCERS

STELLENBOSCH

Anwilka	Ken Forrester	Rudera
Cirrus	L'Avenir	Rust en Vrede
De Toren	Meerlust	Rustenberg
De Trafford	Morgenhof	Simonsig
Glenelly	Morgenster	Thelema
Jordan (available	Mulderbosch	Vergelegen
as Jardin in the	Neil Ellis	Vriesenhof
United States)	Raats Family	Waterford
Kanonkop		

PAARL

Fairview	Nederburg	Vilafonté
Glen Carlou	Veenwouden	

FRANSCHHOEK

Boekenhoutskloof	Boschendal	Graham Beck

SWARTLAND

A. A. Badenhorst Family	Porseleinberg	Sadie Family
Mullineux		

WALKER BAY

Ashbourne	Bouchard-Finlayson	Hamilton Russell

CONSTANTIA

Constantia Uitsig	Klein Constantia	Steenberg

ELGIN

Paul Cluver		

> **– BEST RECENT VINTAGES OF WESTERN CAPE WINES –**
> 2006* 2007 2008* 2009** 2010 2011*
> 2012* 2013* 2014 2015
> * EXCEPTIONAL VINTAGE ** EXTRAORDINARY VINTAGE

> **5 BEST VALUE SOUTH AFRICA WINES WINES UNDER $30**
> Doolhof Dark Lady of the Labyrinth Pinotage • Ken Forrester Sauvignon Blanc •
> Rustenberg 1682 Red Blend • Thelema Cabernet Sauvignon •
> Tokara Chardonnay Reserve Collection •

See page 316 for a complete list

THE WINES OF CANADA

Commercial winemaking in Canada began in the early 1800s, and its wine history closely follows that of New York. Both began by growing the winter-hardy *labrusca* grapes (Concord, Catawba, Niagara). Like New York, many of Canada's wineries specialized in producing fortified wines often labeled with borrowed European names, such as Port and Sherry. Like America, Canada also had a period of national prohibition, 1916–1927. The first major change in Canadian viticulture occurred during the 1970s, when several small producers began experimenting with French hybrid grapes. Over the last 40 years, the best Canadian wines have come from European *vinifera* grapes.

The major white grapes are:

Chardonnay	Pinot Gris	Vidal
Gewürztraminer	Riesling	

The major red grapes are:

Cabernet Franc	Merlot	Syrah
Cabernet Sauvignon	Pinot Noir	

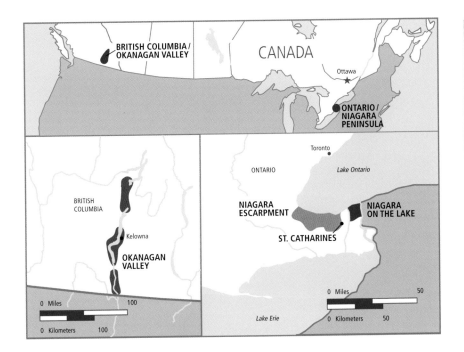

Many people think that Canada sits too far north to make great wine. Just as in other cool-climate wine regions, such as Germany, most of **THE BEST VINEYARDS** lie near water, which tempers the climate. Ontario has Lake Ontario and Lake Erie, and British Columbia has Okanagan Lake.

ONTARIO	
15,074 acres	130 wineries

BRITISH COLUMBIA	
9,500 acres	212 wineries

QUEBEC AND NOVA SCOTIA also grow grapes, primarily hybrids.

60 percent of **VQA WINES** come from white grapes.

Canadians **DAN AYKROYD** and **WAYNE GRETZKY** both have invested in Canadian wineries.

Canada has two major wine-producing regions: British Columbia on the Pacific Coast and Ontario in the eastern Great Lakes region, and each makes a grab bag of different wines:

British Columbia / Okanagan Valley: Chardonnay, Pinot Gris, Merlot, Cabernet Sauvignon, Syrah, Gewürztraminer, Pinot Noir, Riesling, Viognier, Malbec

Ontario / Niagara Peninsula: Chardonnay, Riesling, Pinot Noir, Vidal, Cabernet Franc

The Vintners Quality Alliance (VQA) formed to regulate the wines of Ontario in 1988 and British Columbia in 1990. A VQA designation stipulates that the wine comes from 100 percent *vinifera* varieties, and it also controls varietal percentages. If a label lists the grape variety, the wine must contain at least 85 percent of that variety. If the label names a Designated Viticultural Area (DVA), 95 percent of the grapes must come from that area. If a vineyard appears, 100 percent of the wine must come from that vineyard. More than 100 wineries produce VQA wines.

MY FAVORITE CANADIAN WINERIES

Amisfield	Jackson-Triggs
Château des Charmes	Le Clos Jordanne
Greywacke	Mission Hill
Henry of Pelham	Sumac Ridge
Inniskillin	

CANADIAN ICE WINE

The first new winery in Ontario since 1927, the Inniskillin Winery was founded in 1975 and produced its first ice wine in 1984 after an unseasonably cold winter.

To make ice wine, grapes are allowed to freeze on the vine before being picked by hand. They're pressed carefully while still frozen, yielding a small amount of concentrated juice high in sugar and other components. Canadian law requires that ice wine come only from *vinifera* grapes, usually Riesling and the French hybrid Vidal. It also must contain at least 125 grams of residual sugar per liter. Most ice wines are expensive and sold in half bottles.

TEST YOUR KNOWLEDGE of the wines of Canada by trying the quiz on page 345.

— BEST RECENT VINTAGES OF CANADIAN WINES —

ONTARIO: 2005 2006* 2009 2010* 2011 2012 2013 2014
BRITISH COLUMBIA: 2005 2006 2009 2010 2011
2012 2013 2014 2015
* EXCEPTIONAL VINTAGE

——— FURTHER READING ———

Canadian Wine for Dummies by Tony Aspler

Vintage Canada by Tony Aspler

The Wine Atlas of Canada by Tony Aspler

THE WINES OF AUSTRIA

Grape growing and winemaking in what is now Austria date back to the fourth century B.C., but only in the past quarter century has the country earned a reputation for producing quality wines, specifically some of Europe's most elegant and best-tasting white wines, both dry and sweet. Its Grüner Veltliners and Rieslings pair beautifully with food, which accounts in part for the recent success of Austrian wines in America. Both chefs and sommeliers agree that these wines work well with nearly any dish, from fish and poultry to most meats. Austria's wines also hold their own when paired with Asian spices.

The country contains four wine regions: Lower Austria, Vienna, Burgenland, and Styria, all located along its eastern borders. The Danube River and the fertile valley that surrounds it define the northern wine regions,

Visit the village of Klosterneuburg on the Danube River to see a monastery that dates from 1114. While there, taste the Grüner Veltliner of Donauland. Also visit **THE KLOSTERNEUBURG SCHOOL OF ENOLOGY,** the oldest in the world, founded in 1860.

including Lower Austria—which produces 60 percent of the country's wine—and Vienna, one of the world's most beautiful cities and the only major city to be a wine region. The two most important of these regions, their wine districts, and specialties are:

Burgenland: (red and dessert wines) Neusiedlersee, Mittelburgenland, Neusiedlersee-Hügelland

Lower Austria: (white wines) Wachau, Kamptal, Kremstal, Donauland

The main white varietals are:

Grüner Veltliner   Sauvignon Blanc   Riesling   Chardonnay (Morillon)

and the main red varietals are:

Blaufränkisch (Lemberger)   St. Laurent   Pinot Noir

Austria largely follows the same criteria used in other European countries, specifically Germany, with regard to wine labeling, although it maintains even stricter control. Grape ripeness and the sugar content of the fermenting must determines quality levels, the three broadest being:

Tafelwein   Qualitätswein   Prädikatswein

The Austrian wine board tastes and chemically analyzes Qualitätswein and higher levels of wine, giving consumers a guarantee of taste, style, and quality. If a label lists a specific grape, the wine must contain at least 85 percent of that grape. If a label indicates a vintage, the wine must contain a minimum of 85 percent of that vintage. If the label names a wine region, 100 percent of the wine must come from that region.

WACHAU WINES

STEINFEDER: maximum alcohol 10.7%

FEDERSPIEL: maximum alcohol 12.5%

SMARAGD: minimum alcohol 12.5%

(Sommelier Journal)

Grüner Veltliner accounts for **MORE THAN ONE-THIRD** of Austrian grape plantings.

Austria produces **70 PERCENT** white wine.

TRY BLAUFRÄNKISCH blended with Cabernet Sauvignon.

The **ZWEIGELT** grape is a cross between Blaufränkisch and St. Laurent.

TEST YOUR KNOWLEDGE of the wines of Austria by trying the quiz on page 345.

—— **FURTHER READING** ——

The Ultimate Austrian Wine Guide by Peter Moser

The Wines of Austria by Philipp Blom

As with German wines, most Austrian wines are white, but, unlike German wines, most of Austria's wines are dry, with higher alcohol and more body, resembling the wines of Alsace. Gradation of ripeness indicates the amount of residual sugar left in the wine after fermentation. In Austrian wines, it ranges from the very dry Trocken to the very sweet Trockenbeerenauslese.

GRADATIONS OF RIPENESS

DRY	SWEET	VERY SWEET
TROCKEN	TAFELWEIN	AUSLESE
HALBTROCKEN	LANDWEIN	EISWEIN
LIEBLICH	QUALITÄTSWEIN	BEERENAUSLESE
	KABINETT	AUSBRUCH
	PRÄDIKATSWEIN	TROCKENBEERENAUSLESE
	SPÄTLESE	

Ausbruch, one of the world's great dessert wines, comes from the village of Rust in Burgenland and has a history that dates back as far as 1617. On par with French Sauternes, German Beerenauslese, and Hungarian Tokay, it's made with botrytized grapes, primarily Furmint.

MY FAVORITE AUSTRIAN WINE PRODUCERS

Alzinger	Hirtzberger	Rudy Pichler
Bründlmayer	Knoll	Prager I
F. X. Pichler	Kracher	Schloss Gobelsburg
Hirsch	Nig	

– BEST RECENT VINTAGES OF AUSTRIAN WINES –

2006** 2007* 2008** 2009* 2010 2011
2012 2013 2014 2015**

* EXCEPTIONAL VINTAGE   ** EXTRAORDINARY VINTAGE

---

5 BEST VALUE AUSTRIAN WINES WINES UNDER $30

Alois Kracher Pinot Gris Trocken • Hirsch "Veltliner #1" • Nigl Grüner Veltliner Kremser Freiheit • Schloss Gobelsburg • Sepp Moser Sepp Zweigelt •

See page 309 for a complete list

THE WINES OF HUNGARY

The wine industry of Hungary traces back as far as the Roman Empire, and it has thrived culturally and economically for nearly 1,000 years. Tokay, its most famous wine, has been produced continuously since the sixteenth century, and Tokaj received the world's first vineyard classification in 1700. The reputation of Hungarian wine suffered a major decline under Communist rule from 1949 to 1989. In that time, a state monopoly shifted production to bulk wine with little regard to maintaining or improving existing quality wines.

Since the fall of Communism, however, emphasis has returned to quality wines, with an influx of capital from Italian, French, and German winemakers. The introduction of Sauvignon Blanc, Chardonnay, and Pinot Gris grapes, new vineyard techniques, and modern equipment have helped rebuild Hungary's wine industry. The famous vineyards of Tokaj received the first wave of attention, but investment has expanded throughout the country.

THE HUNGARIAN LANGUAGE can prove difficult for anyone—especially after a glass of wine! This table will help you understand the style of the wine behind the name.

Hungarian name	AKA
Kékfrankos	Blaufränkisch
Tramini	Gewürztraminer
Szürkebarát	Pinot Gris
Zöld Veltlini	Grüner Veltliner

TOKAJ: The name of the village
TOKAJI: From the region
TOKAY: English version of Tokaji

DISZNÓKŐ
TOKAJI ASZÚ
5 PUTTONYOS
2000

The major grapes are:

	NATIVE TO HUNGARY	INTERNATIONAL
WHITE	FURMINT	CHARDONNAY
	HÁRSLEVELÜ	PINOT GRIS (SZÜRKEBARÁT)
	OLASZRIZLING	SAUVIGNON BLANC
RED	KADARKA	CABERNET SAUVIGNON
	KÉKFRANKOS	MERLOT
	PORTUGIESER	PINOT NOIR

The country has 22 wine regions, seven of which you should know along with their most important wines:

Badacsony: Olaszrizling
Eger Kékfrankos: Pinot Noir
Somoló: Furmint
Sopron: Kékfrankos
Szekszárd: Kadarka, Merlot, Cabernet Sauvignon
Tokaj: Furmint, Hárslevelü
Villány-Siklós: Cabernet Sauvignon, Kékfrankos

TOKAJI ASZÚ

This "liquid gold" wine—on par with French Sauternes and German Trockenbeerenauslese—comes from Tokaj, a village in Hungary's northeastern corner and one of the oldest wine regions in the world. *Aszú* refers to the dried, shriveled, botrytized grapes used to make the wine.

Tokaji Aszú usually blends four grapes native to Hungary, primarily Furmint. Throughout the fall harvest season, the grapes affected by the *Botrytis cinerea* mold—or aszú—are picked, lightly crushed, and made into a paste. Unaffected grapes ferment into the base wine. Workers collect the aszú paste in baskets, called *puttonyos*, then blend those into the base wine according to the desired sweetness, measured in *puttonyos* on the label of all Tokaji Aszú. The more paste buckets that go into the base wine, the sweeter the outcome.

Puttonyos wine has four levels:

3 Puttonyos

60 grams of
sugar per liter

4 Puttonyos

90 grams of
sugar per liter

5 Puttonyos

120 grams of
sugar per liter

6 Puttonyos

150 grams of
sugar per liter

The sweetest Tokaj wines—called "Essencia" or "Eszencia"—contain a whopping 180 grams of sugar. Due to its high concentration of sugar, Essencia may take years to finish fermentation, and even then it will have an alcohol content of only 2–5 percent. It's one of the most unique wines in the world!

MY FAVORITE TOKAY PRODUCERS

Chateau Dereszla

Chateau Pajzos

Disznókö

Hétszölö

Oremus

Royal Tokaji Wine
Company

Szepsy

– BEST VINTAGES OF TOKAJI ASZÚ –

2000*   2002   2003   2005*   2006*   2009
2010   2011   2012   2013   2014   2015*

* EXCEPTIONAL VINTAGE

SZAMORODNI is another style of wine made in Tokaj. It ranges from semidry to semisweet but has fewer grams of sugar than three *puttonyos*.

A french Sauternes has 90 **GRAMS OF SUGAR** and a German Trockenbeerenauslese has 150 grams of sugar.

The traditional squat Tokaji Aszú bottles contain **500 MILLILITERS** versus the normal 750 milliliters.

TEST YOUR KNOWLEDGE of the wines of Hungary by trying the quiz on page 345.

———— **FURTHER READING** ————

Wine Guide Hungary by Gabriella Rohaly and Gabor Meszaros

THE WINES OF GREECE

Wine production in the Peloponnese began 7,000 years ago, and wine has played an important role in Greek culture and life since at least the seventh century B.C. It has always ranked as one of the most traded commodities throughout Greece and other Mediterranean countries.

Prior to 1985, most Greek wines were somewhat ordinary. Large bulk-wine producers exported them mainly to Greek communities abroad. Greece joined the European Union in 1981, prompting tremendous investment in winemaking technology and the vineyards there. As a result, especially over the last 25 years, the Greek wine industry has been concentrating on making quality wines. EU subsidies, along with winemakers' dedication, have helped finance state-of-the-art wineries throughout the country.

GREECE

MACEDONIA

AMYNDEO

NAOUSSA

Aegean Sea

PATRAS

Athens ★

NEMEA

SAMOS

MANTINIA

PELOPONNESE

Mediterranean Sea

SANTORINI

RHODES

0 Miles 100

0 Kilometers 200

CRETE

"The wine urges me on, the bewitching wine, which sets even a wise man to singing and laughing gently and rouses him up to dance and brings forth words which were better unspoken."
—Odysseus, *The Odyssey* (14.463–466)

"Shall we not pass a law that, in the first place, no children under 18 may touch wine at all, teaching that it is wrong to pour fire upon fire either in body or in soul . . . and thus guarding against the excitable disposition of the young? And next, we shall rule that the young man under 30 may take wine in moderation, but that he must entirely abstain from intoxication and heavy drinking. But when a man has reached the age of 40, he may join in the convivial gatherings and invoke Dionysus, above all other gods, inviting his presence at the rite (which is also the recreation) of the elders, which he bestowed on mankind as a medicine potent against the crabbedness of Old Age, that thereby we men may renew our youth, and that, through forgetfulness of care, the temper of our souls may lose its hardness and become softer and more ductile."
— Plato, *Laws* 666b

Of Greece's more than 3,000 islands, only **63 ARE INHABITED.**

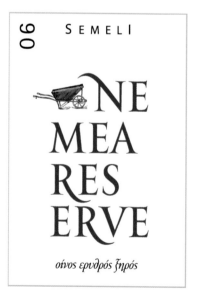

The major white grapes are:

Assyrtiko **Moschofilero** **Roditis**

and the major red grapes are:

Agiorgitiko **Mavrodafni** **Xinomavro**

THE BEST WINE-GROWING REGIONS AND THEIR DISTRICTS

NORTHERN GREECE	SOUTHERN GREECE	AEGEAN SEA

MACEDONIA:
  AMYNDEO
  NAOUSSA
	PELOPONNESE:
	  MANTINIA
	  NEMEA
	  PATRAS
		THE ISLANDS:
		  CRETE
		  SAMOS
		  SANTORINI
		  RHODES

Describing a typical Greek wine poses no easy task. Look at a map of the country and note its many islands and mountains and proximity to the Aegean and Ionian seas of the Mediterranean. It's the third most mountainous country in Europe, and most of its vineyards lie on the slopes of mountains or on remote islands. A typical vineyard here covers less than one hectare (2,471 acres).

Enormous diversity characterizes Greece's wine regions. Some of the climate is distinctly Mediterranean (hot summers; long autumns; short, mild winters), but the mountain regions feature a more typically continental climate: lots of sunshine, cool evenings, dry summers, and mild winters. Some of the islands' volcanic soils make a very different style of wine depending on whether the vineyards lie on flatlands or on steep mountain slopes. Some vineyard owners harvest in August, others in October. According to myth, Dionysus gave wine to the Greeks in Attica, the region containing Athens. Known today for its Retsina and Salvatiano, Attica fosters some of the most exciting experimentation.

Many of the better wines fall into the two governmental categories: OPAP (Wines of Appellation of Origin of Superior Quality, mostly dry) and OPE (Wines of Appellation of Controlled Origin, only sweet). Both designations indicate wines that come from viticultural areas defined in 1971. Nemea is an OPAP wine, and Muscat of Patras an OPE wine. Look for the red stripe at the top of the bottle for an OPAP wine and a blue stripe for an OPE wine. The Greek equivalent to table wine, Epitrapezios Oenos (EO), doesn't include an appellation of origin and may blend wines from many different regions. Exports of Greek wine to America have increased by 30 percent over the last five years, and the next ten years will define the broader future of the new Greek wines.

RETSINA

Adding pine resin as a flavoring agent to wine creates Retsina. In ancient times, winemakers used pine resin to create an airtight seal on amphorae—large ceramic wine vessels—to prevent wine from oxidizing during transportation and storage. The resin sometimes leaked into the wine, and eventually the Greeks developed a taste for the distinctive flavor. A friend describes its pungent aroma as an "acquired taste." (Think turpentine!)

MY FAVORITE GREEK WINE PRODUCERS

Alpha Estate	Oenoforos	Semeli
Driopi	Pavlidis	Sigalas
Gaia Estate	Manoussakis	Skouras
Gerovassiliou	Mercouri	Tselepos
Kir Yianni	Samos Cooperative	

BEST RECENT VINTAGES OF WINES FROM GREECE

2005　2007　2008*　2009　2010　2011
2012　2013　2014　2015*

* EXCEPTIONAL VINTAGE

TEST YOUR KNOWLEDGE of the wines of Greece by trying the quiz on page 345.

TEST YOUR KNOWLEDGE of the wines of Greece by trying the quiz on page 345.

—— **FURTHER READING** ——

The Illustrated Greek Wine Book by Nico Manessis

The Wines of Greece by Konstantinos Lazarakis

THE GREATER WORLD OF WINE

WINE AND FOOD PAIRINGS ✳ FREQUENTLY ASKED
QUESTIONS ABOUT WINE ✳ THE BEST OF THE BEST ✳
THE WORLD'S BEST VALUE WINES $30 AND LESS ✳
WINE RESOURCES

ANDREA ROBINSON worked at Windows on the World and is one of only 15 women in the world to hold the title of master sommelier, awarded by the Court of Master Sommeliers. She has written several books on wine and food, and the James Beard Foundation named her Outstanding Wine & Spirits Professional in 2002.

In 2013, the *New England Journal of Medicine* reaffirmed that a Mediterranean diet rich in olive oil, nuts, beans, fish, fruit, vegetables, **AND WINE** is good for you.

I cook with wine; sometimes I even add it to food.

—Attributed to W. C. Fields

Are you a menu maven or a wine-list junkie? I look at the wine list first, choose my wine, and then make **MY MEAL SELECTION,** as follows:

- What kind of wine do I like?
- Texture of food (heavy or light)
- Preparation (grilled, sautéed, baked, etc.)
- Sauce (cream, tomato, wine, etc.)

WINE AND FOOD PAIRINGS

BY KEVIN ZRALY AND ANDREA ROBINSON

YOU'VE TASTED YOUR way through eight classes, nearly eighty wines, and discovered a shopping cart's worth of bottles that you enjoy. Why? Food! The final stop on our wine odyssey—and really the whole point of the trip—is the dining table. Wine and food were meant for each other. Just look at the dining habits of the world's best eaters, the French, Italians, and Spanish. The American table always features salt and pepper shakers, but in Europe it's the wine bottle because wine enlivens even everyday dishes.

THE BASICS

Forget everything you've ever heard about pairing food and wine. Only one rule applies when it comes to matching the two: The best wine to pair with your meal is whatever wine you like. No matter what! If you know what you want, drink it. Worried that Chardonnay with sirloin isn't "right"? The only palate you must please is your own.

When cooking with wine, try to use the same wine or style that you're going to serve.

HOW MUCH?

Allow one bottle for every five people—that is, one five-ounce glass per person—for each food selection.

SYNERGY

Sounds like a gourmet computer game or a management meeting, right? But it's really not that complicated. If until now you haven't often had wine with dinner, a great adventure awaits you. Remember, the European tradition of wine with meals didn't result from a shortage of milk or iced tea. It developed from the synergy of wine and food. Pairing the two makes both taste better.

How does this concept work? The same way that combining certain foods improves their overall taste. For example, you squeeze fresh lemon juice onto oysters or sprinkle grated Parmesan cheese over spaghetti marinara because that combination of flavors improves the overall dish. It's really that simple. Different foods and wines have different aromas, textures, and flavors. Pairing them provokes more interesting flavors than if you drank just water with dinner. You need only some basic information about wine and food styles to pick wines that will enhance your meals. The first rule of thumb: The more flavorful the food, the more flavorful the wine you should drink.

The addition of **SALT** to food highlights both the tannins and the alcohol in wine.

ACIDITY

Acid turbo-charges flavor. You probably have seen TV chefs using lemons and limes—high-acid ingredients—in many dishes. Even dishes that you wouldn't call sour have a touch of acidity to amp up their flavor. Drink a high-acid wine with dishes featuring cream or cheese sauces to enhance and lengthen the flavor of the dish.

TEXTURE

As we've seen with tannins, wine has a definite texture. It also has flavor nuances that can make it adequate, outstanding, or unforgettable with a meal. Full-bodied wines have a mouth-filling texture and bold, rich flavors that you notice on your palate. But when it comes to food, these wines overwhelm delicate dishes and clash with boldly flavored ones. Remember, you want harmony and balance. The sturdier the food or fuller in flavor, the more full-bodied the wine should be. Pair milder foods with wines that have a medium or light body. Once you understand wine texture, food pairings are easy. You'll find two lists (one for red, one for white) on pages 285–286 with suggestions based on texture and the foods that the wines can match.

BITTERNESS in wine comes from the combination of high tannin and high alcohol, and these wines are best served with grilled, charcoaled, or blackened food.

WINE AND CHEESE

As in all matters of taste, the topic of wine and cheese comes with its share of controversy and debate. Wine and cheese naturally go together. For a good cheese and wine, each enhances the flavors and complexities of the other. Also, the protein in cheese softens the tannins in a red wine. The key here lies in carefully selecting the cheese, and now you see the controversy. Some chefs and culinary experts caution that some of the most popular

Do you drink your tea with milk or lemon? The milk coats your mouth with **SWEETNESS**, whereas the lemon leaves your tongue with a **DRY CRISPNESS**.

Probably one of the reasons that classic **FRENCH CUISINE IS NOTED FOR ITS SUBTLETY** is because the French want to let their wines "show off." This is an especially good idea if the wine is a special or splurge bottle.

cheeses pair badly with wine because they overpower it. Ripe Brie offers a classic example. So let's keep it simple. The best cheeses for wine are:

Cheddar	Manchego	Parmigiano-Reggiano
Chèvre	Monterey Jack	Pecorino
Fontina	Montrachet	Taleggio
Gouda	Mozzarella	Tomme
Gruyère		

These are my favorite cheese-and-wine pairings:

Chèvre with Sancerre or Sauvignon Blanc

Manchego with Rioja or Brunello di Montalcino

Montrachet or aged (dry) Monterey Jack with Bordeaux or Cabernet Sauvignon

Pecorino or Parmigiano-Reggiano with Chianti Classico Riserva, Brunello di Montalcino, Cabernet Sauvignon, Bordeaux, Barolo, or Amarone

What to drink with Brie? Champagne or sparkling wine. Blue cheeses, because of their strong flavor, overpower most wines except—get ready for this—dessert wines! The classic and truly delicious pairings are :

Roquefort with Sauternes

Stilton with Port

HORS D'OEUVRES AND APPETIZERS

Champagne and sparkling wine have a magical effect. Whether served at a wedding or at home, Champagne remains a symbol of celebration, prosperity, romance, and fun, but don't forget about Cava, Prosecco, and California sparkling wine.

WHITE WINES

LIGHT BODY	MEDIUM BODY	FULL BODY
ALBARIÑO	CHABLIS PREMIER CRU	CHABLIS GRAND CRU
ALSACE PINOT BLANC	CHARDONNAY	CHARDONNAY
ALSACE RIESLING	GAVI	CHASSAGNE-
CHABLIS	GEWÜRZTRAMINER	MONTRACHET
FRASCATI	GRÜNER VELTLINER	MEURSAULT
GERMAN KABINETT	MÂCON-VILLAGES	PULIGNY-MONTRACHET
AND SPÄTLESE	MONTAGNY	VIOGNIER
MUSCADET	POUILLY-FUISSÉ	
ORVIETO	POUILLY-FUMÉ	
PINOT GRIGIO	SANCERRE	
PINOT GRIS	SAUVIGNON BLANC /	
SAUVIGNON BLANC	FUMÉ BLANC	
SOAVE	ST-VÉRAN	
VERDEJO	WHITE GRAVES	
VERDICCHIO		

FOOD PAIRINGS		
CLAMS	BASS	BELL PEPPERS
CORN	BELL PEPPERS	CAULIFLOWER
CUCUMBERS	CAULIFLOWER	DUCK
EDAMAME	GREEN BEANS	EGGPLANT
FLOUNDER	EGGPLANT	LOBSTER
OYSTERS	PEAS	PEAS
SALAD	SCALLOPS	ROAST CHICKEN
SOLE	SIRLOIN STEAK	SALMON
VEAL PAILLARD	SNAPPER	SQUASH
	SQUASH	SWORDFISH
	TOMATOES	TOMATOES
	ZUCCHINI	TUNA
		ZUCCHINI

* Some of these wines come in a range of styles, from light to full, depending on the producer. If you don't know a winery's particular style, ask the sommelier or wine merchant for help.

My favorite **WHITE WINE FOR PICNICS** is a chilled German Riesling Kabinett / Spätlese. On a hot summer day, I can think of no better white wine. The balance of fruit, acid, and sweetness as well as the lightness (low alcohol) makes these wines a perfect match for salads, fruits, and cheese. If you prefer a drier-style Riesling, try one from Alsace, Washington, or the Finger Lakes region of New York.

Many Chardonnays (especially from California) are red wines masquerading as white wines, which, in my opinion, makes them a **PERFECT MATCH FOR STEAK**.

VEGETABLES ARE VERY VERSATILE both on their own and when included as an ingredient in a larger recipe, so keep that in mind when considering your wine pairings.

My favorite **RED WINE FOR PICNICS** is Beaujolais. A great Beaujolais is the essence of fresh fruit without the tannins, and its higher acidity blends nicely with all picnic fare.

Most Pinot Noirs are white wines **MASQUERADING AS RED WINES,** which makes them perfect wines for fish and fowl.

YOUNG RED WINES with a lot of tannin taste better when paired with foods that have high fat content. The fat softens the tannins.

Eat your greens, but I don't recommend having them with wine. Artichokes, asparagus, kale, spinach, and other green or leafy vegetables all contain a compound that will make the wine you drink with them **TASTE BITTER.**

RED WINES

LIGHT BODY	MEDIUM BODY	FULL BODY
BARDOLINO	BARBERA	BARBARESCO
BEAUJOLAIS	BORDEAUX	BAROLO
BEAUJOLAIS	(CRUS BOURGEOIS)	BORDEAUX
-VILLAGES	BURGUNDY PREMIERS	(GREAT CHÂTEAUX)
BORDEAUX	AND GRANDS CRUS	CABERNET SAUVIGNON
(PROPRIETARY)	CABERNET	CHÂTEAUNEUF-DU-PAPE
BURGUNDY	SAUVIGNON	HERMITAGE
(VILLAGE)	CHIANTI CLASSICO	MALBEC
PINOT NOIR	RISERVA	MERLOT
RIOJA-CRIANZA	CÔTES DU RHÔNE	SYRAH / SHIRAZ
VALPOLICELLA	CROZES-HERMITAGE	ZINFANDEL
	CRU BEAUJOLAIS	
	DOLCETTO	
	MALBEC	
	MERLOT	
	PINOT NOIR	
	RIOJA RESERVA AND	
	GRAN RESERVA	
	SYRAH / SHIRAZ	
	ZINFANDEL	

FOOD PAIRINGS		
BELL PEPPERS	EGGPLANT	BEEFSTEAK (SIRLOIN)
CORN	GAME BIRDS	GAME MEATS
DUCK	GREEN BEANS	LAMB CHOPS
EDAMAME	LEEKS	LEEKS
PEAS	MUSHROOMS	LEG OF LAMB
SALMON	SQUASH	MUSHROOMS
SWORDFISH	PORK CHOPS	POTATOES
TUNA	POTATOES	SWEET POTATOES
TOMATOES	ROAST CHICKEN	VEAL CHOP
ZUCCHINI	SWEET POTATOES	

* Some of these wines come in a range of styles, from light to full, depending on the producer. If you don't know a winery's particular style, ask the sommelier or wine merchant for help.

NO-FAULT WINE INSURANCE

Drinking wine with food should add enjoyment, not stress, to your meal, but the latter happens all too often. Faced with so many choices, you might choose something familiar—even if the wine doesn't pair well with what you're eating. But it's just as easy to choose the right wine. These user-friendly wines go well with virtually any dish. They all have a light-to-medium body and feature ample fruit, acidity, and low tannins. Which means that you'll taste a harmonious balance of flavors from both the wine and the food. Neither will overwhelm the other. Also, if you want the food to play center stage, these wines are your best bets. These wines work well for what I call restaurant roulette—where one person orders fish, another orders meat, and so on. They also match well with distinctively spiced foods that otherwise might clash with a full-flavored wine. (It goes without saying that they're enjoyable on their own!)

USER-FRIENDLY WINES

ROSÉ	WHITE	RED
VIRTUALLY ANY ROSÉ OR WHITE ZINFANDEL	CHAMPAGNE AND SPARKLING WINES GERMAN RIESLING, KABINETT, AND SPÄTLESE MÂCON-VILLAGES PINOT GRIGIO POUILLY-FUMÉ AND SANCERRE SAUVIGNON BLANC / FUMÉ BLANC	BEAUJOLAIS-VILLAGES CHIANTI CLASSICO CÔTES DU RHÔNE MERLOT PINOT NOIR RIOJA CRIANZA

FAIL-SAFE FOOD: When in doubt, order roast chicken or tofu, which acts as a blank canvas for almost any wine style—light-, medium-, or full-bodied.

SAUCES

Sauces are game-changers. They can alter the entire taste and texture of a dish. Is the sauce acidic, heavy, spicy? Subtly flavored foods allow the wine to play the starring role. Dishes with bold, spicy ingredients can overpower the nuances and complexity that distinguish a great wine. Consider the chicken breast. A simply prepared chicken paillard might match well with a light-bodied white wine, but if you add a cream or cheese sauce, you

For food with **SPICY SAUCES**, try something with carbon dioxide, such as a Champagne or a sparkling wine.

might prefer a high-acid, medium-bodied, or even full-bodied white wine. A tomato sauce calls for a light-bodied red. Always consider the sauce!

DESSERT

Beerenauslese, Port, Sauternes, Tokay—all very different wines—have sweetness in common. They count as dessert wines because their sweetness closes your palate and makes you feel satisfied after a good meal. But dessert holds only one part of the story. In America, coffee is more common with dessert, but more restaurants are adding by-the-glass dessert wines to their menus. (A full bottle of a rich dessert wine isn't practical unless the whole table shares it. For dinner at home, go for dessert wines in half-bottles.) Try a dessert wine a few minutes before the dessert itself to prepare your palate and recalibrate it. These are some of my favorite wine-and-dessert combinations:

Asti Spumante with fresh fruit or biscotti

Beerenauslese and late harvest Riesling with fruit tarts, crème brûlée, or almond cookies

Madeira with milk chocolate, nut tarts, crème caramel, or coffee or mocha desserts

Muscat Beaumes-de-Venise with crème brûlée, fresh fruit, fruit sorbets, or lemon tart

Port with dark chocolate desserts, walnuts, poached pears, or Stilton

Sherry (Padro Ximénez) on top of vanilla ice cream, and with raisin-nut cakes or other desserts containing figs or dried fruit

Sauternes or Tokay with fruit tarts, poached fruits, crème brûlée, caramel and hazelnut desserts, or Roquefort cheese

Vin Santo with biscotti (dipped in the wine)

Vouvray with fruit tarts or fresh fruit

Try serving a dessert wine as the dessert itself. That way you can concentrate on savoring the complex and delicious flavors with a clear palate. It's especially convenient at home. All you have to do is pull a cork! Also, if you're counting calories, one glass of dessert wine affords the satisfying sweetness of a dessert with zero fat!

—— FURTHER READING ——
Great Wine & Food Made Simple by Andrea Robinson

Perfect Pairings by Evan Goldstein

FREQUENTLY ASKED QUESTIONS ABOUT WINE

DOES CALIFORNIA OR FRANCE MAKE THE BEST WINES?

Nice try! California and France both make great wines. The French make the best French wines, and California makes the best California wines. Each region has a distinct profile. Both California and France grow many of the same grape varieties. They also have many differences, including climate, soil, and tradition.

The French regard their soil with reverence and believe that the best wines come only from the greatest soil. When vineyard owners planted California's original grapes, soil didn't determine which grapes grew where. Over recent decades, however, vineyard owners have given this consideration much more importance. Today winemakers cite their best Cabernet Sauvignons as coming from a specific vineyard or even area. As far as weather, temperatures in Napa and Sonoma obviously differ from Bordeaux and Burgundy. European vintners grow gray hair over cold snaps and rainstorms in the growing season, but Californians can count on nearly abundant sunshine and warm temperatures.

It's tradition that really separates the two. Vineyard and winery practices in Europe have remained virtually unchanged for generations, and these age-old techniques—some written into law—define each region's style. In California, where few traditions exist, vintners can experiment and create new products based on consumer demand. If you've ever had a wine called Two Buck Chuck, you know what I mean. Burgundy has been making white wines for more than 1,500 years, but the California wine renaissance only just reached its fiftieth anniversary.

Best to buy how you feel on a given day: Do you want to end up in Bordeaux or the Napa Valley?

DOES VINE AGE AFFECT WINE QUALITY?

As a vine ages, especially beyond 30 years, it starts losing its production value. In commercial vineyards, vine production slows at about 20 years, so most vines are replanted by their fiftieth birthday. French wine labels sometimes use the term *vieilles vignes* ("old vines"). In California, many Zinfandels come from vines more than 75 years old. Many wine tasters, including me, believe that these old vines create a different complexity and taste than younger vines. In many countries, grapes from younger vines don't go into a winery's top wine. In Bordeaux for example, Château Lafite-Rothschild produces a second wine, Carruades de Lafite-Rothschild, from the youngest vines (fewer than 15 years old).

WHO HAS THE BEST WINE SERVICE?

The James Beard Foundation recognizes the following restaurants with the Outstanding Wine Service Award:

1994 Valentino, Santa Monica
1999 Union Square Café, New York
2001 French Laundry, Yountville, California
2002 Gramercy Tavern, New York
2003 Daniel, New York
2004 Babbo, New York
2006 Aureole, Las Vegas
2007 Citronelle, Washington, D.C.
2008 Eleven Madison Park, New York
2009 Le Bernardin, New York
2010 Jean Georges, New York
2011 The Modern, New York
2012 No. 9 Park, Boston
2013 Frasca Food and Wine, Boulder, Colorado
2014 The Barn at Blackberry Farm, Walland, Tennessee
2015 A16, San Francisco
2016 Bern's Steakhouse, Tampa, Florida

Winners of the James Beard Award for Wine and Spirits Professional of the Year include:

1991 Robert Mondavi, Robert Mondavi Winery
1992 Andre Tchelistcheff, Beaulieu Winery
1993 Kevin Zraly, Windows on the World, New York
1994 Randall Grahm, Bonny Doon Vineyard, Santa Cruz
1995 Marvin Shanken, *Wine Spectator*
1996 Jack and Jaimie Davies, Schramsberg Vineyards
1997 Zelma Long, Simi Winery
1998 Robert M. Parker Jr., *Wine Advocate*
1999 Frank Prial, *New York Times*
2000 Kermit Lynch, writer and importer
2001 Gerald Asher, writer
2002 Andrea Robinson, author

2003 Fritz Maytag, Anchor Brewing Co.
2004 Karen MacNeil, author
2005 Joseph Bastianich, Italian Wine Merchants, New York
2006 Daniel Johnnes, The Dinex Group, New York
2007 Paul Draper, Ridge Vineyards
2008 Terry Theise, importer, Terry Theise Estate Selection
2009 Dale DeGroff, author and master mixologist, New York
2010 John Shafer and Doug Shafer, Shafer Vineyards
2011 Julian P. Van Winkle III, Old Rip Van Winkle Distillery, Louisville, Kentucky
2012 Paul Grieco, Terroir, New York
2013 Merry Edwards, Merry Edwards Winery, Sebastopol, California
2014 Garrett Oliver, Brooklyn Brewery, Brooklyn, New York
2015 Rajat Parr, Mina Group, San Francisco
2016 Ron Cooper, Del Maguey Single Village Mezcal, Ranchos de Taos, New Mexico

WHAT ARE THE HOT AREAS IN WINE?

These areas in particular have seen major growth and improvement in quality, over the last 20 years:

Argentina: Malbec
Austria: Grüner Veltliner
Chile: Cabernet Sauvignon
France: Rosé
Italy: Prosecco

Hungary: Tokaji
New Zealand: Sauvignon Blanc, Pinot Noir
South Africa: Sauvignon Blanc, Pinot Noir, Syrah

HOW LONG SHOULD I AGE MY WINE?

The *Wall Street Journal* reported that most people have one or two bottles of wine that they've been saving for years for a special occasion. Not a good idea! More than 90 percent of all wine—red, white, rosé—is made to be consumed within a year. Some wines—dry Riesling, Sauvignon Blanc, Pinot Grigio, Beaujolais—are ready to drink immediately. But keep in mind the following guidelines for aging wine from the best producers in the best years:

WHITE	
CALIFORNIA CHARDONNAY	2–10+ YEARS
FRENCH WHITE BURGUNDY	3–8+ YEARS
GERMAN RIESLING (AUSLESE, BEERENAUSLESE, AND TROCKENBEERENAUSLESE)	3–30+ YEARS
FRENCH SAUTERNES	3–30+ YEARS
RED	
CALIFORNIA / OREGON PINOT NOIRS	2–5+ YEARS
CALIFORNIA MERLOT	2–10+ YEARS
FRENCH RED BURGUNDY	3–8+ YEARS
CHIANTI CLASSICO RISERVAS	3–10+ YEARS
ARGENTINEAN MALBEC	3–15+ YEARS
BRUNELLO DI MONTALCINO	3–15+ YEARS
CALIFORNIA CABERNET SAUVIGNON	3–15+ YEARS
CALIFORNIA ZINFANDEL	5–15+ YEARS
SPANISH RIOJAS (GRAN RESERVAS)	5–20+ YEARS
BAROLO AND BARBARESCO	5–25+ YEARS
HERMITAGE / SYRAH	5–25+ YEARS
BORDEAUX CHÂTEAUX	5–30+ YEARS
VINTAGE PORTS	10–40+ YEARS

Exceptions to the rules always apply, particularly when it comes to generalizing about aging wine (especially with variations in vintages). I've had Bordeaux wines more than a century old that were still going strong, and you're not likely to find a great Sauternes or Port that couldn't do with more age after 50 years. But these age spans represent more than 95 percent of the wines in their categories.

The oldest bottle of wine still aging in Bordeaux is a 1797 Château Lafite-Rothschild!

DO ALL WINES NEED CORKS?

Most corks come from oak trees in Portugal and Spain, but only tradition calls for corks to seal wine bottles. Most wines don't need them. Since you should drink 90 percent of all wines within one year, a screw cap works just as well if not better. Think about what that means: no need for a corkscrew, no broken corks, and no more wine ruined by contaminated cork. Certain wines—those that age for more than five years—benefit from corks, but also keep in mind that a cork's life span lasts approximately 25 to 30 years. After that, drink the wine, or find somebody to recork it!

Many wineries around the world use the Stelvin screw cap, especially in California (Bonny Doon, Sonoma-Cutrer, etc.), Australia, New Zealand, and Austria. Screw-cap wines represent less than 10 percent of all bottled wine, but 93 percent of New Zealand's bottles use them as do 75 percent of Australia's.

WHAT'S A "CORKED" WINE?

This is a serious problem for wine lovers. Some estimates indicate that faulty corks contaminate between 3 and 5 percent of all wines. The culprit? TCA or 2,4,6-trichloranisole. If you've ever encountered a corked wine, it's a smell you won't soon forget! It's dank, wet, and moldy; some describe it as reminiscent of wet cardboard. It overpowers the fruit in the wine and makes it undrinkable, and it can happen to a $10 bottle or a $1,000 bottle.

DECANTING AND AERATING

A good rule to follow: Do as the Romans do—or in this case, the French. For example, in Burgundy, they never decant their Beaujolais or other delicate wines, but in Bordeaux they decant their Cabernet Sauvignon and Merlot most of the time, especially when young. Decant a Vintage Port but not a Ruby or Tawny Port.

To Decant

1. Remove the entire capsule, or protective sleeve, from the neck of the bottle so you can see the wine clearly as it passes through the neck.
2. Light a candle. Most red wines come in dark green glass bottles, making it difficult to see the wine pass through the neck of the bottle. A candle gives the extra illumination you need and also adds a theatrical touch. (If you don't have a candle handy, a flashlight will suffice.)
3. Grasp the decanter—which can also be a carafe or glass pitcher—firmly in hand.
4. With the bottle in your other hand, gently pour the wine into the decanter. Hold both over the candle so that you can see the wine pass through the neck of the bottle.
5. Keep pouring until you see the first signs of sediment. Stop decanting as soon as you see sediment!
6. If there's still wine left, let it stand until the sediment settles. Then decant the rest.

WHAT'S THAT ON THE BOTTOM OF THE CORK?

Tartaric acid, or tartrate, sometimes appears on the bottom of a cork or wine bottle. This harmless crystalline deposit looks like glass or rock candy. These crystals take on a rusty, reddish-brown color from the tannins in red wines. Wineries remove most tartrates by lowering the temperature of the wine before bottling, but this strategy doesn't work with all wines. If you keep your wine at a very cold temperature for a long period of time (for example, in your refrigerator), you can end up with this deposit on your cork. Cool-climate regions, such as Germany, have a greater chance of producing this crystallization.

WHY DO I GET A HEADACHE AFTER DRINKING WINE?

Probably overconsumption! In all seriousness, though, more than 10 percent of my students over the years have been medical doctors, and none has been able to give me the definitive answer to this question. Some people get headaches from white wine, others from red, but dehydration always plays a role in how you feel the next day. For every glass of wine you consume, drink *two* glasses of water to stay hydrated.

Many factors influence how your system metabolizes alcohol. The top three are your health, genetics, and gender. Red wines have differing levels of histamines, which can affect you if you have allergies, causing discomfort and headaches. I myself have a slight allergy to red wine, and I "suffer" every day. Doctors have told me that food additives also contribute to headaches. Research also increasingly points to genetics as a cause for chronic headaches. As for gender, because of certain enzymes, women absorb more alcohol into their bloodstream than men. For women, one glass of wine a day represents a safe limit, but equally healthy men can drink two glasses safely.

WHAT IF I CAN'T FINISH THE BOTTLE?

This is one of the most frequently asked questions in the Wine School—although I've never had this problem! If you still have wine left over, whether red or white, recork the bottle and refrigerate it. Don't leave it on your counter. Bacteria grow in warm temperatures, and a room-temperature kitchen will spoil wine very quickly. If refrigerated, most wines won't lose their flavor over a 48-hour period. (Some swear that the wine tastes better, but I'm not among their number.)

Eventually the wine—any wine with an alcohol content between 8 and 14 percent—will oxidize. Ports, sherries, and other wines with an alcohol content between 17 and 21 percent will last longer, but don't keep them longer than two weeks. Remember, the less contact with oxygen, the longer a wine will last. Consider buying an affordable wine bottle air pump. Some wine collectors even introduce an inert gas into the bottle, such as argon or nitrogen, which has no odor or taste but which preserves the wine from oxygen.

If all else fails, you have a great cooking wine!

WHAT COUNTRIES OR REGIONS WILL YOU BE WRITING ABOUT IN 2025?

America, Argentina, Australia, China, and Eastern Europe, specifically Bulgaria and Romania

WHAT ARE THE MOST IMPORTANT BOOKS FOR YOUR WINE LIBRARY?

First, thank you for buying my wine book, which I hope you have found useful. As with any passion, people always thirst for more. At the end of each section or chapter of this book, I recommend specific books. Beyond those, these are suggestions for required reading:

> *Great Wine Made Simple* by Andrea Robinson
> *Hugh Johnson's Modern Encyclopedia of Wine*
> *The Oxford Companion to Wine edited* by Jancis Robinson
> *Oz Clarke's New Encyclopedia of Wine*
> *Oz Clarke's New Essential Wine Book*
> *Oz Clarke's Wine Atlas*
> *Parker's Wine Buyers Guide* by Robert M. Parker Jr.
> *Sotheby's Wine Encyclopedia* by Tom Stevenson
> *The Widow Clicquot* by Tilar Mazzeo
> *The Wine Bible* by Karen MacNeil
> *Wine for Dummies* by Ed McCarthy and Mary Ewing-Mulligan
> *The World Atlas of Wine* by Hugh Johnson and Jancis Robinson

If you find the above too encyclopedic, try one of these three pocket guides:

> *Andrea Robinson's Wine Buying Guide*
> *Hugh Johnson's Pocket Encyclopedia of Wine*
> *Oz Clarke's Pocket Wine Guide*

THE BEST OF THE BEST

I have spent more than 40 years traveling, tasting, and studying wine, more than 40 years reading, writing, lecturing, and teaching about wine. I have seen it all: the wines, publications, writers, "experts," lists, controversies, events, and so on. The wine world has changed. From the select few wine drinkers of yore to today's great international wines, the following are the best of the best, based on credibility, creativity, experience, impact, and longevity. As with a favorite wine, these are all *personal* selections.

THE WINES

BEST CABERNET SAUVIGNON

Bordeaux, France (Médoc)
Runner-up: California; best value: Chile

In my opinion, the greatest wines of the world come from the châteaux of Bordeaux, and with 7,000 of them there's plenty to choose at all different price points!

The best Cabernet Sauvignon from California comes from the North Coast counties, especially Napa and Sonoma. Napa Cabernets usually have more intensity of fruit and body; Sonoma Cabernets generally taste softer and more elegant.

The price of a vineyard acre in Chile is so far below that of Napa Valley and Bordeaux that you will find tremendous quality and value in Chilean Cabernets.

BEST CHARDONNAY

Burgundy, France
Runner-up: California

As much as I like the best producers of California Chardonnay, nothing else in the world matches the elegance and balance of fruit and acidity of a white Burgundy. Non-oaked Chablis; Montrachets fermented and aged in barrels; the light, easy-drinking Mâcons; and the world-famous Pouilly-Fuissé—there are a style and a price for everyone.

As with Sauvignon Blanc, the best California Chardonnays come from the cooler climates, such as Carneros and Santa Barbara. I'm not a fan of high-alcohol, overly oaked Chardonnays.

BEST MERLOT

Bordeaux, France (St-Émilion, Pomerol)
Runner-up: California

The great châteaux of St-Émilion and Pomerol primarily produce wines made from Merlot, which is the number-one red grape planted in Bordeaux. The major differences between the two regions are availability and price. Pomerol has 1,986 acres, but St-Émilion has more than 23,000. For the better value, go with St-Émilion.

Napa Valley in California produces some superb Merlots as well.

BEST PINOT NOIR

Burgundy, France
Runners-up: Oregon and California

The wine history and tradition of Burgundy run deep. Vines have been growing there for more than a thousand years, and, aside from Beaujolais, French law allows only the sensuous Pinot Noir to grow there. The only problem with a great Pinot Noir from Burgundy is availability and price tag. Oregon makes America's best Pinot Noirs and also great Chardonnays, so many people call Oregon the Burgundy of America. In California, the best Pinot Noirs also grow in cooler climates.

BEST RIESLING

Germany
Runners-up: Alsace, France; and the Finger Lakes District, New York

Many professionals and wine connoisseurs consider Riesling the best white wine in the world. The German diversity of style—some wines being dry, off-dry, semisweet, and very sweet—is why I rank German Rieslings as the world's best. 95 percent of all Alsace Rieslings are dry. Finger Lakes producers make dry, semidry, and sweet Rieslings.

BEST SAUVIGNON BLANC

Loire Valley, France
Runners-up: New Zealand and California

Sauvignon Blanc produced in the Loire Valley is best known by regional names, Sancerre and Pouilly-Fumé. The best of the New Zealand Sauvignon Blancs are sold under the producer's name. The stylistic differences between the two are striking. Both have light to medium body and high acidity and work well with fish and poultry, but New Zealand Sauvignon Blancs have what some call a very tropical aroma, which you either like or don't. (I like it!) After Chardonnay, Sauvignon Blanc is the second-highest-quality white grape grown in California. In my opinion, the best Sauvignon Blancs come from cooler climates, have no oak, and are lower in alcohol content.

BEST FLYING WINEMAKER

Michel Rolland

Over the last 30 years, the demand for high-quality wine around the world has exploded. Like many other businesses, winemakers often hire consultants. Known as the flying wine consultant, Michel Rolland, a Bordeaux native, works with more than 100 wineries on 4 continents. His influence on the quality and style of wine produced all over the world is enormous.

BEST WINE TASTER

Robert M. Parker Jr.

Bob and I started studying wine around the same time but took different paths. His scoring system has changed the way people taste and rate wine. No other human being has tasted more wines. Until a few years ago, he tasted *10,000 wines a year*—more than 25 every day on average! Recently he told me that he scaled down to 5,000 per year, still a prodigious number. *Wine Advocate* publishes all of his reviews as does his website, eRobert-Parker.com. Regardless of whether you agree with his assessments, you have to admire his stamina, perseverance, and red tongue!

Through Christie's wine department, Michael Broadbent, another admirable wine taster, possibly has tasted more older wines than Parker. He doesn't use a numbering system but describes wines in his own British, poetic fashion. Also look for Stephen Tanzer, who has his own publication, *International Wine Cellar*. Many writers and tasters around the world have developed an expertise on specific wines—Bordeaux, Burgundy, California, Tuscany, and so on—and I recommend them throughout this book.

BEST CORK

Frog's Leap Winery, Napa, California

John Williams—owner and winemaker of Frog's Leap and one of California's premier winemakers—adds humor to drinking wine with the inscription "Ribbit" on every Frog's Leap cork.

STORING AND AGING

BEST INVESTMENT

The great châteaux of Bordeaux and California Cabernet Sauvignons

For the last 40 years, I've invested in wine. I have never sold any of my collection, but if I did I'd realize a better return than any money market fund. Even if the market for wine tanks, I can still drink it! From 2000 to 2010, Bordeaux produced the best wine ever, with great vintages in 2000, 2003, 2005, 2009, and 2010 and excellent vintages in 2001 and 2006. The other four vintages were quite good, too, and 2015 also will be exceptional.

It's getting harder to buy California's best Cabernet Sauvignons, specifically Napa Valley, where Cabernet Sauvignon thrives. Napa also has had great vintages recently, especially 2012, 2013, 2014, and 2015. You can still buy many of these for less than $50.

BEST WINE TO CELLAR FOR YOUR CHILD'S 21st BIRTHDAY OR YOUR 25th WEDDING ANNIVERSARY

Few wines age well beyond 20 years, but sharing these aged wines makes for one of the greatest joys of collecting wine.

1990 Bordeaux, California Cabernet Sauvignon, Rhône, Burgundy, Tuscany, Piedmont, Sauternes, Champagne, Germany (Auslese and above)

1991 Rhône (North), Port, California Cabernet Sauvignon

1992 Port, California Cabernet Sauvignon and Zinfandel

1993 California Cabernet Sauvignon and Zinfandel

1994 Port, California Cabernet Sauvignon and Zinfandel, Rioja

1995 Bordeaux, Rhône, Rioja, California Cabernet Sauvignon

1996 Burgundy, Piedmont, Bordeaux (Medoc), Burgundy, Germany (Auslese and above)

1997 California Cabernet Sauvignons, Tuscany (Chianti, Brunello, etc), Piedmont, Port, Australian Shiraz

1998 Bordeaux (St-Émilion / Pomerol), Rhône (South), Piedmont

1999 Piedmont, Rhône (North), California Zinfandel

2000 Bordeaux

2001 Napa Cabernet Sauvignon, Sauternes, Germany (Auslese and above), Rioja, Ribera del Duero

2002 Napa Cabernet Sauvignon, Germany (Auslese and above), Burgundy (Grand Cru), Sauternes

2003 Northern and Southern Rhône, Sauternes, Bordeaux, Port

2004 Napa Cabernet Sauvignon, Piedmont

2005 Bordeaux, Sauternes, Burgundy, Southern Rhône, Piedmont, Tuscany, Germany, Rioja, Ribera del Duero, Southern Australia, Napa Cabernet Sauvignon, Washington Cabernet Sauvignon

2006 Bordeaux (Pomerol), Northern Rhône, Barolo, Barbaresco, Brunello di Montalcino, Germany (Auslese and above), Argentina Malbec

2007 Sauternes, Southern Rhône, Napa Cabernet Sauvignon, Port

2008 Bordeaux, Napa Valley Cabernet Sauvignon

2009 California Cabernet Sauvignon

2010 Bordeaux, Rhône Valley, Brunello

2011 Port

2012 Napa Cabernet Sauvignon

2013 Napa Cabernet Sauvignon

2014 Napa Cabernet Sauvignon

2015 Bordeaux, Napa Cabernet Sauvignon

BEST WINE TO AGE

The great châteaux of Bordeaux

Many great wine regions produce red wines that will age for 30 years or more, but no other region produces both red and white wines that you can drink a *century* later!

BEST BOTTLE FOR AGING

Magnum

My wine collector and winemaker friends say that their best wines will last longer and mature more slowly in a magnum than in a standard bottle. One theory for this difference points to the amount of air in the bottle—between the wine and the cork—versus the quantity of wine. It's also more fun to serve a magnum at a dinner party.

BEST TEMPERATURE FOR STORAGE

55 degrees Fahrenheit

If you have a wine collection or are planning on collecting wines, you must protect your investment. All the great wineries store and age their wine at this temperature, and studies have shown that it's the best temperature for long-term storage. The same studies also show that storing wine at 75 degrees ages wine twice as fast. Just as warm temperatures will prematurely age the wine, temperatures too cold can freeze the wine, pushing out the cork and immediately ending the aging process. Buy a wine refrigerator or build your wine cellar with the proper air conditioning.

BEST HUMIDITY FOR STORAGE

75 percent relative humidity

If you're going to age your wines for more than five years, this is important. (If not, don't worry about it.) If the humidity is too low, your corks will dry out and wine will seep out of the bottle. If wine can get out, air can get in. Too much humidity, and you likely will lose your labels. Personally, I'd rather lose my labels than my corks!

WITH FOOD

BEST RED WINE WITH LUNCH

Pinot Noir

Most of us have to go back to work after lunch, so the light, easy-drinking style of a Pinot Noir won't overpower your usual light fare of soups, salads, and sandwiches.

BEST WHITE WINE WITH LUNCH

Riesling

Depending on what you're having for lunch, you could go with the low-alcohol (8–10 percent) German Riesling Kabinett. Its slight residual sugar blends nicely with food, especially salads. If you prefer a drier style, French Alsace, Washington, Australia, or Finger Lakes Rieslings are also great choices.

BEST CHEESE WITH WINE

Parmigiano-Reggiano

Now we're getting personal! I love Italian food and wine, but Parmigiano-Reggiano also goes extremely well with Bordeaux and California Cabernets.

BEST RED WINE WITH FISH

Pinot Noir
Runners-up: Chianti Classico, Beaujolais, and Rioja

Pinot Noir is light, easy, and not overpowering. Usually it has high acidity and low tannins and blends nicely with different types of food. It's really a white wine masquerading as a red. Pinot Noir is the perfect wine for a dinner of six or eight where everyone is having something different, whether fish, poultry, or meat.

Other choices include Chianti Classico and Spanish Riojas (Crianza and Reserva). For barbecued or grilled fish or shrimp in the middle of the summer, try a chilled Beaujolais-Village or Cru.

BEST WHITE WINE WITH MEAT

Chardonnay

Whoever coined the rule of white wine with fish was probably thinking of Riesling, Pinot Grigio, and Sauvignon Blanc because a vast majority of Chardonnays will overpower fish dishes—except possibly tuna, salmon, or swordfish steak. Many Chardonnays are red wines masquerading as whites, especially the big, oaky, high-alcohol Chardonnays from California and Australia. Usually, the more expensive the Chardonnay, the more oaky it will taste. With its flavor, weight, and tannins, the perfect match for Chardonnay is something like a sirloin steak!

BEST WINE WITH CHICKEN

Anything

Chicken itself doesn't have an overpowering flavor, and it can go with almost any wine—red or white, light, medium, or full.

BEST WINE WITH LAMB

Bordeaux or California Cabernet Sauvignon

The people of Bordeaux have lamb with breakfast, lunch, and dinner! Lamb has such a strong flavor that it needs a strong wine, and the big, full-bodied Cabernet Sauvignons from California and Bordeaux pair with it perfectly.

BEST WINE AFTER DINNER

Port

You don't need to drink a lot of Port to enjoy it fully. One glass of this sweet and fortified wine ends a meal with a satisfying taste. I consume most Port—whether Ruby, Tawny, or Vintage—from November until March, the cooler months in the Northeast. The best way to have Port is when the dishes have been washed, your children are tucked away and dreaming, you're sitting in front of your fireplace, with your dog by your side, while it snows outside.

BEST WINE WITH CHOCOLATE

Port

For me, chocolate and Port together signal the end of the meal. They're both rich, sweet, and decadently satisfying together.

BEST WINE TO ORDER BY THE BOTTLE IN A RESTAURANT

Anything under $75!

I've worked in the restaurant business most of my life, but it's one of the worst places to experiment with wine tasting. Restaurants are notorious for marking up their wines, sometimes triple what you would pay retail. It's easy for me to choose $100+ bottles of wine, but it's more interesting to find a $25 bottle of wine that tastes like a $50, a $50 bottle that tastes like a $100, and so on.

A few years ago, while working with Tim and Nina Zagat, I reviewed more than 125 restaurant wine lists in New York City. Tim and I discovered that neither of us spends more than $75 for a bottle of wine in a restaurant . . . unless someone else is paying! As I was reviewing these wine lists, I looked at the percentage of wines under $50, under $75, and under $100. To my surprise, most of them had a large percentage of affordable wines. Restaurants with high-priced wines and very few less than $75 don't get my money.

BEST WINE FOR A PARTY OR RECEPTION

Champagne
Runner-up: any sparkling wine

These are some of the world's most versatile wines.

BEST WINE FOR VALENTINE'S DAY

Château Calon-Ségur

At one time the marquis de Ségur owned Château Lafite, Château Latour, and Château Calon-Ségur. He said, "I make my wines at Lafite and Latour, but my heart is at Calon." Hence the label.

BEST WINE FOR THANKSGIVING

?

The problem with Thanksgiving is that it's not just turkey. Everything else served with it—sweet potatoes, cranberries, butternut squash, stuffing—can create havoc with wine. This is also America's big family holiday; do you really want to share your best wines with your relatives? Try more user-friendly wines instead: easy-drinking, inexpensive wines from reliable producers. Look at the Wine and Food Pairings section again, and check out the lists on pages 282–288 for more specific wines.

At my Thanksgiving family dinner, I serve a Tawny Port after the turkey with a selection of nuts and fruits.

OTHER BESTS

BEST WINE GLASS

Riedel

This Austrian glassmaking family has crusaded for more than 30 years to elevate drinking wine to a new level with their specially designed varietal glassware. They have designed glasses to accentuate the best components of each grape variety following the principle that, because Cabernet Sauvignon and Pinot Noir are different wines, the glasses from which you drink them should also be different. Riedel glasses come in many different styles, and they make wineglasses for both everyday wine usage and special occasions. The top of the line is the handcrafted Sommelier series. Next comes the moderately priced Vinum collection. If you don't want to spend a lot of money on glassware, look for the Ouverture line.

BEST WINE PUBLICATION

Wine Spectator
Runners-up: *Decanter* **and** *Wine Enthusiast*

Marvin Shanken bought *Wine Spectator,* a worthwhile publication with a few subscribers, in 1979. Over the last 30+ years he has grown the subscription base to 2.8 million. It's a must-read for the articles and ratings.

Decanter magazine has a totally different format and point of view. This British publication includes feature articles by Michael Broadbent, Clive Coates, Hugh Johnson, Linda Murphy, Steven Spurrier, Brian St. Pierre, and others.

Another important read is *Wine Enthusiast*, a magazine created by Adam Strum, whose primary business is selling wine cellars, glassware, and wine accessories.

BEST WINE EVENT

Wine Spectator's New York Wine Experience

In 2016, *Wine Spectator* celebrated the thirty-fifth anniversary of the New York Wine Experience, and I have to admit a proud bias since I cofounded the event. What makes this event the best is that we established it on three principles: 1) Only the best wineries of the world would be invited, 2) the winemaker or owner had to be present, and 3) proceeds go to scholarships.

BEST WINE REGIONS TO VISIT

Bordeaux, France
Napa Valley, California
Tuscany, Italy

A great vacation for me consists of great wine, fabulous restaurants, pleasant climate, proximity to the ocean, beautiful scenery, and nice people. (Am I asking too much?) These three wine regions fulfill my needs.

BEST WINE LIE

All wines improve with age.

Think of all of the wines that you used to drink in college and your early 20s. Now think about how much you paid for those wines. I'm sure they didn't last very long!—which is exactly the way it should be. You should drink 90 percent of all wines within one year, and the next 9 percent shouldn't age longer than five years. Only that last 1 percent of wines made should age more than that.

BEST WINE MYTH

Everyone tastes wine alike.

No one tastes wine or anything else alike! Taste and smell are like fingerprints or snowflakes—no two are alike. The average person has between 5,000 and 10,000 taste buds. It's difficult to measure how many taste buds someone has, so I can trust only my own judgment and no one else's. As you should do.

TOP VALUE WINE REGIONS

Chianti (Italy)

Côtes du Rhône (France)

Maipo (Chile)

Marlborough (New Zealand)

Mendoza (Argentina)

Rioja (Spain)

THE WORLD'S BEST VALUE WINES $30 AND LESS

A few years ago I traveled to 15 countries, 80 regions, and 400 appellations and tasted more than 6,000 wines—all in one year! The experience opened my eyes about the availability of high quality wines at all price points, which is certainly good news for you. The greatest wines always will remain expensive, and unfortunately only a few will consume them, but the recent worldwide recession actually benefited the pricing of most wines. It helped change the concept that a good wine has to cost a lot of money. Today, hundreds of wines less than $30 are equal in quality to wines that I've tasted that cost more than $100. Bottom line: This is the best time ever to buy very good wine at reasonable prices.

This list would have included many more of the world's great wine values, but many aren't available in all markets, so I haven't listed them here. Most of the wines below cost $30 or less, but I've also included some that are great values even if they run more than $30.

AMERICA

States such as North Carolina, Pennsylvania, Virginia, New York, and many others make great value wines, but unfortunately most of these wines are available only locally. California represents the lion's share of the American market (90 percent) with great Sauvignon Blancs and Chardonnays for the whites and Cabernet Sauvignon, Merlot, Pinot Noir, Zinfandel, and Syrah for the reds. Washington, the second largest producer, makes very good value Sauvignon Blancs, Merlots, Chardonnays, and Cabernet Sauvignons. You also can find some Pinot Noirs and Chardonnays from Oregon at reasonable prices. Here are some of my favorite American producers and their value wines:

RED

A to Z Wineworks Pinot Noir

Acacia Carneros Pinot Noir

Acrobat Pinot Noir

Alexander Valley "Sin Zin" Zinfandel

Andrew Will Cabernet Sauvignon

Argyle Pinot Noir

Artesa Pinot Noir

Atalon Cabernet Sauvignon

Au Bon Climat "La Bauge" Pinot Noir

Au Bon Climat Pinot Noir

B. R. Cohn Silver label Cabernet Sauvignon

Beaulieu Coastal Merlot

Beaulieu Rutherford Cabernet Sauvignon

Benton-Lane Pinot Noir

Benziger Merlot

Beringer Knights Valley Cabernet Sauvignon

Bogle Zinfandel

Bonny Doon "Le Cigare Volant" Syrah / Shiraz

Broadside "Margarita Vineyard" Cabernet Sauvignon

Buena Vista Pinot Noir

Byron Pinot Noir

Calera Pinot Noir

The Calling "Rio Lago Vineyard" Cabernet Sauvignon

Cambria Julia's Vineyard Pinot Noir

Cartlidge & Browne Pinot Noir

Castle Rock Pinot Noir

Chappellet Mountain "Cuvee Cervantes" Meritage

Chapter 24 "Two Messengers" Pinot Noir

Charles Krug Merlot

Chateau Ste Michelle "Canoe Ridge" Merlot

Chateau Ste Michelle "Indian Wells" Cabernet Sauvignon

Cline Syrah / Shiraz

Cline Zinfandel

Clos du Bois Reserve Merlot

Cloudline Pinot Noir

Columbia Crest Merlot

Cooper Mountain Pinot Noir

De Martino Syrah / Shiraz

Dry Creek Cabernet Sauvignon

Elements by Artesa Cabernet Sauvignon

Ex Libris Cabernet Sauvignon

Ferrari-Carano Merlot

Fess Parker Syrah / Shiraz

Fetzer Vineyard Valley Oaks Merlot

Foley Pinot Noir

Folie a Deux Cabernet Sauvignon

Forest Glen Cabernet Sauvignon

Forest Glen Merlot

Forest Glen Syrah / Shiraz

Francis Ford Coppola "Director's Cut" Pinot Noir

Freemark Abbey Cabernet Sauvignon

Frei Brothers Merlot

Frog's Leap Cabernet Sauvignon

Frog's Leap Merlot

Gallo of Sonoma Cabernet Sauvignon

Garnet Pinot Noir

Geyser Peak Reserve Cabernet Sauvignon

Hess Select Cabernet Sauvignon

Hogue Merlot

Joel Gott Cabernet Sauvignon

Joel Gott Zinfandel

Justin Syrah / Shiraz

Kendall Jackson Merlot

L'Ecole No. 41 Shiraz

Laurel Glen Quintana Cabernet Sauvignon

Loring Pinot Noir

Louis M. Martini Sonoma Cabernet Sauvignon

Markham Merlot

McManis Cabernet Sauvignon

Miner Family "Stage Coach" Merlot

Mt. Veeder Winery Cabernet Sauvignon

Napa Ridge Merlot

Pinot Noir "Sharecropper" Pinot Noir

Ponzi "Tavola" Pinot Noir

Qupe Bien Nacido Vineyard Syrah / Shiraz

Ravenswood "Belloni" Zinfandel

Red Lava Vineyards Syrah / Shiraz

Rex Hill Pinot Noir

Robert Mondavi Merlot

Robert Mondavi Napa Cabernet Sauvignon

Rodney Strong Cabernet Sauvignon

Rutherford Vintners Cabernet Sauvignon

Saint Francis Cabernet Sauvignon
Saint Francis Merlot
Sean Minor Cabernet Sauvignon
Sebastiani Cabernet Sauvignon
Seven Hills Cabernet Sauvignon
Seven Hills Merlot
Siduri Pinot Noir
Silver Palm Cabernet Sauvignon
Souverain Merlot
Stag's Leap Wine Cellars "Hands of Time"
    Cabernet Sauvignon

Swanson Merlot
Trefethen Eshcol Cabernet Sauvignon
Vista Verde Vineyard Pinot Noir
Waterbrook Merlot
Wild Horse Pinot Noir
Willamette Valley Vineyards Pinot Noir
Wolffer Estate Merlot
Wyatt Pinot Noir
Zaca Mesa Syrah / Shiraz

WHITE

Acacia Chardonnay
Argyle Chardonnay
Arrowood Grand Archer Chardonnay
Beaulieu Coastal Sauvignon Blanc
Benziger Chardonnay
Bergström "Old Stones" Chardonnay
Beringer Chardonnay
Beringer Sauvignon Blanc
Boundary Breaks "Ovid Line North"
    Riesling
Buena Vista Sauvignon Blanc
Calera Central Coast Chardonnay
Cambria "Katherine's Vineyard"
    Chardonnay
Channing Daughters "Scuttlehole"
    Chardonnay
Chateau Montelena Sauvignon Blanc
Chateau Saint Jean Chardonnay
Chateau Saint Jean Sauvignon Blanc
Chateau Ste Michelle Chardonnay
Chateau Ste Michelle "Eroica"
    Riesling
Clos Pegase Mitsuko's Vineyard
    Chardonnay
Columbia Crest Sémillon-Chardonnay
Covey Run Chardonnay
Covey Run Fumé Blanc
Cristom Vineyard Pinot Blanc / Gris

Cuvée Daniel (Au Bon Climat)
    Chardonnay
Dr. Konstantin Frank Riesling
Elk Cove Vineyards Pinot Blanc/Gris
Estancia Chardonnay
Ferrari-Carano Fumé Blanc
Fetzer Vineyard Valley Oaks Chardonnay
Francis Ford Coppola "Director's Cut"
    Chardonnay
Frog's Leap Sauvignon Blanc
Geyser Peak Sauvignon Blanc
Girard Sauvignon Blanc
Grgich Hills Fumé Blanc
Groth Sauvignon Blanc
Hall Winery Sauvignon Blanc
Heitz Cellars Chardonnay
Hermann J. Wiemer Riesling
Hess Select Chardonnay
High Hook Vineyards Pinot Blanc / Gris
Hogue Columbia Valley Chardonnay
Hogue Fumé Blanc
Honig Sauvignon Blanc
Joel Gott Chardonnay
Joel Gott Sauvignon Blanc
Kendall-Jackson Grand Reserve
    Chardonnay
Kendall-Jackson Vintner's Reserve
    Sauvignon Blanc

Kenwood Sauvignon Blanc

King Estate "Signature Collection" Pinot Blanc / Gris

La Crema Pinot Blanc / Gris

Landmark "Overlook" Chardonnay

Mason Sauvignon Blanc

Matanzas Creek Sauvignon Blanc

Mer Soleil "Silver" (unoaked) Chardonnay

Merryvale Starmont Chardonnay

Morgan Chardonnay

Ponzi Pinot Blanc / Gris

Provenance Sauvignon Blanc

Rodney Strong Sauvignon Blanc

Rutherford Ranch Chardonnay

Sbragia Family Sauvignon Blanc

Silverado Sauvignon Blanc

Simi Chardonnay

Truchard Chardonnay

ARGENTINA

Argentina's reputation rests on the Mendoza region and the Malbec grape, but the country makes other wines, such as Bonarda, Cabernet Sauvignon, and Chardonnay, that also are great values. Here are some of my favorite Argentinean producers and their value wines:

RED

Achaval-Ferrer Malbec

Alamos Malbec

Alta Vista Malbec Grand Reserva

Bodega Norton Malbec

Bodegas Esmeralda Malbec

Bodegas Renacer "Enamore"

Bodegas Weinert Carrascal

Catena Malbec

Catena Zapata Cabernet Sauvignon

Clos de los Siete Malbec

Cuvelier Los Andes "Coleccion"

Domaine Jean Bousquet Malbec

Kaiken Cabernet Sauvignon Ultra

Michel Torino Torrontes "Don David"

Miguel Mendoza Malbec Reserva

Perdriel Malbec

Salentein Malbec

Susana Balboa Cabernet Sauvignon

Susana Balboa Malbec

Terrazas Malbec Reserva

Tikal Patriota

Trapiche Oak Cask Malbec

Valentin Bianchi Malbec

WHITE

Alamos Chardonnay

Alta Vista Torrontes Premium

Bodegas Diamandes de Uco Chardonnay

Catena Chardonnay

Michel Torino Torrontés Don David Reserve

AUSTRALIA

Thirty years ago, Australia took the world by storm with great wines at great prices, and that still holds true today. The most famous red grape, Shiraz, often blends with Cabernet Sauvignon, but this huge country has so many other wine regions that it's easy to find great Cabernet Sauvignons, Chardonnays, and Sauvignon Blancs at unbelievable prices. Here are some of my favorite Australian producers and their value wines:

RED

Alice White Cabernet Sauvignon

Banrock Station Shiraz

Black Opal Cabernet Sauvignon or Shiraz

Chapel Hill Grenache "Bushvine"

Chapel Hill Shiraz "Parson's Nose"

d'Arenberg "The Footbolt" Shiraz

d'Arenberg Grenache The Derelict Vineyard

d'Arenberg "The Stump Jump" Red

Jacob's Creek Cabernet Sauvignon

Jacob's Creek Shiraz Cabernet

Jamshead Syrah

Jim Barry Shiraz, "The Lodge Hill"

Jim Barry "The Cover Drive" Cabernet

Kilikanoon "Killerman's Run" Shiraz

Langmeil Winery "Three Gardens" Shiraz / Grenache / Mourvedre

Leeuwin Estate Siblings Shiraz

Lindeman's Shiraz Bin 50

Marquis Philips Sarah's Blend

McWilliam's Shiraz

Mollydooker "The Boxer" Shiraz

Nine Stones Shiraz

Penfolds "Bin 28 Kalimna" Shiraz

Peter Lehmann Barossa Shiraz

Rosemount Estate Shiraz Cabernet (Diamond Label)

Salomon Estate "Finnis River" Shiraz

Schild Shiraz

Taltarni T Series Shiraz

Two Hands Shiraz "Gnarly Dudes"

Yalumba Y Series Shiraz Viognier

Yangarra Shiraz Single Vineyard

WHITE

Banrock Station Chardonnay

Bogle Sauvignon Blanc

Cape Mentelle Sauvignon Blanc-Semillon

Grant Burge Chardonnay

Heggies Vineyard Chardonnay

Lindeman's Chardonnay Bin 65

Matua Valley Sauvignon Blanc

Oxford Landing Sauvignon Blanc

Pewsey Vale Dry Riesling

Rolf Binder Riesling "Highness"

Rosemount Estate Chardonnay

Saint Clair "Pioneer Block 3" Sauvignon Blanc

Saint Hallett "Poacher's Blend" White

Trevor Jones Virgin Chardonnay

Yalumba Y Series Unwooded Chardonnay

AUSTRIA

The two major white grapes are Grüner Veltliner and Riesling, perfect wines to serve with all kinds of foods, easy to drink, and readily available. Here are some of my favorite Austrian producers and their value wines:

RED

Glatzer Zweigelt

Sepp Moser Sepp Zweigelt

WHITE

Albert Neumeister Morillon Steirsche Klassik

Alois Kracher Pinot Gris Trocken

Brundlmayer Grüner Veltliner Kamptaler Terrassen

Forstreiter "Grand Reserve" Grüner Veltliner

Franz Etz Grüner Veltliner (Liter)

Hirsch Grüner Veltliner Heiligenstein

Hirsch "Veltliner #1"

Knoll Grüner Veltliner Federspiel Trocken Wachau Loibner

Nigl Grüner Veltliner Kremser Freiheit

Salomon Grüner Veltliner

Salomon Riesling Steinterrassen

Schloss Gobelsburg

Walter Glatzer Grüner Veltliner "Dornenvogel"

CHILE

The best value in the world for Cabernet Sauvignon is Chile. Also look for their Merlot, Carménère, and Sauvignon Blanc. Here are some of my favorite Chilean producers and their value wines:

RED

Arboleda Carmenère

Caliterra Cabernet Sauvignon or Merlot

Carmen Carmenère

Casa Lapostolle "Cuvée Alexandre" Merlot

Concha y Toro Puente Alto Cabernet

Cono Sur 20 Barrels Cabernet

Cousiño-Macul Antiguas Reserva

Errazuriz Cabernet Sauvignon

Los Vascos Reserve Cabernet

Montes Alpha Merlot Apalta Vineyard

Montes Cabernet Sauvignon

Santa Carolina Cabernet Sauvignon

Veramonte Primus "The Blend"

Veranda Pinot Noir Ritua

Viña Aquitania Lazuli Cabernet

WHITE

Casa Lapostolle Cuvee Alexander Chardonnay

Casa Lapostolle Cuvee Alexander Valley Sauvignon Blanc

Cono Sur "Bicycle Series" Viognier

Veramonte Sauvignon Blanc

Vina Aquitania "Sol del Sol" Chardonnay "Traiguen" 2008

FRANCE

France sometimes has a reputation for very expensive wines (great châteaux of Bordeaux, domaines of Burgundy, etc.), but it always has offered great values. From Alsace: Rieslings, Pinot Blancs, and Pinot Gris; from the Loire Valley: Muscadet, Sancerre, and Pouilly-Fumé; from Burgundy: Beaujolais, Mâcons, Chablis, and Bourgogne Blanc and Rouge; from the Rhône Valley: Côtes du Rhône and Crozes-Hermitage; from Bordeaux: Petit Château and Cru Bourgeois; and the wines from Provence, Languedoc, and Roussillon. Here are some of my favorite French producers and their value wines:

RED

"A" d'Aussières Rouge Corbières
Baron de Brane
Brunier Le Pigeoulet Rouge VDP Vaucluse
Brunier "Megaphone" Ventoux Rouge
Chapelle-St-Arnoux Châteauneuf-du-
    Pape Vieilles Vignes
Château Bel Air
Château Cabrières Côtes du Rhône
Château Cap de Faugeres
Château Caronne-Sainte-Gemme
Château Chantegrive
Château d'Escurac "Pepin"
Château de Maison Neuve
Château de Mercey Mercurey Rouge
Château de Trignon Gigondas
Château de Villambis
Château Greysac
Château Haut du Peyrat
Château Labat
Château La Cardonne
Château La Grangère
Château Lanessan
Château Larose-Trintaudon
Château Le Bonnat
Château Le Sartre
Château Malmaison
Château Malromè
Château Maris La Touge Syrah
Château Pey La Tour Reserve du Château
Château Peyrabon

Château Puy-Blanquet
Château Puynard
Château Saint Julian
Château Segondignac
Château Thébot
Château Tour Leognan
Cheval Noir
Clos Siguier Cahors
Côte-de-Nuits-Village, Joseph Drouhin
Croix Mouton
Cuvée Daniel Côtes de Castillon
Domaine André Brunel Côtes-du-Rhône
    Cuvée Sommelongue
Domaine Bouchard Pinot Noir
Domaine d'Andezon Côtes-du-Rhône
Domaine de la Coume du Roy Côtes du
    Roussillon-Villages "Le Desir"
Domaine de Lagrézette Cahors
Domaine de'Obrieu Côtes du Rhône
    Villages "Cuvée les Antonins"
Domaine de Villemajou "Boutenac"
Domaine Michel Poinard Crozes-
    Hermitage
Domaine Roches Neuves Saumur-
    Champigny
Georges Duboeuf Beaujolais-Villages
Georges Duboeuf Morgon "Cave Jean-
    Ernest Descombes"
Gérard Bertrand Domaine de L'Aigle
    Pinot Noir

Gérard Bertrand Grand Terroir Tautavel

Gilles Ferran "Les Antimagnes"

Guigal Côtes du Rhône

J. Vidal-Fleury Côtes du Rhône

Jaboulet Côtes du Rhône Parallèle 45

Jaboulet Crozes-Hermitage Les Jalets

Jean-Maurice Raffault Chinon

Joseph Drouhin Côte de Beaune-Villages

La Baronne Rouge "Montagne d'Alaric"

La Vieille Ferme Côtes du Ventoux

Lafite Réserve Spéciale

Laplace Madiran

Le Medoc de Cos

Louis Jadot Château des Jacques Moulin-à-Vent

M. Chapoutier Bila-Haut Côtes de Rousillon Villages

Maison Champy Pinot Noir Signature

Marc Rougeot Bourgogne Rouge "Les Lameroses"

Marjosse Reserve du Château

Mas de Gourgonnier Les Baux de Provence Rouge

Michel Poinard Crozes Hermitage

Montirius Gigondas Terres des Aînés

Nicolas Thienpont Selection Saint-Emilion Grand Cru

Perrin & Fils Côtes du Rhône

Rene Lequin-Colin Santenay "Vieilles Vignes"

Thierry Germain Saumur-Champigny

Villa Ponciago Fleurie La Réserve Beaujolais

WHITE

Ballot-Millot et Fils Bourgogne Chardonnay

Barton & Guestier Sauternes

Bertranon Bordeaux Blanc

Bouzeron Domaine Gagey

Cairanne, Domaine les Hautes Cances

Château Bonnet Blanc

Château de Maligny Petit Chablis

Château de Mercey Mercurey Blanc

Château de Rully Blanc "La Pucelle"

Château de Sancerre

Château du Mayne Blanc

Château du Trignon Côtes du Rhône Blanc

Château Fuissé

Château Graville-Lacoste Blanc

Château Loumelat

Château Martinon Blanc

Clarendelle

Claude Lafond Reuilly

Domaine de Montcy Cheverny

Domaine Delaye Saint-Véran "Les Pierres Grises"

Domaine des Baumard Savennières

Domaine Jean Chartron Bourgogne Aligoté

Domaine Mardon Quincy "Très Vieilles Vignes"

Domaine Paul Pillot Bourgogne Chardonnay

Domaine Saint Barbe Macon Clesse "Les Tilles"

Faiveley Bourgogne Blanc

Francis Blanchet Pouilly Fumé "Cuvée Silice"

Georges Duboeuf Pouilly-Fuissé

Helfrich Riesling

Hugel & Fils Gentil

Hugel & Fils Riesling

Hugel Pinot Gris

J.J. Vincent Pouilly-Fuissé "Marie Antoinette"

Jeanguillon Blanc

Jonathon Pabiot Pouilly Fumé

Laroche Petit Chablis

Louis Jadot Macon

Louis Jadot Saint-Véran
Louis Latour Montagny
Louis Latour Pouilly-Vinzelles
Maison Bleue Chardonnay
Marjosse Blanc Reserve du Château
Mas Karolina Côtes Catalanes Blanc
Michel Bailly Pouilly Fumé
Olivier Leflaive Saint-Aubin
Pascal Jolivet Attitude
Pascal Jolivet Sancerre
Robert Klingenfus Pinot Blanc
Sauvion Pouilly-Fumé Les Ombelles

ROSÉ
Château Miraval Côtes de
    Provence Rosé "Pink Floyd"

Sauvion Sancerre, "Les Fondettes"
Simonnet-Febvre Chablis
Thierry Germain Saumur Blanc Cuvée
    "Soliterre"
Thierry Pillot Santenay Blanc "Clos
    Genet"
Trimbach Gewurztraminer
Trimbach Riesling
William Fèvre Chablis
Willm Cuvèe Emile Willm Riesling
    Rèserve
Zind Humbrecht Pinot Blanc

GERMANY

You will find the great value white wines of Germany in the Kabinett and Spätlese styles. Here are some of my favorite German producers and their value wines:

WHITE
Josef Leitz Rüdesheimer Klosterlay
    Riesling Kabinett
Kerpen Wehlener Sonnenuhr Kabinett
Kurt Darting Dürkheimer Hochbenn
    Riesling Kabinett
Leitz "Dragonstone" Riesling
Meulenhof Wehlenuhr Sonnenuhr
    Riesling Spätlese

Saint Urbans-Hof Riesling Kabinett
Schloss Vollrads Riesling Kabinett
Selbach Piesporter Michelsberg Riesling
    Spatlese
Selbach-Oster Zeltinger Sonnenuhr
    Riesling Kabinett
Weingut Max Richter Mülheimer
    Sonnelay Riesling Kabinett

ITALY

Italy is making its best wines ever!—and you can find great values all over. From Tuscany: Chianti Classico Riserva, Rosso di Montalcino, and Rossi di Montepulciano; from Piedmont: Barbera and Dolcetto; from Veneto: Valpolicella, Soave, and Prosecco; from Abruzzi: Montelpulciano d'Abruzzo; from northern Italy: Pinot Grigio and Pinot Bianco; and from Sicily: Nero d'Avola. Here are some of my favorite Italian producers and their value wines:

RED

Aldo Rainoldi Nebbiolo

Aleramo Barbera

Allegrini Palazzo della Torre

Allegrini Valpolicella Classico

Antinori Badia a Passignano Chianti
   Classico

Altesino Rosso di Altesino

Antinori Santa Cristina Sangiovese

Antinori Tormaresca Trentangeli

Baglia di Pianetto "Ramione"

Braida Barbera d'Asti "Montebruna"

Bruno Giacosa Barbera d'Alba

Cantina del Taburno Aglianico Fidelis

Caruso e Minini I Sciani Sachia

Casal Thaulero Montepulciano d'Abruzzo

Cascata Monticello Dolcetto d'Asti

Castellare di Castellina Chianti Classico

Castello Banfi Toscana Centine

Castello Monaci Liante Salice Salentino

Col d'Orcia Rosso di Montalcino

Di Majo Norante Sangiovese Terre degli
   Osci

Einaudi Dolcetto di Dogliani

Fattoria di Felsina Chianti Classico
   Riserva

Francesco Rinaldi Dolcetto d'Alba

Guado al Tasso-Antinori Il Bruciato

La Mozza Morellino di Scansano
   "I Perazzi"

Le Rote Vernaccia di San Gimignano

Librandi Ciro Riserva "Duca San Felice"

Lungarotti Rubesco

Manzone Nebbiolo Langhe "Crutin"

Marchesi de' Frescobaldi Chianti Rúfina

Marchesi di Barolo Barbera d'Alba

Masi "Campofiorin"

Melini Chianti Classico Riserva
   "La Selvanella"

Michele Chiarlo Barbera d'Asti

Mocali Rosso di Montalcino

Monchiero Carbone Barbera d'Alba

Morgante Nero d'Avola

Montesotto Chianti Classico

Podere Ciona "Montegrossoli"

Poggio al Casone La Cattura

Poggio al Tesoro Mediterra

Poggio il Castellare Rosso di Montalcino

Principe Corsini Chianti Classico
   "Le Corti"

Regaleali (Tasca d'Almerita) Rosso

Ruffino Chianti Classico "Riserva Ducale"
   (Tan label)

Ruffino "Modus"

San Polo "Rubio"

Sandrone Nebbiolo d'Alba Valmaggiore

Silvio Nardi Rosso di Montalcino

Taurino Salice Salentino

Tenuta dell'Ornellaia Le Volte

Tenuta di Arceno Arcanum Il Fauno

Tolaini "Valdisanti"

Tormaresca "Torcicoda"

Travaglini Gattinara

Valle Reale Montepulciano d'Abruzzo

Zaccagnini Montepulciano d'Abruzzo
   Riserva

WHITE

Abbazia di Novacella Kerner
Alois Lageder Pinot Bianco
Alois Lageder Pinot Grigio
Anselmi Soave
Antinori Chardonnay della Sala Bramito
   del Cervo
Antinori Vermentino Guado al Tasso
Bolla Soave Classico
Bollini Trentino Pinot Grigio
Boscaini Pinot Grigio
Botromagno Gravina Bianco
Cantina Andriano Pinot Bianco
Caruso e Minini Terre di Giumara Inzolia
Ceretto "Blange" Langhe Arneis
Clelia Romano Fiano di Avellino "Colli di
   Lapio"
Coppo Gavi "La Rocca"
Eugenio Collavini Pinot Grigio
   "Canlungo"
Jermann Pinot Grigio
Kellerei Cantina Terlan Pinot Bianco

ROSÉ

Antinori Guado al Tasso
   Scalabrone Rosato

PROSECCO

Adami
Bortolomiol
Le Colture

Zenato Valpolicella
Zeni Amarone della Valpolicella

La Carraia Orvieto Classico
Le Rote Vernaccia di San Gimignano
Maculan "Pino & Toi"
Malabaila Roero Arneis
Marchetti Verdicchio dei Castelli di Jesi
   Classico
Marco Felluga Collio Pinot Grigio
Mastroberardino Falanghina
Paolo Scavino Bianco
Peter Zemmer Pinot Grigio
Pieropan Soave
Pighin Pinot Grigio
Sergio Mottura Grechetto "Poggio della
   Costa"
Sergio Mottura Orvieto
Soave Classico Pra
Terenzuola Vermentino Colli di Luni
Teruzzi & Puthod "Terre di Tufi"
Terredora Greco di Tufo (Loggia della
   Serra)

La Tordera
Mionetto
Zardetto

NEW ZEALAND

The two most important grapes of New Zealand are Sauvignon Blanc and Pinot Noir. The former—with their tropical aromas and taste with a crisp, citrus finish—have become world famous, but also look for the latter for quality wines. Here are some of my favorite New Zealand producers and their value wines:

RED

Babich Pinot Noir
Brancott Estate Pinot Noir Reserve
Coopers Creek Pinot Noir
Crown Range Pinot Noir
Kim Crawford Pinot Noir
Man O' War Syrah
Mt. Beautiful Pinot Noir Cheviot Hills
Mt. Difficulty Pinot Noir
Neudorf Vineyards Pinot Noir
   "Tom's Block" (Nelson)

Oyster Bay Pinot Noir
Peregrine Pinot Noir
Saint Clair Pinot Noir "Vicar's Choice"
Salomon & Andrew Pinot Noir
Stoneleigh Pinot Noir
Te Awa Syrah
The Crossings Pinot Noir
Yealands Pinot Noir

WHITE

Ata Rangi Sauvignon Blanc
Babich Sauvignon Blanc
Babich Unwooded Chardonnay
Brancott Estate Sauvignon Blanc
Cloudy Bay "Te Koko"
Coopers Creek Sauvignon Blanc
Cru Vin Dogs "Greyhound" Sauvignon
   Blanc
Giesen Sauvignon Blanc
Glazebrook Sauvignon Blanc
Isabel Estate Sauvignon Blanc
Kim Crawford Sauvignon Blanc
Kumeu River Village Chardonnay
Man O' War Sauvignon Blanc
Mohua Pinot Gris
Mohua Sauvignon Blanc
Mount Nelson Sauvignon Blanc

Mt. Difficulty Pinot Gris
Neudorf Chardonnay
Neudorf Sauvignon Blanc
Nobilo Sauvignon Blanc
Oyster Bay Sauvignon Blanc
Pegasus Bay Chardonnay
Peregrine Pinot Gris
Saint Clair Sauvignon Blanc
Salomon & Andrew Sauvignon Blanc
Seresin Sauvignon Blanc
Stoneleigh Chardonnay
Stoneleigh Sauvignon Blanc
Te Awa Chardonnay
Te Mata "Woodthorpe"
Villa Maria "Cellar Selection" Sauvignon
   Blanc

SOUTH AFRICA

The diversity of the South African wines, from Chenin Blanc and Sauvignon Blanc to Cabernet Sauvignon and Pinotage, offers a lot of different choices at great value. Here are some of my favorite South African producers and their value wines:

RED

Boekenhoutskloof "Chocolate Block"
    Meritage
Doolhof Dark Lady of the Labyrinth
    Pinotage
Jardin Syrah
Kanonkop Pinotage
Mount Rozier "Myrtle Grove" Cabernet
    Sauvignon

Mulderbosch Faithful Hound
Kanonkop Kadette Red
Rupert & Rothschild Classique
Rustenberg 1682 Red Blend
Thelema Cabernet Sauvignon

WHITE

Boschendal Chardonnay
Ken Forrester Sauvignon Blanc

Thelema Sauvignon Blanc
Tokara Chardonnay Reserve Collection

SPAIN

From the time I started studying wine more than 40 years ago, the wines of Rioja have represented great value, especially the Crianzas and Reservas. The Tempranillo grape also shines in Ribera del Duero. Rías Baixas makes good Albariños, and from Penedès we have the great Cavas. Here are some of my favorite Spanish producers and their value wines:

RED

Alvaro Palacios Camins del Priorat
Algueira Ribiera Sacra
Antidoto Ribera del Duero Cepas Viejas
Baron de Ley Reserva
Bernabeleva Camino de Navaherreros
Beronia Rioja Reserva
Bodega Numanthia Termes
Bodegas Beronia Reserva
Bodegas Emilio Moro "Emilio Moro"
Bodegas La Cartuja Priorat
Bodegas Lan Rioja Crianza
Bodegas Leda Mas de Leda

Bodegas Marañones 30 Mil Maravedies
Bodegas Montecillo Crianza or Reserva
Bodegas Muga Reserva
Bodegas Ontañón Crianza
Campo Viejo Reserva
Clos Galena Galena
Condado de Haza Ribera del Duero
Conde de Valdemar Crianza
CVNE Rioja Crianza "Viña Real"
Descendientes de José Palacios Bierzo
    Pétalos
Dinastía Vivanco Selección de Familia

El Coto Crianza and Reserva
Ermita San Felices Reserva Rioja Alta
Finca Torremilanos Ribera del Duero
Joan d'Anguera Montsant Garnatxa
Marqués de Cáceres Crianza or Reserva
Marqués de Riscal Proximo Rioja
Onix Priorat
Ontañón Crianza or Reserva

Pago dee Valdoneje Bierzo
Pesquera Tinto Crianza
Rotllan Torra Priorat Crianza
Scala Dei Priorat "Negre"
Senorio de Barahonda "Carro" Tinto
Torres Gran Coronas Reserva
Urbina Rioja Gran Reserva

WHITE
Albariño Don Olegario
Bodegas Ostatu Blanco
Burgáns Albariño Rías Baixas
Castro Brey Albariño "Sin Palabras"
Condes de Albarei "Condes Do Ferreiro
    Albariño de Albarei"

Legaris Verdejo Rueda
Licia Galicia Albariño
Martin Codax Albarino
Pazo de Senorans Albarino
Terras Guada Albarino
    "O Rosal"

CAVA
Codorníu Brut Classico
Cristalino Brut

Freixenet
Segura Viudas

WINE RESOURCES

PUBLICATIONS

Decanter
decanter.com

Food & Wine
foodandwine.com

Tasting Panel
tastingpanelmag.com

Wine Advocate
erobertparker.com

Wine & Spirits
wineandspiritsmagazine.com

Wine Business Monthly
winebusiness.com

Wine Enthusiast
wineenthusiast.com

Wine Spectator
winespectator.com

RESOURCES FOR RATINGS AND PRICES

Beverage Tasting Institute, tastings.com

Parker's *Wine Buying Guide*

Snooth.com

Wine Price File

wine-searcher.com

Wine Spectator's Ultimate Buying Guide

STORAGE AND EQUIPMENT

International Wine
  Accessories
iwawine.com

Sub Zero Freezer Company
subzero-wolf.com

Western Carriers, Inc. Wine
  Cellar Transportation
westerncarriers.com

Wine Enthusiast Catalog
wineenthusiast.com

SELLERS AND AUCTIONEERS

Aulden Cellars–Sotheby's
  Auction House
sothebys.com/wine

Bonhams & Butterfields
bonhams.com

Chicago Wine Company
tcwc.com

Christie's Auction House
christies.com

Hart Davis Hart
hdhwine.com

Morrell & Company
Morrellwineauctions.com

Wally's Wine Auction
wallysauction.com

Zachy's
zachys.com/auctions

Other online wine auction houses:

auctionvine.com

brentwoodwine.com

munichwinecompany.com

spectrumwine.com

winebid.com

winecommune.com

WINE EDUCATION

For a complete list of wine schools, visit the Society of Wine Educators website, societyofwineeducators.org.

WINE CERTIFICATION PROGRAMS

For the professional or those wishing to become sommeliers:

American Sommelier Association
americansommelier.com

International Wine Center
internationalwinecenter.com

Society of Wine Educators
societyofwineeducators.org

Sommelier Society of America
sommeliersocietyofamerica.org

Wine & Spirit Education Trust
wsetglobal.com

Wine Spectator Wine School
winespectator.com/school

CONSUMER EDUCATION

Kevin Zraly Windows on the World Wine School
kevinzraly.com

Sherry-Lehmann / Kevin Zraly
Master Classes
845-255-1456 or
kevin@kevinzraly.com

FURTHER READING

These books are required reading if you want to delve further into the fascinating subject of wine:

The Essential Wine Book by Oz Clarke

Exploring Wine by Steven Kolpan, Brian H. Smith, and Michael A. Weiss

The Food Lover's Guide to Wine by Karen Page and Andrew Dornenburg

Grapes & Wines by Oz Clarke

Great Tastes Made Simple and *Great Wine Made Simple* by Andrea Immer

Hugh Johnson's Modern Encyclopedia of Wine

Oxford Companion to Wine by Jancis Robinson

Perfect Pairings and *Daring Pairings* by Evan Goldstein

The Ultimate Wine Companion by Kevin Zraly

Vino Italiano by Joseph Bastianich and David Lynch

The Wine Bible by Karen MacNeil

Wine for Dummies by Ed McCarthy and Mary Ewing-Mulligan

The Wine Lover's Guide to the Wine Country by Lori Lyn Narlock and Nancy Garfinkel

World Atlas of Wine by Hugh Johnson and Jancis Robinson

The above are encyclopedic, so I always carry with me one of these three pocket guides:

Food & Wine Pocket Guide

Hugh Johnson's Pocket Encyclopedia of Wine

Oz Clarke's Pocket Wine Guide

BLOGGERS

For lists of wine bloggers worth following, see:
wineblogawards.org
Winebusiness.com
Dinersjournal.blogs.nytimes.com

SELECT CONSUMER EVENTS

Check localwineevents.com for events in your area.

Auction Napa Valley
napavintners.com/anv/

Boston Wine Expo, Winter
wine-expos.com

Charlotte Wine & Food Weekend, every other year
in the Spring
charlottewineandfood.com

Epcot Food & Wine Festival
disneyworld.disney.go.com/parks/epcot/

Finger Lakes Wine Festival
flwinefest.com

Florida Winefest & Auction
floridawinefest.com

Food & Wine Classic in Aspen
foodandwine.com/classic

Grand Wine and Food Affair (Texas)
fortbendwineandfoodaffair.com

Naples Winter Wine Festival
napleswinefestival.com

New York Wine Experience
212-684-4224

New York Wine Expo
wine-expos.com

Newport Mansions Wine & Food Festival
newportmansions.org

Saratoga Wine and Food Festival
spac.org

South Beach Wine & Food Fest
sobewineandfoodfest.com

Washington International Wine & Food Festival
wine-expos.com

Westchester Magazine Wine and Food Festival
winefood.westchestermagazine.com

TRADE EVENTS

American Wine Society
National Conference
americanwinesociety.org

Society of Wine Educators Conference
societyofwineeducators.org/
conference.php

AFTERWORD: LOOKING BACK, WITH GRATITUDE

I always will remember:

- Working with and learning from John Novi at the Depuy Canal House, 1970–76
- My first visit to a winery, Benmarl, in 1970
- My first wine classes in 1971, one where I was a student and the other where I was the teacher
- Hitchhiking to California to visit wine country in 1972
- Teaching a two-credit course as a junior in college (open only to seniors) in 1973
- Father Sam Matarazzo, my early and now spiritual leader
- Living and studying wine in Europe, 1974–75
- Planting my own vineyard (four-time failure) in 1974, 1981, 1992, 2014 and making my own wine in 1984 (so-so)
- The excitement of opening Windows on the World in 1976
- The support and friendship of Jules Roinnel, going back to our earliest days together at Windows
- Wine tastings with Alexis Bespaloff and friends
- Mohonk Mountain House in New Paltz, New York, where ideas come easy
- Evening, late-night, and early-morning wine discussions with Alexis Lichine in Bordeaux
- Adviser and great listener Peter Sichel, whose generosity of spirit inspired the way I teach and share my wine knowledge
- Sharing great old vintages with Peter Bienstock
- Jules Epstein, for his advice and for sharing his wine collection
- Touring the world with wine expert Robin Kelley O'Connor
- Creating and directing the New York Wine Experience, 1981–91
- Those no longer here to share a glass of wine: Craig Claiborne, Joseph Baum, Alan Lewis, Raymond Wellington, and my father, Charles
- Witnessing the success of Michael Skurnik, who worked with me at Windows in the late 1970s and quickly rose to fame as a great importer
- Watching my former student Andrea Robinson turn into a superstar wine-and-food personality and author
- The Food Network's *Wines A to Z*—together with Alan Richman
- Reading and enjoying the observations of the great wine writers and tasters (listed throughout the book)
- Having the opportunity to meet all the passionate winemakers, vineyardists, and owners of the great wineries of the world
- The wine events, wine dinners, and tastings around the country that I have had the privilege of attending
- All the groups that have invited me to entertain and educate them about wine
- Writing the first chapter of this book with Kathleen Talbert in 1983
- The original Sterling Publishing team of Burton Hobson, Lincoln Boehm, and Charles Nurnberg
- Marcus Leaver, former CEO of Sterling Publishing, for his tremendous support on all of my books
- To all my editors over the last three decades, especially Felicia Sherbert, Stephen Topping, Keith Schiffman, Steve Magnuson, Hannah Reich, Becky Maines, Mary Hern, Diane Abrams, Carlo DeVito, and James Jayo

- The Sterling team for this edition: Marilyn Kretzer, James Jayo, Chris Bain, Elizabeth Lindy, Linda Liang, Kevin Ullrich, Rich Hazelton, Rodman Neumann, Hannah Reich, Fred Pagan, Trudi Bartow, Chris Vaccari, and Nicole Vines Verlin as well as Rose Fox, Beth Gruber, Jessie Leaman, Jay Kreider, Maria Mann, Ashley Prine, and Katherine Furman
- Karen Nelson for 25 years of beautiful cover designs
- Jim Anderson, who designed the original edition, and Richard Oriolo for capturing my spirit in subsequent editions
- Barnes & Noble for always supporting my books and ideas
- Carmen Bissell, Raymond DePaul, Faye Friedman, Jennifer Redmond, and Maria Battaglia for their help with the Wine School
- All my pourers at the school over the last 40 years
- Having a great relationship with my New York City wine-school peers, especially Harriet Lembeck (Beverage Program) and Mary Ewing-Mulligan (International Wine Center)
- The Baum-Emil team, who re-created Windows on the World in 1996
- Conducting the Sherry-Lehmann / Kevin Zraly Master Wine Class with Michael Aaron, Michael Yurch, Chris Adams, Shyda Gilmer, and Matt Wong
- Michael Stengel at the Marriott Marquis Hotel NYC for his advice and support since September 11th
- My continuing grief at the loss of those friends and co-workers who lost their lives on September 11th
- Robert M. Parker Jr., who so generously donated his time and talents to aid the families of September 11th
- Alan Stillman, founder, chairman, and CEO of the Smith & Wollensky Restaurant Group
- Being honored for "loving wine" and receiving the 2011 Lifetime Achievement Award from the James Beard Foundation, the only wine professional to receive that honor
- Teaching at Cornell University and the Culinary Institute of America
- Serving as a member of the Culinary Institute's Board of Trustees
- All the special wine friends who have helped deplete my wine cellar over the years, especially Harvey
- Those who have tried to keep me organized in my business life: Ellen Kerr, Claire Josephs, Lois Arrighi, Sara Hutton, Andrea Immer, Dawn Lamendola, Catherine Fallis, Rebecca Chapa, Gina D'Angelo-Mullen, and Michelle Woodruff
- My four best vintages: Anthony (1991), Nicolas (1993), Harrison (1997), and Adriana (1999)
- My mom, Kathleen
- My sisters, Sharon and Kathy
- The 20,000 students who attended the Windows on the World Wine School, which celebrated its 40th anniversary and last semester in 2016
- Everyone who worked at Windows on the World, especially my colleagues in the wine department

SPECIAL REMEMBRANCE

Morley Safer for his wonderful segments on wine for *60 Minutes*, especially the French Paradox (see page 183).

A FINAL NOTE

If this were an award-acceptance speech, the music probably would have drowned me out after the first ten bullets above. No doubt I've forgotten to name at least one or two folks—an occupational hazard of consuming so much wine! To everyone I've ever met or known, from grammar school on: *May all your vintages be great!*

GLOSSARY OF SELECT TERMS

Acid: A component of wine, sometimes described as sour or tart, found on the sides of the tongue and mouth.

Acidification: The process of adding acid, usually tartaric or citric, to grape must before fermentation in order to boost low levels of acidity, creating a more balanced wine.

Aftertaste: The sensation in the mouth that persists after swallowing the wine.

Alcohol: The result of fermentation, which yeast creates by consuming the natural sugars in grapes.

AOC: Appellation d'Origine Contrôlée, the French government laws that control wine production.

Aroma: The smell of the grapes in a wine.

Astringent: The mouthfeel created by tannins.

AVA: American Viticultural Area, the designated wine-producing areas in America.

Balance: The integration of the various components of wine, such as acid, alcohol, fruit, and tannin. For proper balance, no one component should dominate the wine's taste.

Barrel-fermented: Wine fermented in small oak barrels rather than stainless steel. The oak of a barrel adds complexity to a wine's flavor and texture.

Biodynamics: A type of holistic farming created by Rudolph Steiner in the 1920s based on principles similar to those of organic farming. Compost and manure take the place of chemical fertilizers or pesticides.

Bitter: One of the three tastes of wine, found at the back of the tongue and throat.

Blend: A combination of two or more wines or grapes to enhance flavor, balance, and complexity.

Body: The weight of a wine in the mouth. A high-alcohol wine feels heavier than a low-alcohol one.

Botrytis cinerea: Also called "noble rot," a special mold that punctures the skin of a grape, allowing water to dissipate, leaving a higher concentration of sugars and acids. Necessary in making Beerenauslese, Sauternes, Trockenbeerenauslese, and Tokaji Aszú.

Bouquet: The smell of a wine as influenced by winemaking processes and barrel aging.

Brix: A scale that measures the sugar level of unfermented grape juice.

Brut: French term for the driest style of Champagne or other sparkling wine.

Chaptalization: The addition of sugar to the must before fermentation to increase the alcohol level of the finished wine.

Character: Aspects of the wine that are typical of its grape varieties or the overall characteristics of the wine.

Classified châteaux: The winemakers in the Bordeaux region of France that produce the best wine.

Colheita: The Portuguese word for "vintage."

Components: The aspects of a wine's character, style, and taste, including acidity, alcohol, fruit, tannin, and residual sugar.

Cru: An indicator of quality (*Grand Cru, Premier Cru*) for certain French vineyards.

Cuvée: From the French word *cuve*, or *vat*; may refer to a particular blend of grapes or, in Champagne, to the select portion of juice from the pressing of the grapes.

Decanting: Pouring wine from its bottle into a carafe or other serving vessel to separate the sediment from the wine.

Dégorgement: A step of the *méthode champenoise* used to expel sediment from Champagne.

Demi-sec: A Champagne containing a higher level of residual sugar than a brut.

DOC: Denominazione di Origine Controllata in Italy for the laws that control wine production there, and Denominación de Origen Condado in Spain for that country's wine laws.

DOCG: Denominazione di Origine Controllata e Garantita, the Italian government's designation for only the finest Italian wines.

Dosage: The addition of sugar, often mixed with wine or brandy, in the final step of producing Champagne or sparkling wine.

Drip irrigation: System for watering vines that applies water directly to the roots through a network of emitters or microsprayers; drip irrigation conserves water and nutrients and minimizes erosion.

Dry: Wine containing very little residual sugar. The opposite of sweet.

Estate-bottled: Wine made, produced, and bottled on the estate where the grapes grew.

Extra dry: Less dry than brut Champagne.

Fermentation: The process by which yeast transforms sugar into alcohol, turning grape juice into wine.

Filtration: Removal of yeast and other solids from a wine to clarify and stabilize the wine before bottling.

Fino: A type of Sherry.

Finish: The taste and feel that wine leaves in the mouth after swallowing. Some wines disappear immediately while others linger for some time.

First growth: The five highest-quality Bordeaux châteaux wines from the Médoc Classification of 1855.

Fortified wine: A wine, such as Port or Sherry, that has additional grape spirits (brandy, for example) added to raise the alcohol content.

Fruit: One of the components of wine that derives from the grape itself.

Gran Reserva: A Spanish wine that has had extra aging.

Grand Cru: The highest classification for wines in Burgundy.

Grand Cru Classé: The highest level of the Bordeaux classification.

Hectare: A metric measure of area that equals 2.471 acres.

Hectoliter: A metric measure of volume that equals 26.42 U.S. gallons.

Halbtrocken: The German term that means semidry.

Kabinett: A light, semidry German wine.

Maceration: The chemical process by which tannin, color, and flavor are extracted from the grape skins into the wine. Temperature and alcohol content influence the speed at which maceration occurs.

Malolactic fermentation: A secondary fermentation process wherein malic acid converts into lactic acid and carbon dioxide. This process reduces a wine's acidity and adds complexity.

Mechanical harvester: A machine used on flat vineyards that shakes the vines to harvest the grapes.

Meritage: Trademark designation for specific, high-quality American wines containing the same varieties used in Bordeaux wines.

Méthode Champenoise: The method by which Champagne, and sometimes sparkling wine, is made.

Mouthfeel: Sensation of texture in the mouth when tasting wine, such as smooth or tannic.

Must: Unfermented grape juice extracted during the crushing process.

Noble Rot: See *Botrytis cinerea*.

Nose: The term used to describe the combined bouquet and aroma of wine.

Phenolics: Chemical compounds derived especially but not exclusively from the skins, stems, and seeds of grapes that affect the color and flavor of wine. Tannin is one example. Maceration can increase their presence in wines.

Oenology: The science and scientific study of winemaking.

Phylloxera: A root louse that kills grapevines.

Prädikatswein: The highest level of quality in German wines.

Premier Cru: A wine that comes from a specific designated vineyard in Burgundy, France, or is blended from several such vineyards.

Proprietary wine: A wine given a brand name and marketed as such, such as Riunite, Mouton-Cadet.

Qualitätswein: A German term meaning "quality wine."

Residual sugar: Any unfermented sugar that remains in a finished wine. Residual sugar determines how dry or sweet a wine tastes.

Riddling: One step of the Champagne-making process in which the bottles are turned gradually each day for weeks until they are upside down so that the sediment rests in the neck of the bottle.

Sediment: Particulate matter that accumulates in wine as it ages.

Sommelier: The French term for cellarmaster or wine steward.

Sulfur dioxide: A gas used in winemaking and grape growing as a preservative, antioxidant, or sterilizing agent.

Tannin: One of the components of wine, a natural compound and preservative that comes from the skins, stems, and pits of the grapes and also from the wood barrel in which wine ages.

Terroir: All of the elements that contribute to the distinctive characteristics of a particular vineyard site, including its soil, subsoil, slope, drainage, elevation, climate, exposure to the sun, temperature, precipitation, and so on.

Varietal wine: A wine labeled with the predominant grape used to produce the wine. For example, a wine made from Chardonnay grapes would be labeled "Chardonnay."

Vintage: The year the grapes are harvested.

Vinification: Winemaking.

***Vitis labrusca*:** A native grape species in America.

***Vitis vinifera*:** The grape species used in most countries in the world for winemaking.

PRELUDE TO WINE
QUIZ

1. What are the three tastes in wine?

2. What are three sources that can affect a wine's flavor?

3. What species of grape makes the most wine?

4. Name three grapes that have high tannin.

5. What is terroir?

6. What is Brix?

7. What is phylloxera?

8. What is Noble Rot?

9. Sugar + _____ = _____ + Carbon Dioxide

10. What are the percentage ranges of alcohol in sparkling wine, table wine, and fortified wine?

11. What is must?

12. How do red grapes make white wine?

13. What is maceration?

14. What is chaptalization?

15. What is residual sugar?

16. Where does tannin come from?

17. What does a vintage on a bottle indicate?

18. What are two factors that affect whether a wine will last more than five years?

19. What is a "corked" wine?

20. Why do vintners use sulfur dioxide in the winemaking process?

21. What is vertical tasting?

22. What happens to the color of white wines as they age?

23. What happens to the color of red wines as they age?

24. What is the difference between aroma and bouquet?

25. Why should you swirl a wine before smelling it?

Turn the page for the answer key.

PRELUDE TO WINE
ANSWERS

1. Sweet, sour, and bitter

2. Grapes, fermentation, and maturation and aging

3. *Vitis vinifera* makes the most wine.

4. Nebbiolo, Cabernet Sauvignon, Syrah/Shiraz

5. Terroir is how the "somewhereness" of a particular region or vineyard tastes, including soil, geography, sunlight, weather, climate, surrounding plant life, and other elements.

6. The winemaker's measure of sugar in grapes

7. A grape louse that can kill the entire plant

8. *Botrytis cinera*, a mold that slowly pierces grape skins, allowing their water content to evaporate and giving the wine a more intense flavor.

9. Sugar + Yeast = Alcohol + Carbon Dioxide

10. Sparkling wine: 8–12 percent; table wine: 8–15 percent; fortified wine: 17–22 percent.

11. The mixture of grape juice and skins

12. Winemakers remove the skins of red grapes to make white wine from the pulp.

13. Soaking the skins to extract aromas, tannins, and color

14. The process of adding sugar to the must so the yeast generates more alcohol in the final wine

15. When some of the natural sugars in the must remain unfermented by yeast

16. Tannin comes from the skins, pits, and stems of the grapes.

17. A vintage indicates the year that growers harvested the grapes.

18. The grape, the vintage, where the wine comes from, how the wine was made, and storage conditions

19. Corked wine is when trichloroanisole (TCA) from the cork has spoiled a wine.

20. As an antioxidant, preservative, and disinfectant to prevent unwanted oxidation and to inhibit the action of bacteria or wild yeast

21. Comparing wines from different vintages

22. As they age, white wines gain color.

23. Red wines lose color as they age.

24. Aroma represents the smell of the grapes in the wine; bouquet describes the total smell of the wine (usually found in older wines).

25. To allow oxygen to aerate the wine, releasing the esters and aldehydes that combine with oxygen to yield the wine's aroma or bouquet.

·⊱ CLASS ONE ⊰·
THE WHITE WINES OF FRANCE
·⊱ QUIZ ⊰·

1. Match grape variety with wine region

   a. Riesling   _____ Champagne

   b. Sauvignon Blanc   _____ Loire Valley

   c. Chardonnay   _____ Alsace

   d. Sémillon   _____ Burgundy

   e. Gewürztraminer   _____ Bordeaux

   f. Grenache   _____ Côtes du Rhône

   g. Pinot Noir

   h. Cabernet Sauvignon

   i. Chenin Blanc

   j. Syrah

   k. Merlot

2. When were the Appellation d'Origine Contrôlée (AOC) laws first established?

3. How many acres are there in a hectare?

4. How many gallons are there in a hectoliter?

5. Name one difference in style between a Riesling from Alsace and one from Germany.

6. What's the most planted grape in Alsace?

7. Name two important shippers of Alsace wine.

8. What's the grape variety for Sancerre and Pouilly-Fumé wines?

9. What's the grape variety for Vouvray wine?

10. Define the term "sur lie."

11. What does the word "Graves" mean in English?

12. The majority of the white Bordeaux wines use which two grape varieties?

13. Name two classified châteaux of Graves.

14. What's the primary grape used for Sauternes?

15. What are the three classification levels of the châteaux in Sauternes?

16. Name the main regions of Burgundy.

17. Which region of Burgundy produces only white wine?

18. Which region of Burgundy produces the most red wine?

19. Does the Côte d'Or produce more white wine or more red?

20. Name three quality levels of Burgundy.

21. For Chablis, name two Grand Cru vineyards and two Premier Cru vineyards.

22. Which are the three most important white-wine villages in the Côte de Beaune?

23. Name three white Grand Cru vineyards from the Côte de Beaune.

24. From which region in Burgundy does Pouilly-Fuissé come?

25. In Burgundy, what does "estate-bottled" wine mean?

Turn the page for the answer key.

THE WHITE WINES OF FRANCE
ANSWERS

1. Grape variety and wine region

   Champagne: Pinot Noir & Chardonnay

   Loire Valley: Sauvignon Blanc & Chenin Blanc

   Alsace: Riesling & Gewurztraminer

   Burgundy: Pinot Noir & Chardonnay

   Bordeaux: Cabernet Sauvignon, Merlot, Sauvignon Blanc & Sémillon

   Côtes du Rhône: Syrah & Grenache

2. 1930s

3. 1 hectare = 2.471 acres

4. 1 hectoliter = 26.42 gallons

5. Rieslings from Alsace are dry, while most German Rieslings have some residual sugar. Also the alcohol content.

6. Reisling

7. Domaine Dopff au Moulin, Domaine F. E. Trimbach, Domaine Hugel & Fils, Domaine Léon Beyer, Domaine Marcel Deiss, Domaine Weinbach, Domaine Zind-Humbrecht.

8. Sauvignon Blanc

9. Chenin Blanc

10. Wine aged on its "lees" (sediment)

11. Gravel

12. Sauvignon Blanc and Sémillon

13. Château Bouscaut, Château Carbonnieux, Château Couhins-Lurton, Domaine de Chevalier, Château Haut-Brion, Château La Louvière, Château La Tour-Matillac, Château Laville-Haut-Brion, Château Malartic-Lagravière, Château Olivier, Château Smith-Haut-Lafitte

14. Sémillon

15. Grand Premier Cru, Premiers Crus, Deuxièmes Crus

16. Chablis, Côte Chalonnaise, Côte d'Or (Côte de Nuits, Côte de Beaune), Mâconnais, Beaujolais

17. Chablis

18. Beaujolais

19. More red

20. Regional Appellations, Village wine, Premier Cru, and Grand Cru.

21. Grand Cru vineyards of Chablis: Blanchots, Bougros, Grenouilles, Les Clos, Preuses, Valmur, and Vaudésir. Premier Cru vineyards of Chablis: Côte de Vaulorent, Fourchaume, Lechet, Montée de Tonnerre, Montmains, Monts de Milieu, and Vaillon

22. Meursault, Puligny-Montrachet, and Chassagne-Montrachet

23. Corton-Charlemagne, Charlemagne, Bâtard-Montrachet, Montrachet, Bienvenue-Bâtard-Montrachet, Chevalier-Montrachet, Criots-Bâtard-Montrachet

24. Mâconnais

25. The owner of the vineyard makes, produces, and bottles the wine.

AMERICAN WINE AND THE
WHITE WINES OF CALIFORNIA

QUIZ

1. What percentage of wine consumed in America comes from the United States?

2. Approximately how many wineries are there in the United States?

3. How many states have wineries?

4. What is the name of a wine-grape species native to America?

5. When did phylloxera first destroy the vineyards of California?

6. In what year did Prohibition begin?

7. In what year did Prohibition end?

8. What is an American Viticultural Area (AVA)?

9. Approximately how many AVAs does America have?

10. If an AVA appears on a wine label, what percentage of the grapes must come from that region?

11. Name the top five states in wine production.

12. Name the top ten states in wine consumption.

13. What are the main viticultural areas of California?

14. What are the top grapes planted in Napa?

15. What are the top grapes planted in Sonoma?

16. What's the most important white-wine grape grown in California?

17. Name three other major white-wine grapes grown in California.

18. What is the difference between Sauvignon Blanc and Fumé Blanc?

19. What are the major grapes grown in Washington?

20. Does Washington produce more red wine or more white?

21. How many AVAs does Oregon have?

22. What grape does Oregon grow most?

23. Name the three main wine regions of New York.

24. Which Native American varieties of grapes grow in New York?

Turn the page for the answer key.

AMERICAN WINE AND THE WHITE WINES OF CALIFORNIA ANSWERS

1. More than 75 percent

2. More than 6,000

3. All fifty

4. Wine grape species native to America include *Vitis labrusca* and *Vitis rotundifolia*.

5. 1876

6. 1920

7. 1933

8. A specific grape-growing area within a state or region recognized by and registered with the federal government

9. More than 230

10. At least 85 percent

11. California, Washington, New York, Oregon, and Virginia

12. Washington, DC; New Hampshire; Vermont; Massachusetts; New Jersey; Nevada; Connecticut; California; Rhode Island; and Delaware

13. North Coast, North Central Coast, South Central Coast, and San Joaquin Valley

14. Cabernet Sauvignon, Chardonnay, and Merlot

15. Chardonnay, Pinot Noir, and Cabernet Sauvignon

16. Chardonnay

17. Sauvignon Blanc, Chenin Blanc, and Viognier

18. Trick question! There's no official difference between Sauvignon Blanc and Fumé Blanc. Robert Mondavi invented the latter name to increase sales.

19. Chardonnay, Riesling, Cabernet Sauvignon, and Merlot

20. Another trick question! Washington produces 50 percent white wine and 50 percent red.

21. 17 AVAs

22. Pinot Noir

23. Finger Lakes, Hudson Valley, and Long Island

24. Concord, Catawba, and Delaware (all *Vitis labrusca*)

THE WHITE WINES OF GERMANY
QUIZ

1. What percentage of German wines are white?

2. If a German wine has the name of a grape variety on a label, what's the minimum percentage of that grape in the wine?

3. What percentage of the grapes planted in Germany are Riesling?

4. What German grape crosses Riesling and Chasselas?

5. If a German wine lists a vintage on the label, what's the minimum percentage of that year in the wine?

6. How many winemaking regions does Germany have?

7. Name Germany's four most important wine regions.

8. Describe the overall style of German wines.

9. Name the three basic styles of German wine.

10. What does the word "Trocken" say about the style of the wine?

11. What's the average alcohol range for German wines?

12. What are the two main categories of Qualitätswein?

13. Name the levels of ripeness of Prädikatswein.

14. What does "Spätlese" mean in English?

15. What is Eiswein?

16. What is Süssreserve?

17. Match the region to the village.

    a. Rheingau   _____ Oppenheim

    b. Mosel   _____ Rüdesheim

    c. Rheinhessen   _____ Bernkastel

    d. Pfalz   _____ Piesport

                           _____ Johannisberg

                           _____ Deidesheim

                           _____ Nierstein

18. What does "Gutsabfüllung" indicate?

19. What is *Edelfäule*?

Turn the page for the answer key.

THE WHITE WINES OF GERMANY
ANSWERS

1. 85 percent

2. At least 85 percent

3. 21 percent

4. Müller-Thurgau

5. 85 percent

6. 13 regions

7. Rheinhessen, Rheingau, Mosel, and Pfalz

8. A balance of sweetness with acidity and low alcohol

9. Trocken, halbtrocken, and fruity

10. It's dry.

11. Between 8 percent and 10 percent.

12. Qualitätswein bestimmter Anbaugebiete and Prädikatswein.

13. Kabinett, Spätlese, Auslese, Beerenauslese, Trockenbeerenauslese, and Eiswein

14. "Late picking"

15. A sweet, concentrated wine made from grapes pressed while still frozen

16. When winemakers reserve grape juice and add it to the wine after fermentation

17. Oppenheim: Rheinhessen

    Rüdesheim: Rheingau

    Bernkastel: Mosel

    Piesport: Mosel

    Johannisberg: Rheingau

    Deidesheim: Pfalz

    Nierstein: Rheinhessen

18. Estate-bottled

19. The German word for *Botrytis cinerea.*

1. What are the main red wine–producing regions in Burgundy?

2. What are the two grape varieties used in making red Burgundy wine?

3. How did the Napoleonic Code affect the vineyards of Burgundy?

4. What grape variety is Beaujolais made from?

5. What are the three quality levels of Beaujolais?

6. How many Cru Beaujolais are there?

7. Name three Cru Beaujolais villages.

8. When does Beaujolais Nouveau release?

9. Name two wine villages of the Côte Châlonnaise.

10. What are the four quality levels of the Côte d'Or?

11. Name the two regions within the Côte d'Or.

12. How many Grand Cru vineyards does the Côte d'Or have?

13. Name two wine villages from the Côte de Beaune known for producing red wine.

14. Name two red Grand Cru vineyards of the Côte de Beaune.

15. Name two wine villages from the Côte de Nuits known for making red wine.

16. Name two red Grand Cru vineyards from the Côte de Nuits.

17. Where in France does the Rhône Valley lie?

18. What are the three major quality levels of the Rhône Valley?

19. What percentage of Côtes du Rhône wines come from grapes grown in the southern region?

20. How many Crus does the Rhône Valley have?

21. Name two Crus from the Northern Rhône.

22. Name two Crus from the Southern Rhône.

23. What two main red-grape varieties grow in the Rhône Valley?

24. What's the primary red grape used in the Northern Rhône?

25. What is Tavel?

26. How many different grape varieties can go into Châteauneuf-du-Pape?

27. Name the four most important grapes used to make Châteauneuf-du-Pape.

28. What's one difference between a Côtes du Rhône and a Beaujolais?

29. Which wine will age longer, a Côtes du Rhône Villages or a Hermitage?

30. Name two white wines from the Rhône.

Turn the page for the answer key.

THE RED WINES OF BURGUNDY AND THE RHONE VALLEY
ANSWERS

1. The Côte d'Or (Côte de Nuits, Côte de Beaune), Beaujolais, and Côte Châlonnaise

2. Pinot Noir and Gamay

3. It instituted equal inheritance laws for heirs, thereby fragmenting the vineyards of Burgundy.

4. 100 percent Gamay grapes

5. Beaujolais, Beaujolais-Villages, and Cru

6. Ten Crus

7. Brouilly, Chénas, Chiroubles, Côte de Brouilly, Fleurie, Juliénas, Morgon, Moulin-à-Vent, Régnié, and St-Amour

8. The third Thursday of November

9. Mercurey, Givry, and Rully

10. Regional (Bourgogne), Village, Premier Cru, and Grand Cru.

11. The Côte de Beaune and Côte de Nuits

12. 32 Grand Cru vineyards

13. Aloxe-Corton, Beaune, Pommard, and Volnay

14. Corton, Corton Bressandes, Corton Clos de Roi, Corton Maréchaude, and Corton Renardes

15. Chambolle-Musigny, Flagey-Échézeaux, Gevrey-Chambertin, Morey-St-Denis, Nuits-St-Georges, Vosne-Romanée, and Vougeot

16. Bonnes Mares, Musigny, Échézeaux, Grands-Échézeaux, Chambertin, Chambertin Close de Bèze, Chapelle-Chambertin, Charmes-Chambertin, Griotte-Chambertin, Latricières-Chambertin, Mazis-Chambertin, Mazoyères-Chambertin, Ruchottes-Chambertin, Clos de la Roche, Clos des Lambrays, Clos de Tart, Clos St-Denis, La Grande-Rue, La Romanée, La Tâche, Malconsorts, Richebourg, Romanée-Conti, Romanée-St-Vivant, and Clos de Vougeout

17. Southeastern France, south of Burgundy

18. Côte du Rhône, Côte du Rhône Villages, and Côte du Rhône Crus (Northern and Southern)

19. More than 90 percent

20. 13 Crus

21. Château-Grillet, Condrieu, Cornas, Côte-Rôtie, Crozes-Hermitage, Hermitage, St-Joseph, and St-Peray

22. Châteauneuf-de-Pape, Gigondas, Lirac, Tavel, and Vacqueyras

23. Grenache and Syrah

24. Syrah

25. A dry rosé made primarily from the Grenache grape.

26. 13 different grapes

27. Grenache, Syrah, Mourvèdre, and Cinsault

28. Côtes du Rhône has more body and alcohol than Beaujolais.

29. Hermitage

30. Condrieu and Chateau Grillet

THE RED WINES OF BORDEAUX
QUIZ

1. What is the English word for red Bordeaux wine?

2. How many appellations does Bordeaux have?

3. What approximate percentage of red wine does Bordeaux produce?

4. What are the three major red grapes that grow in Bordeaux?

5. What red grape grows primarily on the left bank of the Garonne River?

6. What red grape grows primarily on the right bank of the Dordogne River?

7. Name the three quality levels of Bordeaux wine.

8. Approximately how many wine-producing châteaux does Bordeaux have?

9. What percentage of Bordeaux wine costs between $8 and $25 retail?

10. In what year did wine brokers classify the best châteaux of the Médoc?

11. How many châteaux did they classify?

12. What percentage do the Grands Crus Classés Châteaux represent of the total volume of Bordeaux?

13. Name one château from each of the five growths.

14. In what year were the wines of Graves first classified?

15. In what year were the wines of St-Émilion first classified?

16. What's the primary red grape used in St-Émilion wine?

17. Name three great recent vintages from the left bank of the Garonne River.

18. Name three great recent vintages from the right bank of the Dordogne River.

19. Name two second-label wines of classified châteaux.

Turn the page for the answer key.

CLASS SIX

THE RED WINES OF CALIFORNIA
QUIZ

1. Are Americans drinking more red wine or white wine?

2. Does California grow more red grapes or white?

3. What are the three most planted red grapes in California?

4. What does the word "Reserve" mean on a California wine label?

5. In which French wine region do you find great Cabernet Sauvignon?

6. What is the most planted red grape in the Napa Valley?

7. In which two French wine regions do you find great Pinot Noir?

8. Which county in California has the most plantings of Pinot Noir?

9. What California grape has the same DNA as the Italian grape Primitivo?

10. In which French wine region do you find great Syrah?

11. Which California counties have the most Syrah planted?

12. What was the most planted red grape in California in 1970?

13. What is a Meritage wine?

14. Name two Meritage wines.

Turn the page for the answer key.

CLASS FIVE
THE RED WINES OF BORDEAUX
ANSWERS

1. Claret

2. 57

3. 85 percent of Bordeaux wine is red, and 15 percent is white.

4. Merlot, Cabernet Sauvignon, and Cabernet Franc

5. Cabernet Sauvignon

6. Merlot

7. The three quality levels are Bordeaux Appellation, Appellation Region, and Region + Chateau.

8. 7,000

9. 80 percent

10. 1855

11. 61

12. Less than 5 percent

13. See pages 166–167 for the complete list.

14. 1959

15. 1955

16. Merlot

17. 1990, 1995, 1996, 2000, 2003, 2005, 2009, 2010, 2015

18. 1990, 1998, 2000, 2001, 2005, 2009, 2010, 2015

19. Carruades de Lafite, Le Clarence de Haut-Brion, L'Espirit de Chevalier, Les Forts de Latour, Pavillon Rouge du Château Margaux, Le Petit Mouton, Le Petit Lion, Réserve de la Comtesse, La Réserve Léoville-Barton, Les Tourelles de Longueville

CLASS SIX
THE RED WINES OF CALIFORNIA
ANSWERS

1. Red

2. Red grapes

3. Cabernet Sauvignon, Zinfandel, and Merlot

4. The word has no legal meaning. Each winery that uses it defines the term individually.

5. Bordeaux

6. Cabernet Sauvignon

7. Burgundy and Champagne

8. Sonoma

9. Zinfandel

10. The Rhône Valley

11. San Luis Obispo and Sonoma

12. Zinfandel

13. A red or white wine made in America from a blend of the classic Bordeaux grape varieties

14. Examples include: Cain Five, Dominus, Insignia, Magnificat, Opus One, and Trefethen Halo.

THE WINES OF SPAIN AND ITALY

QUIZ

SPAIN

1. Name three of Spain's major winemaking regions.

2. What does *cosecha* mean in English?

3. Name two Spanish wine regions that historically make high-quality wine?

4. What two primary red grapes make Rioja wines?

5. What percentage of Rioja grapes are red?

6. What does *vinos de pagos* indicate about a wine?

7. What are the three levels for aging Rioja wines?

8. In which wine region would you find Bodegas Montecillo, CVNE, and Marqués de Cáceres?

9. In which wine region would you find Vega Sicilia and Pesquera?

10. What major red grapes go into the wines of Ribera del Duero?

11. What is Spanish sparkling wine called, and which region produces most of it?

12. What major grapes make the wines of Priorat?

13. In which region would you find the wines of Alvaro Palacios, Mas Igneus, and Pasanau?

14. Where in Spain does Rueda lie?

15. What major grape makes the majority of wine from the Rías Baixas region?

Turn the page for the answer key.

ITALY

1. How many wine regions does Italy have?

2. Historically what are Italy's top three wine-producing regions?

3. According to Italian wine laws, what's the highest quality level?

4. Name the three different quality levels of Chianti.

5. In which Italian wine region do you find Chianti, Vino Nobile di Montepulciano, and Brunello di Montalcino, and what primary grape makes these wines?

6. What's the minimum amount of time that a Brunello di Montalcino must age in oak?

7. What is a "Super Tuscan" wine?

8. What are the three major red grapes of Piedmont?

9. What's the biggest difference between France's AOC laws and the DOC wine laws of Italy?

10. What's the only grape that can produce Barolo and Barbaresco wines?

11. Under DOCG wine laws, which must age longer, a Barolo or Barbaresco?

12. From which Italian wine region do Valpolicella, Bardolino, Soave, and Amarone come?

13. Define the following terms: Ripasso, Classico, Superiore.

14. What are three different ways that Italian wines are named?

15. What are some other important regions in Italy?

Turn the page for the answer key.

THE WINES OF SPAIN AND ITALY
ANSWERS

SPAIN

1. Rioja, Ribera del Duero, Penedès, Priorat, Rueda, Rías Baixas, Jerez

2. Harvest or vintage

3. Rioja and Priorat

4. Tempranillo and Garnacha

5. Red grapes account for 90 percent of Rioja grape production.

6. The wine comes from a single estate.

7. Crianza, Reserva, and Gran Reserva

8. The Rioja region

9. The Ribera del Duero region

10. Tempranillo, Cabernet Sauvignon, Merlot, Malbec, and Garnacha

11. The Penedès region produces Cava.

12. Garnacha, Cariñena, Cabernet Sauvignon, Merlot, and Syrah

13. Priorat

14. North-central

15. Albariño

ITALY

1. 20

2. Veneto, Piedmont, and Tuscany

3. DOCG / Denominazione di Origine Controllata Garantita

4. Chianti, Chianti Classico, and Chianti Classico Riserva

5. Tuscany, and the primary grape is Brunello.

6. Two years

7. Super Tuscan wines are high-quality table wines from Tuscany that include previously DOC-forbidden grapes, such as Cabernet Sauvignon.

8. Barbera, Dolcetto, Nebbiolo

9. Italy's DOC mandates aging requirements.

10. Nebbiolo

11. Barolo

12. The Veneto

13. Ripasso is the adding back of grape skins from Amarone wine to Valpolicella, giving it extra alcohol and more flavor. Classico means the vineyards lie in the historical part of the region. Superiore means higher levels of alcohol and longer aging.

14. Italian wines are named by grape variety, village or district, or a proprietary designation.

15. Some other important wine regions in Italy are Abruzzo, Fruili-Veneza Giulia, Trentino-Alto Adige, Lombardy, Umbria, Campania, and Sicily.

CHAMPAGNE, SHERRY, AND PORT
QUIZ

CHAMPAGNE

1. What do Champagne, Sherry, and Port have in common?
2. Where in France does the Champagne region lie?
3. What are the four main areas of the Champagne region?
4. What three grapes go into making Champagne?
5. What are the three major types of Champagne?
6. What's the Champagne making process called?
7. What's the minimum amount of time that a nonvintage Champagne and a vintage Champagne must age in the bottle?
8. What is *liqueur de tirage*?
9. Define the following terms: riddling, disgorging, dosage.
10. What are the seven levels of dryness/sweetness in Champagne?
11. What is a Blanc de Blanc Champagne? A Blanc de Noir?
12. Roughly how many pounds per square inch of pressure does a Champagne bottle contain?
13. What are the names for sparkling wine from Spain, Italy, and Germany?
14. From which region in Italy does Prosecco come?

Turn the page for the answer key.

SHERRY

1. What is a fortified wine?
2. What's the alcohol range in a fortified wine?
3. Name the three towns in Spain that form the Sherry triangle.
4. What two grapes make Sherry?
5. Name the five types of Sherry.
6. Which wine did George Washington serve at the signing of the Declaration of Independence?
7. In the context of Sherry, what's a *bodega*?
8. What percentage of Sherry is lost to evaporation each year?
9. What's the Solera Method?
10. Sherry usually is aged in what type of oak?

Turn the page for the answer key.

PORT

1. Where does true Port come from?
2. When is the neutral brandy added to Port wine?
3. Name the two main categories of Port.
4. What kind of Ports are Late Bottled Vintage, Vintage Character, Quinta, and Vintage?
5. What kind of Ports are Ruby, Tawny, and Colheita?
6. How long does Vintage Port age in wood?
7. What's the approximate alcohol content of Port?
8. What percentage of all Port does Vintage Port represent?

Turn the page for the answer key.

CHAMPAGNE, SHERRY, AND PORT
ANSWERS

CHAMPAGNE

1. They're all blended wines, and the shipper is responsible for all phases of production.

2. Northeast of Paris

3. Marne Valley, Côte des Blancs, Reims Mountain, and Aube

4. Pinot Noir, Pinot Meunier, and Chardonnay

5. Nonvintage/multiple vintage, vintage, and "prestige" cuvée

6. Méthode Champenoise

7. Nonvintage Champagne: 15 months; vintage Champagne: 3 years

8. A mixture of sugar and yeast added to the base wine after the blending process to begin the second fermentation.

9. Riddling: gradually turning Champagne bottles while slowly tipping them upside down. Disgorging: freezing and removing the sediment in the neck of a Champagne bottle. Dosage: A mixture of wine and sugar that replaces the wine lost during disgorging.

10. Brut nature, extra brut, brut, extra sec / dry, sec, demi-sec, and doux

11. Blanc de Blanc Champagne comes from 100 percent Chardonnay, Blanc de Noir from 100 percent Pinot Noir.

12. 90 PSI

13. Cava, Spumante, and Sekt

14. The Veneto

SHERRY

1. A wine that contains added neutral brandy to raise the wine's alcohol content

2. 15–20 percent

3. Jerez de la Frontera, Puerto de Santa María, and Sanlúcar de Barrameda

4. Palomino and Pedro Ximénez

5. Manzanilla, Fino, Amontillado, Oloroso, and Cream

6. Madeira

7. An aboveground structure used to store wine

8. At least 3 percent

9. Fractional blending or the continuous blending of several vintages to maintain the house style

10. American oak

PORT

1. The Douro region in northern Portugal

2. During fermentation

3. Cask-aged and bottle-aged

4. Bottle-aged

5. Cask-aged

6. Two years

7. Around 20 percent

8. Only 3 percent

WINES OF THE WORLD

QUIZ

CHILE

1. Name the two major white grapes and the four major red grapes that grow in Chile.

2. What percentage of Chile's total grape acreage does Cabernet Sauvignon represent?

3. Name Chile's three most important winemaking regions.

4. What Chilean grape was mistaken for Merlot?

5. If a grape name appears on a Chilean wine label, what minimum percentage of that grape must the wine contain?

Turn the page for the answer key.

ARGENTINA

1. Where does Argentina rank in worldwide wine production?

2. When were the first grapes planted in Argentina?

3. Name two major white grapes and two major red grapes that grow in Argentina.

4. Name Argentina's three main wine regions.

5. If a grape name appears on an Argentinean wine label, how much of that grape must the wine contain?

Turn the page for the answer key.

AUSTRALIA

1. Name the two top red grapes and the two top white grapes grown in Australia.

2. Name the four Australian states known for wine production and one wine district from each state.

3. What Australian wine region is known for its sparkling wines?

4. If a label specifies a wine growing district, what percentage of the wine must originate from that district?

5. What are some recent good vintages for Australian wine?

Turn the page for the answer key.

NEW ZEALAND

1. When did New Zealand record its first vintage?

2. Name New Zealand's three main grape varieties.

3. Name three of the most important winemaking regions of New Zealand.

4. Does New Zealand produce more red wines or white?

5. What are the flavor characteristics of a Marlborough Sauvignon Blanc?

Turn the page for the answer key.

WINES OF THE WORLD
ANSWERS

CHILE
1. White: Chardonnay, Sauvignon Blanc; red: Cabernet Sauvignon, Carménère, Merlot, and Syrah
2. 32 percent
3. Casablanca Valley, Maipo Valley, and Rapel Valley / Colchagua
4. Carménère
5. 85 percent of the grape variety

ARGENTINA
1. Fifth
2. 1544
3. White: Torrontés Riojano and Sauvignon Blanc; red: Malbec and Cabernet Sauvignon
4. North, Cuyo, and Patagonia
5. 100 percent

AUSTRALIA
1. Red: Shiraz and Cabernet Sauvignon; white: Sauvignon Blanc and Chardonnay
2. South Australia: Adelaide Hills, Clare Valley, Coonawarra, Barossa Valley, McLaren Vale; New South Wales: Hunter Valley; Victoria: Yarra Valley; Western Australia: Margaret River.
3. Tasmania
4. 85 percent
5. 2010, 2012, and 2013

NEW ZEALAND
1. 1836
2. Sauvignon Blanc, Pinot Noir, and Chardonnay
3. Gisborne, Hawke's Bay, Martinborough / Wairarapa, Marlborough, and Central Otago
4. White
5. Crisp, mineral, acidic flavors of grapefruit, lime, or other tropical fruit

WINES OF THE WORLD

QUIZ

SOUTH AFRICA

1. Describe the South African winemaking terrain.
2. Name the three major white grapes and three major red grapes grown in South Africa.
3. Name the three WOs within the Coastal Region.
4. What are some of the ways to make a great Pinotage?
5. In a South African vintage or varietal wine, what minimum percentage must a wine contain of a specific year or grape?

Turn the page for the answer key.

CANADA

1. When did Canadian commercial winemaking begin?
2. Name three major white grapes and three major red grapes grown in Canada.
3. What are Canada's two major wine-producing regions?
4. In a Canadian varietal wine, what minimum percentage must the wine contain of a specific grape?
5. How is ice wine made?

Turn the page for the answer key.

AUSTRIA

1. What are Austria's four main wine regions?
2. Name three major white grapes and three major red grapes that grow in Austria.
3. What are the three major quality levels of Austrian wine?
4. What is Austria's great dessert wine?
5. What qualities of wine do Riedel glasses enhance?

Turn the page for the answer key.

HUNGARY

1. Name the three major white grapes and three major red grapes native to Hungary.
2. Name three major wine regions of Hungary.
3. How is Tokaji Aszú made?
4. What are the four levels of Puttonyos wine?
5. What is the name of the sweetest of the Tokaji wines?

Turn the page for the answer key.

GREECE

1. Roughly when did Greek winemaking begin?
2. What are the characteristics of the Mediterranean climate?
3. Name the three major white grapes and three major red grapes that grow in Greece.
4. Name two of the most important winemaking regions of Greece.
5. What is the winemaking terrain of Greece?

Turn the page for the answer key.

WINES OF THE WORLD
ANSWERS

SOUTH AFRICA
1. Vineyards lie at altitudes from 300 feet above sea level to 1,300. Some have cool, coastal climates, and in others summer days exceed 100 degrees Fahrenheit.
2. Chenin Blanc (Steen), Sauvignon Blanc, Chardonnay; red: Cabernet Sauvignon, Shiraz, Pinotage
3. Constantia, Stellenbosch, and Paarl
4. Vines planted in cooler climates, at least fifteen years old, low per-acre crop yield, long skin contact, maceration in open fermenters, at least two years of oak aging, blending with Cabernet Sauvignon, at least ten years of bottle aging
5. 85 percent

CANADA
1. The early 1800s
2. White: Chardonnay, Pinot Gris, Riesling, Gewürztraminer, Vidal; red: Pinot Noir, Cabernet Sauvignon, Merlot, Cabernet Franc, and Syrah
3. Ontario / Niagara Peninsula and British Columbia / Okanagan Valley
4. 85 percent
5. By pressing naturally frozen, hand-picked grapes

AUSTRIA
1. Lower Austria, Vienna, Burgenland, and Styria
2. White: Grüner Veltliner, Riesling, Sauvignon Blanc, and Chardonnay (Morillon); red: Blaufränkisch (Lemberger), St. Laurent, Pinot Noir
3. Tafelwein, Qualitätswein, and Prädikatswein
4. Ausbruch
5. Aroma, bouquet, and taste

HUNGARY
1. White: Furmint, Hárslevelü, and Olaszrizling; red: Kadarka, Kékfrankos, and Portugieser
2. The major wine regions of Hungary include: Badacsony, Eger, Somoló, Sopron, Szekszárd, Tokaj, and Villány-Siklós.
3. Grapes affected with *Botrytis cinerea* are made into a paste. Unaffected grapes ferment into the base wine, and workers blend in baskets of the noble rot paste according to the desired sweetness level.
4. 3 baskets, (60g sugar / liter), 4 baskets (90g), 5 baskets (120g), and 6 baskets (150g)
5. Essencia

GREECE
1. 5000 B.C.
2. Hot summers; long autumns; and short, mild winters
3. White: Assyrtiko, Moschofilero, and Roditis; red: Agiorgitiko, Xinomavro, Mavrodafni
4. The most important wine-making regions in Greece include: Macedonia, Peloponnese, and the Islands.
5. Most vineyards lie on the slopes of steep mountains or remote islands.

IMAGE CREDITS

age Fotostock: © Tim Graham: 56; © Paul Hudson: 128; © John Miller: 72; © Hans-Peter Siffert: 58; © Kevin Saitta: 86; © San Rostro: 60

Alamy: © allOver Images: 271; © Rosa Betancourt: 122; © Bon Appetit: 65, 78; © Cephas Picture Library: 11; © Design Pics Inc.: 109; © Michael Dunlea: 160; © Elena Elisseeva: 28; © Greg Balfour Evans: 262; © FreeProd: 172; © Hemis: 162; © Peter Horree: 239; © Peter Huggins: 267; © Melissa Jensen: 117; © Jon Bower New Zealand: 261; © Kuttig - Travel: 276; © Iain Masterston: 126; © Angela McComiskey: 264; © Eric Nathan: 274; © National Geographic Creative: 251; © NSP-RF: 245; © OAS Images: 2; © Prisma Bildagentur AG: 237; © Kseniya Ragozina: 246; © Ian Shaw: 301; © Jachen Tack: 136; © Greg Vaughn: 111; © Juhani Vilitanen: vi; © Andrew Watson: 256; © Westend61 GmbH: 31; © Zoonar GmbH: 118

Chris Bain: viii, 23,26, 27, 155, 195

Corbis: © Photocuisine: 184

Depositphotos: © eveleen: 22, 25

eStockPhoto: © SIME: 96

Getty Images: © Danita Delimont: 215; © Tom Hopkins: 95; © Johner Images: 125; © Ray Kachatorian: 226; © Martin Kreuzer/LOOK-foto: 204; © Dennis MacDonald: 114; © MarkSwallow: 68; © moodboard: 227; © New York Daily News Archive: xviii; © Ian O'Leary: 233; © Ina Peters: 139; © Caroline Purser: 45; © RapidEye: 179; © Robert A Sanchez: 198; © Tetra Images: i; © Topical Press Agency: 90; © Vsevolod Vlasenko: 216; © Westend61: 179; © Frank Wing: 9; © Walter Zerla: 210

iStock: © John Alves: 180; © aprott: 289; © chokkicx: xxi; © Creativeeye99: 182; © gilaxia: 36; © halbergam: ii; © Kesu01: 284; © Maudib: 293; © Kevin Miller: 269; © pavlinec: 19; © Peopleimages: 283; © philipimage: 280; © Andreas Prott: 208; © Shaiith: 302; © SilviaJansen: 299; © Mark Swallow: 27, 133; © zorashuang: 188

Shutterstock: © 279photo: 231; © Africa Studio: 41; © Brandon Bourdages: 187; © James M. Cortez: 191; © digieye: throughout (parchment); © Donjiy: 4; © Fotoluminate LLC: 120; © Gyuszko-Photo: 131; © Jeges- Varga Ferenc: 17; © MariyanaM: 294; © Hein Nouwens: 23, 24, 25; © Teri Virbickis: 253

StockFood: © Marian Montoro: 326

Stocksy: © Lumina: 234

Superstock: xix; © Austrophoto/F1 ONLINE: 48, 135; © Walter Bibikow: 105, 223; © Blend Images: 15; © Gary Crabbe: 84; © Cultura Limted: 100; © Thomas Dressler/ardea.com/PA/Pantheon: 207; © Exactostock-1598: 5; © Exactostock-1672; 176; © Michele Falzone/Jon Arnold Images: 240; © foodanddrink-photos: 243; © Owen Franken/Exactostock-1672: 148, 159; © Tim Graham/robertharding: 142, 147, 202, 230; © hemis.fr: 169; © NHPA: 201; © PhotoAlto: 151; © Radius: 154; © robertharding: 140, 196, 219, 224, 228; © Christian Sarramon/hemis.fr: 171; © Christof Sonderegger: 145; © Stockbyte/Exactostock-1491: 83; © Stock Connection: xxiv; © Universal Image Group: 165

Thinkstock: © nickfree: 296

courtesy of Wikimedia Foundation: 219

Rioja *(continued)*
  quality levels, 201
  region, 200, 201–203
  Reserva, **201**
  shippers/producers,
    202–203
  tasting wines of, 222
Ripasso method, 217
ripeness, importance of, 8–9
Riunite, 217
Robert Mondavi
  Cabernet Sauvignon, **185**
  Chardonnay, 106
  Fumé Blanc, **107**
  Mondavi Reserve, 186
  origin, 99
  Sauvignon Blanc, 107
Robert Sinskey, 186
Robertson's, 241
Robert Vocoret, 76
Robert Voerzio, 216
Robert Weil, 134
Robert Young Estate, 104
Robinson, Andrea, xiv, xvi,
  282, 288, 290
Roblin, 64
Rochioli, 186
Roditis grapes, 2, 278
Roederer Estate, 102, 232,
  235
Roero, 209
Roger Sabon & Fills, 156
Roinnel, Jules, xviii
Rolland, Michel, 254, 295
Romanée-Conti, 149, 152
Romanée-St-Vivant, 149
Ropiteau Frères, 80
rosé
  best values $30 and less,
    312, 314
  Champagne, 234
  food and, 287
  Rhône Valley (Tavel), 154,
    155, 156
  user-friendly, 287
Rosenblum, 187
Roshambo, 187
Rotaliano, 218
Rothschild, Baron Philippe
  de, 102, 168, 191. *See also*
  Baron Philippe de Roth-
  schild
Royal Tokaji, **273**, 275
Ruche di Castagnole Mon-
  ferrato, 209, 216
Ruchots, 149
Ruchottes-Chambertin, 149
Rudd, **51**, 106
Rudera, 263, 266
Rudy Pichler, 272
Rueda, 200, 207
Ruffino, **212**
Rugiens, 148

Ruinart Père & Fils, 232
Rully, **79**, 146
Russian River Valley, 93
Rustenberg, 266
Rust en Vrede, 266

Sacred Hill, 261
Sadie Family, 266
Sagrantino di Montefalco,
  210
Sagrantino grapes, 219
Saint-Amour, 144
Saint Clair, 261
Saintsbury, 106, 186
Saintsbury, George, 50
Salcheta, 213
Salentein, 254
Salmanazar, 22, 23
Salon, 232
Samos Cooperative, 279
Sancerre, 64, 66, 284, 285,
  287. *See also* Château de
  Sancerre
Sandeman, 238, 241
Sanderson, Bruce, xiv
Sanford, 186
Sangiovese, 3, 5, 15, 210, 219
Sanlúcar de Barrameda, 236
San Luis Obispo County, 96
San Pedro, 248
Santa Anastasia, 219
Santa Barbara County, 96
Santa Carolina, 248, 250
Santa Clara County, 96
Santa Cruz Mountain, 93
Santa Rita, 248, 250
Santa Sofia, 217
Santenay, 148
Santenots, 148
S. A. Prüm, 134
Sassicaia, 210, **214**
Sauternes, 69–71, 82, 217,
  265, 275, 284, 288, 291, 297
Sauvignon Blanc
  aging, 16
  Austria, 271
  best place on earth for,
    295
  California, 96, 105, 107,
    108
  Cloudy Bay, **260**
  Dog Point, **259**
  flavors, 5
  food and, 108, 284, 285,
    287
  grapes, 58, 69, 87, 107,
    200, 218, 247, 253, 256,
    260, 263–264
  Klein Constantia, **265**
  New Zealand, 259, 260
  regions, 2, 58, 64, 67
  tasting, 82, 124
Sauvion (producer), 64, **65**

Savigny-lés-Beaune, 148
savoring wine, 50
Savory and James, 238
Saxum, 189
Sbragia, Ed, 108, 189, 193
Sbragia Family, 106, 185, 187
Scanzo, 210
Scarecrow, 192
Scharffenberger, 235
Schiavenza, 216
Schloss Gobelsburgz, 272
Schloss Johannisberg, 134
Schloss Vollrads, 134
Schrader, 185, 192
Schramsberg, 235
Screaming Eagle, 185, 192
screw caps, xx, 257, 291
Scuppernong, 86, 87, 120
Sea Smoke, 186
Sebastiani, 91
Sebastiani, Samuele, 98
second growths, 70, 165, 166,
  168–169
second-label wines, 176, 178
Seghesio, 187
Sekt, 235
Selbach, Johannes, 137
Selbach-Oster, 134, **137**
Seléctoin de Grains Nobles, 61
Semeli, **278**, 279
Sémillon, 2, 58, 67, 69–70,
  82, 256
Seña, 250
Señor de San Vicente, 203
Seppelt, 255
Septima, 252, 254
Seresin, 261
Seven Hills, 112
Seyval Blanc, 4, 87, 115, 121,
  122
Sforzato di Valtellina, 210
Shafer, Doug, 290
Shafer, John, 290
Shafer Vineyards, 106, 185,
  188
Shanken, Marvin, 290
Shaw & Smith, 258
Shea, 117
Sheldrake Point, 114
Shelton Vineyards, 120
Sherry, 236–238
  alcohol content, 12, 236
  Angels Share, 237
  buying, 227
  choosing, 238
  clarifying process, 238
  controlled oxidation, 238
  evaporation of, 237
  food and, 238
  grapes for, 237, 238
  Jerez, 200, 236, 237, 238
  Port vs., 236
  production locations, 236

production process,
    236–238
  shelf life, 238
  Solera method, 238
  top producers, 238
  types of, 237
Shinn Estate, 114
shippers
  of Alsace wines, 62
  of Beaujolais, 145
  of Bordeaux, 160
  of Burgundy (red), 152
  of Chablis, 76
  of Champagne, 228, 232
  of Chianti, 212
  of Côte Châlonnaise, 146
  of Rioja, 202–203
  of Sauternes, 70
Shiraz. *See also* Syrah
  aging, 16, 291
  d'Arenberg, **257**
  Fairview, **264**
  flavors, 5
  food and, 286
  Grant Burge, **256**
  grapes, 3, 256, 264
  Hardy's, **256**
Sichel, 163
Sicily, 219
Siduri, 186
Sigalas, **278**, 279
Signorello, 187
Silvaner grapes, 129, 133
Silverado, 106, 107
Silver Oak, 185
Simi, 91, 107, 263
Simi, Giuseppe and Pietro,
  98
Simmonet-Febvre, 76
Simon, Andre L., 55
Simonsig, 265, **266**
Sin Qua Non, 189, 192
Skalli, Robert, 103
Skouras, 279
Skurnik, Michael, xiii
Sloan, 192
S.L.V., 104
smell, sense of
  abilities over lifetime,
    36–37
  accounting for taste and,
    38–39
  aroma categories and, 43
  aromas and flavors chart,
    52–53
  author perspective on,
    26–28
  common language of taste
    and, 43
  common wine descrip-
    tors, 47
  disorders and treatments,
    40–42

mechanics/biology of,
    30–33
  mechanics of, 35
  memory and, 29, 30
  preferences/cultural dif-
    ferences and, 38–39
  scents that arouse women
    and men, 37
  sources and resources, 43
  taste and, together, 35
  tasting wine and, 26–43,
    46–48. *See also taste/
    tasting references*
  things affecting, 40–42
  training/strengthening,
    42–43
  Wendy Dubit perspective
    on, 28–29
Soave, 217, **220**, 285
Soave Superiore, 210
Sogrape Vinhos, 252
Sokol Blosser, 117
Solaia, 210
Soldera, 213
Solera method, 238
Sonoma County, 96, 99
Sonoma Valley, 93
Soter, 117
South Africa, 262–266, 345,
  346
  best values $30 and less,
    316
  best vintages, 266
  dessert wines, 265
  foreign investment in, 263
  grapes, 263–264, 290
  labels, 2
  Pinotage, 264, **265**
  regions, 262–266
  regulatory agency (WO),
    263, 265
  top producers, 266
Southern Rhone, 154
Spain, 199–207
  grapes of, 2, 3, 200, 201,
    204, 205, 207
  regions of, 200
  Sherry production,
    236–238
Spanish wines, 199–207
  age categories, 201
  best values $30 and less,
    316–317
  Penendés, 205
  phylloxera and, 201, 206
  Priorat, 200, 206
  Rías Baixas, 207, 285
  Ribera del Duero, 200,
    204
  Rioja, 200, 201–203
  Rueda, 200, 207
  Sherry, 200, 236–238
  sparkling wine, 242